KEEPERS OF THE ANIMALS

The hearts of little children are pure, and, therefore,
the Great Spirit may show to them many things
which older people miss.
—Black Elk
Black Elk Speaks

KEEPERS OF THE ANIMALS

Native American Stories and Wildlife Activities for Children

Michael J. Caduto and Joseph Bruchac

Foreword by Vine Deloria, Jr.
Story illustrations by John Kahionhes Fadden and David Kanietakeron Fadden
Chapter illustrations by D.D. Tyler and Carol Wood

Fulcrum Publishing
Golden, Colorado

Book Design by Chris Bierwirth
Jacket Mechanical by Ann E. Green, Green Design

Cover Image: "Dream Quest" © 1991 John Kahionhes Fadden
Back Cover Image: "Brown Bat" © 1991 Diana Dee Tyler

Library of Congress Cataloging-in-Publication Data

Caduto, Michael J.
    Keepers of the animals : Native American stories and wildlife activities for children / Michael J. Caduto, Joseph
Bruchac ; illustrations by John Kahionhes Fadden and David Kanietakeron Fadden ; chapter illustrations by
D.D. Tyler and Carol Wood.
        p.   cm.
    Includes bibliographical references and index.
    ISBN 1-55591-088-2
    1. Indians of North America—Legends. 2. Animal ecology—Study and teaching (Elementary) 3. Human
ecology—Study and teaching (Elementary) I. Bruchac, Joseph, 1942–   . II. Title.
    E98.F6C11 1991
    398.2'08997—dc20   91–71364
                                                                                                         CIP

Printed in the United States of America

0 9 8 7 6

Fulcrum Publishing
350 Indiana Street
Golden, Colorado 80401

for Kahionhes and Tehanetorens

who have done
so much
to care
for the children
and the animals

Permissions

Permission to reprint the following is gratefully acknowledged:

The map, "Native North America" on pages xiv–xv, showing the culture regions of the Native North American groups discussed in this book, is printed with permission of Michael J. Caduto (© 1991). Cartography by Stacy Miller, Upper Marlboro, Maryland.

The photographs on pages 4, 86, 111, 126, 162, 178, 199 and 234 by Alan C. Graham are reprinted with his permission.

The quote from Black Elk that appears on page 5 is from John G. Neihardt's *Black Elk Speaks: Being the Life Story of a Holy Man of the Oglala Sioux* (1979) and is reprinted with permission of the University of Nebraska Press, Lincoln, Nebraska.

The quote on page 9 is from *Basic Call to Consciousness* (1978), Akwesasne Notes (eds.) and is reprinted with permission of Akwesasne Notes, Rooseveltown, New York.

The poem "Songs of Small Things" on page 9 is from Joseph Bruchac's *Entering Onondaga* (1978), published by Cold Mountain Press, Austin, Texas, and is reprinted with permission of the author.

The photograph on page 15 by Arthur Swoger is reprinted with his permission, courtesy Audubon Society of Rhode Island.

The photograph on page 16 is reprinted with permission of the Audubon Society of Rhode Island.

The list of problem-solving skills on page 16 was adapted from William B. Stapp and Dorothy A. Cox's *Environmental Education Activities Manual* (1979), published by Thomson-Shore, Inc., Dexter, Michigan, and is reprinted with permission of the authors.

The photographs on pages 18, 21, 65 and 143 by Don Blades are reprinted with his permission.

The illustration on page 24 was adapted from Donald J. Borror and Richard E. White's *A Field Guide to the Insects of America North of Mexico* (© 1970) and is reprinted with permission of Houghton Mifflin, Boston, Massachusetts.

The photographs that appear on pages 32, 105 and 242 by Michael J. Caduto are reprinted with his permission.

The photographs on pages 44, 113, 167 and 176 by Peter Hope are reprinted with his permission.

The quote from Uncheedah that appears on page 53 is from Charles A. Eastman's *Indian Boyhood* (1971) and is reprinted with permission of Dover Publications, Inc., New York.

The quote from the Absaroke (Crow) that appears on page 53 is from Frank B. Linderman's *Plenty-Coups, Chief of the Crows* (1957) and is reprinted with permission of Harper & Row, New York.

The quote from John Fire/Lame Deer that appears on pages 53–54 is from John Fire/Lame Deer and Richard Erdoes's *Lame Deer, Seeker of Visions* (1972) and is reprinted with permission of Simon & Schuster/Touchstone Books, New York.

The activity on page 55 is adapted from 'Flight of Fantasy' by Michael J. Caduto, which first appeared in the "Birds, Birds, Birds" issue of *Ranger Rick's NatureScope*, © 1985 and 1989, vol. 1, no. 4, pp.10-11, and is reprinted with permission of the National Wildlife Federation.

The photographs on pages 57 and 128 by Cecil B. Hoisington are reprinted with her permission.

The illustrations on pages 75, 78 and 98 are adapted from Deborah A. Coulombe's *The Seaside Naturalist* (© 1987) and are redrawn with permission of Prentice-Hall Press, a division of Simon & Schuster, New York, New York.

The illustration on page 85 courtesy Joseph Bruchac is reprinted with his permission.

The photograph on page 100 by Robert S. Michelson of Photography by Michelson, Inc., is reprinted with his permission.

The list of habitat and food requirements of adult amphibians on page 115 from Anne Orth Epple's *The Amphibians of New England* (1983), published by Down East Books, Camden, Maine, is reprinted with permission of the author.

The activity "Beauty in the Beast" on page 133 is adapted from an activity found in Mary Lynne Bowman's *Values Activities in Environmental Education* (1979) and is used with permission of the ERIC Clearinghouse for Science, Mathematics and Environmental Education, Columbus, Ohio.

The quote from the Song of the Long Hair Kachinas on page 140 is from Frank Waters's *Book of the Hopi* (© 1963 by Frank Waters) and is reprinted with permission of Viking Penguin, a division of Penguin Books USA, Inc.

The illustration on page 154 is adapted from the Massachusetts Audubon Society's *Curious Naturalist Supplement No. 2* and is redrawn with permission of the Massachusetts Audubon Society, Lincoln, Massachusetts.

The rules for playing the activity "Unscrambling Mammals" on page 169 are adapted from "Common Squares" found in William B. Stapp and Dorothy A. Cox's *Environmental Education Activities Manual* (1979), published by Thomson-Shore, Inc., Dexter, Michigan, and are used with permission of the authors.

Portions of the information describing several urban animals in the "Discussion" section beginning on page 175 of Chapter 14 are adapted from Michael J. Caduto and Lori D. Mann's *Ann Arbor Alive: The Ecology of a City* (1981), published by the Ecology Center of Ann Arbor, Ann Arbor, Michigan, and are used with permission of the authors.

The poem "Feeder" on page 182 is from Joseph Bruchac's *Near the Mountains* (1987), published by the White Pine Press, Fredonia, New York, and is reprinted with permission of the author.

The photograph on page 181 by Adrienne Miller is reprinted with her permission and that of the Roger Williams Park Zoo, Providence, Rhode Island.

The quote from Old Keyam on page 184 is from Edward Ahenakew's *Voices of the Plains Cree* (© 1973, Ruth M. Buck, ed.), published by McClelland & Stewart Limited, Toronto, Ontario, and is reprinted with permission of Ruth M. Buck.

The photograph on page 196 is reprinted with permission of the Vermont Institute of Natural Science.

The poem "Tracking" on page 198 is from Joseph Bruchac's *Tracking* (1986), published by Ion Books, Inc./Raccoon, Memphis, Tennessee, and is reprinted with permission of the author.

The photograph on page 212 by John A. Korejwa is reprinted with his permission.

The photograph on page 231 by David F. Boehlke is reprinted with his permission.

The stories by Joseph Bruchac throughout this book are reprinted with his permission.

The activities and information by Michael J. Caduto throughout this book are reprinted with his permission.

The story illustrations by John Kahionhes Fadden throughout this book are reprinted with his permission.

The illustrations by David Kanietakeron Fadden throughout this book are reprinted with his permission.

The illustrations by Diana Dee Tyler throughout this book are reprinted with her permission.

The illustrations by Carol Wood that accompany the activities and discussion throughout this book are reprinted with her permission.

Contents

Foreword

Vine Deloria, Jr.

It is often said that we take our cues about what constitutes proper behavior from the people around us. Most probably we get most of our knowledge about the world we live in from our surroundings, although we like to pretend that, with our great colleges and universities, our massive libraries and complex computer retrieval systems, we have more access to information than did people in earlier times. The immensity of the data available to us poses a problem. How do we make this information our own in the sense of using it in a practical manner? Here we lag far behind all previous societies and may indeed be abstracting ourselves from the natural world to an alarming and self-threatening degree. With some rare exceptions, would or could any of us survive in a wholly natural setting? Or are we condemned to remain restricted within the artificial institutional universe that we have constructed?

Our knowledge of birds, animals and the natural world, when we have any ideas about them at all, is derived primarily from television, textbooks and unfortunately, from cartoons that feature cuddly and all-too-human bears, energetic roadrunners and inept coyotes. Other than in petting zoos at supermarkets and roadside cages, few of our children ever see animals, and they never see them in their natural habitats. Animal stories, therefore, are fraught with the possibility of misunderstanding unless some effort is made to provide a context in which the stories take place that is true to the natural setting and behavior of the animals.

Native North Americans saw themselves as participants in a great natural order of life, related in some fundamental manner to every other living species. It was said that each species had a particular knowledge of the universe and specific skills for living in it. Human beings had a little bit of knowledge and some basic skills, but we could not compare with any other animals as far as speed, strength, cunning and intelligence. Therefore it was incumbent on us to respect every other form of life, to learn from them as best we could the proper behavior in this world and the specific technical skills necessary to survive and prosper. Man was the youngest member of the web of life and, therefore, had to have some humility in the face of the talents and experience of other species.

Native North Americans made a point of observing the other creatures and in modeling their own behavior after them. Many of the social systems of the tribes were patterned after their observations of the birds and animals, and in those tribes that organized themselves in clans, every effort was made to follow the behavior of the clan totem animal or birds. Teaching stories for children emphasized the virtues of the animals, and children were admonished to be wise, gentle, brave, or cheerful in the same manner as certain birds and animals. Some of the tribes even developed a psychology of birds and animals, describing human personality traits as being similar to those of coyotes, beavers, elk, bears and so forth. These psychological descriptions are amazingly accurate in terms of predicting individual behavior and frequently surprise casual observers.

The technical skills of birds, animals and reptiles were such that Native North Americans could take cues from them for their own welfare. If birds consistently built nests out of certain materials, it meant that they recognized and adjusted to the fact of harsh or mild weather in a certain location. The building of beaver dams in certain parts of rivers gave information on the depth of water, its purity, the kinds of fish and other water creatures in the locale and the kinds of roots, berries and medicine roots that would be available at that place. Animal trails were carefully observed by the people because inevitably the game animals would take the shortest and easiest path through mountains, prairies and desert and would not be far from water and edible plants.

Hunting and gathering techniques also varied according to the information received from observing animals. A surplus of some small animals would indicate the sparsity of population of their natural enemies and a paucity would indicate that these predators were in abundance in the area. A determination of the edibility of plants was obtained from watching animals; the presence of medicine roots was often indicated by the presence of the animals who primarily used these roots and had passed their knowledge on to humans. Gradually, as the people improved their knowledge of the relationships between the various life forms that inhabited the lands they developed, a species-specific pharmacology evolved, so that they could treat birds and animals for diseases specific to them. Thus a medicine man or woman was credited with having "elk," "deer," "horse" or other kinds of medicine and could cure these animals.

Much of the religious ceremony and ritual of the tribes was derived from information provided to them by birds, animals and reptiles. The famous Hopi "Snake Dance" enabled the people to live in an arid high plateau desert because the snakes could bring water to assist the Hopi in growing corn. In almost every ritual of the tribes, other species participated as full partners. Some of these ceremonies involved the bird or animal in sacrificing its life in order to ensure that the ceremony was properly done. Modern people have a difficult time understanding the nature of these ceremonies or how, after an eagle has been killed in a ceremony, one can look skyward and see eagles circling the site as if they were giving their approval of what had taken place.

The relationship was so close between humans and other forms of life that it was believed that humans could take the shape of the birds and animals for some time after their deaths. Thus it was not uncommon, following the death of an old person, to see a hawk or woodpecker circling the camp or village. Owls sometimes gathered in large numbers on the approaching death of a medicine man. I have personally seen a gathering of nearly three hundred owls on the prairie where there is hardly a blade of grass to sustain life, so I know that many of these stories are to be taken literally and do not merely illustrate a teaching lesson.

Interestingly, many tribes had classifications among the birds and animals that enabled them to explain complicated relationships and provided them with additional knowledge not obtainable from any one species. Thus the Plains Indians saw a grand distinction between two-legged and four-legged creatures. Among the two-leggeds were humans, birds and bears. Bears were included because when feeding, they often stand on two legs. Since the two-leggeds are responsible for helping to put the natural world back into balance when it becomes disordered, birds, bears and humans share a responsibility to participate in healing ceremonies and indeed the cumulative knowledge of these three groups is primarily one of healing.

Over the centuries, certain birds, animals and reptiles and particular human families became very closely associated. They were, in most respects, one intimate family and consequently these families depended upon their animal relatives to warn them of impending dangers or crises of a transitional nature. It is not uncommon to see a family animal in the vicinity of a Native North American home or to find unusual bird and animal appearances happening among some native families. Only the most knowledgeable medicine men or women know the depth of these relationships, but they are very sophisticated, and many people make decisions based on the appearance of the animal people who signal whether a proposed course of action is proper or not.

The stories in this book present some of the basic perspectives that Native North American parents, aunts and uncles use to teach the young. They are phrased in terms that modern youngsters can understand and appreciate. Much of the information about the weather, the particularities of the land and the continuing relationships with birds and animals is not included because we no longer live in a natural setting. Nevertheless, at the most basic level of gathering information, these tales have much to tell us. They enable us to understand that while birds and animals appear to be similar in thought processes to humans, that is simply the way we represent them in our stories. But other creatures do have thought processes, emotions, personal relationships and many of the experiences that we have in our lives. We must carefully accord these other creatures the respect that they deserve and the right to live without unnecessary harm. Wanton killings of different animals by some hunters and sportsmen are completely outside the traditional way that native people have treated other species, and if these stories can help develop in young people a strong sense of the wonder of other forms of life, this sharing of Native North American knowledge will certainly have been worth the effort.

Acknowledgments

From the Authors: We are deeply grateful to the many people who have contributed their time, energy and ideas in order to make this book possible. Bob Baron, Carmel Huestis, and the rest of the staff at Fulcrum, Inc., have crafted the manuscript and accompanying photographs and artwork for *Keepers of the Animals* into the handsome book you now hold in your hands.

The illustrators—John Kahionhes Fadden, Melody Lightfeather, D. D. Tyler and Carol Wood—have created the beautiful images that grace these pages. Their respective work can be distinguished as follows: Kahionhes has illustrated nineteen of the stories and signed his artwork; Melody Lightfeather has illustrated five of the stories and signed her artwork; D. D. Tyler's animal illustrations are credited as such in the captions; and Carol Wood's artwork comprises the balance of the illustrations that accompany the chapters, especially the "Activities" and "Discussion" sections. We are also grateful to the many people, and to the Vermont Institute of Natural Science, whose striking photographs appear on these pages.

Our thanks to the following people for the help, inspiration, friendship and vision they have provided as a foundation for this book: John Kahionhes Fadden, Tehanetorens Ray Fadden, Jeanne Brink, John Lawyer, John Moody and the friends and families of the authors. We are grateful to the Abenaki Nation of Vermont, Chief Homer St. Francis and Tribal Judge Michael Delaney for carrying their traditions forward in a modern world that often forgets the good lessons for relating well to Earth.

There is also a long list of people whose help was crucial during the thorough and extensive process by which the manuscript was reviewed, and to whom we are greatly indebted. The following people reviewed the overall manuscript: Dr. Cheryl Charles, Director, Project Wild; Walter Ellison, Avian Ecologist; John Moody, Ethnohistorian and Independent Scholar; and Dr. Helen Ross Russell, Author, Environmental Biologist, Consultant. In addition, numerous people checked the manuscript for accuracy in their respective areas of expertise: T. Charles Dauphiné, Jr., Endangered Species Coordinator, Canadian Wildlife Service; Walter Ellison, Avian Ecologist; Alan C. Graham, Entomologist; Dr. Thomas P. Husband, Associate Professor of Natural Resources Science, University of Rhode Island; Paul R. Nickerson, Chief, Division of Endangered Species, Northeast Region, United States Fish and Wildlife Service; Dr. Helen Ross Russell, Author, Environmental Biologist, Consultant; Richard S. Stemberger, Aquatic Ecologist, Dartmouth College, Hanover, New Hampshire; Prentice K. Stout, President, Biological Media Services, Inc.; Tom Tyning, Master Naturalist, Massachusetts Audubon Society; and Erik van Lennep, Director, Arctic to Amazonia Alliance.

Thank you to the following parents, teachers, naturalists, environmental educators and youth leaders who donated large amounts of their time and consideration as they field-tested and evaluated the activities newly designed for this book: Mary Bryant; Carli Carrara, Third Grade Instructor, Henry Barnard Lab School, Rhode Island College; Martha Cheo, Assistant Director, Environmental Education Center, W. Alton Jones Campus, University of Rhode Island; Steven Cleaver; Nancy Cyr; Pamela R. Erickson; Lynn Faugot; Mary K. Fitzgerald; Laurie Giard, Environmental Educator; Diane S. Girard; Donna Broman Goldstein, Elementary Math/Science Teacher; Timothy J. Greenwood, English/History Teacher; Claudia Jane Hall; Lucy Hanouille; Laura K. Hathorn, Educator; Judy Intraub; Pamela A.

Korejwa; Cynthia LeBlanc; Betsy Rybeck Lynd; Amy W. Marquis; Karyn Molines; Susan Nellen; Cheryl C. Norton, Director of Education, Audubon Society of Rhode Island; Theresa M. Quinn; Robert J. Rouse, Field Teacher/Naturalist; Claire Schwarzbach, Jamestown School, Rhode Island; Bora Simmons, Assistant Professor of Outdoor Education, Northern Illinois University; Theresa M. Symancyk; William H. Tihen; Krystal Tolley, Instructor, Lloyd Center for Environmental Studies; Bill Tyler, Audubon Society of Rhode Island; Kathleen Valvo; Claudia Wagner; Joanna Waldman; and Ellenor Yahrmarkt.

From Michael Caduto: I want to reiterate my appreciation to all of those people and organizations listed above. I wish to express my gratitude to Ken Maskell of the Abenaki Nation for his aid and guidance in helping me to better understand and share the traditions of the "People of the Dawn," Joel Monture (Teyonhehkwa) of the Six Nations Kanienkahageh (Mohawk) Nation for sharing so openly the rich traditions of his people, my dear friends Paul and Mary Feeney for their support during the preparation of the manuscript and Gail M. Vernazza who miraculously typed the first draft of the manuscript from my handwritten copy. The help of my wife, Marie Levesque Caduto, and her support in so many intangible yet crucial ways, enabled me to carry on and meet each deadline. A special mention and note of appreciation goes to my friends and colleagues on the staff of the Atlantic Center for the Environment, for the example they set in the environmental community by presenting educational and environmental programs that recognize the importance of addressing the inseparable needs of both the human family and all our relations here on Earth.

Finally, my appreciation and respect to the native peoples of North America for the gift of their rich and enduring cultures, and the joy, meaning and wisdom found in their stories. Thank you to the stories themselves, and to the animals, "all our relations," without whom our experience as members of the great family of living things on Earth would be a lonely existence indeed. Most of all, my deep respect, gratitude and best wishes to the parents, teachers and youth leaders of all kinds who will bring these stories and experiences to life in the hearts and minds of children, who are the future. Nyaweh gowah.

From Joseph Bruchac: In addition to those people already mentioned, my special thanks go to the Traditional Elders Circle for their continued example of strength, caring for and commitment to our Mother Earth and all beings and to the Clan Mothers, Chiefs and Storytellers of the Haudenosaunee (Iroquois) Nations, especially to Onondaga Clan Mothers Dewasentah and Gonwaianni, to Chief Oren Lyons (Jo-ag-quis-ho) of the Onondaga Nation, to Wolf Clan Chief Tom Porter and Bear Clan Chief Jake Swamp of the Mohawk Nation for continuing to share their stories and their ancestral visions. I am grateful to Stephen and Margaret Laurent, the Bowman family and Gordon Day for the way they continue to help me tell the old stories of our Abenaki people in the best way I can. It would be difficult for me to continue without the inspiration given me so often by our singers—both traditional and contemporary—so special acknowledgment to Floyd Red Crow Westerman, Willie Dunn, and Joanne Shenandoah and to Roy "Poncho" Hurd. May It All Come To Be. ... And first, last and always on the circle, the thanks of my heart, the breath of my life to All My Relations, to the Birds and Animal People.

Cultural areas and tribal locations of Native North Americans. This map shows tribal locations as they appeared around 1600, except for the Seminole Indians in the southeast and the Tuscaroras in the northeast. The Seminoles formed from a group which withdrew from the Muskogee (Creek) Indians and joined with several other groups on the Georgia/Florida border to form the Seminoles, a name which has been used since about 1775. In the eastern woodlands the Haudenausaunee (Iroquois) consist of six nations, the Cayuga,

BAFFIN
BAY

Iglulik

DAVIS STRAIT

BAFFINLAND
INUIT (ESKIMO)

T (ESKIMO)

Iglulingmiut

C
T
C

LABRADOR
SEA

SATLIRMIUT
(SOUTHAMPTON INUIT)
(ESKIMO)

LABRADOR INUIT
(ESKIMO)

HUDSON
BAY

Montagnais

Naskapi

WEST
MAIN
CREE

EAST
CREE

GULF OF
ST. LAWRENCE

MICMAC

ANISHINABE

(OJIBWAY or CHIPPEWA)

Algonquin

MALISEET
PASSAMAQUODDY

PENOBSCOT

WABANAKI PEOPLES

Nipissing

HAUDENOSAUNEE
(IROQUOIS)

ABENAKI

EASTERN

Huron
(Wyandot)

Ottawa

MOHAWK
ONEIDA
ONONDAGA
CAYUGA
SENECA
TUSCARORA

Susquehannock

PENNACOOK

Massachuset

Wampanoag

TEE

Menominee

Sauk

Neutral

Narragansett
Mohegan, Pequot

Mesquakie

Potawatomi

Erie

Munsee

Winnebago

Fox

Kickapoo

Delaware

(Lenni
Lenape)

Iowa

WOOD-

Miami

Shawnee

souri

Illinois

LAND

Nanticoke

Powhatan

OSAGE

CHEROKEE

TUSCARORA

East Coast Algonquians

Quapaw

Chickasaw

Catawba

Caddo

Muskogee (Creek)

SOUTHEAST

Natchez

CHOCTAW

ATLANTIC

OCEAN

GULF OF MEXICO

Seminole

NATIVE NORTH AMERICA

Mohawk, Oneida, Onondaga, Seneca and Tuscarora. The Tuscaroras were admitted to the Iroquois League in 1722 after many refugees from the Tuscarora Wars (1711–1713) in the southeast fled northward. The Wabanaki Peoples include the Abenaki, Maliseet, Micmac, Passamaquoddy, Pennacook and Penobscot. In addition to the traditional southwestern location of the Yaqui as marked on this historical map, a contemporary population of from 8,000 to 10,000 Yaqui now exists in southern Arizona along an arc reaching from Tucson to Scottsdale and over to Yuma.

Introduction

As we created and interwove the many pieces of *Keepers of the Animals*, the book began to breathe with a life of its own. Through stories, facts and activities the animals reveal themselves in a vital new light—speaking with urgency about their need to be understood, cared for and related to in a good way by human beings. While you share these stories with children an eagle soars high above Earth and brings a young boy to the beautiful sky land, home of the Eagle People; a tiny spider gives strength to a wandering chief and his people by teaching the power and wisdom of patience; four faithful dogs make the ultimate sacrifice by giving their lives to save their master from being killed by a terrible monster; and the Salmon People teach human beings how to live in a healing, balanced way with the animals by honoring the great circles of life.

Keepers of the Animals continues the tradition established by its highly popular and critically acclaimed predecessor, *Keepers of the Earth*. Here each parent, teacher, naturalist and storyteller is given the tools to bring the wonder and magic of the stories and lessons into the lives of children by empowering them with the knowledge, skills and enjoyment found in the activities. This book is about learning to understand, live with and care for the animals: a gathering of carefully selected Native North American animal stories and hands-on activities that promote an understanding of, appreciation for, empathy with and responsible stewardship toward all animals on Earth,* including human beings. *Keepers of the Animals* is a valuable aid for those who want children to be excited by and connected with the animals, the beings many Native North Americans refer to by saying "all our relations." When the stories and activities in this book, and its companion teacher's guide, are followed carefully as children progress from kindergarten through the primary grades, roughly ages five through twelve, they provide a complete program of study in the important concepts and topics of wildlife ecology; the environmental and stewardship issues that are particularly important to animals; and the natural history of every kind of North American animal from mollusk to mammal, and from every kind of habitat from tidepool to mountaintop.

Tell children a story and they listen with their whole beings. Lead children to touch and understand a frog, listen to a bird's song and see the flash of its wings as it darts by, taste and smell a bee's honey and discover the tracks of a wild animal, and you begin to establish connections between children and the animals in their surroundings. Have them listen to and look at a cricket: feel it, study the way it lives, how it creates its song and what that song communicates to other crickets. Help them to understand how the cricket is part of a field or vacant lot community of plants, animals, rocks, soil and water—all fueled by the plant-growing energy of the sun. Visit places where people have affected the cricket's home to help children appreciate their stewardship role in the world and how all things are intertwined. Keep the children at the center of their learning encounters. Build on these experiences with activities that help them to care for, and to take care of, the animals and other human beings so that they may develop a wildlife conservation ethic. The Kiowa story "The Passing of the Buffalo" shows us that we need to live in balance within the family of animals to ensure their future survival.

As the stories unfold and you help the children bring the activities to life, a holistic, interdisciplinary approach to teaching about the animals and Native North American cultures begins. With their close ties to the animals, and all parts of Earth, Native North American cultures are a crucial link between human society and animals. The story characters are voices through which the wisdom of Native North Americans can speak in today's language, fostering listening and reading skills and enhancing understanding of how the native people traditionally live close to the animals. Each story is a natural teaching tool, which becomes a springboard as you dive into the activities designed to provoke curiosity among children and facilitate discovery of the animals and their environments and the influence that people have on those surroundings. Pedagogically sound, these activities have been extensively field-tested. They involve the children in creative arts, theater, reading, writing, science, social studies, mathematics and sensory awareness, among other subjects. The activities engage a child's whole self: emotions, senses, thoughts and actions. They emphasize creative thinking and synthesis of knowledge and experiences.

---

* As used here, *Earth* refers to all of our surroundings: plants, animals and the physical environment, which includes water, air, rocks and sky. Although, by convention, people are often referred to separately in the text, here they are considered to be *part* of Earth, as Native North Americans believe them to be.

Because of the active and involving nature of the experiences found in this book, children who have special needs physically, mentally and emotionally respond well with proper care and skilled instruction.

These stories and activities have been used and enjoyed by families and children at home, in camp settings, nature centers, environmental education programs, public and private schools, library story hours and in both rural and urban settings. Churches and other spiritual groups have found Native North American traditions to be an inspiration for developing environmental stewardship and deeper ties with animals and Earth as part of creation. While the stories and activities arise from North America, with some adaptations for local conditions, they are relevant and useful to people and places in other lands as well.

Native North Americans see themselves as *part* of nature, not apart from it. Their stories use natural images to teach about relationships between people, and between people, animals and the rest of Earth. To the native peoples of North America, what was done to a frog or a deer, to a tree, a rock or a river, was done to a brother or a sister. This perspective has important implications throughout this book where it deals with endangered species, wildlife stewardship and related environmental problems and solutions.

Native North Americans emphasize a close relationship with nature versus control over the natural world. In many stories the lessons are taught both directly and through metaphors. A good example is the Haida story, "Salmon Boy," in Chapter 9. Salmon Boy treats the salmon disrespectfully and does not listen to his parents when they show him how to express gratitude and proper behavior toward the salmon. So the Salmon People make him one of their own and teach him how to live well in the great circles of life, especially the circle of giving and receiving, of showing respect for the gifts of the animals. Salmon Boy is then caught by his mother and turns back into a human who lives among his people as a great healer, teaching them all that he has learned and healing them when they are sick. Like Salmon Boy, we each need to take a journey into the realm of our animal relations in order to better understand them and their needs for survival. *Keepers of the Animals* provides a path for this journey, and the means for sharing these insights and this knowledge with children so they may learn to live in a healing relationship with the animals.

STEPS FOR USING THIS BOOK EFFECTIVELY

The book is divided into two parts, and there is a separate teacher's guide. Part I offers thoughts and suggestions for facilitating the use of stories, guided fantasies, puppet shows and activities, as well as procedures for caring for animals in captivity. If you would like to further round out your background in certain areas before beginning Part II, the teacher's guide discusses the nature of Native North American stories and the cultures from which these particular stories come. It also considers the important educational philosophies and approaches upon which this book is based.

Part II is the heart of the book. In this section we use stories as an introduction to the subjects explored in the activities. In some cases the activities follow directly from the story, while in others the story is a stepping-stone that leads into the activities in a more general way. Stories and activities are arranged under broad topical headings in the Contents. The "Index of Activities by Subject" (page 253) describes the specific lessons taught by the activities and their locations throughout the book.

Each story is followed by a "Discussion" section that provides background information on the topics it introduces. These discussion sections in themselves constitute a unique collection of essays that enhances understanding of the Native North American context of the stories, as well as covering the natural history and environmental issues related to every major group of North American animals. Relevant "Questions" then offer further help in bridging the stories and activities. Chapters end with suggestions for "Extending the Experience."

Following the title of each activity are several symbols that provide a quick reference to both the setting(s) and the topic(s) of that activity.

These two symbols identify activities that occur

 outdoors, or

 indoors (Many of these activities can also be done outdoors, although it is not necessary to do so.)

When an activity is marked with both the indoor *and* outdoor symbols, it means that parts of the activity are better conducted outdoors while other parts are better conducted indoors.

In addition, the activities focus on one or more of the following four subject areas, each of which is represented by a corresponding symbol:

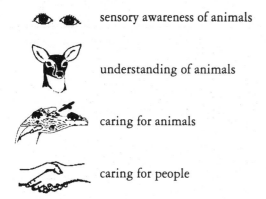

sensory awareness of animals

understanding of animals

caring for animals

caring for people

Begin by sharing a story and illustrations with the children or by having them present the story. Lead a discussion using the background information from the "Discussion" section and the "Questions" at the end of the story. Some leaders prefer to conduct some or all of the activities before sharing the story, in order to give the children some prior background in that subject. It is a matter of approach.

Each "Activity" begins with a title and a brief description of what the children will do during the activity. Broad educational "Goals" are also included. Conduct the activities that are at the appropriate "Age" as indicated in the text. Activities are marked as being appropriate for younger children (roughly ages five to eight) and older children (roughly ages nine to twelve). Some activities are appropriate for both age groups and are so marked. Many of the activities can be adapted to work well with different ages, and this book has been widely adapted for use with children from thirteen to fifteen years of age. All of the "Materials" you will need to conduct the activity are also listed. Virtually all of the materials needed for the stories and activities can be found outdoors, in the learning center and at home: they are simple, common and inexpensive.

A detailed "Procedure" is provided for each activity. These sections use a simple, cookbook-like approach that has been found to work very well with leaders from all backgrounds working in every kind of learning situation. Use the activities described under "Extending the Experience" at the end of each chapter to reinforce and supplement the lessons of the stories and activities. Another valuable tool is the "Glossary and Pronunciation Key to Native North American Words and Names."

Explore, with the children, the Native North American group from which the story comes. The map on pages

xiv–xv shows the cultural areas and tribal locations of the Native North American groups discussed in this book. These specific cultures, and their larger cultural groupings, are described in detail in the teacher's guide.

We encourage you to be creative and use this book as a complement to your family experiences or your educational program for elementary age children. The section "Further Resources on Native North Americans and Environmental Studies" in the teacher's guide provides lists of books for learning and teaching about Native North Americans, animals and Earth, as well as guides to environmental and outdoor education, values education and to facilitating storytelling, guided fantasies, puppet shows, animal care in captivity and interdisciplinary studies. There is also an extensive section in the teacher's guide that lists "Further Reading by Chapter for *Keepers of the Animals.*" This offers a chapter-by-chapter list of books for both children (categorized as being appropriate for either younger or older children, or both) and adults, covering the Native North American group(s) from which the story(ies) in each chapter come, and the animals and other environmental topics addressed in each chapter.

AUTHORS' NOTES
Use of Gender and Terms for Native Peoples

The use of gender varies among individuals and cultures. In order to maintain the accuracy and spirit of word usage and meaning among the writings contributed to this book by other authors, we have included them in their unedited forms. The balance of the text has been written to avoid any gender bias.

Although, by convention, we use the terms *Native American* and *American Indian* interchangeably in this book, not all Native North Americans are American Indians. The Inuit (Eskimo) peoples of the far north (see Chapter 16) comprise a culture that is distinct from the North American Indians who inhabit this continent.

In the United States, American Indian and Native American are terms used interchangeably to refer to the native aboriginal inhabitants of North America, Central America and South America. In Canada, the terms *Native, Indian, Métis* or *Aboriginal* are commonly used rather than *Native American*. In this book, we have used *Native North American* to refer to native peoples of the United States and Canada, and *Native American* or *American Indian* when referring to the native aboriginal inhabitants of North America, Central America and South America. In all cases, it is best to refer first to the person with regard to the individual tribal nation, for example, *Lakota* or *Cree* or *Abenaki.*

Hunting as a Subject
of Environmental Education

A number of the stories in *Keepers of the Animals*, as well as the "Discussions," "Questions" and "Activities" in several chapters (particularly Chapters 9, 13, 15, 16 and 17) address, among other subjects, the topic of hunting. We have included hunting for several reasons. First, hunting is, and has been, an integral part of the lives and cultures of Native North Americans. For these people hunting was, and in some cases still is, a matter of survival. For animals hunting is always a matter of survival.

The same kind of skills that enable hunters to stalk and capture their prey can help children to become more aware and sensitive in their relationship with the animals, such as when they try to get close to an animal in the wild to observe it and learn about it.

Further, hunting needs to be taught about because it is a reality in our world, and we believe that education should be inclusive and not gloss over controversial subjects. The stories and discussion sections of Chapters 16 and 17 are quite graphic and direct because we want the children to be exposed to and to understand the differences between traditional Native North American hunting practices and the realities of modern hunting, and the important issues related to each.

And last, we want to show in these two chapters that, since hunting is commonplace, there are ways it can be managed to assure that animal populations are maintained in a healthy state.

Hunting is one part of the relationship between people and animals. Here we do not advocate or condemn hunting, and we encourage users of this book to study the methods given in Chapter 2, page 17, and in the various values education resources listed in the teacher's guide, for approaching values and controversial issues in education.

PART I

A GUIDE FOR USING AND ENJOYING THIS BOOK

They danced and sang and beneath them Earth took shape.

CHAPTER 1

✤ All Our Relations: Of Humans and Animals ✤

Silver Fox and Coyote Create Earth

(Miwok—West Coast)

Back then, Silver Fox was the only one living. There was no earth, only water. Silver Fox walked along through the fog, feeling lonely. So she began to sing:

I want to meet someone,
I want to meet someone,
I want to meet someone,
I want to meet someone.

So she sang and then she met Coyote.

"I thought I was going to meet someone," Silver Fox said. "Where are you traveling?"

"Where are you traveling?" Coyote said. "Why are you traveling like this?"

"I am traveling because I am lonely," Silver Fox said.

"I am also wandering around," said Coyote.

"Then it is better for two people to travel together," Silver Fox said.

Then, as they traveled, Silver Fox spoke. "This is what I think," Silver Fox said. "Let's make the world."

"How will we do that?" Coyote said.

"We will sing the world," said Silver Fox.

So the two of them began to sing and to dance. They danced around in a circle and Silver Fox thought of a clump of sod. Let it come, Silver Fox thought, and then that clump of sod was there in Silver Fox's hands. Silver Fox threw it down into the fog and they kept on singing and dancing.

"Look down," Silver Fox said, "do you see something there below us?"

"I see something," Coyote said, "but it is very small."

"Then let us close our eyes and keep dancing and singing," said Silver Fox. And that was what they did. They danced and sang and beneath them Earth took shape.

"Look down now," Silver Fox said.

Coyote looked down. "I see it," said Coyote. "It is very big now. It is big enough."

Then the two of them jumped down onto Earth. They danced and sang and stretched it out even more. They made everything on Earth, the valleys and the mountains and the rivers and the lakes, the pines and the cedars and the birds and the animal people. That was what they did way back then.

A child's eyelids grow heavy with the deepening darkness as she stares into the flames of the storytelling fire. Fantastic creatures conjured by the storyteller dance and sing in the realm of the child's night mind. In this dreamworld, where stories are born, everything is truly related and can even change form from one being to another. Stories remind us that in the land of wakefulness, too, we are related to everyone and everything else: the plants, animals, rocks, water and wind.

This Miwok story of how Silver Fox and Coyote created Earth was told to generations of children around the fires in the shadow of Mount Tamalpais near San Francisco Bay, California, where the Miwok people have lived for more than five thousand years. It shows the power and importance of animals in Native American traditions.

All of us, regardless of our cultural backgrounds, trace our ancestors back thousands of years to traditional societies living close to Earth. We all began as native people somewhere on this planet. In those places, around a fire, our ancestors once listened to stories while the rustling of leaves and the cries of nocturnal animals stirred their imaginations.

"Long ago, back when the animals could talk and people could understand them . . ." so some of the old tales begin. Today, people ask what it was like back then, back when animals could talk. It is like today for the animals still can talk, it is just that most people no longer know how to listen (Figure 1-1). Western culture teaches us, from childhood, to draw lines between humans and animals. Even the words *human* and *animal* make those distinctions clear. But to the people of Native North America and to many other "traditional" people all over the world, those lines between humans and animals were not so clearly drawn. This is why, in some Native American ceremonies when the participants enter to purify themselves, they say "all my relations" as a greeting to all relations on this Earth. In many cases, in Native American stories, we hear the animals referred to as the "animal people." They are spoken of in this way because it is hard, in the English language, to speak of them in the old way. Most Native American languages do not have words such as *animal* in them. Fifty years ago, when a man named Jaime de Angulo was living with the Pit River Indian people (Achumawi) in California and studying their language, he asked them what the word was for "animal" in their tongue. They had no word like that, and in their stories, animals and people were all mixed in together. The closest thing they could come up with for animal was *qaade-wade toolol aakaadzi*, which means "the beings

which are world-over, all-living." But that term included people, too, and even the rocks; all things, it seemed, were alive. And what did the Pit River people call the people of European descent, those who didn't see the world in that way? De Angulo was taken aback to discover that the word the Pit River people used for the Europeans was *inallaaduwi*, a word which means, literally, "tramps," people who are not connected to anything, people who are "dead themselves" because they believe nothing is alive.

There is, though, one important distinction that we see all over Native North America between human people and animal people. The distinction is this: in Native American stories it is the animals who came first. In fact, in many stories, it is the animals who created the people! Thus it is common for the tales to refer to animals as our elder relatives and as our teachers and, again and again, in the traditional stories which are still told, when an animal being speaks to a human being, it is always wise for that human to pay very close attention, to listen and to learn.

In North America today people are realizing that we have not listened well, that we have neglected our relations on this Earth and that Native American stories hold power and wisdom for helping us learn how to live in balance with other forms of life. Through the lessons of

Figure 1-1. Many Native American tales say that, back in the early days, human beings could understand animal languages, such as the calls of this tiny male spring peeper. These 3/4-inch (1.9-centimeter), ground-dwelling, brownish treefrogs congregate in large numbers each spring in wetland habitats where they belt out their loud sleighbell-like mating choruses. Photo by Alan C. Graham.

ecology—the study of the relationships between living things and their environments—we have reaffirmed the ancient knowledge of the stories. Science and myth may offer different ways of viewing the world, but they teach us the universal truth that there is an empirically obvious relationship between people and Earth: we should not pollute and destroy our Mother, our Provider, rather we should nurture and protect her. The lessons for survival today come from listening to the old stories and from studying the laws of how natural systems sustain themselves.

Native North Americans did not separate empirical knowledge from myth, art, music, dance and other ways of viewing and experiencing the world: all ways of being were important. We are discovering today that Native Americans possessed a highly sophisticated understanding of nature derived from thousands of years of systematic observation of the natural world. Modern science has benefited from their skills and their knowledge of such topics as astronomy, ecology, population control, nutrition, medicinal uses of plants and animals and chemical properties of plants. Their intimate knowledge of the natural history of thousands of plant and animal species and many technologies such as ceramics, metallurgy, stonework, insulation, building construction, architecture, engineering and the use of paint and pigment has contributed greatly to our own.[1] Native Americans developed the use of plants for nutritional purposes (such as vitamin C), latex, steroids, narcotics, cathartics and psychotherapy. Quinine, curare and ipecac are just a few of the powerful medicines contributed by Native Americans to modern medicine.[2] Six of the world's thirteen major food staples come from the native peoples of North and South America, including maize, potatoes, sweet potatoes, common brown beans, peanuts and cassava (Figure 1-2).[3] A thorough familiarity with the ecology and natural history of local animals was simply a part of their day-to-day lives.

Plains Indians are perhaps best known as a people who lived respectfully and responsively to the rhythms of their centrally important animal relation, the buffalo or American bison. Their seasonal movements were in direct response to the migration of the buffalo herds. Every aspect of their cultures—spirituality and myth, food, clothing, drink, shelter, fire, tools and seasonal migration—was inseparable from the lives of the vast herds of buffalo. It is this relationship with the animals, and with the land—the places where they lived—that gave Native

Americans a deep sense of meaning and the kind of knowledge that enabled them to live well with the animals. The seasonal cycles, moons and endless number of ways that nature works in unending circles were the basis for Plains culture. In the words of Black Elk, a holy man of the Oglala Lakota Sioux:

> Everything the Power of the World does is done in a circle. The sky is round, and I have heard that the Earth is round like a ball, and so are all the stars. The wind in its greatest powers whirls. Birds make their nests in circles, for theirs is the same religion as ours. The sun comes forth and goes down again in a circle. The moon does the same, and both are round. Even the seasons form a great circle in their changing, and always come back again to where they were. The life of a man is a circle from childhood to childhood, and so it is in everything where power moves.[4]

The cycle of giving and receiving—maintaining the circle of life—is fundamental to Native North American culture. Traditionally, when Native Americans prepared for the hunt, they offered prayers and gifts to Creation and to the spirit of the animal to be hunted. If these offerings were made in a respectful, reverential way, the animals accepted them and *presented* themselves for the people. The Creator, they say, forgives us because human beings must eat in order to survive. Additional gifts to the animal's spirit were offered while preparing the meat and again when the meal was over. The bones were returned back to Earth with one final prayer. This Cree story, "How the People Hunted the Moose," tells of the hunter's cycle as seen from the animal's viewpoint.

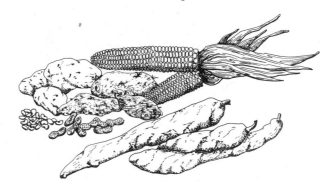

Figure 1-2. Six of the world's thirteen major food staples come from the native peoples of North and South America. Clockwise from the upper right are maize, cassava, peanuts, common brown beans and potatoes. In the center are sweet potatoes.

Sweet-smelling smoke came from the long pipe and it circled the lodge, passing close to each of the Moose People.

How the People Hunted the Moose

(Cree—Subarctic)

One night, a family of moose was sitting in the lodge. As they sat around the fire, a strange thing happened. A pipe came floating in through the door. Sweet-smelling smoke came from the long pipe and it circled the lodge, passing close to each of the Moose People. The old bull moose saw the pipe but said nothing, and it passed him by. The cow moose said nothing, and the pipe passed her by also. So it passed by each of the Moose People until it reached the youngest of the young bull moose near the door of the lodge.

"You have come to me," he said to the pipe. Then he reached out and took the pipe and started to smoke it.

"My son," the old moose said, "you have killed us. This is a pipe from the human beings. They are smoking this pipe now and asking for success in their hunt. Now, tomorrow, they will find us. Now, because you smoked their pipe, they will be able to get us."

"I am not afraid," said the young bull moose. "I can run faster than any of those people. They cannot catch me."

But the old bull moose said nothing more.

When the morning came, the Moose People left their lodge. They went across the land looking for food. But as soon as they reached the edge of the forest, they caught the scent of the hunters. It was the time of year when there is a thin crust on the snow and the moose found it hard to move quickly.

"These human hunters will catch us," said the old cow moose. "Their feet are feathered like those of the grouse. They can walk on top of the snow."

Then the Moose People began to run as the hunters followed them. The young bull moose who had taken the pipe ran off from the others. He was still sure he could outrun the hunters. But the hunters were on snowshoes, and the young moose's feet sank into the snow. They followed him until he tired, and then they killed him. After they had killed him, they thanked him for smoking their pipe and giving himself to them so they could survive. They treated his body with care, and they soothed his spirit.

That night, the young bull moose woke up in his lodge among his people. Next to his bed was a present given him by the human hunters. He showed it to all of the others.

"You see," he said. "It was not a bad thing for me to accept the long pipe the human people sent to us. Those hunters treated me with respect. It is right for us to allow the human beings to catch us."

And so it is to this day. Those hunters who show respect to the moose are always the ones who are successful when they hunt.

The harmony and balance in which Native Americans have traditionally lived with nature come directly from the reciprocity of the circle. In the circle all things are considered of equal value. Even the smallest of things in nature is important. The Haudenosaunee (Iroquois), "People of the Longhouse," from the East believe in the principle, as taught by the great Peacemaker in the mid-fourteenth century, that creation is intended for the benefit of all equally—the birds and animals, trees and insects, as well as humans—and that the world is the property of the Great Creator and not of human beings.[5]

There are now over 5 billion people living in the world and, at the present rate of growth, there will be over 10 billion by the year 2029. And we are not treating our relatives, the animals, very well. Habitat destruction, overhunting, overfishing and pollution such as global warming have put one-quarter of the world's plants and animals in danger of becoming extinct in the next twenty years. From four thousand to six thousand species are now becoming extinct every year as a result of deforestation alone. This is ten thousand times greater than the rate of extinction that existed during prehistory, before human beings appeared on Earth.[6] This represents the greatest setback to the numbers and kinds of plants and animals since Earth formed over 4 billion years ago, even greater than the mass extinction of 65 million years ago when the dinosaurs disappeared! Since merely 1.7 million of Earth's approximately 30 million life-forms have been described to date, hundred of thousands may disappear by the year 2000 before we even knew they existed. The passenger pigeon, sea mink, Carolina parakeet, great auk, blue walleye and Labrador duck will never be seen again.

Some North American animals are in imminent danger of becoming extinct, including the black-footed ferret (Figure 1-3), desert tortoise, red wolf, California condor, right whale and Kemp's ridley turtle. The dusky seaside sparrow, which became extinct in June 1987, is the first bird to disappear since the United States Endangered Species List

Figure 1-3. The black-footed ferret. One of North America's most endangered mammals. Size (including tail): 20–24 inches (50.8–61.0 centimeters).

was created in 1966. A Hawaiian species of honeyeater, the Kauai O'o, is the most recent avian extinction in the United States, having disappeared from its home in Alak'ai Swamp in February 1989. Eighty plants and animals have become extinct in the United States alone while waiting to be listed by the federal government as endangered species under the Endangered Species Act of 1973.

One in forty of Canada's eighteen hundred species of vertebrate animals is either threatened or endangered. The black-footed ferret has been extirpated in Canada, and the whooping crane is experiencing a slow, steady recovery from near-elimination. A number of species, however, including the wood bison and American white pelican, have been brought back from the verge of extinction in Canada. The swift fox, which had been extirpated in Canada for fifty years, is gradually being reintroduced into the prairie region from the more southerly population in the United States. Acid rain is largely responsible for the endangered status of the aurora trout and Acadian whitefish.

In the United States 60,000 acres (24,300 hectares) of ancient forest are cut each year. Tropical rain forests, however, which cover 7 percent of Earth's land area and harbor 50 to 80 percent of all plants and animals, are being cleared or converted to farmland at the rate of 23,000 square miles (59,570 square kilometers) per year. This amounts to an area the size of the state of West Virginia. One-half of all tropical forests have already been destroyed and, at present rates—clearing an area the size of a football field each second—they will disappear entirely by the year 2135.

This loss, of millions of plants and animals, decreases the world's *biological diversity*, the countless characteristics and genetic traits of each life-form that make it unique and help it to adapt and survive in a dynamic world. As diversity declines, we not only lose the beautiful colors, songs, tastes, scents and textures of the plants and animals around us, we also reduce the collective ability for life on Earth to adapt to changing conditions. We diminish ourselves and the relations with which we share this planet.[7]

We have set ourselves apart from nature and, in so doing, have tried to dominate, control and manipulate the natural world to our ends in ways that have proven to be self-defeating and unsustainable. In fact, human beings, too, are governed by natural laws, along with every other form of life with which we share this Earth home. Despite the hubris of Western society and our greatest efforts to subdue nature, the ecological events of today prove that we are inextricably linked to the natural world.

The frog does not drink up the pond in which he lives.
—Teton Sioux proverb

In order to ensure the survival of animals, and ultimately humankind, we can incorporate the wisdom that Native Americans have gained through their experience of living close to nature since Pleistocene times. We need an economic, political, intellectual, material and spiritual way of life that is ecologically based and environmentally sustainable. The Haudenosaunee (Iroquois) Message for the Western World states:

What is needed is the liberation of all the things that support life—the air, the waters, the trees—all the things which support the sacred web of life. [8]

Today, many people *are* working to take care of the animals. Since the banning of the pesticide DDT in 1972 by the United States Environmental Protection Agency, and as a result of dedicated work to reintroduce the animals that were harmed by this poison, the peregrine falcon, bald eagle, brown pelican and others have made dramatic comebacks in regions where they were exterminated, or nearly so, for several decades. Some nearly extinct species, such as the red wolf, black-footed ferret and California condor, are being captive-bred in hopes of reintroducing them and reestablishing viable populations in the wild. Habitat protection and management schemes are being conducted with increasing frequency, efficiency and urgency in order to protect animal homes throughout North America. Many wildlife management and animal rights groups continue to work for the protection of endangered animals and the welfare of them all. Environmental education for the protection and wise

management of wildlife has grown to be a worldwide movement that is educating millions of children and adults and is becoming increasingly influential in guiding government policies that affect animal life. Perhaps, we hope, the governments of the world will be able to work quickly and cooperatively to undertake the massive global cleanup of environmental pollution that is badly needed to assure a healthy home for Earth's residents.

Ultimately, in traditional Native American cultures, the children are regarded as the future. Decisions are made in light of how they would affect the next seven generations. The stories and activities in this book help us to continue healing our relationships with the animals—our brothers and our sisters—by educating the children through the wisdom of science and myth. For young minds have the power to see what adults often fail to perceive because our ways of thinking and acting are often set, habitual and patterned: We tend to see what we expect to see. It is the light touch of a child's hand, the excitement at a new discovery, the innate curiosity and compassion which children possess that give us hope. We place our faith in the smallest humans among us to care for and nurture the smallest of all our relations.

SONGS OF SMALL THINGS

Sitting on the meadow path
mowed through tall July grass
I watch as two leaf hoppers
flick from one knee to the other.

A black cricket
perches on my shoe.

What would we think
if these tiny creatures
like that ant zigzagging
through the hairs of my arm
were birds?

Wouldn't we marvel
at the way so much
which is alive and hidden
from roads and houses
accepts us without thought?

I bend my head
to listen
to the songs of small things.

—Joseph Bruchac
Entering Onondaga

NOTES

1. Janet W. Brown, "Native American Contributions to Science, Engineering, and Medicine," *Science* 189, no. 1 (July 4, 1975): 38–40.

2. Jack Weatherford, *Indian Givers: How the Indians of the Americas Transformed the World* (New York: Fawcett Columbine, 1988), 175–96.

3. Brown, "Native American Contributions."

4. John G. Neihardt, *Black Elk Speaks: Being the Life Story of a Holy Man of the Oglala Sioux* (Lincoln, Nebr.: University of Nebraska Press, 1979), 194–95.

5. Akwesasne Notes, eds., *Basic Call to Consciousness* (Rooseveltown, N.Y.: Akwesasne Notes, 1978), 8.

6. Edward O. Wilson, "Threats to Biodiversity," *Scientific American* 261, no. 3 (September 1989): 108–16.

7. Ibid.

8. Akwesasne Notes, *Basic Call*, 53.

CHAPTER 2

Tips and Techniques for
✤ Bringing This Book to Life ✤

TELLING THE STORIES

Stories form a link between our imagination and our surroundings. They are a way of reaching deep into a child's inner world, to the places where dreams and fantasies are constantly sculpting an ever-growing world view. The emotional identification a child forms with a story character, such as Eagle Boy in Chapter 5, Turtle in Chapter 6, Coyote Woman in Chapter 13 or the fawn in Chapter 15, leads that child to actually *become* that character, to experience the sounds, sights, smells, sensations and emotions through which the character lives. Stories build a bridge between a child's life and the lessons the stories teach.

Each chapter in Part II of *Keepers of the Animals* begins with a Native American story that is the key to unlocking a child's imagination while evoking useful images and exciting interest in the subjects that are then explored in the activities. The natural curiosity with which children regard American Indians is a window to educational opportunities. Several chapters contain supplemental stories that introduce or enhance the lessons of the activities.

Although none of the Indian stories appears in the original native language in which it was first told, we have tried in our retellings to capture the motion and the imagery of the original tales and to make sure that the central message of each story is kept intact, for stories are powerful tools used for teaching and discipline in Native North American cultures. If you decide to retell these stories, to memorize them rather than read them from the book, or to develop them into puppet shows, plays or skits, we urge you to pay close attention to the way these stories work. They are, however, meant to be *told*, rather than read silently.

Among Native North American cultures there were certain stories that were usually told at specific times of the year. Northeastern Indians told stories during the long cold season between the first and last frosts. Although you may not be able to restrict your use of these stories to this period of time, it is good to point out to children the traditional storytelling seasons. With this in mind, we'd like to suggest some ways to approach the oral use of these stories.

Seeing the Story

To begin with, you should read each story aloud to yourself several times before you try to read it to children or to tell it from memory. Let the story become a part of you. This was the method of the old-time American Indian storytellers, who listened again and again to each tale, rehearsing the story alone before trying to share it with an audience. After a story has become part of you, you may find yourself "seeing" the story as you tell it. At that point you may wish to bring your telling to life with descriptions of those things you see as you tell the tales aloud. When the story is a part of you and you are sharing it effectively with the listeners—creating the "reality" of that story—the characters and events will live and move in their mind's eye.

But be careful as you do this and do not try changing the endings or combining these stories together. The elements of a story create a whole, a living being unto itself. Stories, to many Native North Americans, are *life;* they help to maintain the cultural integrity of the people and to keep the world in balance. When you "see" a story, it is like seeing an animal after having only heard about it before. It comes alive for you. But one animal is different from another and so, too, is each story. Some stories may be wolves. Some may be turtles. But to combine the two does not work.

Be sure to look up the meaning of any unfamiliar Indian words or names that appear in the story before you share it with the children. These terms are identified and explained in the Glossary at the end of this book. In this way, when the children ask "What is a Clan Mother?" or "What is a longhouse?" you will be ready with an informed response.

Once you "see" a story and feel comfortable with its telling, you may find it helpful to have a way of recalling the story at the proper time. The Iroquois storyteller or *Hage'ota* carried a bag full of items that acted as mnemonic devices—each item represented a story. The *Hage'ota*, or perhaps a child in the audience, would pull an item out of the bag, the item would be shown to the people and the story would begin. This process also transforms the storytelling into a shared experience by bringing the children into the act of choosing the stories to be told.

Making a storyteller's bag is an easy project. You and your children can gather things from the natural world or make things to add to the bag. Feathers, stones, nuts, small carvings, anything that can be jostled around in a bag without breaking can be part of your collection. Read the stories in this book carefully and then use your imagination.

The Setting of the Story

In many Native North American cultures, everyone was allowed to have a say and people listened with patience. People would sit in a circle during the time of storytelling because in a circle no person is at the head. All are "the same height." Remembering this may help you and it is good to remind your listeners—who are not just an audience but part of the story—of that.

Pay close attention to the setting in which you read or tell a story. If it is in a quiet place where people can sit comfortably in a circle, whether in chairs or on the floor, you are already one step ahead. But if other things are going on around you, if some people are seated outside the group or where they cannot hear well, your story will lose some of its power. We have often waited until we have brought a child into the circle before beginning a story. It is amazing how quiet and involved someone who was standing outside a group and acting uninterested or hostile will become when "brought in." Be sure that you are comfortable as you do your storytelling. Pay attention to how you feel as you speak from a standing position or while seated in a chair. There is no *one* right way for everyone. Some people do best while sitting in a chair or on the floor, others feel more assured while standing or even walking around. Find *your* way.

Speaking the Story

One of the greatest orators among the Iroquois was a man named Red Jacket. He credited his deep sonorous voice to his habit of standing next to the great falls at Niagara and speaking over their roar. While this may have been part of Red Jacket's secret, another part which has not been spoken of so often is that Red Jacket knew the right way to breathe when he spoke. In his youth he was one of the greatest runners among his people, and no one can run great distances without knowing the secrets of deep and even breathing. Breathing is one of the most important things for a storyteller. Too many people try to speak while breathing from high in the chest. This tightens your chest and can strain your voice. Your breath—and your voice—should come from your diaphragm, that part of your body which is just below your

ribs and above your stomach. Place the tips of your fingers there and breathe in. If your diaphragm does not move out, then your breathing is wrong. Native North American people see that area as the center of power for the body, and it is certainly the source of power for oral presentations. Your voice will be stronger, project farther and sound better when it comes from the diaphragm.

When Red Jacket spoke above the roar of the great falls, he was also learning that resonance is a vital part of a good speaking voice. Try humming as an exercise to develop that natural resonance. One common method of voice training is to hum the vowel sounds, first with the letter "M" before them and then with the letter "B." Clarity is as important as resonance, so when you read or tell your stories, be sure you do not let your voice trail away, especially on significant words. Remember that you are the *carrier* of the story. You must bring it to everyone in the room with you. Lift your chin up as you speak and look to the very back of the room. Imagine your voice as beginning in front of your mouth and reaching to the farthest wall. You do not have to shout to be heard.

Pace is also important in telling a story. Many people tend to either speak too fast or too slow. If the story has truly become a part of you, then you should be able to sense its pace and follow it in your reading or telling. But you may wish to check yourself by tape-recording a story as you read or retell it from memory. See if there are places where you speak too quickly, if there are words that are not well enunciated and if you have placed emphasis on the points in the story that should be emphasized.

You may want to make use of any one of a number of formulaic beginnings and endings traditionally used by Native American people when telling stories. One way that the Abenaki people begin a story is with the words, "Here my story camps." They then close the story with such phrases as "That is the end" or "Then I left." The Iroquois often begin by saying, "Would you like to hear a story?" as do many other Native American people. They then end with the words, "*Da neho!*" which mean, "That is all." Such simple beginnings and endings may be of help to you as a storyteller because they give you a clear way into and out of the tale.

Involving the Listeners

A good story cannot exist without a good listener. There are certain things which you, as a reader or teller, can do to help your listeners be more effective and more involved. We have already mentioned the setting in which the story is told, but there are other ways to bring the listeners into the tale. One device is the use of "response words." Tell the listeners that whenever you say "Ho?" they are to respond with "Hey!" That will let you know that they are still awake and listening. The "Ho?" and "Hey!" can also be used as pacing elements in the story or to make the listeners feel themselves entering the tale. For example:

"Then he started to climb . . ."

"Ho?"

"HEY!"

"He climbed higher and higher . . ."

"Ho?"

"HEY!"

"He climbed so high . . ."

"Ho?"

"HEY!"

"That the people looked like ants . . ."

"Ho?"

"HEY!"

As you tell your story, do not look at the same person in your audience all the time. If you are telling stories to a large group of children, make eye contact with different people and see them as individuals, not just a faceless mass. Ask questions that can be answered by someone who has been listening to the story. For example:

"And so that bright red suit of feathers went to who?"

"Cardinal!"

"Yes! Then Buzzard tried on another suit of feathers. It was blue with a black-streaked crest. But that suit was not fine enough, either, for the messenger of all the birds. So that blue suit went to who?"

"Bluejay!"

If there is singing, chanting, movement or hand clapping in your story, teach it to the children before the story begins. Then, at the appropriate time in the story, have everyone join in.

As you tell a story, you should also be aware of how you use your hands, your facial expressions, the motions of your body. Some storytellers or readers prefer to sit quite still and to let their voices do all of the work. Others become theatrical. Again, you should find the way you are most comfortable. Flailing your arms about aimlessly can be distracting or overly dramatic. One way to make your hand gestures more meaningful and to give the eyes of your listeners something really significant to focus upon is to incorporate American Indian sign language in your tellings. Many of the signs are the same as those used by the deaf, and the *lingua franca* sign language that Native Americans developed because of widespread trade across pre-Columbian America is both effective and beautiful to watch. Two

inexpensive and easy-to-use books that teach American Indian sign language through photographs and simple drawings are *Indian Sign Language* by William Tomkins (New York: Dover Publications, 1969) and *Indian Talk: Hand Signals of the North American Indians* by Iron Eyes Cody (Happy Camp, Calif.: Naturegraph Publishers, 1970).

We find that, when sharing longer stories with very young children, it sometimes helps to take a brief break halfway through. Use this interlude to share and discuss the story illustration(s) as they relate to events that are unfolding. This technique prolongs the children's attention span.

LEADING THE GUIDED FANTASIES

Guided fantasies are also used in *Keepers of the Animals* to create firsthand learning experiences that would not be possible otherwise. Some examples are "Flight of Fantasy" (Chapter 5), "The Life of a Salmon" (Chapter 9) and "In the Eyes of a Rattlesnake" (Chapter 11). In all cases the supplemental stories and guided fantasies build upon the subjects introduced by the Native American stories that open each chapter.

While reading the fantasies, have the children

• assume a comfortable position (we often have them lie on their backs)
• close their eyes
• relax
• take a few slow deep breaths
• clear their minds to make them more receptive to the images conjured up

Have them visualize that they are in a safe quiet place, or one they love best, to help them relax. Since some children respond well to the fantasies, while others might find themselves wanting to giggle, make sound effects or move around, ask everyone to remain quiet throughout so that those who are into the journey will not be disturbed. Reassure those children who have difficulty sitting still and imagining the fantasy—not every kind of activity works well with everyone. Incorporate sounds into the fantasy, such as music, a drumbeat or sound effects to enhance the experience. Use different voices and be dramatic!

PERFORMING THE PUPPET SHOWS

Have fun with the children while preparing them for puppeteering. You can begin by having them make finger puppets with which to practice puppet motions (Figure 2-1). Sculpt the head out of salt dough or clay. Have the children make a small (about 1-inch [2.5-centimeter]) head of one of the animals in the puppet shows in this book. Each child should press a thumb up about the length of a fingertip into the bottom of the head to leave a hole just larger than a finger needs to fit into. Paint the head when it dries. The "body" of the puppet will be a simple, tube-shaped piece of cloth (an infant's sock works well), with the closed end pressed and glued up into the hole on the bottom of the puppet's head. To work a puppet, the child pulls the sock down over her or his finger and pushes the fingertip up into the hole under the head.

Now, with everyone's puppet in place, have someone run across in front of the group as each child works her or his puppet to imitate a person running. Continue having someone demonstrate different motions as the puppeteers mimic these actions, such as hopping, skipping, crawling, walking, climbing and jumping. Have the puppets talk to each other and express being sad, surprised, happy, shy and other emotional states.

With this experience the children will be better able to perform the puppet shows. The puppets to be used in the shows could be simple, one-sided or two-sided crayon-colored cardboard-on-a-stick puppets (Figure 2-1), or elaborate three-dimensional puppets with arms and wings that move. As the children practice working their puppets behind a stage, have them imagine that they *are* that puppet—doing, thinking and feeling all that it does, thinks and feels. It helps when they look up at their puppets as they bring them to life. Encourage them to develop a puppet's

character and voice and to stick with it, trying to be as consistent as possible. A lot of energy and movement will help to make the puppet an expressive one. Puppet animals should enter the stage from an appropriate place. A ground-hog may pop up from a burrow or a bat may fly in from above, a squirrel could climb down from a tree or a fox might trot in from the side of the stage.

Sound effects enhance the performance. The sound you make by rapping on a hollow coconut shell sounds like a woodpecker's pecking. Imitate clomping feet by clapping the two halves of the shell together. Shake a piece of metal flashing to create thunder. Spray mist from a bottle from behind the stage to mimic a rainstorm or fog. Use your imagination to make your own original sound effects!

A number of useful books are available on puppeteering, including *Puppets: Methods and Materials* by Cedric Flower and Alan Jon Fortney (Worcester, Mass.: Davis Publications, 1983); *Introducing Puppetry* by Peter Fraser (New York: Watson-Guptill Publications, 1968); and both *Puppet Shows Made Easy!* and *Puppetry and the Art of Story Creation* by Nancy Renfro (Austin, Tex.: Nancy Renfro Studios, 1979).

CONDUCTING THE ACTIVITIES

The following checklist provides specific ideas for creating experiences that are meaningful, informative and fun.

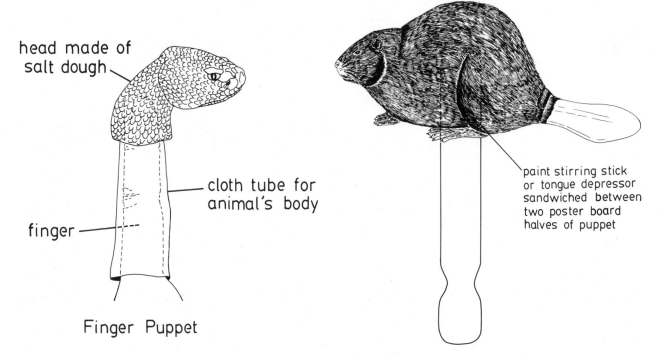

head made of
salt dough

cloth tube for
animal's body

finger

Finger Puppet

paint stirring stick
or tongue depressor
sandwiched between
two poster board
halves of puppet

Figure 2-1. Two kinds of puppets you can make: a finger puppet (left) and a double-sided stick puppet (right).

Plan Wisely and in Detail

Consider the time available. List your activities and the time needed for each one. Plan a few extra activities to be sure there is always something to do if the activities move along quickly. If some children or groups finish a project earlier than others, you can provide meaningful tasks or projects for them to work on while waiting for others to finish. Prioritize the last few activities. This way, in case you begin to run out of time, you can be sure to include those activities that are most important and allow enough time to lead the final activity without rushing through it.

Choose and Adapt Activities for the Children's Levels

Young children need concrete experience and are not yet adept at the second-order, abstract thought used to build concepts. They may understand that rain falls from a cloud because they can see it coming down, but it may be hard for them to visualize how a cloud forms from invisible water vapor that evaporates from ponds, lakes, rivers, oceans and leaves. Older children understand concepts more readily, such as the water cycle, and they are challenged by longer activities that probe a subject in greater depth.

With younger children, the activities need to be brief and active with hands-on exercises throughout. Allow plenty of time for facilitating social interaction and answering questions, questions and more questions! As anyone who works with children knows, two of the most frequently spoken words are, "But why?"

Set the Stage

Prepare the children with one or two pre-activities to help them focus on the intended theme. Use a story, a puppet show, a slide show, a filmstrip, a movie or an activity.

Link the Activities in a Meaningful Way

Provide connections between activities. Discussion and leading questions help the children to discover these links themselves. Keep tying the meaning of each activity in with the overall theme. A focused summary at the end of each activity is a good way to do this. Ask the children, "What happened?" "What does it mean?"

Put the Children into the Center of the Experience

Use and design activities that have the children exploring and asking questions. Facilitating and sharing the experience is more effective and exciting than a show-and-tell approach. Establish your goals and let the children participate in the planning to reach those goals. Early involvement increases motivation later on. Let the children take turns leading or co-leading the group.

Teach by Example

Children love to imitate adults as they grow and search for their own identities. Consistency between your actions and words is crucial. Being a role model is among the most powerful teaching tools.

Use Firsthand, Sensory Experiences Whenever Possible

Help the children to experience the subject firsthand (Figure 2-2). If the lesson is about trees, then take them to a tree in the backyard, or to a forest, a park or a grove of trees on the school grounds. If you are studying water, visit a pond. Avoid prolonged discussion. To see it, smell it, hear it, touch it or taste it is to know it better. This is true for all ages, especially young children. The active approach also aids in motor skill development.

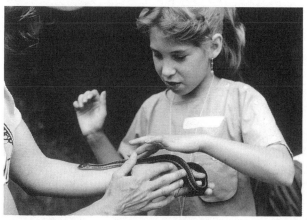

Figure 2-2. There is no substitute for firsthand experience. This child is enthralled as she touches a snake for the first time. Photo by Arthur Swoger, courtesy Audubon Society of Rhode Island.

Use Creative Questions and Answers

Emphasize the children's own discoveries. Questions can be used to direct their attention to important objects or subjects of inquiry. Avoid giving the answers away. Here is an example:

Child: "Why do some animals have whiskers?"
Leader: "Well, have you ever touched an animal's whiskers?"
Child: "Yes, I've touched my cat's whiskers."

Leader: "How does your cat react when you touch its whiskers?"

Child: "It flinches its mouth or turns its head away, even when I've snuck up on it and it didn't know I was there. Oh, I get it, whiskers help an animal to know what is going on around it!"

Leader: "Right! Whiskers are one way that an animal senses its environment. Good thinking!"

If you do not know the answer to a question, it is okay to say so. Children and adults alike can usually tell if you are using questions or other devices as a smoke screen to mask a lack of knowledge. Use an unanswered question as a shared learning experience while you probe the possible solutions together.

Emphasize Positive Feelings as Well as Knowledge

A child who empathizes with someone or something is more likely to want to learn about that person or thing. You can *say* that a spider carries an egg sac, has eight legs and eyes and traps insects in a web. But watch what happens when you read *Charlotte's Web* by E. B. White, then create a giant web of yarn and play the "Sticky Web" game in Chapter 3. Instead of squishing the spider living in a corner of the ceiling, adopt it as a pet and care for it. Observe the spider as it catches flies and other insects in its web and feeds on them. This leads into a discussion of how things die to provide food for other living things. With these activities children become excited and motivated; they laugh at times, and some even cry if the spider gets swatted by someone else. They care.

Figure 2-3. Working in small groups fosters positive social skills. These children are sampling the life in a tidal river. Photo courtesy Audubon Society of Rhode Island.

Provide a supportive atmosphere—a trusting and respectful experience throughout—as a compassionate means to a compassionate end. This approach reinforces efforts to establish positive self-esteem, behavior and environmental attitudes. A child who values and cares for herself or himself is more likely to value Earth and trust other people.

Foster Aesthetic Appreciation

Allow quiet time for observing a flower and drawing its many parts. Share your poetry, photographs or memories with the children. Have them share theirs with you. Allow them slow, quiet moments by building these times into the rhythms of each day. Late afternoons, when energy starts to wane, are good times for this. You could also set a contemplative tone for the day by beginning it with a story.

Emphasize Group Work and Positive Social Interaction

Use teams and small groups to practice positive communication, cooperation and conflict resolution skills (Figure 2-3). This approach fosters self-knowledge and a sense of connection with others—of feeling safe, open and confident in social interaction. Involve everyone. No matter how great or small one child's contribution may seem to you, it is that child's whole world and the basis for his or her self-esteem.

Foster Problem Solving/Research Skills

Here is a process to facilitate decision making and problem solving for environmental concerns:

- recognize the problem(s)
- define the problem(s)
- listen with comprehension
- collect information about the problem(s)
- organize the information
- analyze the information
- generate alternatives for possible solutions to the problem(s)
- develop a plan of action
- implement the plan of action[1]

These are also valuable skills for researching and solving personal problems.

Use Long-term Projects

Watch migrating birds in springtime and autumn. Find out what you can do to protect the tropical rain forest that many migratory birds overwinter in. Keep a pet and teach responsible caring. Adopt an endangered species and make a commitment to do all you can to save it until (hopefully) it recovers and is able to sustain a healthy wild population on its own. If, through your activities at home or your teaching at an environmental education or nature center, you have lots of children come through who are only present for short periods of time, have them work on long-term projects anyway. A bird feeder tended by many children over time still gives each child a feeling of continuing a tradition of nurturing wild birds.

Include a Connection With Other Communities and Countries

We are all part of the global environment. Children can be taught to understand their relationship with other cultures and distant lands. How does our heavy reliance in North America on the natural resources imported from other countries affect those societies, their environments and the animals that live in them? What are the ecological problems associated with acid rain, nuclear energy and other environmental issues that so clearly transcend cultural and political boundaries? These are among the many environmental issues that link North Americans to the lives of other peoples and animals around the world.

Include Moral Issues: Environmental and Social Ethics

Native American stories and Earth activities involve values and moral issues as well as knowledge because they teach about life—human relationships and interactions between people and our environments. Moral issues include our thoughts, feelings and actions toward ourselves, other people and the environment. *Value* can be defined as a strong and enduring preference, by an individual or groups of people, for a specific object, behavior or way of life.[2]

> We are one in relationship with the Earth and other people. Doing good supports this relationship. Love and moral goodness are inseparable; they are the elemental components of a life ethic.[3]

It is important to foster caring, nurturing and compassion in children's lives. Empathy is the tangible sense of our interconnectedness. When we feel what another person feels and when we understand that Earth is a living organism whose parts also have an awareness, even though different from our own, we want to help because we share that emotional experience.

A child's level of moral development is another important consideration when planning values activities.

Face Problems and Controversy and Deal With Them Constructively and Positively

Accept problems as part of reality when studying the environment and other cultures. Emphasize positive approaches to problems.

Controversial issues need to be approached cautiously. One way to avoid biased teaching of controversial issues is to analyze the subjects of bias, prejudice and ideology. Children who are fluent in the ideas of controversy are better able to approach moral issues objectively. Experience with controversial issues motivates and involves children in seeking solutions to problems such as water pollution, acid rain and world hunger.

Respect Spiritual and Religious Beliefs

Spiritual beliefs and religious practices are major factors in determining a child's orientation toward Earth and other people. Each individual's form of spiritual expression needs to be acknowledged and respected when the children's inevitable concerns arise. A child may say: "This story says that Earth was created by Grandmother Spider and Tawa, the Sky God, but that's not what I was taught to believe." We have found a good response to be: "Yes, people believe in different accounts of creation, and this story tells us about the beliefs of certain Native American cultures." Spirituality can be a part of environmental activities in appropriate settings.

Respect the Privacy of Personal Beliefs and Feelings

When asking questions of other people's children, give them the right not to answer if the response will reveal sensitive personal beliefs or self-knowledge. One example is Study Question 5 in Chapter 3, which asks the children how they believe the world was created.

Discipline Compassionately and Decisively

If there are children in your group who insist on diverting attention away from the center of learning, try to involve them in the activity or discussion by asking them for help in solving a problem or completing a task. You may need to stand near an overly active child or even put your arm around her or his shoulders. These techniques help to comfort or give attention to the attention seekers in a positive way while avoiding a confrontation. If a rule is questioned, explain the meaning behind it and turn the experience into a constructive dialogue. This approach also fosters the development of positive personal moral standards.

Avoid using power plays or demeaning methods of punishment. A child who is a severe problem and a continual distraction may have to leave the group so the learning can continue. This can be a positive experience if the child is asked to sit and reflect on what has happened, why and how he or she could learn from the experience.

Don't send mixed messages. Establish the rules and the consequences of excessively disruptive behavior early in the lesson and be consistent in applying both.

Keep a Sense of Humor, Joy and Appreciation

A light touch opens hearts and minds. Be watchful for "teachable moments" in nature that can captivate and enthrall—a butterfly emerging from its chrysalis or a snake shedding its skin. You may want to build up a repertoire of nature puns for older children; for example:

Question: "What did the wild grape say when the deer stepped on it?"
Answer: "Nothing much, it just let out a little 'wine.' "

Question: "Does anyone know what we call this white, milk-colored stone?"
Answer: "That's called quartz, isn't it?"
Response: "Yes, it's a beautiful stone. Let's not take it for granite."

Some children will laugh and some groan (just like adults), but they love it!

Be Yourself

Use whatever works best for your personality. Some adults take a high-energy approach to leading activities, while others use a more low-key style. There are many ways of leading; if you are well prepared and promoting a positive relationship with the children, you are doing well.

Providing a Culminating Activity or Experience

Wrap up, synthesize and summarize a lesson with an activity that brings it all together. A good example is "Save a Species" in Chapter 17.

TAKING YOUR CHILDREN OUTDOORS

Waves tumble over sands; wind rushes through pine boughs; flowers scent the breeze over a field; a pungent smell wafts from the pavement near a vacant lot after a rain—these and more are waiting to be experienced

outdoors. There is adventure in the unknown, and even the familiar looks different when it is visited with the intent of discovering what has been looked at and not yet seen, heard yet never listened to. Whether in the back-yard, the school grounds, a vacant lot, nature-center lands, a wilderness area or a vest-pocket park in the city, there are discoveries awaiting (Figure 2-4).

Figure 2-4. This nest of red-eyed vireo chicks is one of the endless animal discoveries awaiting you and your children outdoors. Photo by Don Blades.

A trip into natural surroundings or the local community is a chance to study the environment firsthand. It is a time to visit plants and animals in their homes and to learn wilderness survival skills. You might take a trip to a local market to study the food that feeds our bodies, the most personal environment of all. Of course, not every child's experience will be filled with wonder and aesthetic beauty; fear is also a natural part of discovering the new. Some fears are well founded, such as being afraid to disturb a bee's nest. Other fears are irrational.

We once led a group of children from a very large urban neighborhood on an excursion to a pond. There were the usual shrieks when a frog jumped in and swam for its life. But the toughest-looking young boy became pale when a frog we were looking at jumped out of our hands and touched him. This streetwise child recoiled from a harmless amphibian. With a little help from his friends, we coaxed him into touching the frog's skin. By the end of our pond study, he understood frogs better and would even hold one at arm's length. He didn't like them, but he accepted them. It was a start.

Planning the Outdoor Excursion

Once you have chosen your activities, scout out the area you intend to take your children to and become familiar with the site. Note the plants, animals and physical aspects of that place and include them in your activities. If there is a nature trail present, you may want to use it for access. If not, plan a route that will do minimal damage to the plant and animal communities along the way. When multiple trips are planned into a wild area, you can establish a path to reduce widespread trampling of the plants, or vary the route in and out to spread the traffic and control wear on the habitat. Consider the access carefully if your group includes children in wheelchairs or with other special needs: No one wants to be left behind.

Choose activities that fulfill your goals and objectives. Think of a theme for the entire program; something broad like "survival" allows for focus and flexibility. Children love to play games en route to a site. You can use the "deer walk" to create suspense and interest. First have them cup their hands behind their ears to create "deer ears." Listen carefully and compare the intensity of sounds heard with and without the deer ears. Ask the children why deer can usually hear people coming before the people notice the deer.

"Because they listen quietly?"

"Right, and that's how we'll walk, with our deer ears alert and as quiet as can be," you reply. "Deer will signal danger by raising their tails and showing the white patch underneath. Whenever you see a white flag (hold up a sample flag), quietly gather around and we'll look at whatever our fellow deer thinks is interesting to see." (Pass out white flags to everyone.) In this way the walk becomes part of the experience. Puppets, stuffed animals, stories or other fun props keep the children's interest. Some leaders find it useful to carry an index card with a general outline of the program written on it, along with a list of intended activities.

Conduct the whole program in your mind's eye beforehand and plan for all contingencies that you can anticipate: transportation, proper attire for seasonal weather conditions (especially rain, snow, cold and extreme heat), materials you will need for each activity and name tags. If you are planning a program at a nature center, a letter sent home beforehand to parents, or to the visiting classroom, will help to ensure that the children come prepared with proper clothing. Parents, teachers, seniors, older students or other community volunteers are all excellent resources for helping with the excursion. Try to keep the ratio of adults to children in each group at around one to five or six.

Above all, be prepared! A complete first aid kit is a must, including anti-bee sting serum in case someone in your group is allergic. Your trail kit should also include these items:

- small knife
- compass
- insect repellant
- trash bags
- water, especially during hot days and on long walks

Since most kinds of weather can be enjoyed if you are prepared for them, it is a good policy to go outside under all but the worst conditions. Heavy rains, winds, lightning or other severe weather can come unexpectedly depending upon the weather patterns in your region. Be ready with a full complement of "rainy day" activities just in case.

Conducting the Field Trip (With Special Tips for Larger Groups)

It's time to go! The children are anxious to begin and energy is high.

"There are a few things that I want to say before we go outside," you begin. "We're visiting the plants and animals in *their* homes, so how do you think we should act?"

"On our good behavior," someone says.

"Right, if you take a rock off the path or turn a log over, you're removing the roof of an animal's home. When a leaf gets pulled off a plant, it's part of a living thing. Do you think you'd like it if someone visited your home and carried the roof away or pulled a piece off of *you*?"

"No!" they respond, laughing.

"O.K., then what should you do if you look under a log or rock?"

"Put it back the way we found it!"

You continue, "Since there are so many of us, we need to respect each other when someone is talking. Please raise your hand if you want to say something and listen whenever someone is talking. If you see me raise my hand, that is the signal to raise your hand and listen because there's something to see, do or discuss."

The tone of empathy and caring is set for the whole walk during the crucial first few minutes. This is also a good time to orient the children, in a general way, to the theme of the field trip and to what they can expect. But don't forget to keep plenty of surprises up your sleeve!

You are on the trail now and there is something you want to point out. Walk past that spot far enough so that roughly one half of the group has passed it. Then backtrack to the spot, and you will be standing in the middle of the group to make it easier for the children to hear. Always try to stand facing the sun so that it falls on their backs and does not glare in their eyes. Ask questions to help them discover what you want them to see. Draw the children in and include everyone. These are great times to tell stories or to listen to one of the children's stories. But be careful! You may need to limit their storytelling. Children love to share stories, and some children can talk so long that the flower you are looking at will have gone to seed by the end of the story. You can handle this tricky issue by allowing special times for their stories toward the end of the field trip.

Approach the excursion with "structured flexibility," being open to the special encounter—the unexpected find or event. One of our favorite activities along the trail is the camouflage game. First hold a brief discussion and answer period about what camouflage is and how animals use camouflage, such as cryptic coloration, hiding behind things and under leaves or being shaped like a natural object. Be sure to have pictures of some well-camouflaged animals to hold up as you talk. Tell the children you want them to camouflage themselves whenever you yell "Camouflage!" Give them 10 seconds to hide and tell them not to go more than 20 feet (6.1 meters) away. Close your eyes as you count. Call out the names or locations of children that you can see when you open your eyes.

After you have played the game once, tell the children that the counting time will be shortened by one second during each round of the game, which can come at any time along the trail when you suddenly yell "Camouflage!" This adds an undertone of anticipation to the excursion.

When children are quiet and listening, they often see special things. Suppose a child comes up to you after the camouflage game and says, "I saw a spider with a moth caught in its web! It's over behind that big rock." Postpone the next planned activity and use the occasion as a time to marvel at the event while letting the children generate their own questions. Or, use some creative questioning to tie the sighting in with your lesson and quell some fears about spiders at the same time.

Snack breaks are good times to share special moments. They are also opportune for reading or telling one of the stories in this book that relates to the theme of your walk.

Don't forget to include quiet time during the outdoor excursion. Children can enjoy keeping a journal in which they write, draw pictures, make bark rubbings or practice other creative forms of expression. Their sketches and writings range from humorous stories and comic-strip variety pictures to beautiful drawings and sensitive poetic verse.

"WATERFALL"

It is sometimes very noisy
It is beautiful
water rushing down,
down to a lake or
stream.
Peaceful now.

Projects also get the children involved. You could pile brush for small mammal homes, pick up trash or build a wood duck nesting box for a pond if it is a long-term study with multiple visits. These kinds of activities are found throughout this book. Projects, along with team activities, provide the means for small group cooperation and social development.

When you are ready to wrap up the visit, it is more effective to conduct a summarizing activity on site or on the way back *before* coming within sight of the house, school bus, learning center or other final destination. While the children are in the midst of the excitement and involvement at the site, their attention is still focused there. If you try to wrap up away from the site, the element of concentration on that place and the day's events is weakened and the children's thoughts are already turning to their next experience.

CLASSIFYING AND IDENTIFYING ANIMALS

Identification is an important part of getting to know an animal. In this book, we encourage a knowledge of animals through observation, experience, stewardship and story, but we also realize the value of classifying animals and learning how they are related to one another. This brief section is a bit more technical than the balance of this book because it provides a general overview of animal classification. Numerous field guides are available for identifying animals in the wild and the reader is encouraged to make use of these as well.

Be careful to not get caught up in naming for its own sake. The importance of studying animals is to further the children's understanding of and appreciation for the animal's natural history and its ecological relationships, as well as to develop both empathy and stewardship toward the animal. Identification is simply one means of furthering these important ends.

Taxonomy is the branch of biology that is concerned with the systematic classification of living things. Through time there have been many systems devised for grouping living things according to such distinctions as cell structure, evolutionary relationships and details of reproductive cycles. At one time there were two major groupings or *kingdoms* recognized—*Plantae* and *Animalia*. Then it was noted that bacteria have cells that are more simplified and smaller than those of other organisms, reproduce almost exclusively by asexual division of the cells and almost always occur as single-celled individuals. These *prokaryotic* cells are distinguished from *eukaryotic* cells, which are larger and more highly evolved, reproduce by relatively complex sexual and asexual means and are often parts of multicellular organisms. Bacteria were separated, sometimes along with other organisms, into a third kingdom called the *Monera*. There have since been many other systems of classification created.

Today it is widely recognized that organisms can be divided into five kingdoms, based on a system that was first proposed by Robert H. Whittaker: *Monera* (bacteria); *Protoctista* (including protozoans and algae); *Fungi* (molds and mushrooms); *Plantae* (flowering plants, conifers, ferns and mosses); and *Animalia* (animals with and without backbones).[4]

This book uses the terms *plant* and *animal* frequently and, where helpful, gives some specifics to indicate a more detailed classification of organisms. The names of the different divisions used to classify organisms, moving from the broadest categories to the most specific, are as follows: kingdom, phylum (botanists use "division"), class, order, family, genus and species. A *species* is a population of organisms that are closely related through similarities in their anatomy and historical evolutionary development and which are capable of reproducing among themselves but cannot successfully breed with members of another species. The three-kingdom system (*Monera*, *Plantae* and *Animalia*) is used in this book.

The animal kingdom has thousands of representatives that are diverse and challenging to identify. Those animals with backbones, called *vertebrates*, are most conspicuous. Overall, however, there is a far greater number of *invertebrates*, animals without backbones.

The invertebrate phyla form an amazing and interesting array of animals, including:

• protozoans or single-celled animals, including the familiar *Amoeba* and *Paramecium*
• sponges
• hydras and jellyfish
• rotifers
• bryozoans or moss animals, also classified by some biologists in the phylum *Ectoprocta*
• worms and wormlike forms: flatworms, proboscis worms, nematodes, horsehair worms, roundworms and segmented worms such as earthworms and leeches
• arthropods, the largest animal group, which in numbers comprises 80 percent of all known animals. Included here are the crustaceans, spiders and mites (arachnids) and insects. Arthropods have an *exoskeleton* to which muscles are attached and which must be shed as the animal grows.
• water bears or tardigrades, which live among the plants and sand grains
• mollusks, including two main groups: the snails (*Gastropoda*) and the clams and mussels (*Pelecypoda*)

Vertebrates are actually a subgroup of the phylum *Chordata*. Members of this group have a divided nerve cord running along the back or *dorsal* side, with a segmented backbone, a circulatory system on the front or *ventral* side and an enclosed brain case. Other characteristics include paired appendages and, in some groups, warm-bloodedness or *homeothermy*. Over one-half of all vertebrates are bony fishes. Vertebrates also include amphibians, reptiles, birds and mammals.

CATCHING ANIMALS AND CARING FOR THEM IN CAPTIVITY

Emphasize that this is a visit to the *animals'* homes. Our philosophy is to enjoy and observe animals in their own habitats (Figure 2-5). Treat the logs, rocks, ponds, flowers, nests, burrows and other homes with respect. We encourage

Figure 2-5. The chipmunk is such a captivating and entertaining little creature we may forget that it is a wild animal and that we are intruding on its habitat as we pass through. Children can be taught to respect wildlife and to leave the homes of animals as they found them. Size (including tail): 8–10 inches (20.3–25.4 centimeters). Photo by Don Blades.

you and the children to "capture" the animal with a photograph or an illustration. If you feel you *must* capture animals as part of your studies, we offer the following humane suggestions for catching animals and keeping them well and for a short period of time in captivity.

If the children want to collect animals (insects, frogs, snakes, turtles), they should simply observe the animals briefly in the wild and return them to their homes unless they know how to properly care for them at home or in the classroom or nature center. Even animals kept for observation should be returned to their homes after a week or so. *Wild animals are not pets.* Be especially careful not to collect mammals, birds or other animals that may carry diseases. Special permits are often required for collecting these animals.

We realize, however, that the instinct among children to capture animals and look at them up close is a powerful one. This experience also dispels fears of animals and brings the children to a greater understanding of their relations in the wild. If animals must be captured, they should only be kept for a brief period of observation, and only when there is a healthy population of that kind of animal present. *Never collect any rare, threatened or endangered species.* If a rare animal is sighted, keep it a secret and report the finding to the appropriate protectors of wildlife in your area. Refrain from conducting experiments of any kind involving animals. Simply have the children learn by observing a brief period of the animal's growth, development and behavior.

Always have the children show respect and appreciation for the animals they catch. This will be accomplished if they

• ask permission of the animal to catch it and keep it for a brief time;
• are careful to make certain that they are leaving a healthy population of the animal behind for future generations;
• collect an animal only during its active seasons; do not capture and try to keep insects, amphibians, reptiles and other animals while they are dormant;
• take good, responsible care of the animal while it is in captivity;
• give thanks to the animal for what it has given them;
• release the animal well, unharmed and in exactly the same place where it was found.

Catching Animals

To begin with, become familiar with the dangerous and poisonous animals in your area. If you have any notion that the animal at hand poses a threat, leave it alone and keep your distance.

It is very important for children to treat animals with great care when capturing them. A child's attitude toward an insect or other animal in hand is a good indication of how he or she regards animals in general. This is an excellent opportunity for encouraging greater understanding and a positive, caring relationship.

Simple things make a big difference when handling animals. Catching a butterfly in a net by gently sweeping it off a flower is preferable to sneaking up on it and pinching its wings, which can damage the wings and rub off protective scales. When catching a toad, salamander, frog or lizard, it is best to cup a hand over the animal first, then hold it gently around the body. Powerful leapers, such as pickerel frogs and bullfrogs, need to be grabbed quickly and securely but not too firmly, then held by the body and hind legs. To capture an animal with wet skin, such as a frog or salamander, the children should wet their hands first so they do not damage the protective mucous coating on the animal's skin. This coating keeps the skin moist to enable it to absorb oxygen. It also protects the animal from becoming infected by fungi, bacteria and other pathogens.

Some basic equipment for catching animals includes a capture net, a well-aerated container for storing the animal, a pair of tweezers and a thick glove for protection in case an animal that may bite or sting is accidentally caught.

Many insects and other small terrestrial animals can be caught in a long-handled, cloth net (Figure 2-6). The wooden handle, such as a piece of an old broomstick, should be a minimum of .75-inch (19 millimeters) in diameter and around 3 feet (91.4 centimeters) long. Make the wire rim of at least number 8-gauge wire with about a 1-foot (30.5-centimeter) diameter opening. Bend the ends of the wire over so that at least 3 inches (7.6 centimeters) of wire can be inserted into a snug hole drilled into the end of the handle, and secure these ends with an epoxy glue. Make the bag about 2 feet (61 centimeters) long and out of a light, airy material.

Insects and small animals can be caught by sweeping the net through grass or other plants, or by stalking and capturing a specific individual. Remove the animal from the net by isolating it in a fold, placing the fold over the capture container and inverting it to release the animal inside. If you catch a biting or stinging insect, such as a bee, wasp or an ant, use a thick glove to maneuver it into a container and leave the container open on its side somewhere away from the children so the animal can escape. Or, you could take the net off to the side, open it and leave it for a time until the insect is gone.

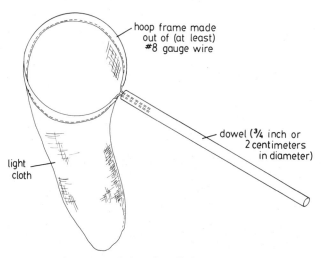

Figure 2-6. Homemade long-handled insect net.

Aquatic insects and small animals are best caught in a strainer. A good, readily available model is a large tea strainer with a 6- to 8-inch (15.2- to 20.3-centimeter) opening. Sweep it through the water, aquatic plants or muck, or pursue and capture specific animals. Pick out any animals that are caught and drop them into their own pond or stream water held in a large, white tub or other white container, which will provide good contrast for viewing the animals. Another technique is to swish the strainer backward through water (backwashing) to sweep any animals off it. Stream critters can be caught by turning rocks over and picking them off, or by placing the strainer downstream from a rock and turning the rock over to allow the current to wash animals into the strainer. A pair of tweezers can be used to pick insects *gently* out of the strainer and place them in the tub, or they can be swished into the water using the backwash technique. Aquatic animals should be placed only in water taken from their own habitat, never in tap water, which often contains poisons such as chlorine. Keep the animals in the shade for an hour or less. Release them where found or nearby in a gentle current, if they were caught in the rapids.

Captured animals can be kept temporarily in a well-aerated jar. Keep terrestrial animals in a dry jar with a few plants for cover. Aquatic animals need some water, but be sure to give frogs, other amphibians and aquatic reptiles a shallow pool of water so they can breathe. When poking holes in the cover of a container to allow air in, work from the outside in, using a hammer and a punch or a nail, then bend over the edges that stick out of the top by gently hammering them flat so that the animal does not get cut on them. Cover the edges with masking tape to further protect animals from cutting themselves. Be sure to punch holes in the tape as well.

Caring for Animals in Captivity

Even if you keep an animal in captivity for a week or less, it is important to give it a clean, adequate home with food, water (if necessary), cover and adequate space. Make sure the cage is roomy so the animal has plenty of space to move around and hide in. A habitat that is too small, or one that lacks a place for the animal to seek seclusion, can create a good deal of stress.

There are many different kinds of insect cages to consider, ranging from simple glass jars to covered flower pots with living plants inside (Figure 2-7). Keep the cage dry and provide just a little water in the form of a damp sponge set in a small plate or jar lid.

Reptiles and amphibians can be kept in one of the following varieties of habitat cages, all of which can be made in a medium-sized aquarium measuring at least 18 inches (45.7 centimeters) long by 12 inches (30.5 centimeters) wide and deep:

- dry habitat with sand or loam as a base;
- terrarium with moist soil, moss and other plants growing;
- semiaquatic terrarium with a plate of water or one-half of the habitat as open water;
- aquarium with aquatic plants in it to keep water oxygenated;
- aquarium with aquatic plants and an aerating device to keep water fresh and oxygenated; or
- outdoor pens protected on top and on all sides to keep the animal in and predators out.

Duplicate the animal's natural condition as closely as possible in its habitat cage. Snakes, for instance, need a dry cage, while frogs, toads and salamanders require a moist environment with a dish of water. Pieces of bark and stones make excellent hiding places. Cover with a weighted screen to allow plenty of air exchange and to prevent the growth of mold and mildew. In an unaerated aquarium in which frogs, tadpoles or amphibian eggs are being kept, change the water every two or three days using new water from the animal's home stream or pond, and replace the aquatic plants that are present with new specimens. Reptiles prefer a temperature of around 75° F to 85° F (24° C to 30° C), while amphibians like it a little cooler at about 70° F (21° C). Place the cage where it will receive some sunlight and some shade every day.

It is beyond the scope of this book to provide a detailed list of the needs of all common insects, reptiles, amphibians and other animals. The discussions and activities in each chapter of *Keepers of the Animals* give further details about the needs of particular animals. In addition, Figure 10-5 in the activity called "Egg-Siting Encounter: From Eggs to Legs" in Chapter 10 provides the food and habitat requirements of many common amphibians. There are a number of books listed in the teacher's guide that give extensive instructions for preparing animal habitat and caring for animals in captivity.

Remind the children that wild animals are not pets and should not be handled, even when kept in a temporary habitat in the home. Children will learn a lot more by observing the animal's undisturbed behavior, such as when it is feeding and being fed, swimming, climbing or flying around the cage. We learn the most about our wild animal friends when we leave them on their own to reveal themselves to us in their own ways.

* * * *

This chapter has provided both ideas and practical suggestions for effectively using and integrating the Native North American stories and environmental activities found in Part II. Now it's time to begin! We hope that you and your children enjoy these stories and activities as much as we enjoy sharing them.

NOTES

1. William B. Stapp and Dorothy A. Cox, *Environmental Education Activities Manual* (Dexter, Mich.: Thomson-Shore, 1979), 16. To obtain a copy write to Environmental Education Activities Manual, 2050 Delaware, Ann Arbor, MI 48103.

2. An adaptation of definitions of value by Milton Rokeach from *Beliefs, Attitudes and Values: A Theory of Organization and Change* (San Francisco, Calif.: Jossey Bass, 1976), 125 and *The Nature of Human Values* (New York: Macmillan, 1973), 5.

3. Michael J. Caduto, *A Guide on Environmental Values Education* (Paris, France: United Nations Education, Scientific and Cultural Organization [UNESCO], 1985), 34.

4. L. Margulis and K.V. Schwartz, *Five Kingdoms: An Illustrated Guide to the Phyla of Life on Earth* (San Francisco, Calif.: W. H. Freeman, 1981).

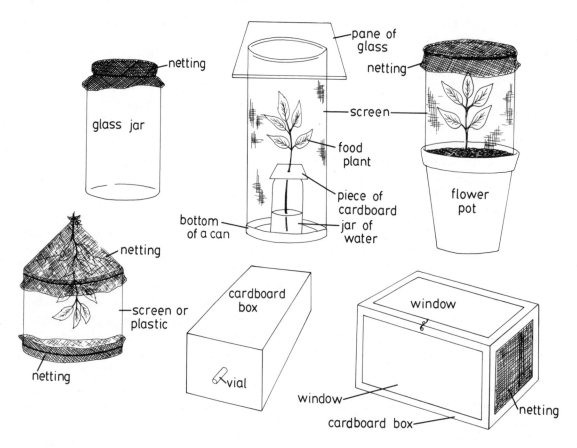

Figure 2-7. Insect cages. Adapted with permission from Donald J. Borror and Richard E. White, A Field Guide to the Insects. *Boston, Mass.: Houghton Mifflin Co., 1970, 25.*

PART II

NATIVE AMERICAN ANIMAL STORIES AND WILDLIFE ACTIVITIES

✦ CREATION ✦

It was left to Grandmother Spider to put things on Earth into order. So Grandmother Spider gathered all of the living creatures around her.

Chapter 3

✤ How Grandmother Spider Named the Clans ✤

(Hopi—Southwest)

After Tawa, the Sky God, and Grandmother Spider had made Earth and all of the things upon it, Tawa went back up into the heavens. Grandmother Spider remained with the animals and all of the people there in the four great caves of the underworld. It was left to Grandmother Spider to put things on Earth into order. So Grandmother Spider gathered all of the living creatures around her. She began to separate the people into the different Indian nations, telling them how it would be from then on for them. So it was that she made the Ute and the Zuni and the Comanche and the Pueblo people and the Hopi and all of the others. She named them and from then on they knew their names. So too she gave all of the animals their names so that they also would know who they were.

Then Grandmother Spider saw that life would not be good for the many animals and people there in the darkness of the underworld. With her two grandsons, the Hero Twins, beside her, she led the animals and the people up out of the four caverns. She led them till they came to an opening into the world above. They came out there next to the Colorado River in the place where the people still go to gather salt. As they came out, the turkey dragged his tail in the mud and his tail has been black-tipped ever since then.

Grandmother Spider sent the mourning dove ahead to find good places for the people to settle, places where there were springs and good soil for corn. Then Grandmother Spider separated the people into clans. She chose one animal to lead each of those groups of people and from then on those people carried the name of that animal. So it was that the Snake Clan and the Antelope Clan, the Mountain Lion Clan and the Deer Clan and the other clans came to be among the Hopi. The people each followed their clan animal and when they came to the place to build their homes, there they settled and there they live to this day.

Suddenly, the chief ran right into a huge spider's web that had been strung between the trees across the trail.

How the Spider Symbol Came to the People

(Osage—Plains)

From the earliest days when they came together on this earth, the Osage people have been divided into two groups. These groups were the Sky People and the Earth People. The nine clans of the Sky People always lived in the northern half of the village. The fifteen clans of the Earth People lived in the southern half of the village. These clans looked to the animals to be their teachers, to serve as symbols for them to live strong lives. Each clan had more than one animal as its symbol. One of these clans was called the Isolated Earth People. This is the story of how the spider became one of the symbols of that clan.

One day, the chief of the Isolated Earth People was hunting in the forest. He was not just hunting for game, he was also hunting for a symbol to give life to his people, some great and powerful animal that would show itself to him and teach him an important lesson. As he hunted, he came upon the tracks of a huge deer. The chief became very excited.

"Grandfather Deer," he said, "surely you are going to show yourself to me. You are going to teach me a lesson and become one of the symbols of my people."

Then the chief began to follow the deer's tracks. His eyes were on nothing else as he followed those tracks and he went faster and faster through the forest. Suddenly, the chief ran right into a huge spider's web that had been strung between the trees across the trail. It was so large and strong that it covered his eyes and made him stumble. When he got back up to his feet, he was very angry. He struck at the spider, which was sitting at the edge of the web, but the spider dodged aside and climbed out of reach. Then the spider spoke to the man.

"Grandson," the spider said, "why do you run through the woods looking at nothing but the ground? Why do you act as if you are blind?"

The chief felt foolish, but he felt he had to answer the spider. "I was following the tracks of the great deer," the chief said. "I am seeking a symbol to give life and strength to my people."

"I can be such a symbol," said the spider.

"How could you give strength to my people?" said the chief. "You are small and weak and I didn't even see you as I followed the great deer."

"Grandson," said the spider, "look upon me. I am patient. I watch and I wait. Then all things come to me. If your people learn this, they will be strong indeed."

The chief saw that it was so. Thus the spider became one of the symbols of the Osage people.

DISCUSSION

Grandmother Spider accomplishes many important things in these two stories. She helps Tawa, the Sky God, create Earth and all things upon it. It is then left to Grandmother Spider to bring order into the formlessness of Creation. She creates and names the Indian nations, brings the people out of the dark underworld and into the light of day, and, finally, separates the people into clans. Each clan is headed by an animal that leads those people to their homeland. Native Americans still follow these clan animals and live in many of these same places.

In "How Grandmother Spider Named the Clans," we

are introduced to the four caverns of the underworld, which are reflected in the four sacred directions of this world. Many Native Americans offer prayers and thanks to the four directions as an essential part of maintaining a balanced and harmonious relationship with the world.

The notion of animals leading people is universal. Many Native American healers are of the Bear Clan and, it is said, those of this clan are apt to be strong and decisive. Members of the Turtle Clan are often described as reserved and deliberate, people who think things through carefully before taking action. Animal *totems* originated among the westernmost woodland peoples, such as the Anishinabe (Ojibway or Chippewa). The role an individual played in society (as healer, warrior, provider of food, leader or teacher) was often determined by that person's totem. Totems were animals or birds, such as Eagle and Bear. A person's link to a totem animal, which was usually determined by a vision or series of events, indicated the closeness he or she felt to the natural world.

In other cultures animals symbolize everything from sports teams and businesses to dance troupes, musical ensembles, art groups and even entire nations. Some spiritual centering practices, such as T'ai Chi Chuan, which originated in China, are based in part on imitating the movements and awareness of particular animals, such as the crane. Animals are and have been leading human beings since the beginning of time.

In the second story, "How the Spider Symbol Came to the People," the clan of the Isolated Earth People needed an animal symbol on which to draw for strength, power, wisdom and life itself. The chief of this clan searches for an animal that will *show itself*. He thinks the deer is the powerful symbol he seeks and so follows its tracks through the woods, oblivious to any other signs or presence. When he runs into Spider's web he becomes angry and tries to hurt her. She reveals her power to the chief but, like many of us, it takes him some time before he sees the value of that which is right in front of him.

"Why do you act as if you are blind?" she asks. "I am patient. I watch and I wait. Then all things come to me. If your people learn this, they will be strong indeed." Finally, the chief sees Spider's strength and wisdom and takes it as a symbol for the Osage people.

While many people today react to spiders with dread and disgust, Native Americans reveal through these stories that they saw virtue in the spider's keen awareness, its patience and the order of its simple existence. Spider webs were a symbol of the *interconnectedness* of all things (Figure 3-1). In a speech made in 1854, Sealth (Chief Seattle) referred

to the "web of life" and how the web connects all things "like the blood which unites one family." We are merely a strand in the web, he said, and whatever we do to the web we do to ourselves: "All things are connected." Even today, in our action-oriented society, we can learn from the spider's example of watching and waiting. We can stop our activity and quiet our inner voice to let the solutions to healing Earth reveal themselves in the stillness.

Figure 3-1. The spider web has become a symbol for the interconnectedness of all things—the great web of life. An action that affects one strand has repercussions throughout the fabric of the web. Photo by Michael J. Caduto.

Spiders

Spiders are related to insects, crustaceans, centipedes and millipedes in the phylum *Arthropoda*. All arthopods have jointed legs and a hard *exoskeleton*. The close relatives of spiders in the class *Arachnida*, which lack antennae or wings, include harvestmen, scorpions and mites. Common ground-dwelling arachnids include the wolf spiders and the harvestmen or "daddy longlegs." Wolf spiders are large, hairy spiders with good eyesight and a keen sense of touch. Harvestmen, which may have long or short legs, feed on live insects and occasionally on plant juices or dead animals. Although harvestmen are commonly referred to as "spiders," they actually comprise an order of arachnid separate from that of true spiders.

So far around thirty-six thousand spiders have been identified, but this probably represents only one-third of the actual number of spiders on Earth. North American spiders range in size from .04-inch (1 millimeter) long to nearly 3 inches (7.6 centimeters). Spiders are so adaptable that they live in every kind of environment in the world, including the Arctic. Except for the black widow, brown recluse and a few others, most species of North American spiders are harmless, though it is always best to observe them from a distance.

ANATOMY. There are two body parts to a spider: the *cephalothorax*, which is a combined head and thorax, and the *abdomen* (Figure 3-2). The cephalothorax contains eight legs, each ending with two or three claws. Most spiders have eight simple eyes on their heads and one pair of jaws called *chelicerae* sporting fanged tips used for puncturing and injecting venom into their victims. The cephalothorax also contains the spider's brain, poison glands and stomach, and it is covered with a protective *carapace*. The eyes of some spiders, such as wolf spiders, seem to glow in the dark when exposed to a flashlight beam or headlight. This *eyeshine* is really caused by light reflecting back from the spider's eyes.

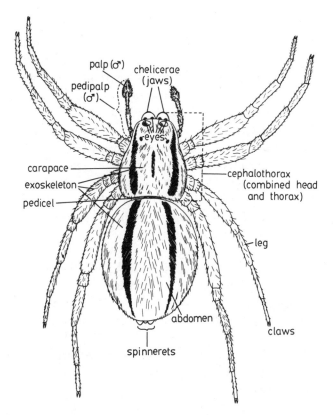

Figure 3-2. The external anatomy of a spider.

A narrow stalk or *pedicel* connects the cephalothorax to the abdomen, which contains the digestive, reproductive and respiratory tracts, the heart, silk glands and silk-making *spinnerets*.

As a spider grows it sheds its hard *exoskeleton* from four to twelve times before becoming an adult. On the whole, spiders live for only one or two seasons. The females of some species of tarantulas, however, can live up to twenty years!

SILK, WEB-WEAVING AND FEEDING. Life as a spider would not be possible without *silk*, which is a fibrous, waterproof strand of protein. Silk emerges as liquid from the spinnerets (of which there are usually six) and hardens instantly once exposed to air. There are many different kinds of silk and uses for it. Some silk is sticky and some is not. Silk is used for weaving webs, to line nests and burrows and to make egg sacs, as a safety *lifeline* or *dragline* for moving to a new spot or escaping from predators, for trapdoor hinges and to wrap prey. Silk is also used for transmitting and receiving information about prey, intruders and potential mates during courtship. Spiderlings use silk for *ballooning*. They climb to a high place and release long strands of silk that catch the wind and carry the young spiderlings away. Silk is handled with the claws on the end of each leg, which, for some unknown reason, do not stick to the silk.

Spiders are fascinating creatures and, using silk as their raw material, are some of nature's most ingenious hunters and engineers. Each spider is uniquely adapted to its way of life. Orb-weaving spiders sit in ambush and wait for an insect to fly into the sticky silk that radiates out in circles from the center of the web. Once the spider feels the vibrations caused by the hapless victim, it moves quickly along the nonsticky cross hairs of the web to subdue its prey with venom. Sometimes the prey is poisoned, killed and eaten on the spot, while other times it is paralyzed and mummified in a silk case where it remains in a comatose state for a later meal. Spiders feed on a live prey by paralyzing it or killing it outright with poison. The spider then uses enzymes to liquefy the prey's body before sucking it into the mouth.

The funnel weaver's web can often be seen in grassy places when the silk threads are covered with morning dew. This spider waits out of sight in the neck of the funnel. When the prey enters and vibrates the web, the spider rushes out, bites its soon-to-be meal and hauls it back inside for the feast.

While all spiders can spin silk, not all of them weave webs. So sophisticated and technologically advanced is the trapdoor spider that it almost defies belief. These denizens of the southern United States live in a silk-lined, tube-shaped hole in the ground covered with a trapdoor which swings on a silken hinge. When a potential victim happens by and vibrates the ground overhead, the spider emerges in a flash from the hole, ambushes the prey and brings it home to eat.

Some crab spiders can change color to blend in with the hues of the particular flower they are waiting upon. When an unsuspecting bee, fly or other insect comes in to sip nectar or gather pollen, it, instead, becomes the spider's fare.

REPRODUCTION. Courtship among spiders ranges from simple to highly complex. Some male wolf spiders and jumping spiders do a dance and wave their legs at their potential mate. The males of some spiders look for draglines set down by females of their own species. By merely touching this silk thread males can tell whether or not a mature female is waiting in the web! One kind of spider simply entices its intended mate beforehand by presenting her with a fly.

The *pedipalps*, a frequently misunderstood pair of reproductive organs on spiders, are located between the jaws and the first pair of legs. On young spiders and females these structures are inconspicuous and leg-like. Males have pedipalps with enlarged tips that sometimes appear to resemble tiny boxing gloves. Fertilization occurs when the male inserts the end or *palp*, containing sperm, into an opening on the underside of the female's abdomen.

About one week after mating the female lays her eggs in a silk *egg sac*. Some females care for the eggs while others abandon them. The female wolf spider carries the egg sac on her spinnerets and the young on her back. The belief that females eat their mates after copulating is only true in some cases, although the males do often die afterward.

OBSERVING SPIDERS. Spiders carry out their interesting lives in the nooks and crannies of foundations and cellars, on tree bark, in windows, in forests, fields, wet areas and even in deserts and arctic environments. Since most spiders are *nocturnal*—active and most apparent at night—they are best seen by flashlight. A keen eye will be rewarded with many discoveries while spider-watching. With spiders, as with many animals, imitation is the best form of observation—watch, wait and be patient in order to understand our eight-legged friends.

WEAVING HOME

Spider in dark nook hiding
      on tangled dust string insect net,
   buzzing bug on the cob is the corn
      for your table.

Sometimes I dream
      of one broom strike. . .
   home no more
      for eight legs on high.

But then,
   we share this place
   and each day I stare upwards
   to see your larder grow.

Patient on silken threads,
   your friends who would spare you are few
   among those you protect
   from becoming mosquito meals.

Eight legs perch on aerial warp.
Eight eyes look down at two
   and ask
"What are you doing in *my* home?"

—Michael J. Caduto

QUESTIONS

1. In the first story, "How Grandmother Spider Named the Clans," Tawa, the Sky God and Grandmother Spider share in creating Earth. Why do you think it is left to Grandmother Spider to put things into order upon Earth while Tawa goes back into the heavens?

2. What does Grandmother Spider do first? Why is it important that she give names to the clans?

3. The mourning dove goes out to find homes for the people. What does the dove look for to help the people live?

4. What animals does Grandmother Spider choose to lead the clans among the Hopi? Why do you think she chooses these particular animals?

5. What are some other Native American creation stories that you have heard? Describe some of the creation stories you know that come from non-Indian people. What do you believe? Are anyone's beliefs in how the world was created any more or less true than anyone else's? Why? Why not?

6. "How the Spider Symbol Came to the People" also begins with beings of Sky and Earth. Why do you think Earth and Sky are so important in Native American creation stories?

7. When the chief of the clan of the Isolated Earth

People runs into the spider's web, why does he try to hurt the spider? What is he angry about?

8. At first, this chief seeks the deer as a symbol and says that the spider is small and weak. Then he questions how the spider could give strength to his people. What qualities does the spider point out that it possesses in order to change the chief's mind? Do you think you would have listened to the spider or kept searching for the deer?

9. Do you like spiders? Why or why not?

10. What do you think is a powerful animal to have as a symbol? To lead a clan?

ACTIVITIES

Symbol Animal

ACTIVITY: Wait in an imaginary web and use the patience and wisdom of the spider while taking a fantasy journey to find an animal symbol that will be a guide and helper, giving strength and wisdom when you need it.

GOALS: Visualize the web of life that connects us to all parts of Earth. Understand how to seek an answer, a guiding animal, by watching, waiting and listening—by being silent and receptive. Understand that we can learn a great deal from animals and that the qualities of animals can help to guide us in our lives.

AGE: Younger children and older children

MATERIALS: Copy of the fantasy "Symbol Animal," pencils, crayons, felt-tipped marking pens, writing paper and construction paper, scissors, strips of newspaper, wheat paste, water, paint brushes, tempera paints, string, small slices of a tree sapling with a hole drilled near the top edge for hanging as a necklace, drill and bit, other supplies as needed for projects chosen.

PROCEDURE: It is time for the children to take a fantasy journey to find their animal symbols. Prepare them for the fantasy as described on page 13 of Chapter 2. Tell them to imagine they are actually doing and experiencing all of the events that occur in the fantasy. Now read *Symbol Animal* to the children.

SYMBOL ANIMAL

You are sitting in the center of your world on a web that reaches out and touches all around you. Every plant and animal, all of the rocks, rivers and oceans, even the sun—everything on Earth and in the sky is connected to you by the strands of the web. If anything moves you can feel the vibrations in your web. Imagine you are holding a strand of the web and plucking it to send vibrations out into the world. Do you feel any coming back to you? Picture all the animals you can and have each one come and pluck a strand of the web.

(*Pause.*) Now imagine that the web and all things living in it are in danger. You see and smell pollution in the air, water and soil. The homes of many plants and animals are being destroyed. Too many animals are being hunted and there are fewer and fewer all the time. Some animals have disappeared forever and will never come back. You are about to begin a journey to help all of the animals, and people too, but you need a special animal, an animal symbol, to guide you on the way. Imagine that there is a wise animal, one that can show you how to take care of all the animals and their homes on Earth and can show people how to take care of each other too, one that is a good healer.

Begin a journey to the home where that animal lives. Imagine that you travel from where you are over the land until you reach the animal's home. You may have to walk a great distance, swim very far, hike over tall mountains, cross the dry desert or even the ocean.

Look carefully and quietly around the animal's home once you get there. Picture the animal slowly coming into your mind. Now you can see its eyes staring into yours and watching. Its ears are alert and listening closely to any sound you make. Suddenly you see its whole head before you. Now the body and legs appear and the animal is complete.

Your animal looks at you and says with its eyes that it wants you to follow and learn what it has to teach you.

That animal is inside you now, in your heart and mind. It stands ready to help you at any time. Here is the animal that will lead you—your symbol animal.

Now, with your animal inside you, it is time to make the return journey to your home. Trace your steps all the way back along the path you took to where your animal lives. Soon you find yourself sitting in the web where you started. Slowly open your eyes.

Now have each child draw a picture of his or her animal in its home. Invite each child to share with the rest of the group as much as he or she chooses to say about the animal. Emphasize that it is their choice to share. Ask each one what makes his or her animal a good leader to help us take care of the other animals. Ask her or him to describe the qualities of that animal. Children often need some help in identifying and relating to the character traits of their animals (e.g., spider = patience). Choose a few animals with such traits as loyalty, friendliness or strength, and share these with the children to help lead them into doing the same with their symbol animals.

Have the children create their own stories in pictures and/or words, of how their symbol animals will lead them on the journey to care for the other animals.

Have each child create a papier-mâché mask that pictures his or her symbol animal. This can be worn or hung to keep the strength of the animal close by.

Lead a brainstorming session to elicit ideas for caring for these symbol animals. Ask each child to make a commitment to follow up on these projects.

In addition, children may adapt a name based on the helping qualities identified in their symbol animals. This helps the children to better appreciate the animal and strengthens their commitment to care for the lives of animals. Have each child write her or his animal name on a wooden medallion, draw a picture of the animal on the other side of the medallion and create a necklace by hanging the medallion from a piece of string.

Create your own extensions to this activity. Keep coming back to these symbol animals as you read the stories and conduct the activities in this book.

Animal Signs of the Times

ACTIVITY: Find several different ways that people use animals for strength and as symbols. Draw pictures of these animals and list the attributes that cause them to be powerful symbols.
GOALS: Understand the many ways and reasons that people use animals to empower their lives and activities. Discover the qualities that we assign to specific animals.
AGE: Older children
MATERIALS: Chalk and chalkboard or markers and newsprint; maps, atlases, magazines, sports journals, encyclopedias and other sources of information about animal symbols; index cards; pencils; crayons; paint and brushes; scissors; animal photos.
PROCEDURE: Facilitate a brainstorming session with the children and have them create a list of the many ways that people use animals as signs and symbols. Have the children conduct research using maps, atlases, magazines, sports journals and encyclopedias to compile their own lists of the ways that different cultures, nations, sports teams, advertisers, individuals and others use animals for power and as symbols. Ask the children to be original and creative. For instance, someone could conduct a survey of the roadside advertising signs that incorporate animals

into their imagery and/or written message.

Before proceeding to the next step, discuss several animals and list some of the qualities and attributes that people assign to them. Have the children practice generating their own list of qualities for several other animals.

Now have each child make up one card for each of the animals discovered in the search. On one side of the card there will be a picture, photo or illustration of the animal. The flip side will list the animal's name, where and how its symbol is used, and the child's own thoughts about what qualities the animal represents for the person or people who are using it—the attributes that those people value. Also in this space, have the children answer these questions: "Why do you think this person or group of people has chosen this particular animal as a symbol?" "What needs does this animal fulfill?"

Making Eight-Leggeds

ACTIVITY: Create model spiders that are anatomically correct.
GOALS: Learn the external anatomy of a spider and understand the function of each body part.
AGE: Younger children and older children
MATERIALS: Small tear-drop-shaped balloons, modeling clay, cloves (for eyes), pipe cleaners, dried flower parts and leaves, tape, glue, scissors, construction paper, magic markers, yarn, enlarged version of Figure 3-2.
PROCEDURE: Have the children create the basic spider body by blowing up one balloon all the way and tying it off at the neck. Make the head by blowing up another balloon about one-third of full size. Tie these two balloons together at the necks to complete the basic spider body. Younger children may have difficulty blowing up the balloons. Have these children use clay or construction paper to make the parts of the spider body. This also creates a more durable spider.

Now lay out the other materials and let the children use their imaginations to accurately complete the spiders. Post an enlarged version of Figure 3-2 for the children to consult as they work. Encourage them to be creative by adding their own touches such as coloring the spider's body with markers or putting hair on the legs and body.

Once they have completed their spiders, hold up the diagram of a spider and have them find each body part. Discuss the function of each part while the children are looking at it. Compare spider anatomy to that of insects and point out the differences between these two groups of arthropod.

Finding Spider Hiders

ACTIVITY: Go looking for spiders. Observe and protect spiders in their natural habitat.

GOALS: Learn some common locations for spider homes. Understand how spiders live in the wild. Develop patience and practice observation skills. Become acclimated to spiders and their day-to-day activities.

AGE: Younger children and older children

MATERIALS: Flashlight, capture jar with holes in the lid for aeration, hand lenses, plastic magnifying cube-boxes, gloves, sweep net, copies of the Golden Guide *Spiders and Their Kin* (New York: Golden Press, 1968).

PROCEDURE: Take the children on a search for spiders around the home or learning center. Look for webs in the nooks and crannies of the cellar, foundation, stairwell, ceilings and windows. Go outside to check in the crevices of tree bark and holes, in dense plant cover or on a dew-covered field or lawn. Swish a sweep net through tall grass to catch spiders in that habitat. Many spiders are nocturnal and some (such as wolf spiders) can be sighted at night when a flashlight beam reflects off their eyes. Web spiders tend to spend the daylight hours waiting at the edge of their webs, but they can be found in the web after dark.

Once you have found a web containing a spider, have the children stand off at a little distance to watch patiently and quietly for any activity. While you are waiting, search the web for old exoskeletons that the spider has shed while growing, the empty skeletons of past meals, the mummified insects that will become future meals and (especially in the late fall and winter months) silk egg cases. This provides an opportunity to discuss how the children feel about the spider's feeding on insects and other small creatures. Watch long enough to really see the spider in action. This may take awhile and is a good time to talk about the incredible patience it takes to live and hunt as a spider.

Now move in close to the spider and use a gloved hand to catch it and place it in a plastic magnifying observation box. Or catch it in a glass jar and have the children observe it with a hand lens. Review the parts of a spider. Have the children count the number of eyes and legs and find the spinnerets. Have older children identify the kind of spider they are watching by using a field guide such as the Golden Guide *Spiders and Their Kin*. Release the spider exactly where it was captured.

The best way to *keep* a spider is to find one living nearby in its own web—to visit and observe it regularly.

Sticky Web

ACTIVITY: Construct a spider web of yarn. Send "insects" through the web while it is held in different locations in a doorway to discover how many insects the "spider" will catch.

GOALS: Understand the structure of a spider's web, how the web works and how its location determines its effectiveness for catching prey.

AGE: Younger and older children

MATERIALS: Hula hoop (a large one having a 40-inch [1-meter] diameter works best), yarn, scissors, Velcro® strips (the hooked component of the Velcro®), double-sided tape, Ping-Pong balls, magic markers, masking tape, a pencil or pen, Figures 3-3 and 3-4 and a doorway.

PROCEDURE: Construct a web using the hula hoop for a frame and yarn for the strands. Cut the yarn into pieces of about 6 inches (15.2 centimeters) longer than the outside diameter of the hula hoop (Figure 3-3). Tie the ends of the cross-threads onto the rim so that they stretch across and through the center of the hoop. Space the cross-

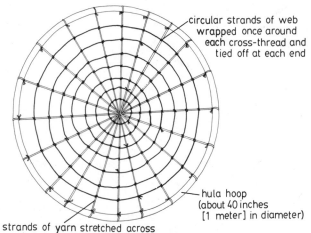

circular strands of web wrapped once around each cross-thread and tied off at each end

hula hoop (about 40 inches [1 meter] in diameter)

strands of yarn stretched across and tied onto the hoop at each end- leave about 4 inches (10.2 centimeters) between each cross-thread along the hoop frame

Figure 3-3. Sticky Web. Make sure the spaces in between strands of the web are about 3 to 4 inches (7.6 to 10.2 centimeters) wide—large enough for the Ping-Pong ball "insects" to pass through.

threads about 4 inches (10.2 centimeters) apart along the rim.

Now create the circular strands of the web. Start with the center piece and work progressively toward the outside, leaving about 3 inches (7.6 centimeters) between each strand. Begin by tying each strand off at one end and then working it around in a circle. Keep the strands from slipping by wrapping them once around each cross-thread where they meet.

As the children do this webbing, mention that on a spider's web the cross-pieces, which the spider walks on, are not sticky and that they function to support the sticky circular strands of the web.

Create the "insects" by attaching sticky Velcro® strips to the outside of Ping-Pong balls (Figure 3-4). Two or three strips of Velcro® reaching all the way around and spaced evenly will suffice. Children can choose to call these creatures any insect that they like, such as a mosquito, moth, fly, etc. Have the children draw directly on the Ping-Pong balls to create their chosen insects.

Divide the children into small groups and designate one child to be the first spider. She or he will stand on the opposite side of the doorway from the rest of the group and will hold the web up in a location that she or he thinks will catch the most "insects." Have the other children

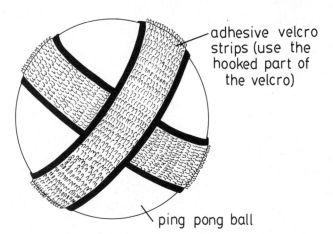

Figure 3-4. Ping-Pong ball "insect" for use with the "Sticky Web."

adhesive velcro strips (use the hooked part of the velcro)

ping pong ball

stand about 10 feet (3 meters) from the doorway and try to throw their Velcro® insects through it without getting them caught in the web. Stick a piece of masking tape on the doorframe next to the spot where each spider holds the web and record her or his name and the number of insects caught. Have each child take turns being the spider until they have all had a turn. Now check the masking tape records to discover which locations of the web resulted in the most insects being caught.

Where would the children weave their webs if they wanted to catch the most insects and to be well-fed spiders?

Which of these "spiders" would most likely survive to reproduce?

How would spiders be affected by the abundance or scarcity of insects near their webs?

EXTENDING THE EXPERIENCE

• Read *Charlotte's Web* by E. B. White with the children and have them write and illustrate original stories, songs and poems about spiders. Begin by allowing them to share their own experiences with spiders.

• Rewrite the story of *Little Miss Muffet* from the spider's point of view. Or rewrite it describing what Little Miss Muffet would do and say if she were *not* afraid of spiders!

• Conduct a search similar to that in "Animal Signs of the Times" for ways that spiders are used as symbols and what they mean to people. Make a list of both the negative and positive attributes that people assign to spiders.

• Study several Native North American nations, the clan animals that appear among them and how each animal affects the lives of the people in its clan.

• Find other creation stories, from Native North American and other cultures, and compare them to the stories in this chapter. Look closely at these stories to find similarities and differences. Which are your favorite stories? Why?

• Create a giant web as a room divider to better understand how intricate and challenging web-building really is and to see and appreciate the beauty and symmetry of a web.

✛ CELEBRATION ✛

The rabbit lifted one of its feet and thumped the ground.

CHAPTER 4

✤ The Rabbit Dance ✤

(Mohawk {Kanienkahageh}—Eastern Woodland)

Long ago, a group of hunters were out looking for game. They had seen no sign of animals, but they went slowly and carefully through the forest, knowing that at any moment they might find something. Just ahead of them was a clearing. The leader of the hunters held up his hand for the others to pause. He thought he had seen something. All of the men dropped down on their stomachs and crept up to the clearing's edge to see what they could see. What they saw amazed them. There, in the center of the clearing, was the biggest rabbit any of them had ever seen. It seemed to be as big as a small bear!

One of the hunters slowly began to raise his bow. A rabbit as large as that one would be food enough for the whole village. But the leader of the men held out his hand and made a small motion that the man with the bow understood. He lowered his weapon. Something unusual was happening. It was best to just watch and see what would happen next.

The rabbit lifted its head and looked toward the men. Even though they were well hidden on the other side of the clearing, it seemed as if that giant rabbit could see them. But the rabbit did not take flight. Instead, it just nodded its head. Then it lifted one of its feet and thumped the ground. As soon as it did so, other rabbits began to come into the clearing. They came from all directions and, like their chief, they paid no attention to the hunters.

Now the big rabbit began to thump its foot against the ground in a different way. Ba-pum, ba-pum, pa-pum, pa-pum. It was like the sound of a drum beating. The rabbits all around made a big circle and began to dance. They danced and danced. They danced in couples and moved in and out and back and forth. It was a very good dance that the rabbits did. The hunters who were watching found themselves tapping the earth with their hands in the same beat as the big rabbit's foot.

Then, suddenly, the big rabbit stopped thumping the earth. All of the rabbits stopped dancing. BA-BUM! The chief of the rabbits thumped the earth one final time. It leaped high into the air, right over the men's heads, and it was gone. All of the other rabbits ran in every direction out of the clearing and they were gone, too.

The men were astonished at what they had seen. None of them had ever seen anything at all like this. None of them had ever heard or seen such a dance. It was all they could talk about as they went back to the village. All thought of hunting was now gone from their minds.

When they reached the village, they went straight to the longhouse where the head of the Clan Mothers lived. She was a very wise woman and knew a great deal about the animals. They told her their story. She listened closely. When they were done telling the story, she picked up a water drum and handed it to the leader of the hunters.

"Play that rhythm which the Rabbit Chief played," she said.

The leader of the men did as she asked. He played the rhythm of the rabbits' dance.

"That is a good sound," said the Clan Mother. "Now show me the dance which the Rabbit People showed you."

The hunters then did the dance while their leader played the drum. The Clan Mother listened closely and watched. When they were done, she smiled at them.

"I understand what has happened," she said. "The Rabbit People know that we rely on them. We hunt them for food and for clothing. The Rabbit Chief has given us this special dance so that we can honor its people for all that they give to the human beings. If we play their song and do their dance, then they will know we are grateful for all they continue to give us. We must call this new song The Rabbit Dance and we must do it, men and women together, to honor the Rabbit People.

So it was that a new social dance was given to the Iroquois people. To this day the Rabbit Dance is done to thank the Rabbit People for all they have given, not only food and clothing, but also a fine dance that makes the people glad.

The Deer Dance

(Yaqui—Southwest)

There was a man who lived in the country far away from any village. He made his living as a hunter, but he always was very respectful of the animals he hunted. This man's name was Walking Man. He always kept his eyes and ears open to everything around him, for he knew how special it was in the wilderness. It was to the wilderness that people went in their dreams, to the place they called Seye Wailo. That name meant many things. It meant the Home of All the Animals. It meant the Home of the Deer. It meant the Place Where Flowers Live. It was said that the best songs always came to people from Seye Wailo.

One day, as Walking Man was out, he heard a sound from a hilltop. It was like a sound he had heard before at the time of year when the deer are mating. It was the clattering of antlers. He knew that the bucks would fight in this way during the mating time, striking their antlers together. But it was not that time of year and this sound was different. It was a softer sound and its rhythm was like that of a song. He went to look, but he could see nothing.

The next morning Walking Man rose before the sun came up and went back to that hilltop. He sat quietly on a fallen tree and waited as the sun rose. He began to hear that sound again, and he looked carefully. There not far from him were two big deer. They had huge antlers and, as they stood facing each other, they rattled their antlers together. Near them was a young deer. As Walking Man watched, he saw that young deer lift its head and lower it. It ran from side to side, leaping up and down. It seemed happy as it did this. Walking Man knew what he was

As he walked he found a newborn fawn where its mother had left it hidden among the flowers.

seeing. He was seeing the deer do their own special dance. Though he had his weapons with him, he did not try to kill them. He watched them dance for a long time.

When Walking Man went down that hill, he had a thought in his mind. There were songs coming into his mind. When he rose the next morning, he went out to walk and as he walked he found a newborn fawn where its mother had left it hidden among the flowers. He made a song for that fawn. Then he went to the village and gathered some of his friends.

"I am going to make songs for the deer," he said.

He took two sticks and put notches on one of them so that he could make the sound of the deer's antlers. He showed one of the boys in the village how the young deer danced and had the boy dance that way as they played the deer song and sang.

So it was that the Deer Dance came to the Yaqui people, a gift from the deer, a gift from Seye Wailo.

DISCUSSION

Celebration

Music, dance and celebration are sometimes seen by people of European heritage as being limited to human beings. Native North American people do not see it that way at all. The rabbit, for one, is regarded as a great dancer and one who loves to have a good time (Figure 4-1). We recall one clear moonlit night when we were walking through new snow in the Adirondack woods. The snow was so soft and deep that it muffled our footsteps and, though a wind had been blowing earlier, it was completely calm now. There was no wind to carry our scent. We came to the edge of the cedars and looked out toward the clear space between the trees where there was a little swamp and a small pond made by a beaver dam. There we saw something that we will never forget. The wind had swept clean the frozen surface of the pond. The new snow lay all around the ice and there were at least four rabbits there. In the light and shadows of moon and trees it was hard to tell how many of them there were. And they were moving so quickly! As we watched, they ran in circles in the snow, making patterns with their feet, going faster and faster until they reached the smooth ice and slid across its surface. It seemed unbelievable, but it was really happening. The light of the moon was bright on the snow and the rabbits danced and played in its light. We watched for a time and then smiled, turned and went on our way.

RABBIT DANCE. It is often said by the People of the Longhouse, the Haudenosaunee (Iroquois), that we learn many things from the animals. This story of "The Rabbit Dance" is one example. It comes from the Mohawk (Kanienkahageh or "People of the Flint") Nation of the Haudenosaunee. By watching the animals closely, the hunters came home with something special. The relationship between Native North American people and the animals they had to hunt for their own survival was very different from that between a modern sportsman who hunts only for his own pleasure and his prey. In story after story among the Haudenosaunee, a hunter goes out and comes back not with game, but with a lesson learned from the animals themselves. The role of animals as wise teachers is a central element in Native North American stories.

CIRCLE DANCE. Each time the animals offer the gift of survival to the people, a *circle* of giving and receiving is begun. This circle is completed when the gift is returned

Figure 4-1. Rabbits, such as these baby cottontails, are known as fun-loving animals that spend a good deal of time engaged in energetic play. Size of adult: 14–17 inches (35.6–43.2 centimeters). Photo by Peter Hope.

by the people. There are numerous traditional practices that move on this circle. In the tradition of the Abenaki Indians of the East, the "People of the Dawn," for instance, the hunter prepares for the hunt by asking permission of the animal and Creation. If this is done in a respectful, reverential way, it is believed, the animal will present itself to the hunter. All of the animal is used without wasting anything, which would be disrespectful. A gift of the animal's bones is then returned to the place where the animal was found, and a final prayer of thanks is said. Circle dances are commonly done to celebrate the gift, to remind people of their interconnectedness with all of life, to strengthen the community and to celebrate the giving circle and the circles of life of which we are all part. These traditional practices, and the circle dance celebration, are important aspects of living in balance with the animals.

DEER DANCE. The second story reminds us that today the Deer Dance remains strong among the Yaqui people. Deer Dances are frequently done by the Yaqui people, who live in Arizona (about six thousand people) and Sonora, Mexico (where the majority of the Yaqui people, about twenty-five thousand, reside). In fact, as Larry Evers and Felipe S. Molina point out in their wonderful book *Yaqui Deer Songs*,[1] the Deer Dance is growing in popularity among the Yaqui people in Arizona. It is closely connected with the very identity of being a Yaqui. Although originally the dances were probably done before going out to hunt the deer—the dance was part of a ritual to give praise and thanks before setting out—today they are done on many different occasions. For example, Deer Dances are part of the village dramas carried out during the Easter season in Yaqui villages. At one point, the Deer Dancers and singers defend the church. The original idea of the Deer Dance gathering "the wilderness world into a symbol of earthly sacrifice and of spiritual life after death," as Evers and Molina explain, certainly lends itself easily to Christianity. If you are in that part of Arizona during the Lenten season, the Deer Dance is a Native American dance that likely you will have an opportunity to see.

The Yaqui people strongly believe that everything in the world of the desert is alive and in communication with everything else. As Evers and Molina put it, "all the inhabitants of the Sonoran desert . . . plants, animals, birds, fishes, even rocks and springs" are part of *huya ania*, the wilderness world.

Unless you have spent some time in that Sonoran desert, it may be hard to understand how different a desert actually is from the pictures we have of it in many books and movies, pictures that show us a lifeless place. We have walked in that desert many times, and each time it has shown us something new—a covey of Gambel's quail scurrying under the cover of the mesquite bushes, a Saguaro wren darting out of the hole in a great cactus, a piece of the desert earth suddenly coming to life as a chuckwalla lizard. When you walk along the dry sandy bed of the arroyos, which may burst into tumultuous (and dangerous) life after a storm in the mountains, you see even more signs of how much life there is in the Sonoran desert. There are tracks everywhere—tracks of javelina pigs, desert hares, coyotes, roadrunners, deer.

The Yaqui people also know the desert world to be a place of flowers. There are few places in North America where flowers leap into life with such beauty and intensity as in the Arizona desert during the brief time of spring rains. Even the stones seem to flower as tiny dry cacti break out in white and yellow blossom and the tall spindly ocotillos become as red as flame with delicate petalled flowers. The desert truly is the "Flower World." All of the Deer Songs of the Yaqui people speak of and give praise to this flower-covered world that is the desert. It is a world that may seem to be dead, but the smallest drops of rain awaken it to life again and the deer go among the new flowers, dancing.

QUESTIONS

1. In "The Rabbit Dance," when the big rabbit is first spotted, one of the hunters raises his bow to shoot. Then the leader makes a motion and the hunter lowers his bow. What does the leader "say" with this motion?

2. Back in the village, the head of the Clan Mothers listens to the song and watches the Rabbit Dance. Why does she say the Rabbit Chief gave the song and dance to the Iroquois people?

3. In the Yaqui story "The Deer Dance," Walking Man waits on a fallen tree and watches the deer dance. Then, on the way down the hill, songs come into his mind. Where do these songs come from?

4. What does the Deer Dance mean to the Yaqui people today?

5. What is the importance of the circle of giving and receiving in our relationship with the animals? How do Native Americans honor this circle in their lives?

6. What are some other ways that we can show our appreciation to the animals?

7. What other animals do you know of, besides deer and rabbits, that celebrate with song, dance and play?

8. Why do animals celebrate?

ACTIVITIES
Circle Dance

ACTIVITY: List the many gifts that humans receive from animals. Perform a circle dance to honor and to give praise and thanks to the animals for the many gifts we receive from them, and to honor the other great circles of life.

GOALS: Appreciate the great richness of the gifts animals give to people. Understand the meaning of the *Circle Dance* and the importance of showing gratitude toward the animals. Celebrate, participate in and understand the many circles of life of which we are all a part: the interconnectedness of the great family of all living things on Earth; the community of people in the circle, with the shape of the circle representing the equality of everyone within it; the circle of giving and receiving; the circles of nature that surround and support us, such as the earth, sun, moon, seasons, day/night and ecological cycles; other circles the children may think of. Realize that "giving thanks" can take the form of celebration and fun.

AGE: Younger children and older children

MATERIALS: Chalkboard and chalk or newsprint and felt-tipped marker, copy of Figure 4-2, drum with a head of rubber or leather, drum striker composed of a stick with a piece of cotton-filled felt wrapped over the striking end.

PROCEDURE: Beforehand, obtain or prepare a simple, hand-held drum with a striker.

Lead a brainstorming session to help the children generate a list of the gifts that animals give to people, such as food, clothing, beauty, song and dance. When the list is completed, tell the children that they will be showing their appreciation for these gifts, and for the great beauty and abundance of nature by honoring and giving thanks to the animals with the *Circle Dance* . Ask the children to recall the important circles revealed through the stories and activities in this chapter. Discuss the circles of life as listed in the "Goals." Ask the children to think of other circles that they can celebrate during the dance.

Gather the children together and have them link arms in a circle standing shoulder-to-shoulder. Tell them they may relax their arms by their sides while you explain the dance and dance step.

Enter the circle and tell them the *Circle Dance* is performed to honor and remind us of the circles you have just discussed. Play the drum to demonstrate the beat. It is a simple, two-part repetition with the drum played harder on the first beat and softer on the second: hard-soft, hard-soft, hard-soft. . . .

Demonstrate the toe-heel step that accompanies the drumbeat. This simple step starts by putting just the toe of one foot down on the first (hard) beat of the drum, then keeping that toe down and bringing the heel of that foot down on the second (soft) beat of the drum, so that the foot is flat. It is called the "toe-heel" step, but younger children sometimes learn it better when it is described as toe-flat, toe-flat, toe-flat. . . . Perform the step in the center of the circle and have the children practice it in place as they watch you moving to the drumbeat.

Say the following to them: "Walking upon Earth is like beating a drum. Let us walk with a light step that shows we are respectful of Earth and its ways."

Now have everyone face clockwise in the circle and hold onto the shoulders of the person in front of them using both hands. Those who are much shorter than the person in front may hold onto that person's waist, or even the back of the knees. This is a silent dance, so they should remain quiet throughout. Ask the children to concentrate on the dance step and on walking in a good way upon Earth and to remember the circles honored by the dance—the circles of life have no end. It is very important that everyone remains connected so that the circle remains unbroken throughout the dance and that everyone takes deliberate, measured walking steps to keep pace with the person in front of them. Running will cause a whip-like effect among the people behind, especially those on the outermost part of the spiral, so, please, *no running!*

Break the circle and enter along it at some point. Someone will be holding onto you from behind and there will be a space in front of you. You will beat the drum but will not hold onto the person in front of you. Instruct the person behind you to hold on and follow wherever you go as you lead the group, since you will leave the circle shape for a while as you spiral in and out.

Lead the group thus, as shown in Figure 4-2: a. circle once clockwise; b. spiral in; c. turn to the left (counterclockwise) and spiral out; d. unravel the spiral, re-form into a counterclockwise circle and go around for one more turn.

EXTENDING THE EXPERIENCE

• Listen to bird calls, insect songs and the voices of other animals that the children like and appreciate. Notice any rhythmic patterns and musical refrains as you listen. Record these onto a cassette using a tape recorder by either tapping out the beats or humming, whistling or

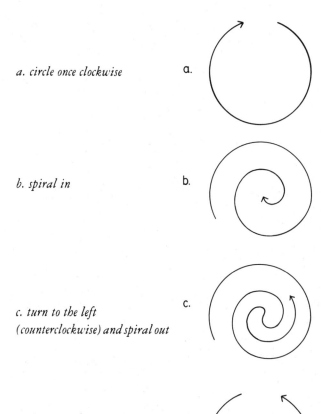

a. circle once clockwise   a.

b. spiral in   b.

c. turn to the left   c.
(counterclockwise) and spiral out

d. unravel the spiral, re-form   d.
into a counterclockwise circle and
go around for one more turn

Figure 4-2. Pattern of movement for leading a group in the "Circle Dance."

singing the music. Play this recording back and use this simple music to write songs for those animals. Add in different instruments, vocals or other accompaniment.

• Observe animal movements for patterns and rhythms as you see them moving through the woods, fields, water or air. Record the rhythms on a tape recorder and remember the dances of these animals. Elaborate upon these basic movements and rhythms to create dances of your own, moving in the style of those particular animals. Mix in drumbeats, rattles and other rhythmic instruments.

• Observe the full or nearly full moon on a clear night. Look for the "Rabbit in the Moon"—a pattern formed by the darker moon landforms that resembles a rabbit with floppy ears. The Rabbit in the Moon's head and ears are on the right side of the moon pointing down! Create and illustrate a story about how the Rabbit in the Moon came to be.

• Use the references listed in the *Teacher's Guide* to enrich the children's understanding and experience of Native North American music and dance.

NOTES

1. Larry Evers, and Felipe S. Molina, *Yaqui Deer Songs: Maso Bwikan* (Tucson, Ariz.: University of Arizona Press, 1987).

✦ VISION ✦

KAHIONHES

The eagle and the boy flew higher and higher until they came to an opening in the clouds.

CHAPTER 5

✧ Eagle Boy ✧

(*Zuni—Southwest*)

Long ago, a boy was out walking one day when he found a young eagle had fallen from its nest. He picked that eagle up and brought it home and began to care for it. He made a place for it to stay, and each day he went out and hunted for rabbits and other small game to feed it. His mother asked him why he no longer came to work in the fields and help his family. "I must hunt for this eagle," the boy said. So it went on for a long time and the eagle grew large and strong as the boy hunted and fed it. Now it was large enough to fly away if it wished, but it stayed with the boy who had cared for it so well. The boy's brothers criticized him for not doing his part to care for the corn fields and the melon fields, but Eagle Boy did not hear them. He cared only for his bird. Even the boy's father, who was an important man in the village, began to criticize him for not helping. But still the boy did not listen. So it was that the boy's brothers and his older male relatives came together and decided that they must kill the eagle. They decided they would do so when they returned from the fields on the following day.

When Eagle Boy came to his bird's cage, he saw that the bird sat there with its head down. He placed a rabbit he had just caught in the cage, but the eagle did not touch it.

"What is wrong, my eagle?" said the boy.

Then the eagle spoke, even though it had never spoken before. "My friend, I cannot eat because I am filled with sorrow," said the eagle.

"Why are you troubled?" said the boy.

"It is because of you," said the eagle. "You have not done your work in the fields. Instead, you have spent all of your time caring for me. Now your brothers and your older male relatives have decided to kill me so that you will again return to your duties in the village. I have stayed here all of this time because I love you. But now I must leave. When the sun rises tomorrow, I will fly away and never come back."

"My eagle," said the boy, "I do not wish to stay here without you. You must take me with you."

"My friend, I cannot take you with me," said the eagle. "You would not be able to find your way through the sky. You would not be able to eat raw food."

"My eagle," said the boy, "I cannot live here without you." So he begged the eagle and at last the great bird agreed.

"If you are certain, then you may come with me. But you must do as I say. Come to me at dawn, after the people have gone down to their fields. Bring food to eat on our long journey across the sky. Put the food in pouches that you can sling over your shoulders. You must also bring two strings of bells and tie them to my feet."

That night the boy filled pouches with blue corn wafer bread and dried meat and fruits. He made up two strings of bells, tying them with strong rawhide. The next morning, after

• 51 •

the people had gone down to the fields, he went to the eagle's cage and opened it. The eagle spread its wings wide.

"Now," he said to Eagle Boy, "tie the bells to my feet and then climb onto my back and hold onto the base of my wings."

Eagle Boy climbed on and the eagle began to fly. It rose higher and higher in slow circles above the town and above the field. The bells on the eagle's feet jingled and the eagle sang and the boy sang with it:

Huli-i-i, hu-li-i-i
Pa shish lakwa-a-a-a . . .

So they sang and the people in the fields below heard them singing, and they heard the sounds of the bells Eagle Boy had tied to the eagle's feet. They all looked up.

"They are leaving," the people said. "They are leaving." Eagle Boy's parents called up to him to return, but he could not hear them. The eagle and the boy rose higher and higher in the sky until they were only a tiny speck and then they were gone from the sight of the village people.

The eagle and the boy flew higher and higher until they came to an opening in the clouds. They passed through and came out into the Sky Land. They landed there on Turquoise Mountain where the Eagle People lived. Eagle Boy looked around the sky world. Everything was smooth and white and clean as clouds.

"Here is my home," the eagle said. He took the boy into the city in the sky, and there were eagles all around them. They looked like people, for they took off their wings and their clothing of feathers when they were in their homes.

The Eagle People made a coat of eagle feathers for the boy and taught him to wear it and to fly. It took him a long time to learn, but soon he was able to circle above the land just like the Eagle People and he was an eagle himself.

"You may fly anywhere," the old eagles told him, "anywhere except to the south. Never fly to the South Land."

All went well for Eagle Boy in his new life. One day, though, as he flew alone, he wondered what it was that was so terrible about the south. His curiosity grew, and he flew further and further toward the south. Lower and lower he flew and now he saw a beautiful city below with people dancing around red fires.

"There is nothing to fear here," he said, and flew lower still. Closer and closer he came, drawn by the red fires, until he landed. The people greeted him and drew him into the circle. He danced with them all night and then, when he grew tired, they gave him a place to sleep. When he woke next morning and looked around, he saw that the fires were gone. The houses no longer seemed bright and beautiful. All around him there was dust, and in the dust there were bones. He looked for his cloak of eagle feathers, wanting to fly away from this city of the dead, but it was nowhere to be found. Then the bones rose up and came together. There were people made of bones all around him! He rose and began to run, and the people made of bones chased him. Just as they were about to catch him, he saw a badger.

"Grandson," the badger said, "I will save you." Then the badger carried the boy down into his hole and the bone people could not follow. "You have been foolish," the badger said. "You did not listen to the warnings the eagles gave you. Now that you have been to this land in the south, they will not allow you to live with them anymore."

Then the badger showed Eagle Boy the way back to the city of the eagles. It was a long journey and when the boy reached the eagle city, he stood outside the high white walls. The eagles would not let him enter.

"You have been to the South Land," they said. "You can no longer live with us."

At last the eagle the boy had raised took pity on him. He brought the boy an old and ragged feather cloak.

"With this cloak you may reach the home of your own people," he said. "But you can never return to our place in the sky."

So the boy took the cloak of tattered feathers. His flight back down to his people was a hard one and he almost fell many times. When he landed on the earth in his village, the eagles flew down and carried off his feathered cloak. From then on, Eagle Boy lived among his people. Though he lifted his eyes and watched whenever eagles soared overhead, he shared in the work in the fields, and his people were glad to have him among them.

DISCUSSION

The Vision Quest

This story "Eagle Boy" is rich in imagery that can be interpreted in many different ways. It could be that Eagle Boy so loves his friend the eagle that he cannot bear to part company, and leaves his family and village behind to join the eagles in the sky world. He becomes an eagle, but, in the end, he is drawn back to his own people.

"Eagle Boy" could also be seen as a metaphor for this Zuni child's vision quest. In spirit, he leaves his people for a time, has a vision of the spirit world where the eagles dwell and ultimately returns to the ordinary world once more. His vision and sense of oneness with the rest of creation are expanded. He is compelled to leave his home to go with the eagle, then he chooses to return. This is only possible because he initially withdraws from his family as he cares for the young eagle. In this solitude he is drawn to the strange and wonderful city of the eagles in the clouds. Eagle Boy, no doubt, gains a great deal of self-knowledge in this quest to a sacred place. The eagle becomes his ally in life—his guide and source of strength.

It is difficult for people from other traditions to understand how powerful and tangible the sky world is to the boy in this story. During the rite of passage quest, the adolescent—through fasting, solitude and spiritual guidance—seeks a vision. This vision is a source of knowledge and strength throughout his or her life.

> There are many secrets which the Great Mystery will disclose only to the most worthy. Only those who seek him fasting and in solitude will receive his signs.[1]
> —Uncheedah, Santee Sioux

In the time of fasting the senses become heightened and more keenly aware of both worlds.

> In you . . . are natural powers. You have a will. Learn to use it. Make it work for you. Sharpen your senses as you sharpen your knife. . . . We can give you nothing. You already possess everything necessary to become great.[2]
> —Absaroke (Crow)

The solitude of this quest, its individual nature, is an essential part of each person's journey.

> He [The Great Spirit] only sketches out the path of the life roughly for all the creatures on Earth, shows them where

to go, where to arrive at, but leaves them to find their own way to get there. He wants them to act independently according to their nature, to the urges in each of them.[3]
—John Fire/Lame Deer, Lakota (Sioux)

The Teachings of the Eagle

It should be of no surprise to anyone living in North America—where the eagle has become an almost universal symbol of such power and majesty—that Native Americans regarded eagles with reverence long before Europeans arrived on these shores. Who has not dreamed of soaring as an eagle? Of catching the rising wind with a broad wing and etching circles in the sky with a slight shift of feathers? Of viewing one's land and life from an expansive aerial vantage on high? Indeed, one of the most common and persistent nighttime experiences for many people is to dream of flying.

The Pawnee story "The Teachings of the Eagle" is a window on the eagle's significance in one Native American culture of the plains.

The Great Eagle is the bird of Tirawa, our Creator. This bird carries many of the lessons which Tirawa has given to the people. Look at Eagle and you will see his teachings. Eagle has two wings and those wings are balanced in strength when it flies. In the same way, a man and a woman are balanced in strength and are two. The right wing is the man and the left wing is the woman and together they are in balance and will continue life on Earth. Eagle also always lays two eggs, reminding us again that things come in pairs. There is the sun and the moon, the day and the night, the body and the spirit, all of them part of Eagle's teachings.

Look upon Great Eagle's feathers. You will see that half of the feather is dark and half of it is white. Just so, we have day and night, winter and summer, sunshine and clouds. Eagle reminds us of this with these sacred feathers, which are special gifts of Tirawa, our Creator.

As Eagle flies, its eyes look in two directions. Just so, we human beings may look in two directions. We may look in the direction of good or we may look in the direction of that which is bad. We may see happiness and we may see sorrow.

So it is that Eagle teaches us and so it is that we wear Eagle's feathers to remind us of these teachings, the teachings Eagle carries as a gift from Tirawa, our Creator.

Eagles

When this story directs us to "see that half of the feather is dark and half of it is white," it describes one of the primary feathers on an immature golden eagle. Ever

since the bald eagle was adopted as the national symbol of the United States in 1782, it has overshadowed North America's only other resident eagle, the golden eagle, even though the golden eagle has always been more common in the West. Unlike the bald eagle, which is in the genus *Haliaeetus* along with the world's seven other species of sea eagle, the golden eagle is one of the booted eagles of the genus *Aquila* and has feathers covering its feet right down to the toes. Golden eagles live in the mountains and desert where they nest on cliffs and feed on small mammals. In its fierce defense of nesting territory, the golden eagle has been known to attack other eagles and even objects that resemble eagles such as light aircraft.

Eagles are best known for their supreme mastery of flight. Their broad, wide wings, which can stretch to 7 feet (2.1 meters) across from tip-to-tip on bald eagles, carry them aloft on rising thermal air currents and where the wind is forced upward along the face of a cliff. While bald eagles are adept at self-powered, level flight and do not *require* thermals or updrafts, golden eagles appear to be more dependent upon thermals. It takes such a great amount of energy to power the muscles that move their huge wings that eagles tend to roost when the wind is still, only to fly up and soar when updrafts are strong enough to hold them aloft. Like other soaring birds, the bald eagle has *primaries* or broad flight feathers on each wing tip, which can be continuously adjusted to the wind by bringing them close together, spreading them out or sweeping them up. Eagles, like other birds, have hollow bones. The total weight of an eagle's bones is, amazingly, less than one-half that of its feathers.[4] When soaring, eagles ride the updrafts as they etch spirals in the sky.

Considering its popularity as a symbol of power and grace, the bald eagle is poorly understood by most people (Figure 5-1). These great birds frequent seacoasts, rivers and lakes where they use their naked yellow feet and sharp black talons to catch mostly fish, some waterfowl, such as mallards and coots, and even small mammals. They have been seen cooperating to catch prey as large as a cormorant or a great blue heron. It is not uncommon for a bald eagle to harass an osprey (a fish hawk that is much smaller) until it drops its fish for the eagle to snatch up. Eagles have even been known to fly under an osprey, turn upside down and grab a fish out of the osprey's talons! When food is scarce, such as in the winter months when waterways are frozen over, the eagle scavenges, and its diet consists largely of *carrion* or dead animals. They will commonly eat dead fish even during the warmer months. Rarely does an eagle ever feed on domestic animals such as sheep and kid goats.

Figure 5-1. The majestic bald eagle is an inspiring symbol of power and grace. As birds of prey, bald eagles are at the top of the food web. Size: body, 30–43 inches (76–109 centimeters); wingspread, 7–8 feet (2.1–2.4 meters). Illustration by D. D. Tyler.

Bald eagles are social birds that will congregate in large numbers when they are not breeding or raising young. Adults are easily recognized by their size, signature "bald" (white-feathered) head and tail and bright yellow, hooked bill. The all-brown immature birds are not so distinctively marked, but their flight feathers are slightly longer than those of the adults, giving them a somewhat greater width. Bald eagles do not attain the snow-white head and tail feathers until they are seven years old.

As inspiring and moving as the eagles' image is to both Native North Americans and immigrant cultures in North America, there was a time not long ago when they were nearly wiped out in the lower forty-eight United States. But that is another part of this story, which continues in the "Discussion" section of Chapter 17.

QUESTIONS

1. Why is the boy allowed to neglect his work in the fields to care for the eagle, even though his family is not pleased that he is doing so?

2. Why does the eagle stay with the boy even when it grows strong enough to fly away?

3. Why does the boy want to become an eagle?

4. Why does the eagle tell the boy to tie bells onto its feet first before it escapes into the sky?

5. Does he really turn into an eagle and fly away with his friend?

6. How can the eagles look like people in the sky world?

7. Why does Eagle Boy fly to the South Land where he is forbidden to go? Have you ever done something because you were curious, even though you had been told not to do it? What was it that you did? What happened to you after you did it?

8. Do you think Eagle Boy is happy when he finally ends up joining the people of his village again?

9. What do you think Eagle Boy learns from becoming an eagle?

10. Have you ever seen an eagle? Have you ever dreamed of becoming an eagle?

11. Why is the bald eagle used as a symbol by so many people? What qualities make it a special bird?

ACTIVITIES

Flight of Fantasy

ACTIVITY: Take a fantasy journey and imagine what it would be like to be an eagle.

GOALS: Understand how a bird's body is structured to enable it to fly. Visualize the ways that a bird's anatomy is different from that of a person's.

AGE: Younger children and older children

MATERIALS: Pencils, paper, crayons, copy of "Flight of Fantasy."

PROCEDURE: What would it be like to soar among the clouds or ride high on a thermal? In this activity, by listening to a special story, your children will get a chance to imagine what it feels like to fly.

Have the children close their eyes and take a few deep breaths. Tell them to relax their bodies and to let their imaginations soar as you read the following story out loud.

FLIGHT OF FANTASY

You are going to travel to places you've never been before, moving high above Earth. But first you must change, for you are now too heavy and would never get off the ground.

Imagine you are an eagle. Each ankle is long and skinny. You have only four toes on each foot, but not all face in the same direction. Three toes are held in front and one sticks out of the back of each foot. The end of each toe has a very sharp, curved toenail. The outside of your feet and ankles are covered with rough, bumpy scales. There is a perch in front of you and you hop over to it and feel your toes close around it. You are now perching.

Your legs are short and your knees are close in to your body. Your short body is tipped forward. You are very slim and compact.

In place of hands you have wings. Flap them a few times and feel how they move.

Your nose and mouth are joined together to form a sharp, curved beak—hooked and strong. You have no teeth.

Your eyes are on the sides of your head and they cannot turn as easily in their sockets. You have to turn your whole head to look around. Your ears are small holes found close to your eyes, beneath and behind them.

Air sacs are found in many places in your body. They are like thin balloons connected to your lungs. Your bones have air spaces in them, which make them much, much lighter than human bones.

Feathers cover you all over except for your beak and feet. Soft down feathers grow close to your body and longer, wider feathers cover your body, shape your wings and form a broad tail. When you try to speak, only a loud, hoarse call comes out.

A great urge to go outside comes over you and you hop down off your perch and hop quickly to the nearest door. As you face outside, the wind calls to you and you jump, flapping your wings quickly and with great force. Up you go—over the trees and buildings and toward the sky. A great, warm gust of wind pushes up under your wings and lifts you higher and higher until the trees look the size of buttons.

A mouse runs across a field far below you and you can see its shape very clearly, even though you are up so high. All of the colors of Earth look beautiful down below—green leaves, brown earth, and blue water. Buildings and cars of all colors are connected with roads that look like thin ribbons.

As you circle on the rising winds the breeze rushes around your body. You see a puffy, white cloud ahead, and with a few flaps of your wings and a tilt of your tail, you glide into the whiteness. It is cool and damp and you feel lost for a moment. Then you come out on the other side and see a great range of mountains on the horizon.

The mountains and sky are your new home. As you fly high above Earth, you let out the long, loud cry of an eagle.

Have the children imagine that they are now back in their seats where they began their journeys. Tell them to open their eyes slowly. Then have everyone stand up and stretch.

Ask them what their favorite part of the journey was. Discuss some of the differences between the anatomy of a human being and that of an eagle. Share with the children the images of a bald eagle in Figures 5-1 and 5-2. Then have the children draw a picture of what they think the eagle might see as it looks down. How would trees look from above? Buildings? Water? Fields? The children's own neighborhoods? Have them write a story that continues where the "Flight of Fantasy" leaves off.

Use Chapter 12 to continue the experience.

Perch of Perception

ACTIVITY: Choose a special tree, bush or other place that feels right in a natural area, such as by the bank of a pond or stream, and sit alone and in silence in that place. Visit the site often, leave gifts of thanks there and practice some activities to heighten your senses of observation, of seeing and hearing and of self-understanding.

GOALS: Understand the importance of silent watching and listening in solitude as a way to better observe nature, heighten sensory awareness and enhance self-knowledge. Develop a relationship with a special place in nature and practice giving to and receiving from that place.

AGE: Younger children and older children

MATERIALS: Paper, pencils, clipboards or cardboard backing for support while writing or drawing, journals, crayons, natural objects, string, yarn and other supplies as needed for the activities chosen.

PROCEDURE: Arrange for a low ratio of children to adults when conducting this activity, such as one adult for each three children in the group. Scout out and choose ahead of time a *safe* natural area for the children to visit. The edges of woodlands, where the forest opens onto some farmland, a field or a park usually afford good dense shrubs and trees with strong lower branches and good views of the surrounding area. Children also have a natural affinity for sitting near streams, ponds and other wet places.

Take the children to the chosen area and tell them that, for this first visit, they are to simply find a shrub to sit beneath, a good lower branch of a tree to climb up to and look out from, the bank of a pond or stream or another reasonably dry, comfortable place to sit. Here, they are

Figure 5-2. A bald eagle spreads its wings for take-off. Size: body. 30–43 inches (76–109 centimeters); wingspread, 7–8 feet (2.1–2.4 meters). Photo by Cecil B. Hoisington.

going to imagine themselves as birds perching—watching and listening closely to everything that is happening around them. Pick a certain bird call, such as a hawk, eagle, owl (or whatever you can best imitate!) and tell the children to stay in their perches until you signal for them to come back with the bird call.

Now have the children search for a special gift to leave at the base of their shrubs, trees or wherever they are sitting at their perches—an acorn, a pretty stone, a colorful leaf or some other natural object will suffice. Tell them that they will use this gift in a circle of giving and receiving with each visit to their perches. Ask them to ask permission of the perches during each visit before taking their places there, and to leave a gift at the perches to say "thank you" for the gift of solitude and the experience the perches have given them.

Have the children search out their own "perches." They will naturally select a place where they feel safe,

comfortable and connected. Station the adults in your group in such a way that all of the children are visible to at least one adult. Allow the children to stay at their own "Perch of Perception" for ten minutes this first time, then use the bird call to gather them together. Have the group sit in a circle and ask the children to take turns sharing what they have seen and heard from their perches.

Visit this site often and have the children continue to ask permission on arriving and leave a gift on departing from their perches. Keep extending the length of their visits by a few minutes each time, and conduct the visits over the course of a few days, weeks or even seasons depending on how long you have contact with the children.

Conduct a variety of directed activities with them during each visit. On appropriate visits, ask each child to do the following.

• Draw a picture of your "Perch of Perception" with you in it.
• Draw a picture of anything you want to during each visit. Draw small things like the ants you see crawling up tree bark and large things like the open area in front of you.
• Listen closely to the birds, insects, wind and other sounds that you hear. Turn those sounds into word sounds and spell them out on paper. Imitate the sounds until you can mimic some of them. Count the number of different sounds you hear during each visit and record that number.
• Make models of the birds and animals (using natural objects) that you hear and see at your perch. Use string to hang them from the branches around your perch.
• Keep a journal of events at your "Perch of Perception." Write or draw a little in this journal each time you visit. Read or look over your journal entries later when you are home and add more to them when something comes to mind.
• During the spring and early summer, bring pieces of yarn and string to your perch and stick the ends of them into the cracks and crevices of nearby bark and branches. Watch to see if the birds take them to use for nest-building in between your visits. Later, search for nests in the area and look for string and yarn in them.
• Leave sunflower seeds, nuts or pieces of soft fruit at your perch for the animals to eat. (Emphasize that this is a one-time gift to the animals and is not meant to supplement their diets.)
• Get into a comfortable position and sit perfectly still and silently for your entire visit. Imagine that you are part of your perch: rooted and growing in the earth. If you move at all, move *very* slowly so that an animal watching you would

not notice. If you learn to be good at "naturalizing"—at becoming part of nature—then the birds, insects and other animals will accept you as part of their surroundings and come very close. One may even land or crawl on you! Watch the ground at your perch, too, during this time to notice any animals passing by. Now imagine yourself as a bird sitting in its perch, with bird eyes and ears. What do you see in your surroundings? What do you hear?

• Look for spiders, ants and other insects living on or walking over your perch. Watch them closely. What are they doing? What are they eating? Do you see any insect eggs? Cocoons? Caterpillars? Keep track of these sightings in your journal.

• Take care of the area around your perch. Keep it clean and free of litter, but be careful not to handle broken glass or rusty metal.

• Gather *a few* natural objects from your perch to keep at home as a reminder of this special place.

• Once you have made a number of visits to your perch, use your journal entries, the pictures you have drawn and events you remember to write and/or illustrate a story of your perch adventures.

EXTENDING THE EXPERIENCE

• Have the children compare their "armspans" to the wingspan of an eagle. Divide the group into teams and give each team some masking tape and a yardstick. Have each team go to a different wall and measure out 7 feet (2.1 meters), the eagle's wingspan, marking the distance with two small pieces of tape. Then have each person go up to a wall and hold his or her arms out. How does each child's armspan compare to an eagle's wingspan?

• Make a life-sized model of an eagle out of cloth and stuffing. Use two broomsticks to give the model some rigidity, one stick running inside and across the wings, and the other running the length of the body. Hang this "eagle" and let it soar up on the ceiling.

• Have the children imagine they are their "Symbol Animals" (see Chapter 3) while in their "Perch of Perception."

• Visit the "Perch of Perception" after twilight for a nighttime experience.

• See Chapter 12 for more stories, information and activities focusing on birds. Use these resources to continue exploring birds and bird life.

NOTES

1. Charles A. Eastman, *Indian Boyhood* (New York: Dover Publications, 1971), 18. Quoted in Frances G. Lombardi and Gerald Scott Lombardi, *Circle Without End: A Sourcebook of American Indian Ethics* (Happy Camp, Calif.: Naturegraph Publishers, 1982), 14.

2. Frank B. Linderman, *Plenty-Coups, Chief of the Crows* (Lincoln, Nebr.: University of Nebraska Press, 1930, 1957), 43. Quoted in Lombardi, 21.

3. John Fire/Lame Deer and Richard Erdoes, *Lame Deer, Seeker of Visions* (New York: Simon & Schuster/Touchstone Books, 1972), 157. Quoted in Lombardi, 14.

4. Jon M. Gerrard and Gary R. Bortolotti, *The Bald Eagle* (Washington, D.C.: Smithsonian Institution Press, 1988), 20.

FEATHERS AND FUR, SCALES AND SKIN

Just as Beaver's tail reached the top of its swing, Turtle let go.

CHAPTER 6

❖ Turtle Races With Beaver ❖

(Seneca—Eastern Woodland)

Long ago, Turtle lived in a small pond. It was a fine place. There were alder trees along the bank to give shade and a fine grassy bank where Turtle could crawl out and sun himself. There were plenty of fish for Turtle to catch. The small pond had everything any turtle could ever want, and Turtle thought his pond was the finest place in the whole world. Turtle spent his time swimming around, sunning himself, and catching fish whenever he was hungry. So it went until the cold winds began to blow down from the north.

"Ah," Turtle said, "It is time for me to go to sleep." Then he dove down to the bottom of the pond and burrowed into the mud. He went to sleep for the winter. He slept so soundly, in fact, that he slept a little later than usual and did not wake up until it was late in the spring. The warming waters of the pond woke him, and he crawled out of the mud and began to swim toward the surface. Something was wrong, though, for it seemed to take much too long to get to the surface of his small pond. Turtle was certain the water had not been that deep when he went to sleep.

As soon as Turtle reached the surface and looked around, he saw that things were not as they should be. His small pond was more than twice its normal size. His fine grassy bank for sunning himself was underwater! His beautiful alder trees had been cut down and made into a big dam.

"Who has done this to my pond?" Turtle said.

Just then Turtle heard a loud sound. WHAP! Turtle turned to look and saw a strange animal swimming toward him across the surface of his pond. It had a big, flat tail and as it came close to Turtle, it lifted up that big, flat tail and hit the surface of the water with it. WHAP!

"Who are you?" Turtle said. "What are you doing in my pond? What have you done to my beautiful trees?"

"Hunh!" the strange animal said. "This is not your pond. This is my pond! I am Beaver and I cut down those trees with my teeth and I built that dam and made this pond nice and deep. This is my pond and you must leave."

"No," Turtle said. "This is my pond. If you do not leave, I will fight you. I am a great warrior."

"Hunh!" Beaver said. "That is good. Let us fight. I will call all my relatives to help me, and they will chew your head off with their strong teeth."

Turtle looked closely at Beaver's teeth. They were long and yellow and looked very sharp.

"Hah!" Turtle said, "I can see it would be too easy to fight you. Instead we should have a contest to decide which of us will leave this pond forever."

"Hunh!" Beaver said. "That is a good idea. Let us see who can stay underwater the longest. I can stay under for a whole day."

As soon as Beaver said that, Turtle saw he would have to think of a different contest. He had been about to suggest that they see who could stay underwater the longest, but if what Beaver said was true, then he would beat Turtle.

"Hah!" Turtle said. "It would be too easy to defeat you that way. Let us have a race instead. The first one to reach the other side of the pond is the winner. The loser must leave my pond forever."

"Hunh!" Beaver said. "That is a good contest. I am the fastest swimmer of all. When I win, you will have to leave my pond forever. Let us begin to race."

"Wait," Turtle said, "I am such a fast swimmer that it would not be fair unless I started from behind you."

Then Turtle placed himself behind Beaver, right next to Beaver's big tail.

"I am ready," Turtle said, "let us begin!"

Beaver began to swim. He was such a fast swimmer that Turtle could barely keep up with him. When they were halfway across the pond, Turtle began to fall even further behind. But Turtle had a plan. He stuck his long neck out and grabbed Beaver's tail in his jaws.

Beaver felt something grab his tail, but he could not look back. He was too busy swimming, trying to win the race. He swung his tail back and forth, but Turtle held on tight. Now Beaver was almost to the other side of the pond. Turtle bit down even harder. Beaver swung his tail high up into the air, trying to shake free whatever had hold of him. Just as Beaver's tail reached the top of its swing, Turtle let go. He flew through the air and landed on the bank! Beaver looked up, and there was Turtle! Turtle had won the race.

So it was that Beaver had to leave and Turtle, once again, had his pond to himself. With its new deeper waters there were soon even more fish than there had been before and Turtle's alders grew back once more. Truly, Turtle's pond was the finest place in the whole world.

DISCUSSION

Turtle is a very special animal for Native American peoples. In many of the stories of Creation, before Earth is made, there is only water. In some of the stories, this is the way it had always been; in others, there had been a great flood. Various animals volunteer to dive down to the bottom of the water to bring up some earth in order to make or remake the world. But when one of them finally succeeds, there is no place to put the earth. The problem is solved when Great Turtle swims up to the surface. "Place Earth on my back," Great Turtle says.

It is because of that story that many Native North American people refer to North America as "Turtle Island," "Turtle Continent" or "Earth on Turtle's Back." Among some of the native people of California, the story goes on to

say that Great Turtle stands on another turtle's back. And below that turtle is yet another turtle, and so on forever. In California, when earthquakes happened, the native people used to say, "Ah, Turtle is stretching its limbs."

If you look at the back of a turtle you will note that there are thirteen large plates on its back. This is as true for land tortoises as it is for sea turtles. Those thirteen plates, many Native American traditions say, stand for each of the moons during the cycle of a year (in Abenaki moons). Little Loon, an Abenaki elder, once told us that those thirteen plates stand for each of the Abenaki nations that belonged to the Wabanaki Confederacy.

Turtle's shell was made to be this way to remind us that everything in the natural world is connected; there is balance and rhythm and a plan to things. Turtle's shell reminds us of this and reminds us to try to keep that balance.

The turtle is also seen to be an animal that is quite clever. In stories from the Northeastern Woodlands, such as this story from the Seneca Nation of the Haudenosaunee (Iroquois) people, Turtle often uses his wits to defeat animals bigger and faster than he is. However, as is the case with anyone who is quick-witted, in some of the stories Turtle outwits himself.

Because turtles live for such a long time, the turtle was associated with longevity. Among many of the Native American nations—the people of the Great Plains, for example—it was common practice to keep the child's umbilical cord and put it into a small stuffed turtle made of deerskin. As the baby played with that little stuffed turtle, it was also asking (though it did not know it at the time) for the blessing of a long life—like Turtle.

Ecological Principles

"Turtle Races With Beaver" is a strong teaching story that introduces many of the important ideas and concepts of *ecology*—those that describe the relationships between plants, animals and their environments. Turtle's pond is the home or *habitat* for an *ecological community*, those plants and animals that live *interdependently* in a particular environment, sharing the available food, water, air, shelter and other resources needed for survival. These vital resources, along with the organisms that live in a particular habitat, are known collectively as an *ecosystem.* "Everything affects everything else" in nature as Turtle's experience proves so well. The *interrelationship* of the pond animals becomes clear when Beaver's dam floods Turtle's grassy banks and prized alder trees. Although we often think of people as the only ones who alter the environment, Beaver shows us that change is a part of the natural order as well: it can bring disaster for some and opportunity for others. Even though Beaver flooded Turtle's favorite haunts along the shore, he also created a greater amount of shoreline habitat and a home for those plants and animals that live in deeper water.

Turtle's pond is a microcosm of the entire living Earth. Those plants that give Turtle a place to sun himself provide more than just habitat. Green plants are ultimately the source of energy for nearly all living things. Only certain kinds of bacteria and a few deep-sea animals do not depend on plants as their source of energy. Plants, in turn, need the air, water, soil and the rocks from which soil forms.

Energy for the growth of green plants comes from the sun. During the crucial process of *photosynthesis*, a reaction

occurs when sunlight strikes the green chlorophyll of the leaf, changing water (H_2O) and carbon dioxide (CO_2) into simple sugars, starches, fats, proteins, vitamins and other nutrients that trap the sun's energy. Water is also produced, along with oxygen, a vital gas used by plants and animals during *respiration* to metabolize their food to get energy for growth and maintenance. Plants, then, provide animals with food, shelter and oxygen. Since animals take in oxygen and give off carbon dioxide during respiration, while plants use carbon dioxide and produce oxygen during photosynthesis, a *gas cycle* occurs as plants and animals exchange these gases (Figure 6-1).

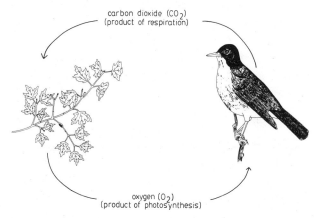

carbon dioxide (CO_2)
(product of respiration)

oxygen (O_2)
(product of photosynthesis)

Figure 6-1. The gas cycle between plants and animals. In the process of respiration, animals use oxygen and produce carbon dioxide. Plants are net producers of oxygen because they give off more oxygen during photosynthesis than they use in respiration.

While green plants are the *producers* of energy, those life forms that live off this energy are *consumers.* When the beaver eats the bark from the trees it has cut down, roughly 90 percent of the energy stored in that bark will be expended as the energy is used for growth, moving around, metabolic processes such as breathing and digestion and for producing heat. The actual amount of energy lost varies greatly depending on the food energy available in the plant or animal eaten, the season and the efficiency of the consumer.

The beaver is an *herbivore* because it eats only plants, but that is only one kind of consumer. The heron that eats fish in the pond is a meat eater or *carnivore.* The turtle is an *omnivore* because it eats both plants and animals. The aquatic earthworm and planaria crawling through the pond mud are called *scavengers:* they feast on *detritus*—the dead remains and wastes of plants and/or animals. On land, the *decomposers,* mostly bacteria and fungi, consume dead plant and animal remains and break them down further into proteins, fats, carbohydrates, minerals and other compounds. Nutrients are released for plant growth once again through leaching from detritus, excretion and on death of the decomposers, in a process called *mineralization*. This process of decomposition completes the *nutrient cycle*, one of the great circles of life on Earth—the circle of life and death that makes continuing life possible for the plants that use sunlight to grow and the animals that eat them.

Underwater, however, where conditions in the pond mud are nearly devoid of oxygen or are *anaerobic*, decomposition occurs very slowly and pond muck accumulates. Some bacteria that can live under those conditions break down detritus chemically, releasing gases such as ammonia, methane (a flammable gas) and hydrogen sulfide, which creates the rotten-egg smell of marsh gas. This is usually what you see when you look across a pond or marsh and see tiny bubbles breaking the surface.

* * * *

Each plant and animal of the pond occupies a certain *niche* or ecological role in the ecosystem, such as producer, consumer, decomposer, pollinator or spreader of seeds. Algae is a producer that is eaten by a tadpole, a consumer. A young bass is a predator that in turn eats the tadpole, then itself falls prey to the swift and agile otter. Plants and animals often compete for the same niche, and a single organism can fill several niches. For instance a beaver is an herbivore that also spreads the seeds that get caught in its fur. In addition, it acts as an agent of change in its habitat by clearing trees and allowing sun-loving plants to grow in the newly sunny forest floor.

Energy flows from the sun to the plants and animals. As energy passes from algae to otter along the steps of the pathway just described, it links those plants and animals together along a *food chain* (Figure 6-2). Bass, of course, also eat small fish, large insects, frogs and even other bass, while otters eat other kinds of fish besides bass. All of these food chains interlock to form an intricate *food web*. And, because energy is lost whenever it passes from one level to the next along the way, a *food pyramid* forms with

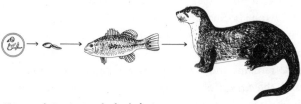

Figure 6-2. A simple food chain.

ever smaller numbers of organisms living at the uppermost levels, being supported by the ones below (Figure 6-3). Since herbivores eat lower on the food pyramid and there is more food energy available to them, any given habitat usually supports a greater population of plant eaters. Conversely, carnivores feed higher up on the pyramid and so, are fewer because there is less energy to support them. Top carnivores are those that eat other carnivores and have no significant predators of their own, such as the otter and osprey. These animals are uppermost on the food pyramid.

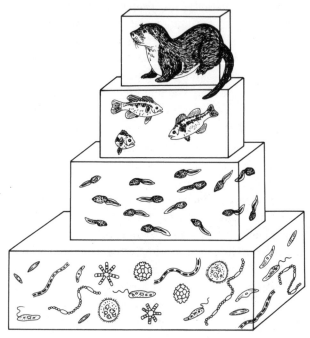

Figure 6-3. Food pyramid.

Freshwater Life

The myriad interactions and adaptations among plants and animals in lakes, ponds, rivers, streams and wetlands, such as swamps, marshes and bogs, make these places fascinating and magical for children and adults alike. From turtles to one-celled amoebas and from crayfish to water striders, there is a host of aquatic creatures to enjoy discovering. They are able to exchange gases, eat, move around, find optimal temperatures, maintain correct body fluid concentrations, excrete waste, reproduce, survive in the current and adjust to seasonal changes.[1] They do all of this while adapting to the challenging life conditions in fresh water: oxygen levels (dissolved oxygen), temperature, pH (acid, neutral or alkaline conditions), availability of food, water quality and water movement (waves and currents).[2]

Dormancy and Other Adaptations to the Seasons

These conditions in fresh water change with the seasons. When the cold winds blow down from the north, the turtle burrows into the mud at the bottom of the pond and falls asleep for the winter. It stays there until the warming waters wake it up and prompt it to come out of the mud and swim to the surface.

Whenever the chilly autumn air arrives each year, bringing short days and the ice and snow of winter that make food scarce, a period of dormancy called *hibernation* begins for many animals. As ponds, marshes and lakes freeze over and the ground begins to harden, the *cold-blooded* animals or *ectotherms*, like the turtle—those whose body temperature fluctuates with and is dependent on that of their surroundings—burrow into the submerged mud or, as with snakes, beneath the frost line on land. During this state of deep hibernation, which often lasts for the entire winter, their metabolism, including heartbeat, circulation and respiration, and rate of growth drop dramatically. A hibernating amphibian, such as a frog, needs so little oxygen that it breathes entirely through its skin. This is also true for certain reptiles. Garter snakes, which usually hibernate in burrows on land, have been found hibernating underwater in the mud at the edges of ponds! *Brumation* is a term used to describe dormancy among cold-blooded animals.

Other kinds of animals adapt to winter conditions with a variety of strategies. They may remain active during cold weather, migrate to a warmer climate (see Chapters 8 and 12), take shelter in a protected place, overwinter in a resting stage such as an egg or hibernate like the turtle.

The fox and hare simply grow a thicker coat and remain active through the winter. Other *warm-blooded* animals or *endotherms*—which produce their own internal heat and maintain body temperature independently from that of the environment—do undergo deep hibernation. Animals in this state of dormancy, such as the meadow jumping mouse, groundhog (woodchuck) and many bats, lower their body temperatures dramatically. Some hibernating bats experience frigid body temperatures as low as 35.6°F (2°C). Groundhogs drop their heart rate from ninety beats per minute when active to ten beats per minute when dormant (Figure 6-4)!

Hibernation is not as clearly defined in all dormant animals, however. Although bears are perhaps most often used as examples of hibernating animals, they really experience a partial hibernation called *torpor*, during which their

Figure 6-4. The heart rate of a hibernating groundhog (woodchuck) is about 10 beats per minute, a dramatic drop from the normal, active rate of 90 beats per minute! A dormant groundhog's body temperature may fall to as low as 37.4° F (3.0° C), down significantly from its active, summer temperature of around 96.8° F (36.0° C). Size (including tail): 20–27 inches (50.8–68.6 centimeters). Photo by Don Blades.

body temperatures may remain as high as 95°F (35°C), while their respiration rate drops to two to three times per minute. Other animals that undergo torpor, such as the raccoon, skunk, chipmunk and many squirrels, also maintain higher body temperatures than do deep hibernators.

During extended periods of extreme heat or drought, some animals enter a period of dormancy similar to hibernation called *estivation*. Many salamanders burrow under debris or into the ground to estivate during hot, dry summer periods when food and water are hard to find. Some desert animals also estivate, such as the spadefoot toad of the southwestern United States. Hummingbirds, and even some bats in temperate regions, undergo a partial dormancy called *diurnation*, which consists of a period of inactivity during summer days.

Still, during the favorable season, when the cooling winds and life-giving rains return to the desert, or when the warm days of spring finally arrive after a cold northern winter, the metabolism and need for oxygen increases among dormant animals. They hop, crawl, swim, fly and scurry out of their resting places to continue the activity of their remarkable lives once again.

QUESTIONS

1. Why does Turtle crawl into the mud at the bottom of his pond to go to sleep? What do we call it when an animal does this?

2. Is Turtle a cold-blooded or a warm-blooded animal?

What is the difference between these two kinds of animals?

3. What does Turtle find when he awakes?

4. Does Turtle *really* win the race with Beaver? How does he beat Beaver to the other shore? Does this way of winning count in a race?

5. Whose pond is it really? Turtle's? Beaver's? Does any one animal own the pond?

6. How many scales are there on the back of Turtle? Why are these scales important in Native North American traditions?

7. Turtle and Beaver have an argument when they discover they are sharing the pond. How do different animals really share the water, food and shelter available where they live?

8. What is the word we use for an animal's home?

9. What is ecology?

10. Why do Turtle and Beaver need the plants in their pond? What do they use the plants for? What would happen to them and the other animals of the pond if the plants were all taken away?

11. How do plants grow? Where do they get their energy from? What do we call the process by which plants produce food from the sun? What else do they produce?

12. What is a food chain? What are the different kinds of food an animal can eat? What do we call the animals that eat plants? Those that eat animals?

ACTIVITIES

Web of Energy

ACTIVITY: Choose and visit a beaver pond or other pond, stream, lake, field, forest, seashore, desert or other local environment, such as a schoolyard, vacant lot, backyard or park, to enjoy and observe the plants and animals living there. Discuss energy flow, photosynthesis and green plants as producers of energy, animals as consumers, and identify each animal as herbivore, carnivore, omnivore or scavenger. Create a food web with the sun at the center.

GOALS: Experience the life of a certain ecological community and the interrelationships of plants and animals in that community. Understand that, through photosynthesis, sunlight grows the green plants that are the primary food for animals. Understand the concepts of energy flow, producer, consumer, food chain and web. Identify and understand the kinds of consumers: herbivore, carnivore, omnivore and scavenger.

AGE: Younger children and older children

MATERIALS: 5x7 index cards, pencils, cardboard backing to write against, felt-tipped markers, crayons, hand lenses, field guides containing the natural history of plants and animals living in the habitat where the scavenger hunt is conducted, pictures of the plants and animals which characterize that habitat, Figures 6-2, 6-3 and 6-5, yellow cap, yarn, scissors.

PROCEDURE: Beforehand, help the children choose a habitat that they want to work with—one that is accessible from your house or learning center. Brainstorm a list of plants and animals they can expect to see in this habitat. Use this list to create scavenger hunt cards listing plants and animals that most likely live in the beaver pond or other habitat you will visit. Include everything you want to be included in the *"Web of Energy"* on the scavenger hunt cards; for example, for a pond: sunlight, algae, lily pads, grass, cattails, bass, tadpole, minnow, water beetle, crayfish, heron, kingfisher, frog, turtle, snake, muskrat and raccoon. Leave blank spaces where the children can write down or draw in additional discoveries.

Copy and pass out the cards and describe what the children can expect to find. Emphasize that the idea is to observe, learn about and make note of—not to collect. Review the basic rules of behavior in animals' homes (see Chapter 2). Pass out the hand lenses and show the children how to use them.

Working in small groups of about three, have the children find, observe for a while and then check off as many of the plants and animals that are listed on their cards as they can, writing or drawing in any new sightings as they go. Gather the entire group together after about 20 to 30 minutes and have each small group report on what they found. Visit the site of particularly exciting findings so that the entire group may share in the experience. Now have the children write the names of everything on the scavenger hunt sheet, *plus* their new findings, onto separate index cards. Younger children can draw pictures of these instead of writing them out.

Define and discuss the concepts of photosynthesis, energy producers and the different kinds of consumers: herbivores, carnivores, omnivores and scavengers. Discuss the interrelationships that tie this community together, and how energy flows along the food chains that make up an elaborate web of energy. Use field guides to research food habits and categorize each animal on an index card as a certain kind of consumer. Have the children write this classification and the specific foods that animal eats onto the back of the appropriate animal's card. Describe how this category helps to define each plant or animal's *niche* or role in this ecological community.

Now gather the children into a big circle. Assign one child as the sun and source of energy and have her or him wear the yellow cap and stand in the center of the circle with hands outstretched. If you have a large group of children, have each one take an index card and become the plant or animal that is named on that card. Children representing plants may need to take several cards because there are more plants than animals. Now have all of the plants receive their energy from the sun by holding one of the sun's hands (Figure 6-5). Have each plant offer its energy to the animals by stretching the still open hand away from the sun in the center toward the other children in the circle. Now have each of the children who represent plants, one by one, call out the plant names and have every animal (herbivore or omnivore) that eats that (these) plant(s) go up and hold his or her hand to extend the spokes of the web further out from the center. When all of the appropriate animals have joined the web, have each one in turn call out its identity and have all of the animals (carnivore or omnivore) that eat that animal go up to hold his or her hand to extend the web of the spokes even further out. Help any animal that has not joined the web to find a correct position.

Discuss how this "web" symbolizes the flow of energy but is not accurate in terms of the relative numbers of plants and animals that one would expect to find in an ecosystem.

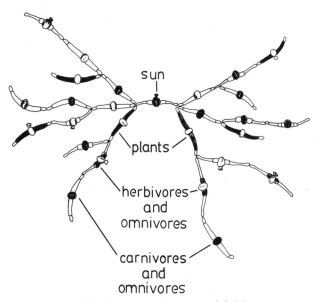

Figure 6-5. "Web of Energy" formation of children.

In reality, there would be more plants than animals, as well as a decreasing number of animals in each category of consumer with increasing distance from the sun. (See the description of *food pyramid* in the "Discussion" section.)

Ask the animals, one at a time, if any of them eat more than just the plant or animal they are connected to. In response, take pieces of yarn and join that "animal" with all of its other "foods" in the web. Do this with each animal in turn until they are all strung onto their food supplies and the web is "complete." Do not tie the ends of the yarn, just have each child hold on lightly to each end.

Now tell the children they are going to see just how important the plants are to the animals. Have the children *gently* lean out away from the sun in the center of the circle. Tell the animals their primary food, the plants, is about to be taken away. Now have all of the plants let go of the animals to send them tumbling down.

Use the same sequence between the sun and plants and send them out of the web to unravel it completely.

Follow this activity with *"Vored to Death"* on page 51 of *Keepers of the Earth* to introduce the concept of the food pyramid. *"Vored to Death"* is set up as a natural sequence using the same introduction and materials gathered for *Web of Energy.*

Whither the Winter of Turtle and Beaver

ACTIVITY: Perform a puppet show comparing the wintering strategies of Turtle, Beaver, a red-winged blackbird, a honeybee and a cricket.

GOALS: Contrast and understand the wintering strategies of a hibernating cold-blooded animal, an active warm-blooded animal, a migrating bird and two insects.

AGE: Younger children and older children

MATERIALS: Paper, cardboard, crayons, felt-tipped markers, scissors, glue, tape, pictures of each animal for children to use as models for the puppets, sticks on which to mount the puppets, table and blue blanket for stage, props for the set (cattails, beaver lodge, lily pad, etc.), script to "Whither the Winter of Turtle and Beaver."

PROCEDURE: Have the children prepare puppets on a stick of a turtle, a beaver, a red-winged blackbird, a cricket and a honeybee. Make a few props suggesting a pond, such as a cattail, water lily and beaver lodge. Set up a stage using props and a blue blanket or bedspread for the water.

Practice and then perform this puppet show with the children. Encourage the puppeteers to adopt voices that they think their animals would sound like.

WHITHER THE WINTER OF TURTLE AND BEAVER

Turtle: (*sitting on beaver lodge while sunning*) Buuurrr! It's getting chilly outside. I can feel that cold north wind. Even the sun doesn't warm me like it did this summer.

Beaver: Hey, who is that? Who said you could sun yourself on my lodge?

Turtle: I'm sorry, Beaver, I hope you don't mind. I *had* to get out of the cold water into the sun. I'm *freezing*. Why, I'm so cold that I'm thinking of going into hibernation.

Beaver: Listen to me, Turtle. You can't sleep your winters away like that. Look at me, I stay active and keep warm by huddling with my family in the lodge. Right now I'm cutting branches and sticking sticks into the mud underwater so we will have some nice, juicy bark to eat when the pond freezes over. Then I've got to repair the lodge, fix a leak in the dam. . . . Busy, busy, busy. How can you even think of sleeping?

Turtle: Beaver, you may have your own body heat and a nice thick coat of fur to hold it in, but I'm just a cold-blooded terrapin with nothing but the shell on my back for a home. I *must* burrow deep into the mud to sleep off the winter. If I tried to stay awake, I would freeze and die!

Redwing: Look at meee! Look at meee!

Beaver: Oh cool it, Redwing. We know you're there already.

Redwing: Beaver, is that you? Why are you in such a bad mood?

Beaver: It's my teeth. I bit into the bark of that tree I cut down over there and some human had driven a nail into it and I chipped my tooth. Ow, it hurts!

Redwing: Sorry to hear it, but that explains your biting remarks. Listen, I overheard and you two are *both* being silly. I just fly away when it gets cold and food becomes scarce. It's warm and food is easy to find down south.

Turtle: Hey, I can't fly!

Beaver: Neither can I!

Redwing: No, come to think of it, I guess you'll just have to adapt to the cold in your own way, won't you? Some of us can fly, and some of us can't. Bye, bye.

Honeybee: (*flies over buzzing*) Buuzzzzzz! I'm glad he'zzzzz gone. Old Redwing might eat me.

Beaver: I suppose you came here to brag about flying south for the winter too. Eh?

Honeybee: Jeezzzzzz Beaver. Are you in a louzzzzzzy mood. I'm not the boazzzzztful type. Beezzzzides, all we honey-bees do is ball up together in our hollow tree to help each other keep warm when Old Man Winter arrives.

Beaver: Yeah, kind of like we beavers snuggle together in our lodge.

Honeybee: Well, sort of, although I'd rather have my stinger than your flat tail any day.

Beaver: Well, I wouldn't mind having a stinger myself. There are a few times I would have used it, I'll tell you. But I couldn't use a stinger to help me pack mud into my lodge and dam.

Honeybee: Beaver, I'd like to talk but I'm very buzzzzzey gathering nectar to make our winter honey supply. Eazzzzzy does it with that tooth! Buzzzzz (*flies off*).

Turtle: Beaver, I heard the way you were talking to Honeybee. You seem quite convinced that your way of doing things is the only *right* way. How about a little humility?

Beaver: Well, you may have a point there, Turtle, though I'm not quite convinced.

Cricket: Chirp, chirp, chirp.

Beaver: Is that you, Cricket?

Cricket: Cheer up, Beaver, life is lots of fun, if only you'd let yourself enjoy it!

Turtle: Beaver's broken a bit off of his tooth, I'm afraid, but he seems to have a chip on his shoulder.

Cricket: I hear you two are talking about winter already. Well, I don't worry about winter. My life is very short. We crickets, and our cousins the grasshoppers, lay eggs in the ground before the cold comes. Eventually, as the weather gets colder and the temperature reaches down below freezing, I'm going to die. Only my eggs will winter over. But don't worry. You can meet my children next spring when the eggs hatch out after spending the winter buried in the ground. Hey, time to lay some eggs! (*hops off*)

Beaver: I've been so foolish. I never had any idea that there were so many ways to survive the winter. Now that I know, I feel lucky to have it so easy, and to have my family to help me through it!

Turtle: I'm glad you've come to your senses. Well, it's time to go look for a good spot in the mud to sleep the winter. So long, Beaver. (*starts to leave but . . .*)

Beaver: Take it slow, Turtle.

Turtle: Very funny, Beaver! Very funny! (*both disappear*)

Cycle Says

ACTIVITY: Play an adaptation of "Simon Says" and act out the movements of animals important to the nutrient cycle.

GOAL: Understand the nutrient cycle and some animals that help to make it possible.

AGE: Younger children and older children

MATERIALS: Information about the nutrient cycle from the "Discussion" section, list of actions of decomposers for the "Cycle Says" game, enough apples for everyone in the group, hand lenses, empty white yogurt cups or other containers to place animals in for observation.

PROCEDURE: Review the nutrient cycle in the "Discussion" section and discuss it with the children. Allow time for questions and answers to be certain they understand the concept and that life on Earth would be impossible without soil, sun and the plants that they nourish at the base of the food chain.

Now tell the children they are going to play a kind of "Simon Says" game, called "Cycle Says," acting out the roles (mostly) of animals involved in the nutrient cycle. Explain that the rules are the same as for Simon Says. Children will line up in a row, shoulder to shoulder with enough space in between them to allow for vigorous movement. When you (the "Cycle") call out one of the actions in the following list, the children will only act it out if you preface the action like this: "Cycle says wiggle like an earthworm." If you demand an action without first saying "Cycle says," the children are *not* to act it out. If someone acts it out at the wrong time, point it out to the child and have him or her continue the game. When all of the actions have been performed at least once, the "nutrients" in the soil have been released and have nurtured a seed that has grown into the form of an apple tree and produced apples. Pass out apples for all to munch on.

Here is the list of actions representing the scavengers, decomposers and others that contribute directly to the nutrient cycle. Repeat them as often and in as many different sequences as you like during the game, being certain that "Cycle Says" to do every action at least once.

- wiggle like an earthworm
- chew like a termite
- stand like a mushroom (fungus)
- creep like a centipede
- spin silk like a spider
- crawl like a beetle
- jump like a springtail
- wave your antennae like a carpenter ant
- inch along like a larva
- move like a millipede
- be small like a bacteria

When the game is over, review each of the actions of animals (plus fungus and bacteria) and their roles in the nutrient cycle. Show the children pictures of these organisms.

Now take a trip outdoors to a wooded area in a forest or park. Have the children choose a spot among the leaves on the ground and slowly peel away the layers of leaves from top to bottom. Point out that the leaves are more decomposed the deeper they peel. Have them use their hand lenses to look for the white threads of fungi called *hyphae*. Mushrooms are the fruiting bodies of these threads. Observe and discuss the decomposer animals that they find and their roles in the nutrient cycle.

Habitat Sweet Habitat

ACTIVITY: (A) Create a model beaver pond, along with Turtle, Beaver, and other plants and animals that live there. (B) Play a game matching the animals from the puppet show "Whither the Winter of Turtle and Beaver" with their survival needs of food, water, oxygen and shelter.

GOALS: Understand that all animals have basic survival needs of food, water, oxygen and shelter. Realize that each animal's specific requirements of food, water, oxygen and shelter are different from those of other animals. Understand that animals often change their environments as they meet their survival needs.

AGE: Younger children (A) and older children (B)

MATERIALS: (A) For each pair of children: one 18-inch (45.7-centimeter) square board, one piece of plastic of similar dimensions, pile of small sticks, lots of clay. For all pairs to share: additional clay, pipe cleaners, scissors, cardboard, construction paper, paints, paintbrushes, toothpicks, water, copy of Figure 6-6, etc. (B) copies of the "Habitat Match-Up (Figure 6-7)," pencils, paper.

PROCEDURE A: *Eager Beaver.* Divide the group into pairs and give each pair a board, pile of small sticks, piece of plastic and lots of clay. Have other materials available in a common area. Each pair will use the clay to create three sides of the perimeter of a beaver pond. Have them paint in a place where a "stream" flows out of the pond on the fourth (open) side. A dam will then be built across the stream using clay and sticks. The pond should now consist of a complete basin capable of being a "pond." Have the children line the pond with plastic, tucking the edges into the top of the clay banks and dam to hide and secure the plastic so that water cannot leak out. Now, have them build a beaver lodge of sticks and clay in the middle of the pond (Figure 6-6).

Figure 6-6. Cross-section showing beavers in their habitat to use as a model for the "Eager Beaver" activity in "Habitat Sweet Habitat."

Have the children use their imaginations to create beavers, turtles, lily pads and lilies, cattails, logs, dragonflies and any other plants, animals and parts of the habitat that the children think of. As you watch them creating, talk about what each animal needs to live and where it would be found in the beaver pond. When the projects are completed, fill the ponds with water to a reasonable level, being sure that the top of the lodge is sticking out above the surface of the water, but that the entryways to the lodge are submerged.

Once they have completed their projects, have each pair share and describe the habitat and how each animal meets its needs there for food, water, oxygen and shelter.

Ask the children to describe how the beaver changes the habitat when it builds its dam and floods the area, creating a pond. Ask them to think of other animals that change their environments by the ways they eat, burrow, build or engage in other activities.

PROCEDURE B: *Habitat Match-Up.* Hand out copies of the following game matching animals from the puppet show "Whither the Winter of Turtle and Beaver" with their appropriate needs for food, water, shelter and oxygen (Figure 6-7). Add additional animals and their needs to create a more challenging game. Have the children draw lines connecting each animal with its food(s) and shelter(s), as well as its supply(ies) of both water and oxygen. Tell them that the animals may use more than one of the kinds of food and/or shelter listed, and may obtain water and oxygen from more than one source. Discuss how all animals need food, water, oxygen and shelter to survive. Describe and discuss the gas cycle.

Allow time for the children to discuss their matches. Have them design their own matching game using other animals from a beaver pond, or with animals from the habitat they visited in "Web of Energy." Have them identify and explain as many examples as they can think of for how animals, like beavers, alter their environments as they eat, create new habitat, burrow and live out their lives.

EXTENDING THE EXPERIENCE

• Think of other things that the thirteen scales on Turtle's back could represent. Use thirteen as a good luck number!

• Make up a list of both cold-blooded and warm-blooded animals, discuss the differences between the two and have children choose which ones are which.

• Make up an original story about two different animals having a race.

• Create a habitat mural showing the sun, the plants it helps to grow and the food web of animals that live in that habitat. Focus on a particular habitat such as the forest, field, stream, pond, lake, marsh, seashore or desert.

• Make a list of some favorite foods. Trace each food to the source plant or animal it comes from. Use these links to make a food web that supports people.

NOTES

1. Michael J. Caduto, *Pond and Brook: A Guide to Nature in Freshwater Environments* (Hanover, N.H.: University Press of New England, 1990), 230–35.

2. Ibid., 31–36.

Figure 6-7

Habitat Match-Up

OXYGEN SUPPLIES

- from water (oxygen dissolved in the water)
- from the air directly

SHELTERS

- hollow tree
- under a log
- grass
- water weeds
- water
- mud
- treetops
- under a rock
- bushes
- lodge

Turtle

Beaver

Red-winged Blackbird

Honeybee

Cricket

FOODS

- grass
- fish
- moth
- nectar
- crayfish
- frog and/or salamander eggs
- tadpole
- bark
- worm
- seeds
- berries
- pollen

WATER SUPPLIES

- pond
- stream
- raindrops
- puddle
- dewdrops on leaves
- flower nectar
- mud

Her braids turned into eight long arms. Four of those arms wrapped around Raven and four around the rock.

CHAPTER 7

✦ Octopus and Raven ✦

(Nootka—Pacific Northwest)

One morning, as the tide went out, the old people came down to sit and watch by the shore. That was the way it was done in the old days. As they sat there, they saw a woman walking along the beach. Her hair was long and it was strung into eight braids. That woman was Octopus. She carried a basket on her back. There was a yew wood digging stick in her hand. She was going to look for clams. She sat down on one of the stones just at the edge of the water and began to dig. Before long, she dug up one clam and then another.

As the people watched, someone else came along the beach. That person was tall with glossy black hair.

"Look," one of the old people said. "Here comes Raven. He has seen Octopus digging for food. Now he is going to bother her."

"Ah," another of the old people said. "That is not a good idea. You shouldn't bother Octopus!"

Sure enough, just as the old people expected, Raven walked right down to the rock where Octopus sat and began to bother her.

"Octopus," Raven said in a loud voice, "what are you doing? Are you digging for clams?"

Octopus didn't answer him or even look up. She just continued to dig with her stick.

Raven stepped a little closer. "Are you digging for clams?" he said, his voice louder still.

Octopus did not look up. She just kept on digging.

Raven came closer. "Are you digging for clams?" he said in an even louder voice.

Octopus didn't answer him. She just kept on digging.

Now Raven came very close indeed. He poked his nose into Octopus' basket. "Are you digging for clams?" he shouted.

Suddenly, Octopus stood up. She dropped her digging stick. Her braids turned into eight long arms. Four of those arms wrapped around Raven and four around the rock.

"Raven," she said, "I am glad you asked me that question. Yes, I am digging clams. It is clams that I am digging."

Raven struggled to get free, but he was caught. The tide had turned now and the water was around his feet. "Octopus," he said, "thank you for answering my question. Now you can let me go."

But Octopus only held him tighter. "Raven," she said, "that is a good question that you asked. Now I must answer you. Yes, I am digging clams. It is clams that I am digging."

The water was growing deeper around them. Now it had reached Raven's knees. He tried to get loose, but Octopus wrapped her arms tighter. "That is a very good answer," Raven said. "I have heard you clearly now. Indeed, you are digging clams. You do a very good job of digging clams. Now please let me go."

But Octopus did not let go. "Raven" she said, "let me answer your question. I am digging clams. It is clams that I am digging."

Now the water was over their waists. Raven saw that it would soon be even deeper. "Octopus," he said, "you do not have to answer me again. It is very clear to me what you were doing. Just let me go now. Please let me go now."

Octopus did not let go. "Raven," she said, "I was digging clams, I was digging clams."

Again Raven begged, but the water continued to get deeper and Octopus held tight. The water came up to their necks and then it was over their heads.

Up on the beach, above the tide line, the old people watched.

"Octopus can hold her breath longer than Raven," one of the old people said.

They watched and finally, after a long time, Raven could hold his breath no longer and he drowned. Octopus let go and Raven floated up to the surface.

"Look," another of the old people said, "Raven has drowned."

"Don't worry about him," the other old people said. "He will come back to life again. He always does. His cousin, Crow, will help."

Then the old people went down and pulled Raven out of the water. They carried him to his cousin, Crow. Crow was very wise and she knew just what to do. The next day, just as the old people said, Raven came back to life again. But it was a long time before he went back to the shore and he never asked Octopus another question.

DISCUSSION

Raven is a great trickster and transformer among the tales of the Pacific Northwest peoples, such as the Haida, Tlingit, Kwakiutl and Tsimshian. Soon after being created beneath the sea, Raven flies off into the mists of the new, formless world. He tricks Wolf into giving him some fresh water from his spring, then brings it to the new land, forming the streams, rivers, lakes and ponds. Raven steals the light from a box and places it in the sky, transforming the primal darkness with the first, brilliant rays of dawn. Finally, Raven forms the first human beings from a chiton.

In this story of Octopus and Raven his curiosity gets the best of him. He sees that Octopus is intent upon her task of gathering clams, yet he pesters her with questions until she becomes annoyed. As the old people sitting on shore watch in amusement, Raven is caught and held by Octopus until he drowns. Yet, as the old people know, Raven is like other tricksters—Coyote in the myths of the Plains peoples and Azaban the Raccoon among the tales of the Abenakis of the Dawn Land to the east—Raven always comes back to life to cause more mischief. In this story, his cousin, Crow, helps him to do so.

Although Raven is not very good at watching patiently, many Native North American peoples believe strongly in teaching children by allowing them to watch and listen quietly while they work. Gradually, if a child shows a sincere interest in learning a particular craft, skill or art, he or she is brought in and allowed to help out. In time, the children or adults find that the knowledge has become a part of them and they are now proficient at that particular task. Of course, not all children watch patiently. Most of us have had the experience of being barraged by an endless string of questions from a curious child, especially the often unanswerable query of, "But why?" So it is easy to identify with how Octopus feels. This may be just the story to share with an overly inquisitive child! Be careful, however, to emphasize that asking questions is a good thing and an important part of learning. Curiosity and questioning are to be encouraged. It is when the same question is asked repeatedly, even after the answer has been given, that people's patience can be stretched.

The Seashore

After sharing the story, take the child for a stroll along the seashore. Few, if any natural environments can equal the enchantment and excitement, the sense of mystery and awe inspired in children by a sojourn seaside. A tidepool, sandy beach or rocky shore, salt marsh, mangrove island or a waving bed of seaweed or eel grass—all are the perfect elixir for a child struck with a feverish curiosity for nature.

The abundance and variety of life at the seashore mirrors the richness of nutrients that are found here where ocean meets land. Seashores are *wetlands*—ecological zones between the open water and dry land where the presence of water determines the nature of the soil and plant and animal

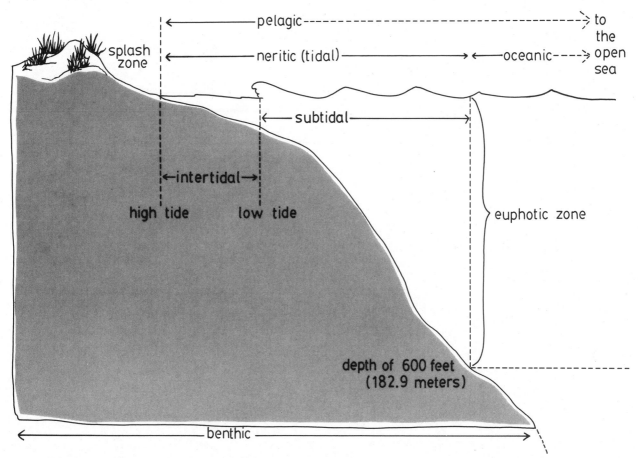

Figure 7-1. Zones of the seashore. Adapted with permission from Deborah A. Coulombe, The Seaside Naturalist. *Englewood Cliffs, N.J.: Prentice-Hall, 6.*

communities present. *Estuaries* are especially rich environments where freshwater rivers and streams deposit their nutrients as they mix with saltwater tidal flows.

TIDES AND TIDAL ZONES. As Raven discovered so painfully in his encounter with Octopus, waves and tides are a dominant force at the seashore. *Tides* are caused by the gravitational pull of the sun and moon. The force of the moon is over twice that of the sun because it is so much closer to Earth. The interplay of these two powerful forces pulling on Earth's surface causes the ocean to bulge and recede on a regular cyclical basis. Tidal cycles vary greatly in different parts of North America. On the Pacific Coast, where this story comes from, there are two high tides and two low tides each day (actually over a period of 24 hours and 50 minutes), with one cycle being more extreme than the other. The East Coast also has two tidal cycles each day, but they are of similar magnitude; the Gulf Coast experiences only one high tide and low tide. The range of change in depth from high tide to low tide varies from only several inches or centimeters on some shores to over 50 feet (15.2 meters) in the Bay of Fundy between Nova Scotia and New Brunswick.

The tidal zone is part of the *pelagic* or open water zone of the ocean. There is an *intertidal* zone between the high tide and low tide lines, a *splash* zone just above high tide and a *subtidal* zone below low tide and down to 600 feet (182.9 meters) deep, which is always submerged (Figure 7-1). The tidal zones are often referred to as the *neritic* zone, while further out past the subtidal zone is the *oceanic* zone. The neritic zone corresponds roughly to the vertical layer of the ocean known as the *euphotic* zone, which ranges from the surface of the sea down to a depth of 600 feet (182.9 meters). Adequate sunlight penetrates the euphotic zone to support photosynthesis. Underlying all of these zones is the *benthic* zone or ocean bottom.

Animals of the Seashore

When the *ebb* tide is strong and the tide going out, some of the *epifauna*—animals that live on the ocean bottom or attached to rocks and other things on the bottom—can be seen. The epifauna make up more than 125,000 of the over 200,000 plants and animals of the sea. These include mussels, crabs, lobsters, snails and sea stars (starfish). Over thirty

Figure 7-2. The sea otter lives in kelp beds and along rocky shores off the West Coast of North America. It feeds on sea urchins, abalones and other marine animals by bringing them up to the surface and using its chest to feed upon. A sea otter will sometimes carry a rock up, place it on its chest and use it to break open the spiny coat of a sea urchin. Size (including tail): 41–49 inches (104.1–124.5 centimeters). Illustration by D. D. Tyler.

thousand kinds of clams, worms and other animals of the *infauna* live in the bottom substrate.

Stroll along any expanse of shoreline that is reasonably unpolluted and you will find a dazzling and sometimes bizarre array of animals carrying out their lives. A gull rises into the sky and drops a mussel onto the rocks to crack the shell and eat the soft flesh inside. Crabs scuttle sideways through the seaweed as they scavenge in the shallows. Offshore a harbor seal lounges on a rock. Or a sea otter floats on its back above a bed of kelp as it uses a rock to break open a sea urchin for a tasty meal (Figure 7-2).

INVERTEBRATES: ANIMALS WITHOUT BACKBONES. Most seashore inhabitants, however, are *invertebrates*, animals without backbones. This chapter focuses on these amazing animals. Step on the sand and a clam withdraws its siphon, squirting water up several inches. Turn over some rotting seaweed and some small shrimp-like amphipods scurry for cover. The clear, squishy bell of a jellyfish may have washed up nearby, transformed out of water from a graceful, swimming umbrella to a gelatinous blob collapsed on the sand. Horseshoe crabs may be mating in the calm bay of a tidal channel, while crabs do their sideways stroll through the shallows in search of a dead animal to scavenge upon. A nearby tidepool is home for hundreds of periwinkles slowly scraping and eating algae off the rocks with their fine-toothed tongues, while some spiny sea urchins are also grazing algae nearby. Turn up a handful of soil from a mudflat and a host of marine worms go wiggling back down seeking cover in the damp dark mud. Depending on where you live and the kind of seashore nearby, you may encounter beds of bluish mussels, sponges, rock-hugging chitons, tunicates, lobsters, sand fleas, microscopic tardigrades or "water bears," corals, sea fans, sea stars, sea urchins, sea anemones and even an octopus.

Arthropods ("joined legs") are among the most conspicuous denizens of the seashore. Seventy-five percent of all animals are members of the phylum *Arthropoda*, including insects, chelicerates (spiders, mites and horseshoe crabs) and crustaceans, such as crabs, shrimps and lobsters. Arthropods have a hard external skeleton or *exoskeleton* composed of a protein called *chitin*. This exoskeleton protects the animal, provides a place to anchor muscles and consists of jointed segments. Since the exoskeleton does not grow with the animal it must be shed periodically when a new skeleton has grown in beneath it. The jointed legs are used for swimming, walking, eating and for sensing the surroundings. Most arthropods have eyes.

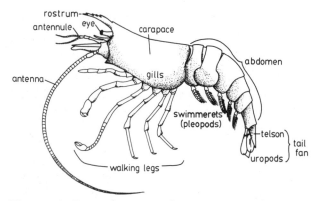

Figure 7-3. External anatomy of a crustacean; in this case, a shrimp.

Crustaceans are the dominant group among marine arthropods. They have a body that is characteristically divided in two sections (Figure 7-3). The *head* has three pairs of feeding appendages and two pairs of antennae. The *trunk* is divided into a *thorax* with gills at the top of the legs, and an *abdomen*. Among crustaceans the exoskeleton contains not only chitin but calcium as well. Female crustaceans typically brood their eggs until they hatch. The young larvae, which look very different from the adult parents, molt as they grow and eventually take on the adult form. A limb that is lost or damaged gradually regenerates with each molt.

Many different kinds of crustaceans inhabit the coast. Barnacles attach to a rock, piling or other substrate where they stick their six, feathery legs out of hard, calcareous shells to trap plankton for food.

Sea spiders, horseshoe crabs, krill, shrimp, crabs and lobsters are all crustaceans, as are the 3/4- to 1-inch (1.9 to 2.5 centimeters) long shrimp-like amphipods and isopods that flit amid the sand grains, between layers of dead seaweed and swim on their sides in tidal pools. These tiny crustaceans also go by the names of beach hoppers, side swimmers, beach fleas, sand fleas and scuds. Some are filter-feeders and others scavenge for their food, eating dead animals, algae and seaweed. Birds, fish and other animals eat large numbers of amphipods.

Hermit crabs are perhaps the most beloved of all seaside crustaceans. They protect their soft abdomen by carrying around a protective, abandoned snail shell for a house as they scavenge the dunes and flats for dead animals to eat. Seemingly never quite satisfied with their old house, hermit crabs are forever searching for a new shell to move into. When a suitable home is found (they never leave their old shell before locating a new one), they quickly pull out of the old shell and back into the new.

Octopus, like the one in this story of Octopus and Raven, is a kind of mollusk classified as a *cephalopod*, along with squid and the nautilus. *Mollusks* are a large group of over 100,000 species of animals that also include, near the shore, the *Gastropoda* (snails and slugs), *Pelecypoda* (clams and their kin) and *Amphineura* (chitons). Mollusks are best known by their other common names of limpet, conch, periwinkle, slipper shells, worm shells, sea hares and sea slugs (nudibranchs). Mollusks have a head, foot and visceral mass that contains most of the major organs. Unlike a crustacean's shell which must be shed as it grows, a mollusk's calcareous shell grows with the animal and is never shed. New layers of shell are produced by the *mantle* in a cross-hatched pattern for strength. Besides providing a place for attaching muscles, the shell protects the animal from predation, injury and dessication in the sunlight. Many forms of mollusk use a *radula*—a tongue holding many minute teeth—for grating, scraping, holding or cutting their food.

Octopi are unusual among mollusks in that they do not have a shell. These soft, yet strong and tentacled animals swim by inhaling water into a mantle cavity and squirting it out a siphon near the mouth, which can be aimed in any direction. An octopus usually creeps along the bottom using its eight arms. Each arm is equipped with suction discs for gripping prey and pulling itself along. While spending much time drawn into its home or *lair* of a small cave or crevice, the octopus comes out to repel an enemy or pursue its prey, usually snails or crustaceans. The hapless victim is trapped and drawn into the mouth by the tentacled arms, injected with poison from the jaws, bitten with a hard, tearing beak and eaten. Octopi have keen eyesight and may be able to detect color. When they are threatened or pursued they can change color quickly to hide, or they will squirt a large splotch of dark ink into the water as a smoke screen to aid in escaping. Male octopi have a specialized arm used for depositing sperm into the female's mantle cavity. The female lays the eggs and secures them to a rock, empty shell or other substrate. She then uses her siphon to keep the eggs clean and well aerated until they hatch. Females of the species called the common octopus die after the eggs hatch.

Another mollusk, the chiton, figures prominently in the stories and diet of the Native North Americans of the Pacific Northwest. The Giant Pacific Chiton grows to be up to 13 inches (33.0 centimeters) long and 6 inches (15.2 centimeters) wide! Chitons have a calcareous shell of eight transverse plates that form a hard, oval protective coat that hugs the rocks on which they graze. Beneath this shell is a wide, oval foot that clings to the rock with a strong suction as the chiton moves slowly along scraping off its food of algae. If dislodged, a chiton can curl up into a ball, protected by its eight-parted armor.

The clams Octopus is digging in the story, and other members of the class *Pelecypoda*, which are also known as *bivalves*, are the most familiar kinds of mollusks to many people. Most bivalves filter fine food particles from the water with their gills. Tiny, hair-like *cilia* create a current on the gills bringing in plankton that is trapped by the gills and by a mucus coating. Water is inhaled in one siphon and exhaled out another. The food is then moved to the mouth. Periwinkles, however, scrape algae off of rocks while whelks prey on bivalves by forcing the shell open and feeding on the soft tissues inside.

Bivalves have a two-parted shell consisting of two halves or *valves* hinged together. They include clams, quahogs, mussels, scallops, oysters, coquina, ship worms (which are really a kind of bivalve) and cockles. Some, like clams and quahogs, live buried in the sand. Mussels and oysters are attached to the bottom while scallops live unattached on the bottom. Scallops have beautiful blue eyes along the mantle fringe and they swim by quickly clapping their shells and forcing water out near the hinge.

Unlike other mollusks, bivalves lack a head and have no radula (Figure 7-4). They burrow by extending their foot forward, enlarging the distant end to act as an anchor, then pulling the shell toward the foot. While snails fertilize their eggs internally before depositing them on the bottom, bivalves release both eggs and sperm directly into the water where fertilization occurs. This strategy apparently works well since bivalves are an abundant form of life along most shorelines and provide food for many kinds of animals.

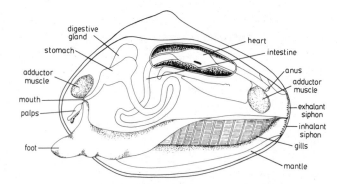

Figure 7-4. Internal anatomy of a bivalve. Water enters via the inhalant siphon, carrying in oxygen and plankton, which is filtered out by the gills for food. Wastes are eliminated when water is pumped out the exhalant siphon. Adapted with permission from Deborah A. Coulombe, The Seaside Naturalist. *Englewood Cliffs, N.J.: Prentice-Hall, 113.*

The sudden squirt of a clam as it retreats from a footstep on the sand is one of a multitude of signs that announce the wonders awaiting in the tidal zone. Whether stooping in silent awe at the edge of a tidepool or gingerly touching the arms of a sea star, children will find the seashore to be an infinite source of new discoveries.

QUESTIONS

1. Why does Octopus become so annoyed at Raven? Do you think it is a good idea for Raven to ask his question so many times? How can you ask questions without making someone impatient?

2. What are some other ways, besides asking questions, that you can learn from someone?

3. What is your favorite thing to do when you go down to the seashore? What do you like to find?

4. How many different animals can you think of that make their home at the seashore? What are some of your favorites?

5. What is an estuary? Name some animals that live there.

6. What causes the tides? Is the pull of the sun or moon stronger? Why?

7. What would make the seashore a good habitat in which to live? Why would it also be a challenging home in which to survive?

8. Would you really expect to find an octopus digging clams along the shore? Where does an octopus really live? What does it really eat?

9. Have you ever dug clams? Why do they live in the sand? What is their food and how do they eat it?

10. What would you eat if you lived along the seashore?

ACTIVITIES

Seashore Charades

ACTIVITY: Play a game of charades to imitate the anatomy and behavior of seashore invertebrates.
GOALS: Become familiar with some common seashore invertebrates. Understand how animals have become adapted to life in the tidal zone.
AGE: Younger children and older children
MATERIALS: Books, magazines and other sources of pictures and information describing some common seashore invertebrates (Figure 7-5), pencil or pen, index file cards, construction paper, scissors, masking tape.

PROCEDURE: Gather from books, magazines and Figure 7-5 some photographs and illustrations of common invertebrates found along the seashore in your area. Be sure to include a diverse sampling of animals representing different groups, such as clams and mussels, crabs and amphipods, snails, lobster and octopus. Research the basic natural history of each animal and record it on an index file card.

Place the pictures and illustrations in a place where the children can see them. Divide the children into groups of three or four and ask each group to choose an animal they want to imitate in the charades game. Now give the groups 20 minutes or so to discuss and plan how they will work together to act out that animal so that others can guess which one it is. Offer them the opportunity to use one or two construction paper props *only* if their animal has some unusual parts to portray. When all groups are ready, have each group take a turn imitating its animal while the other groups try to guess which animal it is. If no one can guess the animal after the acting has gone on for a few minutes, have the active group tell the others which animal they are trying to mimic. Now have someone from that group read the natural history of their animal to the others. If the children are very young, read the information for them.

Mussel Mimicry

ACTIVITY: (A) Create small models of a mussel's filter-feeding system. (B) Go on a scavenger hunt in the tide zone to find and collect specific shells. Create a duplicate arrangement of these objects in the exact same order and appearance as a model arrangement. Take a seaside stroll to look for and watch filter-feeding mollusks.
GOALS: Understand the mechanism of filter-feeding and the kinds of animals that use this method for gathering food. Experience the diversity of filter-feeding life found along the seashore. Sharpen memory and recognition skills.
AGE: Younger children and older children
MATERIALS: (A) Figure 7-4, flexible drinking straws, pipe cleaners, balloons, construction paper, cups from egg cartons and empty plastic Easter eggs or other materials to imitate a bivalve's two shells, masking tape, crayons, felt-tipped markers, tempera paints, paintbrushes, combs, yarn, paste, glue, scissors. (B) Field guide to sea shells in your area, large handkerchiefs, collection of shells from the site you will visit.

PROCEDURE A: *Fantastic Filter Feeders. Note:* Conduct this activity *before* leading "Mussel Beach Multiplication."

Use Figure 7-4 to describe how bivalve mollusks, such as clams, mussels, quahogs, scallops and oysters, use a filter-feeding system to gather microscopic plants and animals and other minute food particles. Have the children use various materials to construct their own, imaginary filter-feeding creatures. They can make any possible kind of strange creature they like, but it must have a workable filter-feeding system of their own design built in.

Once they have completed their "Fantastic Filter Feeders," have them demonstrate to the other children how the "animal" will gather its food.

A variation on this activity is to have the children work in small groups and turn one of its members into a "Fantastic Filter Feeder."

PROCEDURE B: *Mussel Beach Multiplication.* Beforehand, gather nine different bivalve shells (clams, mussels, quahogs, scallops, oysters, etc.) for making an arrangement for older children. Use a smaller number of from four to six shells for younger children. Use shells that are no longer occupied. It is fine to use the same kind of shell more than once but try to find a good variety of shells.

Take the children to visit the rocky tide zone and/or beach where you collected your bivalve shells. Arrange the (nine) shells in a circle or in three rows of three on a towel or large handkerchief (older children), or arrange the four to six shells in a circle (younger children). Allow the children to study them carefully.

Have the children work alone or in small teams and pass out a towel or large handkerchief to each team. Tell them that, when you yell "Mussel Beach," they are to begin a race to see who will be first to duplicate exactly your arrangement of shells on their handkerchief. Emphasize that they are to collect empty shells only, not live animals. Be certain that they are all wearing sneakers or sandals to protect their feet as they rush around. Remind them to be careful for their own safety and for the well-being of the homes of the plants and animals that live there. Tell them to stay out of any ecologically sensitive areas nearby, such as fragile sand dunes. Now, yell "Mussel Beach" to begin the activity.

Have each team yell "Mussel Beach" when their collection is complete. Check each arrangement to make sure it is accurate. Allow time for all teams to finish their arrangements.

When all are done, have them practice their multiplication tables based on multiples of the number of shells in *each* set to calculate the total that have been collected

by all teams. Now describe the kinds of mollusks that have these kinds of shells and look up any unfamiliar ones in a field guide to seashells in your area. Ask the children to describe where they found their shells, and to explain why there is a high concentration of shells at the top of the high tide line. Return the shells to the seashore as a gift of thanks for this experience.

Crustacean Stroll and Tidal Poll

ACTIVITY: (A) Play a guessing game to estimate the direction and degree the tide will change while you visit the shore. (B) Take a quiet walk to a beach and tidepool, rocky shore or other nearby habitat to observe and discover the many different kinds of crustaceans living there.

GOALS: Realize the magnitude and direction of tidal change over a certain period of time. Quietly observe and understand some of the variety of crustaceans living at the seashore.

AGE: Younger children and older children

MATERIALS: (A) One tall wooden pole—such as a broomstick—sharpened on one end, one shorter wooden stake, about 2 feet (61.0 centimeters) long, for each child, masking tape, waterproof felt-tipped marking pens, rubber mallet. (B) Hand lenses, large tea strainers, large pail, collecting cups or jars, "Discussion" section from this chapter, Figure 7-5.

PROCEDURE A: *Tide Pole Poll.* Beforehand, check a tidal chart to plan your visit for a period of time when the tide is at the beginning of the period when it is changing rapidly (coming in or going out). This activity is easier and more effective to conduct when the tide is coming in, enabling the children to set their stakes *above* the advancing tide line.

When you arrive at the beach go down to the water and ask the children to watch the tide for a short time, observing whether the tide is coming in or going out. Then inform the children of what the tidal chart says the tide is doing at that time.

Drive a 5 foot (1.5 meter) tall wooden pole at least 1 foot (30.5 centimeters) into the sand or gravel to mark the very upper edge of the tide to where the waves are reaching when you arrive at the seashore.

Have each child wrap a piece of masking tape around the top of a similar stake at least 3 feet (about 1 meter) long and label it with her or his initials. Now help each child to drive her or his own stake into the sand or gravel above or below the marker pole to estimate where she or he thinks the upper reach of the waves will be in 45 minutes. This period of time

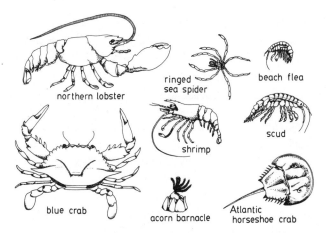

Figure 7-5. An incredible array of crustaceans can be found along the seashore. Shown here, beginning with the top left, are a northern lobster, size: to 3 feet (91.4 centimeters); ringed sea spider, size: leg span to 1/4 inch (6.4 millimeters); beach flea, size: species vary from 5/16 inch (8 millimeters) to over 1-3/16 inches (3.0 centimeters); shrimp, size: species vary from 5/16 inch (8 millimeters) to 10 inches (25.4 centimeters); scud, size: commonly to 1-1/4 inches (3.2 centimeters) but up to 2 inches (5.1 centimeters) among Arctic species; blue crab, size: to 9 inches (22.9 centimeters); acorn barnacle, size: species vary from 3/8 inch (1.0 centimeter) to 1 inch (2.5 centimeters); Atlantic horseshoe crab, size (including tail): to 2 feet (61.0 centimeters).

may need to be shorter if tides change more quickly in your area or longer if the tide change is more gradual. Be sure to drive all stakes in *at least* 1 foot (30.5 centimeters) so they do not topple over and get washed away.

PROCEDURE B: *Crustacean Peregrination.* While the tide is changing, take a walk along the beach to a tidepool or along a nearby rocky shore. Look for crustaceans or the remains of them that may be found there. Tell the children that this group of animals includes crabs, lobsters, barnacles, shrimp, krill, sea spiders and horseshoe crabs. The small (3/4 to 1 inch [1.9 to 2.5 centimeter]) beach fleas, beach hoppers, side swimmers, sand fleas and scuds are also crustaceans. Show Figure 7-5 to the children to demonstrate the diversity found among these crustaceans. Use the strainers to catch some small beach fleas among the sand grains, side swimmers in a tidepool or beach hoppers in a clump of dead seaweed. Place them in collecting containers and have the children observe them with hand lenses. Use the "Discussion" section to share more information about how they feed and reproduce. Keep your eye out for larger crustaceans and signs of them. Allow time for questions and stories. Gently release each animal back into its home when you have finished observing it.

Return to the tide poles in about 45 minutes to check the children's stakes against the old high tide mark at the base of the larger stake and the new high tide mark to where the waves are reaching. Lead a question and answer period to discuss what has happened and how the tide has changed. Have them pull up their stakes and move them to a new location marking where the tide ought to be after another period of time.

Lead another crustacean stroll or other activity, and check on the stakes when the time is up to see how the children's estimates have improved.

Octopus Tag

ACTIVITY: Play a game of tag during which you are "safe" only when part of a blob of four people with eight arms like an octopus.

GOALS: Review the natural history of the octopus and have fun playing tag.

AGE: Younger children and older children

MATERIALS: Large, open area that is fairly level, preferably a beach or other seashore locale.

PROCEDURE: Tell the children they are about to learn how to play octopus tag. Discuss the general form of the octopus—its eight arms of equal length, how it uses them to capture food and other aspects of its life from the "Discussion" section.

Mark boundaries on the ground to delineate a playing area just large enough for a game of tag, and just small enough so the person who is "it" will be able to tag people. The size will depend on the size of your group.

Tell the children that they are to remain inside the boundaries at all times. Since an octopus has eight arms, the players will be safe when they are part of a group of four people (eight arms) holding on to one another—the octopi. That is the *only* time they will be "safe" and immune from being tagged. The person who is "it" can tag anyone who is alone, or anyone in a group of *any* combination of people except four. When a new person is tagged, he or she becomes "it" and a new round of the game begins.

As soon as the game begins, the children are to form into roving groups of four; each group is arranged in single file. Players wanting to join a group must attach to the *rear* of the line. When this new player causes the group to become more than four people, the person on the front of the line *must* detach and look for a new "octopus" which has space to which to attach. That is the rule!

You can also reverse the game and have the "it" be an "octopus" of four people (eight arms) holding hands and sweeping through the playing area to tag someone. A relatively smaller playing area is needed for this version since the "octopus" cannot move about as quickly as the individual players that it is chasing.

Learning to Listen—Listening to Learn

ACTIVITY: Practice learning a skill, craft, art or some other area of expertise by watching, listening patiently and practicing by doing. Practice teaching using the same quiet, experiential techniques to pass knowledge on to another.

GOALS: Realize that a quiet, attentive, interested approach to understanding is a very good way to learning something new. Understand how to teach with an emphasis on patiently *showing* another how to master your knowledge, skill or art form.

AGE: Older children

MATERIALS: Chalkboard and chalk or markers and newsprint, paper, pencils, materials needed for the children's educational projects.

PROCEDURE: Traditional teaching among many Native North American cultures consisted of a patient, hands-on approach. A child would spend time with the person he or she wanted to learn from and would gradually acquire the skill through watchful observation and a willingness to help out when asked.

This activity is meant to foster patience and quiet learning skills, not to discourage healthy curiosity as expressed through asking questions.

Review with the children the salient parts of the story of Octopus and Raven that deal with patience, listening, curiosity and learning. For example, the way the old people look on quietly as Raven gets himself into trouble and how Raven's impatient curiosity disturbs Octopus as he pesters her with questions.

Mention that questioning is a *good* way to learn and that you normally want the children to ask any questions they may have when they want to understand something better. Now tell them that in this activity, they are going to practice learning by *silent* watching and doing.

Have the children write down their names and some skills they have and would like to teach others, such as drawing, riding a bicycle, playing baseball or some other

sport, playing a guitar or some other musical instrument, making clothes, etc. Now compile a list of all these skills and have other children pick one from each child's list so that *all* children have had *one* skill picked from their list. Leave the children's names off the list so that they choose skills to learn and not just their favorite partners. Split the group in half, and have half be learners at first and the rest teachers. Allow time each day for the learning to be carried out in silence—by showing and doing. Encourage the children to set *realistic* learning goals for the time they have. A guitar player, for instance, may be able to teach a song using simple chords, but not an advanced piece.

Later, switch roles so that they are reversed and the knowledge is going the other way. This will take some mixing and matching so that the children who were teachers first get a chance to pick what they want to learn from the children who have switched from learners to teachers.

EXTENDING THE EXPERIENCE

• Write your own story about Raven, the trickster. Or add to the story of Octopus and Raven to describe Raven's next adventure.

• Make giant models of seashore animals. Use an umbrella as a base from which to create a gigantic jellyfish. Take a large beachball and add eight long, thin balloons as arms of an octopus. Or create stuffed animals out of material into which you can even place models of organs for an anatomy lesson.

• Conduct the activity "Circle of the Sea" from Chapter 9 to encourage respect, reverence, solitude and gratitude toward the sea.

• Study water quality along your seashore. Learn where any pollution may be coming from. Explore ways to educate the public about this situation, as well as a means of encouraging cleanup.

• *Periwinkle Pickup.* Pick up and hold a periwinkle for a while. Wait patiently until it feels safe and it will emerge from its shell to crawl over your hand. How does it feel? What could it be looking for? What and how does it eat? Hum to the periwinkle to see if the vibration of your voice draws it out.

• *A Gift for Shore.* Sculpt castles, animals and other creations out of sand as an expression of gratitude to the waves and plants and animals of the seashores. Create your sculptures in front of the advancing tide and watch as the tide rises to receive its gift.

CHAPTER 8

✤ How the Butterflies Came to Be ✤

(Papago—Southwest)

Long ago, not long after Earth-Maker shaped the world out of dirt and sweat he scraped from his skin, Iitoi, our Elder Brother, was walking about. It was just after the time of year when the rains come. There were flowers blooming all around him as he walked. The leaves of the trees were green and bright. He came to a village and there he saw the children playing. It made his heart good to see the children happy and playing. Then he became sad. He thought of how those children would grow old and weaken and die. That was the way it was made to be. The red and yellow and white and blue of the flowers would fade. The leaves would fall from the trees. The days would grow short and the nights would be cold.

A wind brushed past Elder Brother, making some fallen yellow leaves dance in the sunlight. Then an idea came to him.

"I will make something," Elder Brother said. "It will make the hearts of the children dance and it will make my own heart glad again."

Then Iitoi took a bag and placed in it the bright-colored flowers and the fallen leaves. He placed many things in that bag. He placed yellow pollen and white cornmeal and green pine needles in that bag and caught some of the shining gold of the sunlight and placed it in there, as well. There were birds singing around him and he took some of their songs and put them into that bag, too.

"Come here," Elder Brother called to the children, "come here. I have something here for you."

The children came to him and he handed them his bag.

"Open this," he said.

The children opened Elder Brother's bag and out of it flew the first butterflies. Their wings were bright as sunlight and held all of the colors of the flowers and the leaves, the cornmeal, the pollen and the green pine needles. They were red and gold and black and yellow, blue and green and white. They looked like flowers, dancing in the wind. They flew about the heads of the children and the children laughed. As those first butterflies flew, they sang and the children listened.

But as the children listened to the singing butterflies, the songbirds came to Elder Brother.

"Iitoi," the songbirds said, "those songs were given to us. It is fine that you have given these new creatures all the brightest colors, but it is not right that they should also have our songs."

"Ah," Elder Brother said, "you speak truly. The songs belong to you and not to the butterflies."

So it is to this day. Though they dance as they fly, the butterflies are silent. But still, when the children see them, brightly dancing in the wind, their hearts are glad. That is how Elder Brother meant it to be.

The children opened Elder Brother's bag and out of it flew the first butterflies.

DISCUSSION

This beautiful, gentle story unfolds as the flowers bloom and children play happily during the time of rain. Brilliant, colorful butterflies dancing on the wind are created to dispel feelings of sadness, aging and death. Seeing a butterfly lightens the hearts of children and brings gladness to those who have known life's sorrows.

Butterflies have always held a special place in the hearts of many Native North American peoples. Hopi girls of the butterfly clan who had not yet married wore their hair styled in the shape of butterfly wings. Many forms of pottery were, and still are, adorned with butterfly motifs (Figure 8-1). The word for butterfly among the Nez Percé of the Pacific Northwest is Lap Lap, and their home is called Lapwai Valley. It is said that the butterflies came when the Nez Percé children called to them.

Figure 8-1. Hopi symbol for butterfly, from Pictograph Point rock writing. Illustration courtesy Joseph Bruchac.

Insects

The joy that butterflies in this story bring to the children of the Papago, a desert people of the arid Southwest, is one of the many ways that insects enrich our lives. So why have many people come to view insects as adversaries? It is true that insects damage and destroy crops in the field, as well as contaminate and consume stored food and other goods. And each warm season brings out a variety of stinging, biting and sometimes disease-spreading insects.

Although insects can be pests and nuisances in these ways, life would be difficult, less enjoyable and even impossible without our six-legged friends. Imagine a world in which:

• all of the animals that eat insects disappeared (trout, swallows, bluebirds, baby birds, most warblers, toads, moles . . .);

• our multitude of insect-pollinated foods were not available (most orchard fruits such as plums, pears, cherries, apples, citrus; nuts; figs; strawberries; cranberries; blueberries; blackberries; raspberries; squash; melons (pumpkins included); carrots; onions and a multitude of other vegetables and crops);

• silk, beeswax, honey, shellac and other insect-made products could not be found;

• the vital insect scavengers were a missing link in the nutrient cycle and thus the life-giving release of nutrients from dead plants and animals to make new plant growth possible came grinding to a halt;

• the insects used in medicine (treating diseases) and research (i.e., pollution and genetics) were not to be found; and

• the color and beauty of a butterfly's wings, the sound of crickets in summer's heat, the flash of a firefly's glow and the bizarre find of a "walking stick" were just distant memories.

The amazing insects have been evolving for 400 million years, dating back to the Devonian Period. Nearly 350 million years ago, during the Carboniferous Period, the ancestors of modern dragonflies, called *Meganeura*, flew with wingspans of over 3 feet (.9 meters). Insects now inhabit nearly every kind of environment the world over and comprise up to two-thirds of the total number of animals in existence. The ocean is the only environment to which insects have not adapted in any significant numbers. North America alone is home for more than 88,600 species of insect.

ANATOMY. Insects are a type of arthropod, a phylum of invertebrate animals that includes spiders, mites, centipedes, millipedes and the crustaceans, such as crabs, lobster, crayfish and shrimp.[1] All *arthropods* have jointed legs and a hard *exoskeleton* made of a protein called *chitin*. An insect's body is divided into three parts: the *head*, *thorax* and *abdomen* (Figure 8-2). The head includes eyes, mouthparts and *antennae*, which are used for smelling and feeling. Three pairs of legs and, often, one or two pairs of wings are attached to the thorax. Some insects taste with their feet. While not all insects have wings, this is the only group of animals without backbones that possess wings. They breathe air through openings in the body called *spiracles* located on the thorax and/or abdomen. Once the air enters the spiracles it travels through tubes called *tracheae*, which branch to carry oxygen directly to the tissues throughout the insect's body. Insect blood does not carry oxygen via hemoglobin as does the blood found in vertebrates.

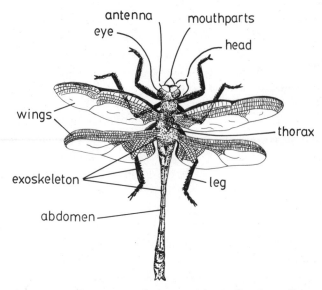

Figure 8-2. Basic parts of an insect (dragonfly). Spiracles—openings through which insects breathe—can be located on the thorax and/or abdomen. Spiracles are found on the sides of the thorax of this dragonfly.

REPRODUCTION. At times, the variety of insects (there are twenty-six different orders of insects) can confuse and astound the observer. The dramatic differences in appearance of the same insect at the various stages of its life further complicate matters. Many insects even live in different habitats as they are growing. The adult mayfly is a graceful, delicate-winged creature that lives for only a day or two, completes the reproductive cycle and dies. They do not even eat (Figure 8-3). Yet, the resulting eggs will hatch into aquatic nymphs that, among some species, live several years underwater.

One form of insect development is called *simple* or *gradual metamorphosis*, during which an egg hatches into a tiny, adult-like *nymph* or *naiad*. Nymphs often resemble the mature insect and live in the same habitat. As the nymph grows, it periodically sheds its exoskeleton until it finally changes into the adult. Each stage between molts is called an *instar*. There are usually from four to eight instars involved, but there can be up to twenty among some insects. Crickets and grasshoppers experience gradual metamorphosis. The four major, common insect orders that undergo gradual metamorphosis are:

- Hemipterans (true bugs)
- Orthopterans (crickets, locusts, grasshoppers)
- Odonates (damselflies and dragonflies)
- Homopterans (cicadas, aphids, leafhoppers)

Some insects develop through four distinct stages en route from egg to adult: *egg, larva, pupa* and *adult*. This process is called *complete metamorphosis* (Figure 8-4). Caterpillars, fly maggots and beetle grubs are common larvae, while cocoons and chrysalises are some well-known forms of pupae. Here are four representative orders of insects that undergo complete metamorphosis:

- Hymenopterans (bees, wasps, ants, ichneumons)
- Lepidopterans (butterflies and moths)
- Coleopterans (beetles)
- Dipterans (gnats, flies, mosquitos)

Dipterans are the only true flies, although the word "fly" appears in many insect names. The names of true flies are here written with two words (for example, black fly) and other fly-like species as one word (mayfly, for instance).

Most insects lay eggs that develop outside of the body, but only if they have been fertilized. Some do give birth to live young. Eggs are usually laid in a protected place, such as the underside of a leaf, a nook in a stone wall or a crack in tree bark. Many eggs are encased in a protective covering.

In some groups of insects, such as the bees, wasps, ants and ichneumons, fertilized eggs develop into females

Figure 8-3. This newly hatched mayfly, which hangs upside-down, looks like an adult, yet it is really the brief stage called a subimago *between the aquatic nymph and the adult. Nymphs hatch into a dull-looking subimago, which again sheds its skin to become the adult. Mayflies are the only insects with a stage that molts after the wings become functional. Adults, which frequently hatch out in great swarms near lakes and rivers, do not feed and rarely survive more than a day or two. Size of body (not including tail): 3/8 inch (1.0 centimeter). Photo by Alan C. Graham.*

Figure 8-4. The four stages of the monarch butterfly on a milkweed plant. The egg has just hatched into a young caterpillar in the lower left corner of the illustration. Appearing from left to right, hanging from the bottom of the leaf, are the striped caterpillar (larva) as it prepares to pupate, two stages in the development of the chrysalis (pupa) and the newly emerging adult as it pumps hemolymph or insect blood through the veins of its wings to inflate them to full size. Monarch caterpillars feed on milkweed, which contains a bitter-tasting milky white sap. The caterpillars in turn develop a noxious flavor. As a result, birds vomit when they feed on the caterpillars. and adults tend to avoid repeating the unpleasant experience. Size of adult (body length): 1.3 inches (3.3 centimeters). Illustration by D. D. Tyler.

while unfertilized eggs produce males. Aphids and some other insects, however, produce only females generation after generation. During this process called *parthenogenesis* ("virgin birth"), overwintering aphid eggs hatch each spring into a generation of wingless females. When mature, these females birth live female young. Aphids can have up to thirteen generations in one summer. Some of these generations have wings. These fly off to colonize other plants. At some point from the middle of summer on, according to each aphid species' life cycle, a generation is born of both females *and* males. These mate and lay the eggs that will overwinter to begin the cycle again next spring. In some species of parthenogenetic insects males are not known to exist at all!

Many North American insects produce one generation each year, while some may have two or more. The life spans of adult insects may range from 20 minutes in one mayfly species to several years for some of the social insect reproductives, such as queen bees, wasps and ants. The cicada is a good example of a long-lived insect. Cicada nymphs live in burrows underground where they feed on the sap of tree roots. Some common species emerge as adults in one to three years, but nymphs of the seventeen-year cicada survive underground for seventeen years before emerging to mate in great numbers. The adults of some insects may require more than one summer to mature, or may survive for several years.

ADAPTATIONS TO THE SEASONS. Insects cope with winter by using a number of strategies. Each group of insect tends to survive the cold months in a particular stage of development. Among the array of insects can be found some that overwinter as egg, larva, pupa, nymph or adult. Even within groups the wintering stage can vary due to climate. Field crickets usually overwinter as eggs in the ground but, in warmer climates, can be found surviving the winter as eggs, nymphs and adults. Ants ball up in a mass deep underground to survive the winter, while honeybees huddle together in a hollow tree to derive the greatest benefit from their collective body heat. Adult monarch butterflies migrate great distances to warm, southwestern climes to weather the winter chill.

COMMUNICATION. The calls or songs of male insects, including crickets and grasshoppers, are intended to attract a mate. Short-horned grasshoppers call by rubbing a series of comb-like projections on their hind legs along a ridge attached to their wings, while crickets and long-horned grasshoppers rub a scraper on one wing against a row of ridges on the other wing (Figure 8-5). A kind of tympanic instrument is used by cicadas to produce their songs that are heard in the steamy heat of summer. The thorax contains a pair of hollow, membrane-covered structures. Muscles are used to vibrate the membranes that serve as a kind of drum head. The cicada's large, mostly hollow abdomen may serve as a resonating chamber to amplify its call.

Observing and Conserving Insects

Keep your eyes and ears alert for insects and they can be found almost anywhere. Look on flowers, the undersides of leaves, on plant stems, under logs and rocks (be sure to roll these back into place afterward), in the basement, garage or woodpile. You may see signs of them in the multitude of *galls* to be found, which are swellings on plants that can be of nearly any size or shape. During the winter months you can find insects clinging to the undersides of rocks in streams.

Watch them hunting other insects; feeding, hiding or reproducing on plants; communicating with each other with songs, displays and a rainbow of colors; or nesting somewhere in your home.

Insects are easily collected by sweeping a net through plants in a field, straining the mud of a pond or looking

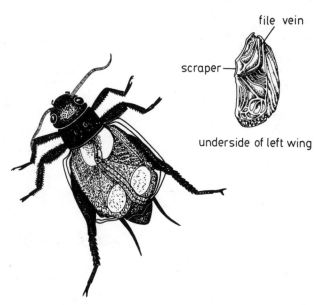

Figure 8-5. A field cricket's "chirp" is created as it vibrates its wings. Each wing has a file-like ridge or vein running along its underside, as well as a sharp scraper on the upper edge. As the two wings are rubbed against one another with a sideways motion, the file-like vein on one wing rubs against the scraper on the other wing to create the beautiful notes, intended to attract a mate, that fill the evening and the night air with a wistful chorus of song. Size: .8 inch (2.0 centimeters).

under rocks in a stream. Keep them in a well-ventilated glass jar for a while and observe them with a hand lens. Children will be both fascinated and horrified by simply looking through a hand lens and watching a caterpillar devour a blade of grass. They will be challenged as they try to perceive the flashing pattern that a particular firefly is using to attract a mate.

Since some insects, such as the iridescent-hued tiger beetles, are incredibly beautiful, they have been collected in great numbers. The habitat of many insects has all but been destroyed, posing even a greater threat to their existence. In order to protect and respect the six-legged ones, please do not keep the insects you collect nor make an insect collection. Once you are through enjoying our insect friends, tell them "thank you" and return them to their homes exactly where you discovered them.

QUESTIONS

1. Why does Elder Brother create the butterflies in this story?

2. Where does Elder Brother get the beautiful colors to make butterfly wings? What are some colors you have seen in butterflies' wings? What colors are among the butterfly wings in this story?

3. Why do the birds become upset when butterflies are given their songs? What do they say to Elder Brother?

4. How does Elder Brother respond when the birds ask to have their songs back?

5. What are some gifts that the insects give to us? What are some things they do that are harmful?

6. Which insects are your favorite? Why? Which ones do you like the least? Why?

7. What makes an insect different from other animals? What is special about insects?

8. Is a spider a kind of insect? How many legs does a spider have? How many legs does an insect have?[2]

9. What kinds of insects live in your home?

10. As an insect grows, what stages does it go through before it becomes an adult? Give an example of these stages from among insects you are familiar with.

11. How does an insect survive the winter?

12. Which insects have a call or song? How do these songs sound? Try imitating them.

13. How should an insect be handled while you observe it? What is the proper thing to do when you are done looking at an insect?

ACTIVITIES
Circle With the Six-Leggeds

ACTIVITY: (A) Make a list of all the gifts we receive from insects. Practice using only what is needed giving thanks when receiving each of these gifts. (B) Create a special gift to return the generosity of the insects.

GOALS: Understand how numerous and varied are the gifts we receive from insects and their activities. Realize that living in balance involves using only what is needed, not being wasteful and giving thanks to complete the circle of giving and receiving.

AGE: Younger children and older children

MATERIALS: (A) chalkboard and chalk or felt-tipped markers and newsprint, masking tape. (B) same materials as in (A) plus: pencils, paper, crayons, construction paper, scissors, glue, tape, very large sheet of paper such as brown postal wrapping paper, pictures or photographs of insects as models for their drawings (younger children), other materials as needed to complete children's own, original projects.

PROCEDURE A: *Opening the Circle—Receiving.* Use the children's ideas, those from the "Discussion" section and your own thoughts to compile a list of the many gifts we receive from insects. Brainstorm a list of insects that help to bring each of the gifts to us. Have the children go through an entire day by saying "thank you" to an insect, or insects in general, each time one of these gifts is used, eaten, worn, etc. An example is "Thank you, honeybee" for honey and beeswax (a common ingredient in lip balm).

Encourage the children to be especially careful to use these gifts wisely—to take only what they need and not be wasteful.

PROCEDURE B: *Completing the Circle—Giving Back.* Now tell the children how this story of "How the Butterflies Came to Be" reminds us that the insects give us many wonderful gifts, and that living in balance with the animals means, in part, to return the gifts we receive by giving something of ourselves back. Ask the children to call out ways they may do this and write them down for all to see. Save them for use later.

Have each of the children write, in his or her own words, a poem or other form of saying "thank you" to the insects. Younger or older children may draw a picture to depict a feeling or experience of gratitude. Very young children may need pictures or photographs of the insect(s) to help them visualize the images for their drawings.

Create, on a large sheet of paper, an outline of a grasshopper or other chosen insect, such as a butterfly. Have each child write her or his form of "thank you" inside this outline. Pictures may be cut out and glued or taped on. The insect could even be entirely filled with pictures or illustrations to form a collage.

Follow through on some of the children's other ways of giving thanks to the insects. Use this activity as a model for completing the circle of giving and receiving with other animals.

Six-Legged Symphony

ACTIVITY: (A) Listen to the instruments and songs of grasshoppers, crickets and cicadas. Discuss how these insects create their sounds. (B) Create your own insect instruments and play a children's chorus back to them.
GOALS: Enjoy the symphony of insect voices. Understand how their sounds are created. Have fun making and playing your own chorus.
AGE: Younger children
MATERIALS: (A) "Discussion" section, diagrams of insect instruments such as in Figure 8-5. (B) Empty oatmeal boxes or cans, rubber gloves to cut up for drum heads, scissors, masking tape, unsharpened pencils with erasers on the end, combs, scrapers to run over the comb teeth.
PROCEDURE A: *Insect Instrumentation. Note:* This activity is best when conducted from mid-summer to early fall in most areas, when the insects are calling most strongly.

Take the children out to a field where crickets, grasshoppers or cicadas are calling. An open area interspersed with shrubs and/or trees is usually best. Have them close their eyes and listen quietly to the six-legged symphony around them. Once they have listened for a few minutes, ask them to keep listening while trying to pick out as many different kinds of insect calls as they can distinguish. Have them make fists and open up one finger for each different sound they hear.

After a few more minutes have passed, ask them to open their eyes and have them take turns describing or imitating what they heard. Discuss why insects call and what they use for instruments. Refer to the information from the "Discussion" section, Figure 8-5 and the diagrams you have created to represent the insect instruments.
PROCEDURE B: *Children's Chorus.* Now have the children create their own insect instruments using combs, scrapers, improvised drums and other original sound makers. Drums can be fashioned using empty oatmeal boxes or cans (opened on one end only) as a base. Be certain to remove or flatten out any sharp edges on the cans. Cut out pieces of sheer rubber such as from a rubber glove, slightly larger than the opening of the box or can. Stretch the rubber snugly over the opening while taping the edge down securely all around. The tighter it is stretched, the higher the pitch that will be produced. Use the blunt, eraser ends of pencils for drumsticks.

Once the instruments are completed, take them to the field where you first heard the six-legged symphony. Have the children play their own version of a chorus back to the insects. How do the insects respond? Do the insects understand the children's chorus? Why? Why not?

Cricket Thermometer

ACTIVITY: Listen to the number of calls made by the snowy tree cricket in 15 seconds and use a formula to calculate the approximate temperature in degrees Fahrenheit and centigrade.
GOAL: Understand that the level of activity of crickets and other insects is directly related to the temperature of their surroundings.
AGE: Younger children and older children
MATERIALS: Wristwatch or stopwatch with seconds indicator, pencil, paper, clipboard or cardboard backing, pocket calculator (optional).
PROCEDURE: *Note:* This activity works well in autumn when studying how insects prepare for surviving the winter.

During the late summer or fall take the children to a field, hedgerow, school yard, ballpark, vacant lot, park or other habitat where snowy tree crickets are calling from amid the grasses and bushes. Snowy tree crickets produce synchronized choruses of low, brief musical chirps, during which they all sing at once in a certain area. Cricket calls are whistle-like and have a musical quality to them and you can sing or hum a note to match that pitch. Grasshoppers make a mechanical sound with which you cannot hum along. These calls are made by the males to attract a mate, to warn other crickets of danger and to defend its own territory, such as a clump of grass, from other males. (In fact you can often return to a certain clump of grass to find the same male calling on different occasions.) Crickets create these calls by rubbing a scraper on one wing with ridges on the other wing. The male and female use their antennae to find each other because it is thought that they mate mostly at night.

Pick out the snowy tree crickets' calls and have the children focus their ears upon it. Discuss how it is making this sound. Explain that in colder weather crickets call more slowly, and that the calling gets faster as the temperature climbs higher and the insects' metabolism increases.

Now call out the beginning of a 15-second period of time and have the children count the number of chirps the cricket makes before you yell "stop" when the interval is over. You can also have the children work in pairs with one child timing the 15 seconds while the other counts chirps. Repeat this procedure at least 2 more times and calculate the average number of chirps per 15 seconds. Add 37 to this number and you will have a rough estimate of the current temperature in degrees Fahrenheit.[3]

CRICKET THERMOMETER FORMULA

_____ (number of chirps in 15 seconds)

$\dfrac{+\ 37}{=\ \underline{\quad}\ ^{\circ}\text{F}}$

The formula to convert Fahrenheit to centigrade is:
$$(^{\circ}\text{F}- 32) \times \tfrac{5}{9} = \underline{\quad}\ ^{\circ}\text{C}$$

Miraculous Metamorphosis

ACTIVITY: (A) Go on a scavenger hunt to look for and observe insects in each of the stages of metamorphosis. (B) Create models of a familiar insect as it grows and experiences the four stages of complete metamorphosis.

GOAL: Understand the process and growth stages of both complete metamorphosis and simple or gradual metamorphosis.

AGE: Younger children and older children

MATERIALS: (A) Pictures of insects in various stages of metamorphosis, as in Figure 8-4 (monarch butterfly illustration); paper; pencils; cardboard backings; Figure 8-6; hand lenses; field guides to basic insect life and structure. (B) Figures 8-2 and 8-4; clay, balloons, egg cartons, etc., to create the insects' bodies; pipe cleaners; toothpicks; construction paper; scissors; tape; paste; string; crayons; felt-tipped marking pens of assorted colors; cardboard.

PROCEDURE A: *Metamorphosis Meander.* Discuss and describe the two basic kinds of insect metamorphosis and the various stages involved in each, using Figure 8-4 as an example of complete metamorphosis. Tell the children

Figure 8-6

Metamorphosis Meander Scavenger Hunt

Place a check (✔) next to those things you can find. Look for:

_____ a caterpillar

_____ a mass of insect eggs in tree bark

_____ a leaf with edges rolled under and woven together with silk to form a tent

_____ a butterfly

_____ spittlebug spit on a plant stem with nymphs living inside

_____ a bee on a flower

_____ insect eggs laid on the underside of a leaf

_____ a grasshopper nymph (too young to have developed wings) (If you pick it up, it may secrete a dark green fluid to scare you into dropping it!)

_____ a cricket

_____ ant eggs under a rock or log

_____ insects caught in a spider's web

that they are going outside on a scavenger hunt to find insects in these stages of growth and to have fun watching insects in their homes and learning about them.

Divide the children into pairs and hand out to each pair a copy of Figure 8-6 with a cardboard backing, a pencil and a hand lens. Emphasize that this is an exercise in finding and observing, not collecting.

Have each pair go out into a defined area. Circulate among them to help answer questions about their discoveries. Use field guides to insects to look up any questions that you are not sure how to answer. Have an older child or adult accompany each pair of very young children to help them record their findings.

Call all the children back after about a half hour has elapsed. Sit in a circle and have them share (describe) what they found to the rest of the group. Then visit the sites of especially interesting findings so that everyone may share the experience.

PROCEDURE B: *Making Metamorphosis.* Place the materials for this part of the activity in several piles distributed among the children. Review the stages of both forms of metamorphosis and the basic parts of an adult insect as described in Figure 8-2. Figure 8-4 provides an example of complete metamorphosis. Have the children work in groups of three to create models of each stage of metamorphosis for a particular insect of their choice. Encourage them to use their findings in "Metamorphosis Meander" as a basis for their creations. Have plenty of pictures of insects and life stages around to give them more ideas.

Once they have all completed their projects, have the entire group take a tour around to see them, with children from each small group acting as interpreters using the models to describe their insect, its various stages during metamorphosis and the full range of parts developed in the adult.

Note: A variation on this activity is to use puzzles to introduce specific insects and their life stages, such as the monarch butterfly (complete metamorphosis) and grasshopper (gradual metamorphosis). Make illustrations of the stages using a single sheet of paper for each insect. Then cut the illustration into puzzle pieces to suit your group's level of difficulty. Use a different colored paper for each insect puzzle.

Hand out the jumbled pieces to children in the group and have them use the paper color as the key to finding those children holding the collective pieces to that insect puzzle. Once they have pieced the puzzle together they may use the illustration as a model for the "Making Metamorphosis" part of their activity.

Monarch Migration Maze

ACTIVITY: Discuss the various ways insects overwinter. Complete a maze simulating the hazardous migratory route of a monarch butterfly on its way to its southern wintering grounds.

GOAL: Understand the various overwintering strategies used by insects. Understand the migration behavior and dangers faced by monarch butterflies en route to their southern wintering roosts.

AGE: Younger children and older children

MATERIALS: "Discussion" section, copy of the description of the monarch migration in this activity, crayons or pens, one copy of the "Monarch Migration Maze" (Figure 8-7) for each child.

PROCEDURE: Use the "Discussion" section to review the many ways and places that insects overwinter. Ask the children to think of examples of insects that use each of these strategies. Now read this description of migratory behavior of the monarch butterfly with the children:

From late summer through autumn each year monarch butterflies begin a migration of hundreds of miles south to their wintering grounds. Each night they rest individually or in groups of only a few to several thousand. They prefer roosting in pines, maples and willows. Large groups may congregate at the edge of lakes, the tips of peninsulas and wherever land projects into a large body of water. When migrating monarchs reach something that blocks their route, such as a mountain, building, cliff face or tall trees, they usually fly up over the obstacle. Monarchs from the eastern part of North America overwinter by the millions in small areas of only 20 to 30 acres (8.1 to 12.2 hectares) in the mountains of southern Mexico. Their western counterparts follow the coast as they migrate south. Their roosts are found in eucalyptus trees and Monterey pines between Los Angeles and San Francisco on the coast of California. When the spring migration begins in March the monarchs work their way northward. Some monarchs do not stop to lay eggs on milkweed until they reach the northern parts of their range in May and June. Some, however, do lay eggs in the south as they push northward.

Lead a question and answer period once you have read this background information. Be sure to ask the children to think of the dangers a monarch would face on its long journey. Now pass out a copy of the "Monarch Migration Maze" (Figure 8-7) to each child. Have them imagine they are monarchs flying south for the winter. They are to begin at the starting point on the outside and work their way to the southern winter roost in the middle. Each hazard a monarch might encounter turns up in the maze as a dead end. Have the children record *all* of their movements in the maze in pen or crayon. Since it is a game, they will be allowed to backtrack out of the dead-ends to continue their journey southward. Tell them that one of the rules is to not erase when they reach a dead end, but to turn around and look for another way south.

Note: You can also enlarge the maze and have the children make or illustrate a monarch butterfly to move through the maze. You can even set up a maze in the home or learning center and have the children walk through and "fly" their monarch southward.

Once their migration mazes are complete, lead a discussion of their journeys and any questions, thoughts or stories that they have to share. Ask how many of them reached the wintering groups *without* heading down a single dead end. These are the *only* monarchs that would have made it safely to the south for certain. Have the children act out their monarch migration adventure as a skit.

Insect Alert

ACTIVITY: Sit quietly in a field while observing the interactions of insects and plants.
GOALS: Realize the many interrelationships that exist between plants and insects. Practice quiet, focused observation.
AGE: Younger children and older children
MATERIALS: Paper; cardboard backing; pencils; crayons; hand lenses; hats; long-sleeved shirts, hats and pants if biting insects are present.
PROCEDURE: Discuss the value of silent observation when learning about and appreciating nature. When our thoughts are silent and our bodies at rest, we are far more receptive to the sights, sounds and experiences surrounding us.

Pass out a pencil, paper with backing and a hand lens to each child. Give younger children several colors of crayons as well. Take the children out to a safe field and define a certain area in which they will work. A field near a pond is usually humming with all sorts of insects. Make the boundaries large enough so the children will be able to be far enough apart to feel alone. Be certain that children who simply cannot keep from talking and making other kinds of nonverbal contact when near each other are not even within sight of each other. Decide on a verbal call to bring everyone back when their time alone is up.

Have each child choose a spot in which she or he feels interested and comfortable. Look for a place where there are a lot of insects to be found, such as a patch of flowers. Encourage the children to focus on one or two specific flowers or other locations to get the most benefit out of their observations. Emphasize that the idea is to focus small but remain open to other things happening nearby and to observe them as well, then return to their original focus. They may use the hand lenses if they like, but sparingly since *the idea is to be very still and be accepted as part of the environment* by the animals. If they sit still they will have some insects crawl up on them or land on them, as grasshoppers and dragonflies often do. For older children, light pencil sketching or taking a few field notes is fine, but the idea is to use their senses to observe, not to draw a picture or write a story. Younger children may be more oriented toward drawing and coloring an illustration of whatever they see.

Use your agreed-upon cue to call them in after about 20 minutes (10 to 15 minutes for younger children) have passed. Sit in a sharing circle and have children describe and share the highlights of their experiences, including their field notes, sketches or illustrations. Complete the experience by encouraging them to continue this kind of activity on their own. This is an excellent way to develop observational and research skills. It can also be used for compiling a record of animal sightings, activities and discoveries in their own backyards and neighborhoods over time.

EXTENDING THE EXPERIENCE

• Make an exhaustive list of the food and other gifts we receive as the result of insect activity. Add your own ideas to those in the "Discussion" section. Go through an entire 24-hour period without eating or using any of these gifts from the insects.

• Write a story about a world in which there are neither insects nor any of the multitude of gifts we receive from them.

• Hold a "Pollination Appreciation" feast using only the foods we receive as a result of insect pollination.

• Write a story about being your favorite insect and having the adventures you might have in that life.

• Have a colorful butterfly festival with butterfly kites, balloons, mobiles, cookies and other fun forms of expression to honor the butterflies.

• Cut out colors and shapes from magazines and paste them together in a collage shaped like a butterfly.

NOTES

1. See Chapters 3, 6 and 7 for more information and activities about arthropods.
2. See Chapter 3 for more information and activities about spiders.
3. Donald W. Stokes, *A Guide to Observing Insect Lives* (Boston and Toronto: Little, Brown and Company, 1983), 207.

Figure 8-7. Monarch Migration Maze.

CHAPTER 9

✤ Salmon Boy ✤

(Haida—Pacific Northwest)

Long ago, among the Haida people, there was a boy who showed no respect for the salmon. Though the salmon meant life for the people, he was not respectful of the one his people called Swimmer. His parents told him to show gratitude and behave properly, but he did not listen. When fishing he would step on the bodies of the salmon that were caught and after eating he carelessly threw the bones of the fish into the bushes. Others warned him that the spirits of the salmon were not pleased by such behavior, but he did not listen.

One day, his mother served him a meal of salmon. He looked at it with disgust. "This is moldy," he said, though the meat was good. He threw it upon the ground. Then he went down to the river to swim with the other children. However, as he was swimming, a current caught him and pulled him away from the others. It swept him into the deepest water and he could not swim strongly enough to escape from it. He sank into the river and drowned.

There, deep in the river, the Salmon People took him with them. They were returning back to the ocean without their bodies. They had left their bodies behind for the humans and the animal people to use as food. The boy went with them, for he now belonged to the salmon.

When they reached their home in the ocean, they looked just like human beings. Their village there in the ocean looked much like his own home and he could hear the sound of children playing in the stream which flowed behind the village. Now the Salmon People began to teach him. He was hungry and they told him to go to the stream and catch one of their children, who were salmon swimming in the stream. However, he was told, he must be respectful and after eating return all of the bones and everything he did not intend to eat to the water. Then, he was told, their child would be able to come back to life. But if the bones were not returned to the water, that salmon child could not come back.

He did as he was told, but one day after he had eaten, when it came time for the children to come up to the village from the stream, he heard one of them crying. He went to see what was wrong. The child was limping because one of its feet was gone. Then the boy realized he had not thrown all of the fins back into the stream. He quickly found the one fin he had missed, threw it in and the child was healed.

After he had spent the winter with the Salmon People, it again was spring and time for them to return to the rivers. The boy swam with them, for he belonged to the Salmon People now. When they swam past his village, his own mother caught him in her net. When she pulled him from the water, even though he was in the shape of a salmon, she saw the copper necklace he was wearing. It was the same necklace she had given her son. She carried Salmon Boy carefully back home. She spoke to him and held him and gradually he began to shed his salmon skin. First his head emerged. Then, after eight days, he shed all of the skin and was a human again.

She spoke to him and held him and gradually Salmon Boy began to shed his salmon skin.

Salmon Boy taught the people all of the things he had learned. He was a healer now and helped them when they were sick.

"I cannot stay with you long," he said, "you must remember what I teach you."

He remained with the people until the time came when the old salmon who had gone upstream and not been caught by the humans or the animal people came drifting back down toward the sea. As Salmon Boy stood by the water, he saw a huge old salmon floating down toward him. It was so worn by its journey that he could see through its sides. He recognized it as his own soul and he thrust his spear into it. As soon as he did so, he died.

Then the people of the village did as he had told them to do. They placed his body into the river. It circled four times and then sank, going back to his home in the ocean, back to the Salmon People.

DISCUSSION

"Salmon Boy" is an allegory of great importance, revealing a series of interlocking circles which, as the story proceeds, run progressively deeper into the life ways of the Haida. Even though the people catch and eat the salmon, they do so with respect and gratitude. When the people live in balance and treat the spirits well the salmon swim upstream and offer their bodies for food. By returning the bones and all they do not eat to the water this *circle of giving and receiving* remains intact—the gift keeps moving. There is an important, interdependent relationship here: The salmon give people food and the people show their appreciation through prayer and reverence.

The salmon take notice when the boy begins to live out of balance by being disrespectful and breaking the circle. Yet, the salmon do not react by getting angry and harming the boy. He is made one of them so that he may more fully understand who they are and how to care for and respect them. Even though he drowns and dies to his own people, Salmon Boy has a new life among the Salmon People at their home in the ocean. We see the great *circle of life and death* and the reality of the spirit world.

Then, in another circle, one of transformation, Salmon Boy returns to his people as a healer to teach them the ways of the Salmon People and to help them when they are sick. This event in the story reveals the Native American's deep sense of *interconnectedness* between this world and the spirit world, and between animals and people.

Finally, after drowning and finding a new life first among the salmon and then again with his own people, Salmon Boy spears his own salmon soul and his human self dies. When his body is placed into the river it circles *four times*—a sacred number—and returns again to life among the Salmon People.

Just as the salmon in this story represent a link between the ordinary world and the spirit world, they also connect us to their mysterious home under the sea. It is believed that salmon once lived only in fresh water, but at some point in their history began to migrate to the sea where food is plentiful.

About Oceans

A vast and intriguing frontier for the imagination, *oceans* cover 71 percent of Earth's 8,000-mile (12,872-kilometer)-wide sphere. An additional 4 percent of Earth is covered by freshwater streams, rivers, lakes and ponds. Our five great oceans—the Atlantic, Pacific, Indian, Arctic and Antarctic—average 2.3 miles (3.7 kilometers) deep!

In a phenomenon known as the *Coriolis effect*, Earth's spinning motion deflects ocean currents to the right in the northern hemisphere and to the left south of the equator. As a result, the major ocean currents to the north of the equator turn clockwise and counterclockwise to the south.

The "salt" in sea water is composed of 84 percent sodium and chlorine, along with over 100 other elements. There are around 3.5 pounds (1.6 kilograms) of salt in every 100 pounds (45.4 kilograms)[1] of ocean water, or 35 parts salt per 1,000 of water. Salt water, as a result, freezes at 28.4°F (-2°C) or below.

What kind of a home does the ocean make? Compared to land the sea is a relatively stable environment. Temperatures in the Persian Gulf and the Red Sea, the warmest ocean waters on Earth, can reach 86° F (30.0° C), and those of the Arctic and Antarctic water can dip down to 28° F (-2.2° C). This hottest to coldest temperature range on land runs from 136° F (57.8° C) in the North African Sahara to -126° F (-87.8° C) in Antarctica! Ocean temperatures generally decrease moving farther from the equator and at greater depths.

Scientists divide the ocean into zones (Figure 9-1). The *pelagic* zone consists of all the water in the sea. Starting at the shoreline and moving toward the open sea, the pelagic zone is divided further into two other zones.

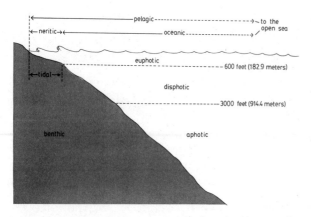

Figure 9-1. Zones of the ocean. Adapted with permission from Deborah A. Coulombe, The Seaside Naturalist. *Englewood Cliffs. N.J.: Prentice-Hall, 6.*

From the uppermost reaches of the tides and out to a depth of 600 feet (182.9 meters) the *neritic* (tidal) zone is found. The *oceanic* zone lies beyond the neritic zone and out to the open sea.

Conditions vary tremendously at the various depths in which ocean animals live and the ocean is divided, accordingly, into three major vertical layers or zones. In the *euphotic* zone, from the surface down to about 600 feet (182.9 meters), there is plenty of light penetration to sustain photosynthesis in green plants. This zone roughly corresponds to the neritic zone. From the bottom of the euphotic zone down to about 3,000 feet (914.4 meters) deep is the *disphotic* zone where light levels are very low. In the great depths below the disphotic zone, where no light penetrates at all, lies the *aphotic* zone which comprises 90 percent of the ocean's volume. The ocean bottom is the *benthic* zone.

Pressure is an important limiting factor for ocean animals. At 1,000 feet deep (304.8 meters) water pressure is nearly 500 pounds per square inch (35.2 kilograms per square centimeter). Pressure reaches 2.2 tons per square inch (.31 metric tons [310 kilograms] per square centimeter) at 10,000 feet (3,048.0 meters).

Ocean Life

Untold numbers and kinds of plants and animals have adapted to life in the sea. Except for some bacteria and some highly specialized marine giants—a 10-foot long (3-meter) tube worm along with a giant clam and crab—the ocean food web is supported by tiny, drifting plants called *phytoplankton*. In size they are microscopic or nearly so. These green plants, through the process of photosynthesis (see Chapter 6, page 63 for a detailed look at photosynthesis), use sunlight to produce food energy and oxygen. They are a major source of oxygen for the

ocean and Earth's atmosphere. Other *pelagic* forms of life, those that live in the open water, include tiny aquatic animals called *zooplankton*. These eat phytoplankton, and in turn become food for larger animals, including the 60-foot (18.3-meter) whale shark and the baleen whales, including the largest animal on Earth, the 100-foot (30.5-meter) blue whale. The benthic or bottom zone of the ocean is itself home for a host of plants and animals called the *benthos*, such as the sea star (starfish), crabs, sea anemones, lobster, clams, seaweed and others.

Fish

For all of its great diversity of life forms, the ocean is the undisputable realm of fish. Fish, along with whales, squid and other strong swimmers of the open water, are called *nekton*. Science tells us that fish are the common ancestors of all land *vertebrates*, animals with a backbone, going back hundreds of millions of years. One survivor, the lungfish, has both gills and lungs and can even walk on its long fins. Some fish, like the Mississippi paddlefish, sea lamprey and sharks, have changed little over the millenia. There are over twenty thousand species of fish and over half of all vertebrate animals are bony fish!

Fish have adapted to every conceivable aquatic environment. Their home is found from the surface to the bottom, along with the open water in between, from frigid polar seas to tepid tropical waters, from ponds to coral reefs to rivers, and from bright waters to the darkest depths where some even create their own light. Water temperature largely determines the distribution of fish because they are cold-blooded. Most species live in temperate waters, though they can survive temperature changes of from 12 to 15° F (6.7 to 8.4° C). Some fish, however, live beneath the pack ice in the Arctic and Antarctic, surviving in waters with temperatures below 32° F (0° C).

There are three major groups of fish. One group, the *Agnatha*, includes the jawless lampreys and hagfishes. Sharks, rays and skates comprise a second group, the *Chondrichthyes*, which have fully cartilaginous skeletons instead of bones. The bony fish or *Osteichthyes*, however, have from seven hundred to eight hundred bones in their bodies. Most well-known fish are bony fish. In fresh water these include trout, bass, catfish or horned pout, sunfish, perch, shiners, suckers, crappies, carp, dace, minnow and salmon. Some familiar saltwater species are the anchovy, bluefish, halibut, herring, goosefish, grunion, tuna, pollack, haddock, flounder, killifish, cod, swordfish and salmon.

An incredible array of rainbow colors are found among fish, unequalled by any other group of animals except, perhaps, insects and birds. Most fish follow a color pattern of being dark above and light below. This patterning, also common among many other kinds of animals, allows fish to blend in with the dark bottom when seen from above and the bright sky when viewed from below.

ADAPTATIONS FOR SURVIVAL. A fish's many adaptations for survival are a direct response to conditions for life beneath the waves. How deep is the water and how clear? What is the water temperature? How strong are the currents? Since water cannot be compressed it must be pushed aside when a fish swims through it. *Streamlining* allows fish to use their pointed head and tapered tail to pass easily through the water with little disturbance and minimal resistance (Figure 9-2). Their fins help them to steer, maneuver and stay upright. Flying fish have evolved fantastic fins that allow them to actually fly along from wave crest to wave crest for up to one minute and to attain heights of up to 10 to 20 feet (3.0 to 6.1 meters) above the water.

Scales overlap to cover a fish from head to tail and are in turn coated with a slimy, antibiotic *mucous*. This light slippery armor lubricates a fish's body and protects it from being infected by bacteria and fungi. During the summer months, as a fish grows faster, annual rings are left on its scales. These can be counted to estimate age.

A distinct line can be seen running along the side of a fish. This *lateral line* marks a system of canals in the skin which are extremely sensitive to water currents, movement and fine vibrations. This "sixth sense" helps a fish to orient in murky waters and dark places and to be keenly aware of any movements in its vicinity.

Breathing, as we know it, is impossible underwater. Fish get oxygen directly from the water. They take water in through the mouth, pass it over the *gills* and out the gill covers. Oxygen is absorbed into the bloodstream through the gill membranes.

Many modern fishes use a *gas bladder* to fine-tune their buoyancy to match that found at a particular depth. This airtight sac expands and contracts to just the right flotation

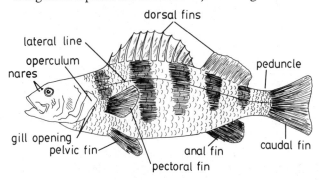

dorsal fins
lateral line
operculum
nares
peduncle
gill opening
pelvic fin
anal fin
caudal fin
pectoral fin

Figure 9-2. Basic parts of a fish (yellow perch). Size of adult: 10–14 inches (25.4–35.6 centimeters).

using gases from the bloodstream. Since a fish's cellular fluid is about the same density as that of water it is better able to remain "weightless" in its home. Some fish, such as sharks, do not possess a gas bladder. Since they sink when at rest, sharks must remain in constant motion.

Saltwater fish tend to *lose* water from their bodies into the concentrated salt of ocean water. They drink large amounts of water to compensate. The salt is then excreted and is also forced out through the gills. They do not usually urinate. Since freshwater fishes have body fluids that are more salty than their surroundings, they tend to *absorb* water over the surface of the skin and gills. As a result, they urinate often and do not drink at all!

Like many wild animals, fish spend much of their time searching for and catching or gathering their food. Fish exploit the entire range of available food, plant and animal, dead and alive, or a combination of several kinds. Plankton eaters, such as herring, mackerel, menhaden and the whale sharks, which stay near their food at the surface, use sieve-like *gill rakers* to filter out these tiny plants and animals. Predators, such as the bluefish, bass, shark and tuna, stalk their prey where they can be found. The masterful archerfish shoots its prey down with a jet of water, then devours it! This is even more amazing since water refracts light and the archerfish must compensate by aiming in front of its intended prey!

A fish's keen senses enable it to survive. They have good eyesight and no need for eyelids underwater where the eyes are always bathed. Fish can even see some color. The senses of hearing, touch and smell are all acute. Taste is unimportant since they gulp their food, though most possess taste buds located outside of the mouth.

REPRODUCTION. Fish would not have survived millions of years without a number of successful means of reproducing. Many fish live on by dint of their great numbers. Cod produce from four to six million eggs in one mating cycle or *spawn*. An average-sized (22 pounds or 10.0 kilograms) king or chinook salmon lays around eight thousand eggs. Most eggs are laid and fertilized in the water, while the eggs of some, such as sharks and guppies, are fertilized internally where they develop until the young are born live. Seasonal temperatures are an important factor in initiating spawning and in the successful development of the eggs. Spawning and growth usually occur during the spring and summer months. Most eggs are tiny, nearly transparent and they mature while afloat, especially among saltwater fish. Many freshwater fish lay eggs that sink to the bottom. In some species the young are cared for after hatching. The male bullhead (horned pout) guards the newly hatched young until they are up to 2 inches (5.1 centimeters) long.

Salmon

The salmon in the story "Salmon Boy" are *anadromous* species that live and grow in salt water, then return to ancestral freshwater spawning grounds when mature (Figure 9-3). The shad and the alewife are also anadromous. A few fish, such as the American eel, are *catadromous*, spending most of their lives in fresh water only to return to the sea to spawn.

Salmon travel immense distances on their life's migration to the sea and back. The king or chinook salmon of Idaho swim west to the central Aleutian Islands where they mature. They then travel 2,500 miles (4,023.4 kilometers) back to spawn in the headwater of the Snake and Columbia Rivers. Pacific salmon, such as the king, chum and red or sockeye salmon, die once they spawn. Some Atlantic salmon survive to spawn again. There are even some landlocked salmon that live their entire lives in fresh water.

No one knows for sure how the salmon navigate to make their epic migrations. They may follow the sun, moon or stars. Some hypothesize that they orient according to salinity, temperature, the unique odor and chemistry of water in their home streams or from some primal memory of how to reach these ancient sites of their origins. One theory surmises that enough salmon survive to assure that enough reach home to spawn just through random migration toward that general coastal area.

Once in their home river systems salmon demonstrate an intense desire to move upstream—leaping up to 10 feet (3.0 meters) high over waterfalls and rapids. Spawning salmon do not eat along their journey.

Conservation of Fish

As in the story "Salmon Boy," people still fish for salmon as well as many other species. Those who remember the traditional ways still maintain a close, respectful relationship with the Fish People. Some traditional Oglala Lakota (Sioux), when fishing, offer the bait saying, "You who are down in the water with wings of red, I offer this to you; so come hither." When a fish is caught it is treated with respect, or else the others will hear of the catch and flee. When little fish are caught they are treated especially well and released so they will not tell the bigger fish and scare them away. [2]

But fishhooks and spears have largely been supplanted by a high technology fishing industry that uses computers, planes and echo sounders to locate fish, and an array of nets and highly effective catching devices. A

Figure 9-3. A recently hatched Atlantic salmon fry *amid the gravel of a streambed. Salmon spawn during the fall in the headwaters of streams. The female hollows out a nest or* redd *in the gravel using powerful strokes of her tail. Here she lays the eggs, which the male fertilizes with a cloud of* milt. *The female covers the eggs once they are fertilized. Unlike Pacific salmon, which die after spawning just once, Atlantic salmon can spawn two or three times. Young salmon remain in fresh water from one to four or five years. During this time the young salmon are called* parr, *named after the "parr marks" on their sides, which are easily seen in this photograph. Salmon mature at three to five years of age or more. When they grow to a length of 5–6 inches (12.7–15.2 centimeters), parr begin their journey to the ocean. They are now called* smolts. *Salmon commonly spend from one to three winters in the ocean before they return to their ancestral streams to spawn. Those individuals that return to spawn after only one winter at sea are called* grilse. *During that first winter, grilse grow from their 6-inch (15.2-centimeter) smolt size to 4 pounds (1.8 kilograms) or more. Older salmon, which have spent up to six winters at sea, can weigh as much as 70 pounds (31.8 kilograms). Weight of adult: 12 pounds (5.4 kilograms) on the average, and up to 100 pounds (45.4 kilograms). Photo by Robert S. Michelson.*

modern fishing fleet often consists of a mother ship, spotters, catchers and factory processing ships where the catch is gutted, cleaned and frozen, all while at sea. As a result of the pressures placed on fish populations by the technology and efficacy of modern fishing fleets, many species of fish that Native North Americans have hunted as food for thousands of years are now greatly depleted. Some species have been so over-fished that they have become scarce and can no longer be used as food.

Salmon and other fish face many other threats to their well-being besides extreme hunting pressures. Dams present obstacles that block migration upstream. Water pollution stresses and weakens the health of migrating fish and masks the natural odors by which salmon recognize their home streams on the return spawning runs. Severe water pollution along a stretch of river can create zones that are so deadly to fish that they cannot be traversed, and so act as barriers to migration. Polluted water can adversely affect the development of fish eggs and young. Acid rain has created numerous bodies of water that are devoid of fish life. Toxic elements in many aquatic ecosystems are causing severe and widespread disease among fish populations, such as birth defects, tumors and many other forms of cancer.

Fortunately, over time, some of the dams that once blocked the flow of many rivers are being fitted with fish passage facilities, such as fish ladders and elevators. And many polluted lakes, ponds and rivers have gradually been cleaned up over the past few decades. There is, however, a long way to go in North America before our waterways are restored to a level of cleanliness and ecological health befitting the amazing fish that inhabit them.

QUESTIONS

1. What do the salmon do when the young boy treats them disrespectfully? What would you have done? Why do the salmon make the boy one of their own?

2. How is the young boy changed by his experience? What does he learn?

3. How can Salmon Boy die and come back to life so many times in this story? What finally happens to him in the end?

4. Identify some of the circles and cycles revealed in this story? Why are they important? Why is it important for our relationship with nature to be practiced with circles?

5. Salmon spend part of their lives in freshwater rivers and part of their lives in the ocean. What do they do in the rivers? Why do they swim down to the ocean? How do they find their way when traveling these great distances?

6. What do you think is the most important food for the ocean animals?

7. Would you want to live in the ocean? Why or why not? What would it be like to live in the deep sea?

8. What are your favorite animals of the ocean?

9. There are many kinds of fish living in the sea. Can you name some of them?

10. What kind of skin does a fish have? Why does it have scales?

11. How does a fish breathe?

12. How did Native North Americans fish using their traditional fishing methods? How do they fish today?

13. Do you eat fish? How do people catch the fish that your family buys? What is happening to the populations of fish as such great numbers of them are caught?

ACTIVITIES

Focus on Fish

ACTIVITY: (A) Assemble the pieces of a fish puzzle. (B) Catch a fish in a net, look at it in a fish bowl, draw a picture of it and release it.

GOALS: Understand the basic external anatomy of a fish, including the purpose and function of its various parts. Understand how a fish swims and feeds at the surface. Practice patience and still-stalking skills. Sharpen reflexes.

AGE: Younger children and older children

MATERIALS: (A) Posterboard or card stock, copies of Figure 9-4 and an enlarged drawing of same, Figure 9-2, scissors, envelopes, pencil, pictures of real fish. (B) Safety equipment for working in water, bathing suits, sandals or old sneakers, towels or rectangular pieces of fish netting (best), fish food from a pet store, slices of bread, minnow bait, minnow trap, goldfish bowls or large glass jars, pails, seine net and/or a long-handled fish net, Figure 9-2, supplies for an aquarium as described in Chapter 2, page 23.

PROCEDURE A: *Bits of a Bluegill.* Beforehand, make a copy of Figure 9-4 to use as a master. Draw lines on this master indicating where you want to cut the fish to turn it into a puzzle. Make the puzzle more or less complicated to suit the age of the children. Copy this master onto posterboard or light card stock and then cut each picture of a fish into puzzle pieces. Label the pieces of each puzzle with all As, Bs, etc., and put them in similarly labeled envelopes to keep matching pieces together. Younger children will be challenged by a four- to six-piece puzzle, while older children will need, for example, a twelve-piece puzzle.

Have the children work in pairs to assemble the puzzles—one puzzle to each pair. Once the puzzles are put together use Figure 9-2 and an enlargement of Figure 9-4 to point out the parts of the bluegill sunfish and their functions. Field questions from the children and allow time near the end for them to share fish stories. Look at pictures of different kinds of real fish and have the children find the body parts on these pictures. Try comparing Figure 9-4 with an illustration of human anatomy and correlate the parts of a fish with the corresponding parts of the human body where they exist.

Check the weather before taking the children outdoors to complete the rest of this activity. Do not venture out on cold, windy days and especially not on stormy days

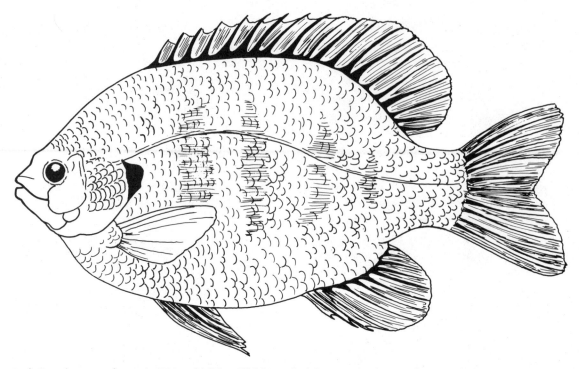

Figure 9-4. Puzzle master for use in "Bits of a Bluegill." Size of adult: can exceed 10 inches (25.4 centimeters).

when lightning may be present. Assuming that it is a warm day with little wind, travel to a pond or lake that has a good supply of small fish along the shore, a gradual, sandy or gravelly shoreline and water with visibility of at least a few feet. Have the children bring a towel and put on a bathing suit and pair of sandals or old sneakers. Bring along a loaf of bread and two goldfish bowls or large glass jars. This is the time to set up an aquarium if you plan to bring a fish back to observe it for a while.

PROCEDURE B: *Fish Watching.* Take the children down to the shoreline and demonstrate how they will work in pairs to catch fish. Each child will hold the opposite corners of a rectangular piece of netting or a towel, with this improvised capture net stretched lengthwise between them. They will stand in waste-deep water, holding this net about 9 inches (22.9 centimeters) to 1 foot (30.5 centimeters) beneath the surface. You will go to each pair and float a piece of tightly wadded-up bread in the water directly over the middle of the net. The children will need to keep the bread over the net. Mention that fish do not naturally eat bread and that bread is used here only as a one-time bait to catch the fish. Bread should not be fed to fish in captivity.

After waiting perfectly still for a few minutes some sunfish—or other small fish—will gather around the edge of the net. In time, a few adventurous ones will test out the net by swimming a little ways over it from the edge. The trick is to wait for a bold fish to go after the bread, then to lift the

net up evenly by all four corners to catch the fish. This is a great opportunity for the children to learn patience, observation and quickness. They love doing this so much that it is sometimes hard to get them to stop.

While the children are catching fish, set up a baited minnow bucket in a quiet area along the shore. Minnow bait, such as bits of mussels, crabs or dead fish, can be obtained at a bait store. Or obtain help from the children catching fish with a seine net and/or long-handled fish net. This way you will have some fish to look at *just in case* the children do not have any luck catching fish using the net/towel method described above.

Once a fish is caught put it into a waiting goldfish bowl or large glass jar in the shade. After a few fish are captured hold them up for the group, review the identifying marks, the basic parts of the anatomy (see Figure 9-2) and the nature of that fish, such as food and feeding habits, nesting and reproduction, breathing, scales and fins. Have each child draw a picture of any fish she or he chooses. Do not feed the fish at this time.

Now, hold a release ceremony for the fish and gently let them go while saying "thank you." Or take a fish or two back to observe for a week or so in the aquarium. Be careful not to keep a large fish in with a small one or the latter could be eaten. Use fish food obtained from a pet store while the animal is in captivity. Release the fish after a week of feeding and observation.

During the off-season (winter) use a fish from the pet store instead of one caught in "Fish Watching." Be sure not to buy an exotic species that may be rare in the wild. Instead, buy a locally occurring, abundant species—preferably one reared in captivity. Native fish can be kept in an aquarium.[3] Use the occasion of the trip to the pet store to discuss the issue of capturing rare and wild fish for pets.

Salmon Survival

ACTIVITY: (A) Listen to a fantasy journey and live out the life cycle of a salmon. (B) Calculate the number of salmon that would be produced if all of the offspring of one pair lived to reproduce.

GOALS: Experience and understand the life cycle of the salmon. Realize that the cycle of life and death (mortality) plays an important role in maintaining a balance for life on Earth.

AGE: Younger children (A) and older children (A and B)

MATERIALS: (A) Copy of "The Life of a Salmon," pencils, crayons or pastels, paper, Figure 9-3. (B) Pencils, paper, calculator, chalkboard and chalk or newsprint and felt-tipped markers.

PROCEDURE A: *The Life of a Salmon.* Lead a question and answer session with the children. Ask them to share what they know about salmon. Use the "Discussion" section to review the basics of fish migration and include examples of both catadromous and anadromous fish.

Now prepare the children for a guided imagery experience. Have them lie down and close their eyes to listen. Read the following story:

THE LIFE OF A SALMON

You have just hatched from an egg as a tiny salmon with a bit of yolk attached to your belly for food. Your new home is the cool, clear water at the top of a rocky riverbed. There are millions of other young salmon swimming all around you.

In a few weeks the yolk is used up and you begin to eat microscopic plants and animals. Your first summer passes, then fall, winter and spring as you grow larger and larger. Now you are eating other fish that are smaller than you. One day you swim past an old log underwater and you see the sinister outline of a fish lurking in the shadows. Quickly, a large trout shoots out to eat you. You swim as hard as you can. Your heart is racing. There is a small crevice in gravel up ahead and you dart in to safety just as the trout's jaws snap at you from behind. Whew! That was close.

Soon it is your second summer and you are a beautiful, two-year-old salmon. Now you feel an overwhelming urge to swim downstream. The river grows deeper, warmer and less shaded as you swim. Wheee! You shoot down some long rapids and high waterfalls. It is really fun! Then you hear a whirring sound and see a great cement dam across the river with a shoot for water to pass through. At first you hesitate and swim from side-to-side looking for another way down, but there is none. So you drop into the dark hole and are soon spun around wildly by the metal blades of a turbine. Then you shoot into the river below the dam. Since you are small you survive with only a minor cut, but you see other young salmon who are hurt badly in the water around you.

Finally you reach the salty sea and swim for several months and thousands of miles. Your new home is a vast, blue-green sea where you swim with many salmon in a great school. Here, where there are plenty of small ocean fish to eat, you live and grow for another two years. Once, when you are about three years old, a great net is dragged up from behind you and you are just able to outrun it to keep from getting caught. But many of your salmon friends are carried away and never seen again. Another time you narrowly escape the sharp teeth of a shark.

In time, your fourth summer arrives and the urge to go home to the stream where you were born drives you to begin a great journey. When you reach the shore you swim for a time before you smell the waters of your home river and head upstream. Someone is fishing from shore but you swim right by the baited hook. In fact, you haven't eaten a thing since you began your journey. You are tired and hungry, but you press on.

Up ahead there is the high cement wall of a large dam. After exploring for a time you find a strong current leading up many small falls into little pools along the side of the dam. Up, rest . . . Up, rest . . . Up, rest you go until you reach the top.

Look! A great waterfall. How will you ever get up. You back up and swim very fast, then leap as high as you can. Now you're in the air! Through the cool mist of the falls you see the sunlight, green leaves and a small rainbow. It is beautiful.

Plop! You land above the falls and push on.

You are weak and growing very thin. There is a fork up ahead and the smell of the river water entering from the left tells you it is the way home. Very sluggishly you near the place where you were born. Now you can recognize some of the large rocks in the riverbed.

This is your destiny. You summon all of your last strength to force a great mass of eggs out a hole beneath your body. There are hundreds of salmon all around you laying eggs and squirting milky sperm into the water. You feel light and relieved, but now you have nothing left to give.

There is a shallow pool up ahead. You flop over to it and feel your life begin to slip away. Your gills are working hard as you roll over on your left side. Your right eye can see the sun shining through the bright green leaves of a tree overhanging the stream. The image of the leaves slowly fades and you feel a deep sense of peace as the world turns dark and still.

Ask the children to open their eyes and sit up. Allow them to share how they feel. What were their favorite parts of the story and which parts didn't they like? Ask them what happened to their fantasy salmon at the end of the story. Ask the children what would happen on Earth if every animal and human being did not die eventually. Have them write and illustrate another story about the life of a young salmon that hatches from one of the eggs laid in this story just before the salmon died.

Point out to the children that not all Atlantic salmon die after spawning. Be sure to mention that the operators of many dams provide fish passage facilities, such as fish ladders and elevators, to help transport fish around the dams during spawning runs.

Further the experience by having them illustrate some of the scenes in "The Life of a Salmon" that most caught their imaginations. Then show them Figure 9-3 so they can see what a young salmon fry really looks like.

PROCEDURE B: *Salmon Calamity.* Tell the children they are going to prove that, without natural death, life could not continue as it is on Earth. This will be done by calculating the approximate number of salmon that would be produced if *every* offspring of one clutch of salmon eggs, and all of *their* offspring for a total of *five* generations lived to reproduce.

A spawning female king or chinook salmon lays an average of about eight thousand eggs. Assume, for the sake of this activity, that half of each generation of eggs produces females. Also assume that half of each successive generation of eggs will produce females. Although in reality each one of these females takes four years to grow to reproductive maturity, for this activity each living female will produce eight thousand eggs each year. The formula, then, looks like this:

1 female x 8,000 eggs =

8,000 eggs x .5 = 4,000 females x 8,000 eggs =

32,000,000 (32 million) eggs x .5 = 16,000,000 females x 8,000 eggs =

128,000,000,000 (128 billion) eggs x .5 = 64,000,000,000 females x 8,000 eggs =

512,000,000,000,000 (512 trillion) eggs x .5 = 256,000,000,000,000 x 8,000 eggs =

2,048,000,000,000,000,000 (2 quintillion) eggs after only 5 generations!

Now lead a question and answer/discussion session focusing on why it would not be a good thing for all of these salmon—or all of any animal—to survive. Stress that the *circle of life and death* allows room for new life to be born. This circle also prevents pollution, overcrowding and the depletion of resources, such as food, space, water and shelter. Also, if nothing ever died, nutrients would not be recycled back into the aquatic or terrestrial food chains.

Circle of the Sea

ACTIVITY: Practice expressing respect, appreciation and thanks for the gifts of the sea. Sit alone with the sea for a while and deepen that sense of connection.
GOALS: Begin to understand and experience a way of completing the circle of giving and receiving with the sea. Appreciate more fully our interconnectedness with the sea.
AGE: Younger children and older children
MATERIALS: Transportation for all, pencils, charcoal or pastels.
PROCEDURE: Travel with the children down to a special, beautiful place along the seashore, preferably one with a bit of a rise overlooking the water. Bring along some sharp pencils or charcoal or pastels capable of writing or drawing on a smooth rock.

Have the children search for and choose a beautiful, smooth, fist-sized or larger stone on which to draw or write. Now pass out the writing and drawing tools to the children. Ask the children to think of as many examples as they can of gifts we receive from the sea, such as food, a cool and fun place to swim, a beautiful setting to visit, a surface to boat on and fascinating plants and animals to learn about.

Sit the children at well-spaced intervals along the shore. Find places where the children can be watched for safety, yet which afford them a sense of being alone with the sea. Have them face the water and sit quietly for a time, ranging from a few minutes (younger children) to 20 minutes (older children).

As the children sit they are to think of one of their favorite gifts from the sea. This could range from something less tangible like the cry of a sea gull or sound of the surf, to a wonderful boat ride they once took to a certain kind of seafood they may like to eat. Have the very young children draw a picture on their rock to represent the gift they receive from the sea. Give older children a choice of either drawing a picture, writing a thank-you note (or whatever else they desire) or creating a short seashore poem expressing their gratitude. Ask those who choose to write a short poem to try to create an image with words. Here is an example:

> crashing thunder waves
> I love to hear your music
> rising from the sea

Once the children have completed their creations have them sit in a circle. Use this time for allowing them to share their gift and expression of thanks *if* they so desire. Discuss the importance of these gifts to the sea. Explain that because we are interconnected and interdependent with the sea it is important to take only what we need from her and not waste anything as Salmon Boy did. Explain that it is good to ask permission before taking anything from the sea and to show appreciation by reciprocating with gifts of our own to the sea to keep the gift moving.

Once this is done walk with the group to a beautiful spot near the water (Figure 9-5). Have each child say a silent thanks to the sea. Or you could all make up a thanks to say out loud such as, "Thank you, Sea, for all of your wonderful gifts. With these presents we complete the circle and show our gratitude!" Keep it simple. Now have the children give their gifts back to the sea by gently tossing their stones into the water.

EXTENDING THE EXPERIENCE

• Create a diorama of an underwater ocean scene (Figure 9-6). Show different kinds of fish, other ocean animals, as well as plants and the many parts of the ocean environment.

• Make a mobile of some small, precious objects collected at the seashore.

• Draw pictures of some favorite freshwater or saltwater fish and create a mural of an underwater scene in which to place the fish. Depict the fish in action positions and use the occasion to discuss how these fish would live and interact with one another in the wild, such as predator, prey, scavenger, herbivore, omnivore or parasite.

• Plan a field trip to a seaport where fishing vessels unload their catch. Arrange for the children to watch the unloading of fish and to get a close look at what kind of fish are in the catch. Have someone hold up the fish and describe how they are used for food. Later, study the natural history of the fish they saw at the seaport. *Or* visit a seafood store and conduct a similar experience and follow-up.

• Set up an aquarium at home or in the learning center and keep some native species of fish for the children to observe.

Figure 9-5. Sunrise and sunset are inspiring times to visit the seashore for completing the "Circle of the Sea." Photo by Michael J. Caduto.

• Make a spring trip to see the migration of an anadromous fish, such as the salmon. Visit a local dam with a fish passage facility and arrange a tour, if possible, or visit a local stream or small river during the height of fish migration to see the fish passing.

NOTES

1. In volume, 100 pounds (45.4 kilograms) of water equals about 12 gallons or 45.4 liters.
2. See Chapter 16 for more information and activities regarding native peoples and animals of the sea.
3. John R. Quinn, *Our Native Fishes: The Aquarium Hobbyist's Guide to Observing, Collecting and Keeping Them.* (Woodstock, Vt.: The Countryman Press, 1990).

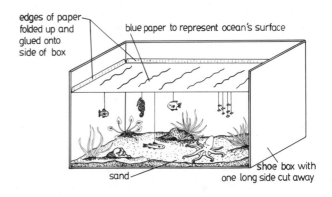

Figure 9-6. Create a diorama of life beneath the ocean waves.

"You are so ugly." she said to the frog. "Even another frog would not want to marry you!" Then she threw the frog back into the lake.

CHAPTER 10

✦ The Woman Who Married a Frog ✦

(Tlingit—Pacific Northwest)

There once was a young woman who was very proud. She was the daughter of the town chief and her family was very respected. Many of the young men wanted to marry her, but she thought none of them were good enough for her. One day, she was walking with her sister beside the big lake near their village. There were many frogs in that lake. A large number of them were sitting on a mud bank in the middle of the lake and she began to make fun of them.

"How ugly these frogs are," she said. Then she bent over and picked one up which was sitting on the muddy shore and looking up at her. "You are so ugly," she said to the frog. "Even another frog would not want to marry you!" Then she threw the frog back into the lake.

That night, when she stepped outside of her lodge to walk while the others were sleeping, she was surprised to see a young man standing there. His clothing was decorated with green beads and he seemed very handsome.

"I have come to marry you," the young man said. "Come with me to my father's house."

The young woman agreed. She thought she had never seen such a handsome man before and wanted to be his wife.

"We must climb the hill to go to my father's house," the young man said and he pointed toward the lake. They began to walk down toward the water, but it seemed to the young woman they were climbing a hill. When they reached the water they did not stop, but they went under.

The next day, her family noticed that she was missing. They searched for her everywhere and when they found her tracks leading to the water, they decided she had drowned. They beat the drums for a death feast. People cut their hair and blackened their faces and mourned.

One day, though, a man walked down by the lake. When he looked out toward its middle he saw on the mud bank many frogs sitting there. There, in the midst of the frogs, was the chief's missing daughter. He began to wade in toward them, but they leaped into the water, taking the young woman with them.

The man went as quickly as he could to the chief's house. "I have seen your daughter," he said. "She has been taken by the frogs. I tried to reach her, but the Frog People took her with them under the water."

The young woman's father and mother went down to the lake. There they saw their daughter sitting on the mud bank surrounded by the Frog People. As before, when they tried to reach her, the frogs dove in and carried her under the lake with them. Then the chief's other daughter spoke.

"My sister insulted the frogs," she said, "that is why they have taken her."

The chief saw then what he must do. He made offerings to the Frog People, asking them to forgive his daughter. They placed dishes of food on the surface of the water. The dishes floated out and then sank. But the frogs would not give up the young woman. They placed robes of fine skins on the bank. The young woman and the Frog People came to the bank and took those robes, but when the chief came close, the Frog People drew her back into the lake. The frogs would not give her up. At last the chief made a plan. He gathered together all of the people in the village.

"We will dig a trench," he said. "We will drain away the water of the lake and rescue my daughter."

The people worked for a long time and the water began to drain away. The Frog People tried to fill the trench with mud, but they could not stop the water from flowing out. The frogs tried to drive the people away, but the people only picked the frogs up and dropped them back into the water. They were careful not to hurt any of the frogs, but they did not stop digging the trench. The water continued to flow out and the homes of the Frog People were being destroyed. At last the chief of the frogs decided. It was his son who had married the young woman.

"We are not strong enough to fight these humans," he said. "We must give my new daughter back to her people."

So they brought the young woman to the trench. Her father and mother saw her and they pulled her out. She was covered with mud and smelled like a frog. One frog leaped out of the water after her. It was the frog who had been her husband. But the people carefully picked him up and dropped him back into the lake.

They took the young woman home. For a long time she could only speak as a frog does, "Huh, Huh, Huh!" Finally she learned to speak like a human again.

"The frogs know our language." she told the people. "We must not talk badly about them."

From that day on, her people showed great respect to the frogs. They learned the songs that the woman brought from the Frog People and they used the frog as an emblem. They had learned a great lesson. They never forgot what happened to that young woman who was too proud. To this day, some people in that village still say when they hear the frogs singing in the lake, the frogs are telling their children this story, too.

DISCUSSION

"You are so ugly," says the young woman, "even another frog would not want to marry you!" This attitude of superiority over other life forms is common among human beings. It comes in such subtle, even cute expressions and story lines that we are often amused. It expresses a common belief that people are better than animals. Yet, the young woman's insulting comments in "The Woman Who Married a Frog" show that, by being too proud and not developing an eye for appreciating the animals around us, we can cause disharmony in the relationships between people and animals.

In the German fairy tale "The Frog Prince," a princess reluctantly keeps her promise and cares for a frog. Her act of kindness breaks a wicked spell and transforms the frog back into his real form as a handsome young prince. The young woman in this Tlingit story, however, pays for her vanity by marrying a handsome young man who, in reality, turns out to be a frog! Then his relatives, the frogs, will not let her go.

But the chief and his people do not use force to rescue his daughter. First they make offerings of food to ask the frogs' forgiveness. Then they present robes of fine skins as gifts. All of these presents are taken by the Frog People but they will not give the chief back his daughter—the frogs do not seem to want to *forgive*. This brings disaster upon them when their home is drained by the chief and his people. Even though the frogs then try to drive the people away, they are gently placed back in the lake. When the frogs finally return the woman to her people, she warns them not to speak ill of the frogs. In the end, the frogs earn the respect of these people and are even used as an emblem.

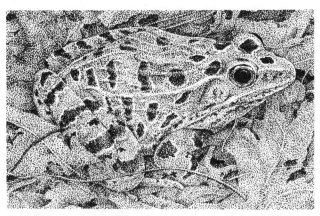

Figure 10-1. The northern leopard frog ranges throughout southern Canada and the northern half of the United States. It is the most well known of North America's five species of leopard frogs because it was the standard frog used for dissection in biology classes for many years. Its voice consists of a series of deep clucking sounds, interspersed with grunts or snores that last from 2 to 3 seconds. Populations of northern leopard frogs are greatly depleted in many areas due to overcollecting for biological supply houses. Size: 2–3-1/2 inches (5.1–8.9 centimeters). Illustration by D. D. Tyler.

Amphibians

Why is it that children are fascinated the most by amphibians, reptiles and other "creepy crawlers" that some adults find the most loathsome? In fact, *herpetology*, the study of amphibians and reptiles, comes from the Greek word *herpetó* which means "a creeping thing." This chapter introduces the *amphibians*, those who lead a double ("amphi") life ("bios"). Most amphibians have a young, aquatic *larval* stage of their life that transforms into a semiaquatic *adult*.

Amphibians first appeared on Earth over 300 million years ago. For a period of several million years they dominated the planet and are thought to have been the first *vertebrates*, animals with backbones, to live partly on land. The three surviving groups of amphibians are:

• *Salientia (Anura)*, the tailless frogs (including toads);
• *Caudata (Urodela)*, the tailed salamanders; and
• *Apoda (Gymnophiona)*, the legless, worm-like *caecilians* of the tropics.

There are about 350 species of salamanders worldwide and over 3,500 known species of frogs and toads (Figure 10-1).

What distinguishes amphibians from reptiles and other animals? Amphibians:

• are the only vertebrates with *naked skin*, which is not covered by fur (hair), feathers or scales. This skin can be smooth or rough, and either wet and slimy or dry to the touch.
• have toes but *no claws*.
• are *cold-blooded* or *ectothermic*. They depend on the environment as their source of heat and their body temperature fluctuates with that of the surroundings.
• have skin containing many glands, including toxic ones in some cases.

An amphibian's skin is shed as the animal outgrows the old one, which is often eaten. Water is absorbed through its skin so it has no need to drink. Oxygen and carbon dioxide are also exchanged through the skin and linings of the mouth and throat. All larvae have gills, while most adults develop a pair of lungs with which to breathe, although they continue to respire through their skin as well. Although amphibians cannot change the *color* of their skin, their pigments are capable of changing, which causes the animal's *shade* to change.

As adults, most species of frogs, toads and salamanders have two pairs of legs with four toes on the front feet and five on the rear, although there are exceptions.

Amphibians, as a group, are highly adaptable, living in habitats ranging from tropical to subarctic, and are quite tolerant of low temperatures. Most of them do, however, function best at an optimal range of body temperature. They seek sunlight and shade at different times in order to regulate body temperature, which affects digestion, respiration, growth, reproduction and overall metabolism. Some salamanders and the spadefoot toad of southwestern deserts will enter a period of summer dormancy called *estivation*, which can last for weeks during periods of extreme heat and drought.

REPRODUCTION. Seasonal changes in temperature and length of day have a dramatic effect on amphibian reproduction. Preparation for the breeding season actually begins during the shortening days of the preceeding autumn as reproductive organs swell and other physiological changes occur prior to hibernation. The warmer, lengthening days of the following spring cause the mating urge to soar. This stirs up a frenzy of mating calls and, sometimes, a territorial defense on the breeding grounds. Spring peepers, wood frogs and other early breeders begin to call even before others, such as bullfrogs, have emerged from hibernation.[1] Some amphibians, such as spotted salamanders, spadefoot toads and wood frogs are *explosive breeders*. These species migrate in great numbers to the breeding pools, court, mate, lay and fertilize their eggs, then leave—all in the span of several days or even a few hours. These eggs and young, which are often laid in

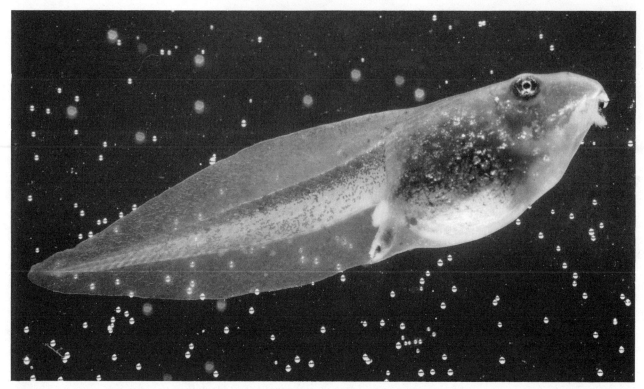

Figure 10-2. At a maximum size of 5 inches (12.7 centimeters) or more in length, the olive-colored bullfrog tadpole is the largest in North America. Over much of their range, bullfrog tadpoles hatch from eggs one summer, overwinter and then metamorphose into juveniles the next summer. In some cases, particularly in northern reaches of their range, these large tadpoles will live through two winters before transforming into juveniles and finally adults. The rear legs on the bullfrog tadpole in this photograph are just beginning to show in the early stages of growth. Photo by Alan C. Graham.

seasonal ponds, must quickly develop and metamorphose into adults before their pools dry. Males of the *prolonged breeders*, like the bullfrog, green frog and northern leopard frog, stake out and defend a mating territory, then attract the female with their persistent calling. Their young develop more slowly. Bullfrog tadpoles in the northern parts of their range grow for up to two years before metamorphosing into juvenile frogs.

Frogs and toads fertilize their eggs *externally*, while nearly all salamanders have *internal fertilization*. The males of some species of salamander use scent to attract and arouse a mate. The male usually rubs his chin or tail on the female's body, and some salamanders even perform a nuptial dance! Males then release small, gelatinous capsules of sperm called *spermatophores* that are picked up by the female's cloaca and stored in a special chamber to await the eggs. The *cloaca* is an opening used for both reproduction and the elimination of wastes. Females may acquire spermatophores from several different males, resulting in a clutch of eggs having more than one father.

Male frogs, however, simply mount a receptive fe-

male from the back and clasp her with forelegs in a position called *amplexus*. As the eggs are laid in the pool the male emits his sperm and, having completed his part, eventually releases his mate. Depending on the species, males will ride attached to the female for a few days, and up to a few weeks, while waiting for her to lay the eggs.

The familiar spring and summer mating calls of chorus frogs, spring peepers, bullfrogs and others serve to advertise and defend the mating territory and attract a mate. Other calls warn against predators and other dangers. A *release call* is issued when a nonreceptive female or a male is inadvertently grasped by a mating male in his enthusiasm to continue the life cycle. Calling is accomplished by passing air quickly over the vocal chords between the lungs and one or two vocal sacs.

Amphibian eggs are fascinating creations to watch because they are usually enclosed in a clear, protective, gelatinous coating. They can be found in pools, ponds, streams and other wet places, either free-floating or attached to a rock, log or branch underwater. Soon after laying, the jelly coating absorbs water and grows up to three times its original size. Some frogs lay eggs in masses and toads lay them in two strings containing hundreds or thousands of eggs. Salamanders lay masses of larger and fewer eggs, consisting of only ten to about one hundred at a time. Most amphibians abandon the eggs but a few kinds of salamanders will remain with them until they hatch. The blackish or brownish eggs develop in a few days to nearly a month depending on the species and the surrounding temperature. Many eggs are eaten by insects, such as dragonfly nymphs, leeches, turtles, adult amphibians such as the red-spotted newt and other predators.

METAMORPHOSIS. Growing embryos begin to squirm and wiggle before they finally hatch into frog or toad *tadpoles* or *larval salamanders*. All of these young are called the *larval* stage and they obtain oxygen through their gills.

A *pollywog* ("wiggling head") or *tadpole* ("toad's head") begins life with a pair of sucking appendages on its mouth to help it anchor underwater. In a few days these disappear along with its small, external gills that are replaced by internal gills. The tadpole takes water into its mouth, runs it over the gills and forces it out of an opening called a *spiracle*, located under or on the left side of its body. The gills are also used to feed by filtering algae and bacteria from the water as they swim along (Figure 10-2). Algae and bacteria are also eaten from rocks and plants by scraping with a toothy beak. Although the carnivorous spadefoot tadpole is known to eat meat, the rest are herbivorous. Both tadpoles and salamander larvae have a *lateral line organ* running along the body which senses vibrations, such as those made by predators.

As they undergo the transformation of *metamorphosis* from tadpole to adult, there comes an awkward juvenile stage that for frogs has been called "froglet" or "toadlet," and even "frogiwog" or "frogpole." First the rear legs appear, then the front limbs. The tail and gills are absorbed for food and lungs develop; now the tadpole surfaces for air. Finally, the digestive tract develops for a carnivorous diet as the adult frog or toad assumes a new niche in the food chain. Adult frogs are tailless, which accounts for their common scientific name of *Anurans*, meaning "without tails."

Salamander larvae differ from tadpoles in that they have three gills externally on each side of their heads. Some larvae have a pair of structures in front of the gills that helps them to keep their balance until the legs appear, which is usually in just a few days. All larval salamanders are carnivorous and some even devour smaller members of their own kind.

FURTHER ADAPTATIONS FOR SURVIVAL. As adults, salamanders continue to be carnivorous, eating worms, insects, spiders and other small salamanders. A few adults are cannibalistic, such as that of the red-spotted newt that feeds on larval newts. The tiny, grasping teeth on a salamander's upper and lower jaws curve inward and serve only for holding prey while it is being swallowed. Aquatic salamanders use their tail or *caudal fin* for swimming. One common belief that seems improbable, but is really true is that when some salamanders are caught by the tail they can thrash and break the tail off. Little or no blood is lost and a new, somewhat shorter tail soon grows in! Many salamanders have vertical bulges or folds called *costal grooves* on the sides of their bodies between the legs. Virtually all salamanders are mute—they lack vocal chords and eardrums. Sounds are sensed as vibrations, through the legs among terrestrial species and via the lower jaw in aquatic forms.

Adult frogs and toads, however, are keenly tuned into sounds with a conspicuous round membrane of skin called the *tympanum* that is stretched over each ear canal. These membranes are part of a frog's smooth, moist, slippery skin, or a toad's rough warty skin that is dry to the touch. Frogs spend most of their lives in damp areas, while a toad's thick skin allows it to take refuge in drier habitats, such as under rocks and logs. Although a toad's bumpy skin glands do secrete a fluid that can irritate eyes and other sensitive areas, *toads do not cause warts* (Figure 10-3). The pair of large *parotoid*

Figure 10-3. Toads, such as this American toad, possess bumpy skin glands that secrete a fluid that is irritating to eyes and other sensitive areas of the skin. This fluid is, in part, an effective defense that causes the toad to have an offensive taste when eaten by a predator. The touch of a toad, however, does not cause warts! Notice the prominent bump, called the parotoid gland, just behind the eye. Size: 2–3-1/2 inches (5.1–8.9 centimeters). Photo by Alan C. Graham.

glands just behind the eyes are most conspicuous. Some frogs have folds of skin called *dorsolateral ridges* that run along their backs beginning from behind the eyes.

Most people who have held a frog or toad know it urinates when caught. This defense mechanism is an attempt to surprise a predator and cause it to release. If held too tightly frogs and toads will scream in pain, sounding much like the cry of a human child. When swimming to safety a frog or toad folds its front legs in and propels with powerful thrusts of its hind legs. Upon resurfacing they will often float with only their eyes and nostrils exposed. Air is taken in through the nostrils, which then close, and the air is pushed down into the lungs. Sometimes, when the throat is pulsing, air is only being drawn into the throat, which contains minute blood vessels for absorbing oxygen. Oxygen can also be absorbed over the surface of the skin.

A frog's eyes, tongue and teeth all work in tandem when it feeds. When a prey is spotted within range the tongue quickly flicks its sticky tip forward to catch it. While most frogs have teeth on their upper jaws, which are used only to hold the prey not to chew it, toads are toothless. (*Neither of them bite human beings.*) The eyes are then lowered in their sockets and protrude into the mouth, helping to force food down the throat. Each eye has three lids: the upper and lower lids that open and close the eye and a third, clear *nictitating membrane* that is raised from behind the lower lid. This clear lid cleans the eye and protects it, especially when swimming underwater.

Although they are superbly adapted to their form of existence, life as an amphibian is not easy. Predators abound, including turtles, snakes, other amphibians, aquatic birds such as herons and gulls, raccoons, skunks and even human pets. In captivity, when well cared for and free from the dangers of a wild existence, some amphibians can live to an impressive old age. One spotted salamander lived twenty-five years, and an American toad survived to see its thirty-first birthday!

Conservation of Amphibians

People now present the greatest threat to the continued existence and well-being of these remarkable animals. In many parts of the world amphibians are disappearing where they were once commonplace. Scientists have discovered a decline of from 50 to 90 percent in various locations around the world, including local extinctions in some temperate mountain lakes and tropical forests. Particularly hard hit are populations in North America, central and northern Europe, and in tropical Central America and South America. Frog and toad populations are also declining in Australia. Although wild animal populations normally experience natural population cycles of ups and downs, amphibian populations are not recovering from the bottom end of these cycles. Of particular concern is that this decline is being experienced even in natural areas such as national parks, wilderness areas and biological preserves. There are also some regions, such as Borneo and East Africa, and some parts of North America, like the northeastern United States, where the number of amphibians seems to be stable.

Western species seem to be taking the brunt of this decline in North America. Native frogs ranging from southern California up to British Columbia and east to the Rocky Mountains are declining dramatically. This includes the boreal toad and leopard frog in the Rocky Mountains, the western spotted frog and Cascades frog in Oregon and the yellow-legged frog living in several mountain lakes in California.

A combination of some specific environmental issues, poor treatment of amphibians by people and a state of general environmental degradation are causing these frogs, toads and salamanders to die off. Acid rain, pesticides, habitat destruction and overhunting are the worst culprits. Acidic snow and rain eventually kill the algae in lakes that are not well buffered, causing starvation that ripples up the food chain. The combined effects of acid rain, pesticides and other pollutants both stress and weaken the animals, causing them to become increasingly susceptible to viruses and other natural diseases as their resistance is lowered. Exotic fish and other animals have been introduced in some places that eat indigenous amphibians and compete with them for food. Amphibians are heavily collected in some localities for food, pets, research and lab experiments. During one year in the early 1970s, just under 600,000 amphibians were imported legally, primarily to be sold as pets.[2] The leopard frog has been nearly wiped out in many parts of its range because it was relentlessly collected over the years for dissection in biology classes and for use in laboratory experiments.

No animal can survive without a home, and there are many forms of environmental change that are disrupting and destroying amphibian habitats. Indiscriminate forms of logging, such as clear cutting, cause erosion, siltation and filling of many streams and ponds. This and other forms of runoff, such as fertilization and septic system leachate, overfertilizes aquatic ecosystems causing oxygen depletion and rapid plant growth. Directly draining

Figure 10-4. The spotted salamander lives in a dark world under soil and leaf litter. They emerge en masse during the first few rainy nights of early spring when temperatures are above freezing and migrate to vernal pools. Males arrive first and, once the females come, deposit sperm on submerged plants. An adult female takes sperm into her cloaca, where the eggs are fertilized, then she lays the eggs in the water. This vital task accomplished, the salamanders return to their dark world until next year's brief mating foray. Size: 6–7 inches (15.2–17.8 centimeters). Photo by Peter Hope.

wetlands and other aquatic environments, such as the people did in the story that begins this chapter, has destroyed an alarming amount of amphibian habitat. In the United States alone an area of wetlands the size of the state of Delaware is destroyed every three years. Ninety-one percent of California's original wetlands are gone, along with 99 percent of Iowa's natural marshes.

If we are to continue enjoying these fascinating animals we will need to understand them better and share this Earth home with them more generously. In some communities in Europe and North America tunnels have been built to allow frogs, toads and salamanders to cross unharmed under roadways during their spring mating migrations.[3] (See Figure 10-4.) We can all help with the larger environmental issues outlined here by actively working to solve these problems. We can make it a point regularly to observe, enjoy and keep records of amphibian behavior and the locations and dates of our sightings. This information is a valuable resource that can be shared with appropriate conservation groups or agencies. Amphibians are vulnerable animals whose care will bring many hours of enjoyment and a lifetime of fascinating surprises.

QUESTIONS

1. Why does the young woman insult the frogs and call one of them ugly? Do you think this is a good thing to do? Why or why not?

2. What does the young woman's father, the chief, do to get her back? Why does he use gifts to persuade the frogs to give back his daughter?

3. Do you think the people were right to drain the frogs' lake when the frogs refused to give back the young woman? What would you have done?

4. What do you do or say when you think an animal is ugly? How do you suppose people appear to frogs and other animals?

5. How do things end up between the frogs and the people?

6. Do you treat small animals with respect? How do you treat a frog when you catch it?

7. What kind of animal is a frog? Can you think of some other kinds of animals that are closely related to frogs?

8. There is something special about the way frogs live. What is it?

9. What do we call a young frog? Can you think of more than one name for it?

10. Have you ever found frogs' eggs? What are they like?

11. Do you know any frog calls or songs? Imitate the ones you know. Why do frogs call?

12. How does a frog breathe?

13. Are people taking care of frogs and their kin today? What are some threats that frogs face? What could you do to help take care of them?

ACTIVITIES
Two Lives Are Wetter Than One

ACTIVITY: Listen to a puppet show that describes amphibian characteristics and the process of amphibian metamorphosis.

GOALS: Understand which traits distinguish amphibians from other kinds of animals. Recognize the stages and process of amphibian metamorphosis.

AGE: Younger children and older children

MATERIALS: Outlines of puppet figures as described in detail in the "Procedure," paper, pencils, crayons, masking tape, scissors, glue, cardboard backing, sticks on which to mount the puppets, copy of puppet show script "When Tadpole Met-a-Morphoses."

PROCEDURE: Create puppets for each character in this puppet show. You will need two frogs, a male bullfrog named "Bullfrog" and a female frog named "Pollywog," a tadpole and a half-metamorphosed tadpole or "froglet" that looks like a tadpole but is larger and has hind legs. (Refer to the photograph in Figure 10-2 on page 86 of *Keepers of the Earth.*) Bullfrog and Pollywog are the two main characters. The tadpole and froglet are just held up briefly during the performance.

Now perform the following puppet show called "When Tadpole Met-a-Morphoses." Follow the puppet show with a question-and-answer period explaining metamorphosis and the characteristics of amphibians.

WHEN TADPOLE MET-A-MORPHOSES

Bullfrog: (*He begins the show by walking across the stage croaking, "Jug-o-rum, jug-o-rum. . . ." loudly.*)

Pollywog: (*She pops up.*) Hi there! Have you seen my friend Tadpole? He used to live in this part of the pond and I thought I would come over to visit him.

Bullfrog: Well, I don't know. If I could find him who should I say is asking for him?

Pollywog: Just tell him it's me—Pollywog.

Bullfrog: Polly . . . Pollywog? . . . Is that you? How are you? I haven't seen you in a frog's age! Don't you recognize who I am? It's me, Tadpole. Now I call myself Bullfrog!

Pollywog: No way!!! My friend Tadpole has a large head, a small tail, two little eyes and a tiny mouth. You don't look like him at all!

Bullfrog: Frog-gone-it, Pollywog—it *is* me. I'm Tadpole and I used to look like you just described me.

Pollywog: But how could you . . . Wait a minute . . . Is it possible? . . . Tadpole, is that really you in that frog suit?

Bullfrog: It's *not* a frog suit . . . (*Pollywog butts in.*)

Pollywog: But if it's not a frog suit then what happened to the old Tadpole, the one I knew so well. He didn't . . . he didn't *croak* did he?

Bullfrog: No, I didn't *croak* , but I do "croak" now that I'm a frog, Bullfrog, that is.

Pollywog: Now I'm really confused. How could you now be Bullfrog when my friend was Tadpole? Life is too complicated.

Bullfrog: Calm down, Pollywog, calm down. Let me explain. Back when you first knew me I used to look like this. (*Hold up tadpole.*) I used to breathe with gills and I ate algae and tiny microscopic bacteria. As I grew older I grew rear legs, then front ones. I absorbed my tail and gills and used them for food. Then I developed lungs and began to breathe in air directly. I looked kind of awkward and felt it too. See! (*Hold up froglet.*) People called me a lot of names because they didn't know what to call me. Some called me froglet. Others called me frogiwog or frogpole. I didn't like it one bit.

Pollywog: Gee, I'm sorry, Tadpole, I mean Bullfrog, that must have been a tough time in your life.

Bullfrog: I'm glad you're finally beginning to understand, Pollywog. Most strange of all is that I then began using my long, sticky tongue to eat insects, smaller frogs and other small animals. (*Take froglet down.*)

Pollywog: Hey, that happened to me a while back. I just kind of lost my appetite for those little plants I used to eat.

Bullfrog: I can't believe you, Pollywog. Are you blind? Don't you know anything? For goodness' sake, take a look at your reflection in the water! Hurry up!

Pollywog: (*Looks slowly down and studies her reflection, then screams.*) Aaahh!! I'm . . . I'm not a pollywog anymore! Leaping legs! I've turned into a . . . a . . . a frog!

Bullfrog: Easy, Pollywog. It's alright. You've obviously been a frog for quite a while now and you're doing fine.

Pollywog: Oh sure, it's no skin off your back!

Bullfrog: Hey, I've been through the same experience. It's a major change called *metamorphosis.* And don't worry about your skin. As I get bigger I simply grow a new skin, shed my old one and eat it. You'll get used to it. Besides, our skin is part of what makes us who we are. We have naked skin with no hair, scales or feathers. We also have toes without claws. We're cold-blooded—we have to get our body heat from the sun and the rest of our surroundings. And we have the three stages to our life beginning with an *egg,* then hatching into a *larva,* which most people call a tadpole or polliwog. Finally, we change into what we are now—*adults* called frogs. We're called *amphibians,* which means "double-life." Toads and salamanders are also amphibians.

Pollywog: Wow! Life will never be the same. I'll be eating insects forever and ever!

Bullfrog: Polly, you're impossible. There's more to life than eats the fly. Life *will* be the same as when you met me today because you've already been a frog for quite a while.

Pollywog: You're amazing Tadpole, er, Bullfrog. You know so much. But why did it take you so long to tell me that I am really a frog?

Bullfrog: Polly, just because it took you a long time to see who you really are, it's no reflection on me. I wanted you to see for yourself.

Pollywog: I guess you're right. Well, I've got to go. Thanks for everything, Bullfrog. I can't wait to tell all my friends.

Bullfrog: Uh, Pollywog, I think they already know. Anyway, good-bye and good luck.

Pollywog: Bye, bye, Bullfrog.

ADULT AMPHIBIAN	TYPE OF TANK	FOOD
Mudpuppy	large aquarium with aerating unit (no land)	worms, fish, insects
Jefferson salamander	woodland terrarium	earthworms, mealworms
Blue-spotted salamander	woodland terrarium	earthworms, mealworms
Marbled salamander	woodland terrarium	earthworms, insects
Spotted salamander	woodland terrarium	earthworms, mealworms, insects
Red-spotted newt	eft stage: woodland terrarium newt stage: aquarium with water; aerating unit not necessary	eft: small insects, small earthworms newt: small water insects and mosquito larvae
Northern dusky salamander	must have cooled, aerated water	insects, insect larvae, worms, snails
Red-backed salamander	woodland terrarium	small earthworms, fruit flies, other small insects
Four-toed salamander	woodland terrarium with sphagnum moss	insects
Spring salamander	must have cooled, aerated water	insects, earthworms
Two-lined salamander	must have cooled, aerated water	insects, insect larvae, earthworms
Eastern spadefoot toad	woodland terrarium, burrows constantly	earthworms, insect larvae
American toad	woodland terrarium	earthworms, insects
Fowler's toad	woodland terrarium	earthworms, insects
Spring peeper	woodland terrarium	small insects, small worms
Gray tree frog	woodland terrarium	insects, earthworms, mealworms
Bullfrog	semiaquatic	insects, earthworms, smaller frogs, salamanders
Mink frog	semiaquatic	earthworms, insects, smaller frogs
Green frog	semiaquatic	earthworms, insects, smaller frogs
Northern leopard frog	woodland terrarium	earthworms, insects
Pickerel frog	woodland terrarium: keep alone because of poisonous skin secretions	earthworms, insects
Wood frog	woodland terrarium	earthworms, slugs, insects

Figure 10-5. Food and habitat requirements for some common amphibians. Used with permission from Anne Orth Epple, The Amphibians of New England. *Camden, Maine: Down East Books, 1983, 126–29.*

Egg-Siting Encounter: From Eggs to Legs

ACTIVITY: Collect a small number of wood frog or toad eggs if it is legal to do so in your state or province. Keep, care for and observe them until they hatch into larvae. Raise the larvae to the froglet or toadlet (immature adolescent) stage and study them as they grow. Then set them free.

GOAL: Experience and understand the developmental stages of an amphibian from egg to larva and froglet or toadlet.

AGE: Younger children and older children

MATERIALS: Supplies needed for an aquarium and

terrarium as described on pages 23 to 24 in Chapter 2, dip net or scoop for collecting the eggs, two collecting pails, pond water from the eggs' home pond or pool, algae-covered rocks and sticks, aquatic plants, stones and/or floating sticks to create dry habitat, appropriate food as described in Figure 10-5, a copy of Figure 10-5, pencils, paper, crayons, camera, film.

PROCEDURE: Set up an aquarium beforehand as described on pages 23 to 24 in Chapter 2. A large goldfish bowl or wide-mouthed glass jar will do. Go out to a nearby pond or vernal pool in early to late spring, soon after the first spring peepers, chorus frogs and wood frogs or other early frogs start calling. Look for the jelly-like masses of wood frog eggs that are deposited early each spring, or the double strings of clear to cloudy gelatinous toad eggs. Collecting salamander eggs from streams, where most salamanders live, is not recommended because special aerating equipment is needed to raise them. Do not collect eggs other than those of toads or the wood frog because it is difficult to raise many other kinds of amphibian eggs. Also, some amphibians take much longer than a few months to reach the froglet stage.

Fill a clean pail half full with water from the pond or pool the eggs are found in. Now carefully place several dozen eggs of the same kind into the pail. Collect only from ponds and pools where the eggs are abundant. Add some small aquatic plants and/or algae to this pail. Now fill the second pail with water from the same location in the pond from which you gathered the eggs.

Fill the aquarium half full with water from the pond or pool. Gently submerge the edge of the pail in the aquarium and let the eggs float out. Then pour in the rest of the water. Place this aquarium/incubator in a shady, warm place out of direct sunlight. Change the water and plants every third day to keep the habitat clean and healthy. Now watch the eggs as they grow, change shape and finally begin to squirm and wiggle.

Keep the first dozen or so larvae that hatch and return the rest of the unhatched eggs to their home pond or pool.

Frog and toad larvae will need algae to eat. Keep them supplied with algae-coated rocks and sticks and keep changing the water at around three-day intervals, using only water from the home pool.

As the larvae grow and develop lungs add some stones with tops exposed above the water, and/or some floating sticks into the aquarium. Once the animals develop legs and become froglets (immature adolescents), they can be placed in a terrarium containing a plate of water. Feed them insects, worms, wood lice and other gradually larger food as they

develop. Consult the chart (Figure 10-5) for the specific habitat and food requirements of some common amphibians.

As the eggs, larvae and froglets develop have the children observe and record—in pictures, charts and words—the growth of the animals. Once the froglets have developed, have the children compile reports, complete with illustrations and photographs, chronicling the journey from egg to froglet. Have them write a story about this journey and title it "From Eggs to Legs," or some other title of their choosing.

Finally, hold a release ceremony back at the animals' home pond. Thank the amphibians for their gift of learning and appreciation as they are gently released into a quiet pool.

Frog Tongue Flick

ACTIVITY: Watch a frog's or toad's tongue as it is feeding. Create a brief moving picture showing in slow motion how the tongue works.

GOALS: Appreciate and experience the speed and accuracy of the feeding action of a frog's or toad's tongue. Learn how to create a simple motion picture.

AGE: Younger children and older children

MATERIALS: Frog or toad and habitat (see Chapter 2, pages 23 to 24 for habitat instructions), food (see Figure 10-5), 4 x 6 inch (10.2 x 15.2 centimeter) index cards, a copy of Figure 10-6 for each child (younger children), pencils, crayons, staples.

PROCEDURE: Have the children observe a frog or toad raised during the "Egg-Siting Encounter: From Eggs to Legs" activity in this chapter, or a different animal caught by the children on a field trip. (See Chapter 2, pages 21 to 24 for tips on catching and keeping animals.) Frogs can be caught at a local pond, while toads are often found living under a rock, log or bush near the home, learning center or in a nearby park.

Have the children closely observe the frog or toad while it is feeding. Describe how the sticky tongue is attached inside the front of the lower jaw and that the tip is somewhat forked. When it is not being used the tongue rests backward, pointing down the throat. To catch prey the tongue flicks out of the mouth and picks off the food with the sticky tip. Mention that toads are toothless and frogs have small teeth on their upper jaws used to hold the prey while it is being swallowed whole, not to chew it. *Neither frogs nor toads bite humans!*

Figure 10-6. Frog Tongue Flick.

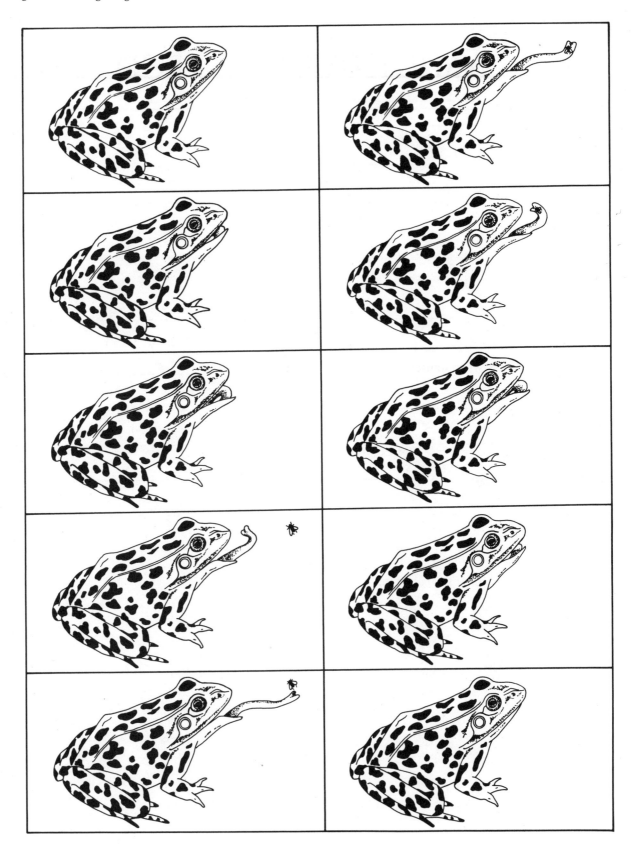

Figure 10-7

AMPHIBIAN WATCH

Date: _____

Time: _____

Location:_____

Name of Observer: _____

Air Temperature:_____°F   or   _____°C

Animal sighted: _____

Activities of animal when sighted: _____

_____

_____

_____

_____

_____

Rough field sketch of animal showing identifying marks:

If you are working with older children, have them draw pictures of a frog's or toad's tongue as it moves from the resting position, to catching its prey and back again. These pictures must show a gradual change in position, must be close to the same size on each card and must be drawn in the same place and position on each card. Figure 10-6 shows ten stages of the tongue in action. Ideally, children should create at least twenty sequential pictures including all of those shown in Figure 10-6 as well as the various stages of movement in between the stages shown in Figure 10-6.

With younger children, simply make copies of Figure 10-6, then have each child cut out the ten "frames" of the movie and paste each one of these onto a separate index card to create a complete sequential deck.

Once the illustrations are completed and placed in order, have the children hold one side of the illustrated deck of index cards tightly (or it can be stapled) and flip the cards in sequence using the open end of the stack. They will see a moving picture of a frog or toad tongue in action! Don't forget to tell them that this is how cartoons are made!

Amphibian Alert

ACTIVITY: Monitor and record amphibian sightings in your area. Take appropriate action for protecting local populations of amphibians.
GOALS: Acquire skills in observing and keeping field records of animal sightings. Realize the importance of records in monitoring animal populations over time. Understand how to respond to protect local amphibians.
AGE: Older children
MATERIALS: Chalk and chalkboard or felt-tipped markers and newsprint, topographic maps, transportation for the group, copies of the "Amphibian Watch" sheets (Figure 10-7), pencils, binoculars, hand lenses, thermometers, field identification and natural history guides to amphibians, flashlights, lined paper, tape recorder, tape of amphibians calling (available at natural history supply shops and bookstores), envelopes, stamps, other supplies as needed for additional projects that are undertaken.
PROCEDURE: Use the human impact section near the end of the "Discussion" section for this chapter as a springboard for exploring this issue with the children. Make an appointment to interview the appropriate naturalist, curator or other expert at a local Audubon society, natural history museum, environmental center or state or provincial nongame wildlife

agency. Prior to the interview, brainstorm with the children to generate a list of questions to ask the amphibian expert. Bring the children in to ask this amphibian expert some questions, such as inquiring about the status of amphibian populations in the area, certain species the children are interested in, publications in which to learn more and keep up with amphibian news, the location of important amphibian breeding grounds and actions that the children can take to preserve amphibians.

Use topographic maps to locate important amphibian habitat within a 1/2- to 1-mile (.8- to 1.6-kilometer) radius of the home or learning center. Use a larger radius if habitat is scarce. Before visiting the sites play some recordings of the amphibian calls they may expect to hear there. Lead seasonal field trips to these sites and have the children record their sightings using the "Amphibian Watch" sheets provided in Figure 10-7. Use the visits as exciting learning encounters to view and learn about local amphibians. Have the children send these records to a local conservation group or agency.

In some locations you will find breeding grounds where each spring, or during the wet season in arid regions, hundreds, perhaps thousands of amphibians emerge and migrate to breed. Lead a daytime or nighttime visit to this or these sites using binoculars, hand lenses and flashlights to observe the courtship and mating rituals. Some common explosive spring breeders are wood frogs, spring peepers and spotted salamanders. Countless numbers of amphibians are killed on roadways near these sites each spring. Work with local traffic authorities to set up a safe roadblock or traffic rerouting system on crucial mating nights. Help the children explore raising funds and environmental awareness to have some small tunnels installed under roadways where crucial amphibian crossings occur, as is done in some European and North American communities for toads.

Write to the World Wildlife Fund, Canadian Wildlife Federation, National Wildlife Federation, National Audubon Society and other private and government conservation groups for ideas on how to help amphibian populations throughout North America.[4] Compile a list of additional projects to get involved with using information and the children's own ideas.

EXTENDING THE EXPERIENCE
• *Collect Calls.* Listen to breeding amphibians calling and make up your own words, phrases and music that mimic those calls. Write down and/or record your phrases and songs.

• Make up a matching game to pair amphibian pictures with phrases or music identifying their calls.

• Play a game of leap frog. See how far the children can leap from a squatting position. Discuss how powerful a frog's or toad's hind leg muscles must be in order to propel it so far. A northern leopard frog has been known to jump 44 inches (3.7 feet or 1.1 meters) horizontally, which is equivalent to a child who is 4 feet (1.2 meters) tall leaping nearly 55 feet (17 meters)!

• Help monitor acid rain and support strong air pollution control laws to prevent the cause of this serious environmental problem. Contact the National Audubon Society, Citizens Acid Rain Monitoring Network, 950 Third Avenue, New York, NY, 10022; (212) 832-3200. In Canada, contact Pollution Probe, 12 Madison Avenue, Toronto, Ontario M5R 2S1; (416) 926-1907.

• Adapt the activity in Chapter 11 called "By the Skin of Their Scales: Conserving Reptiles" for use with amphibians.

NOTES

1. See Chapter 6 for more information and activities on amphibians, hibernation and dormancy.
2. Roger Conant, *A Field Guide to Reptiles and Amphibians* (Peterson Field Guide Series) (Boston: Houghton Mifflin, 1975), 13-14.
3. Thomas F. Tyning, *A Guide to Amphibians and Reptiles* (Stokes Nature Guides) (Boston: Little, Brown and Company, 1990), 6.
4. In the United States write to:
   World Wildlife Fund
   1250 Twenty-fourth Street, NW
   Washington, D.C. 20037
   (202) 293-4800

   National Wildlife Federation
   1412 Sixteenth Street, NW
   Washington, D.C. 20036-2266
   (703) 790-4000

   The Nature Conservancy
   1815 North Lynn Street
   Arlington, VA 22209
   (703) 841-5300

National Audubon Society
950 Third Avenue
New York, NY 10022
(212) 546-9119

U.S. Department of the Interior
Fish and Wildlife Service
Washington, D.C. 20240
(202) 208-4717

State Conservation Agencies

In Canada write to:
   World Wildlife Fund
   90 Eglington Avenue East, Suite 504
   Toronto, Ontario M4P 2Z7
   (416) 489-8800

   Canadian Wildlife Federation
   1673 Carling Avenue
   Ottawa, Ontario K2A 3Z1
   (613) 725-2191

   Canadian Wildlife Service
   c/o Environment Canada
   Ottawa, Ontario K1A 0H3
   (819) 997-1301

   Canadian Nature Federation
   453 Sussex Drive
   Ottawa, Ontario K1N 6Z4
   (613) 238-6154

   Fondation pour la Sauvegarde des Espèces Menacées
   8191 Avenue du Zoo
   Charlesbourg, Québec G1G 4G4
   (418) 622-0595

Provincial Conservation Agencies

CHAPTER 11

✤ How Poison Came Into the World ✤

(Choctaw—Southeast)

Back when the world was new, there was a certain plant that grew in the shallow water of the bayous. It grew in the places where the Choctaw people would come to bathe or swim. This vine was very poisonous and whenever the people touched this vine, they would become very sick and die.

This vine liked the Choctaw people and felt sorry for them. It did not want to cause them so much suffering. It could not show itself to them, because it was its nature to grow beneath the surface. So it decided to give its poison away. It called together the chiefs of the small people of the swamps—the bees, wasps and snakes. It told them that it wished to give up its poison.

Those small creatures held council together about the vine's offer. Until then, they had no poison and they were often stepped on by others. They agreed that they would share the poison.

Wasp spoke first. "I will take a small part of your poison," it said. "Then I will be able to defend my nest. But I will warn the people by buzzing close to them before I poison them. I will keep the poison in my tail."

Bee was next. "I, too, will take a small part of your poison," it said. "I will use it to defend my hive. I will warn the people away before I poison them and even if I should have to use my poison, it will kill me to use it, so I will use it carefully."

Water Moccasin spoke. "I will take some of your poison. I will only use it if people step on me. I will hold it in my mouth and when I open my mouth people will see how white it is and know that they should avoid me."

Last of all, Rattlesnake spoke. "I will take a good measure of your poison," he said. "I will take all that remains. I will hold it in my mouth, too. Before I strike anyone, I will use my tail to warn them. *Intesha, intesha, intesha, intesha.* That is the sound I will make to let them know they are too close."

So it was done. The vine gave up its poison to the bees and wasps, the water moccasin and the rattlesnake. Now the shallow waters of the bayous were safe for the Choctaw people and where once that vine had poison, now it had flowers. From then on, only those who were foolish and did not heed the warnings of the small ones who took the vine's poison were hurt.

The vine called together the chiefs of the small people of the swamps—the bees, wasps and snakes. It told them that it wished to give up its poison.

The Boy and the Rattlesnake

(Apache—Southwest)

Once there was a boy who was very soft-hearted. One morning, as he was walking along he saw a rattlesnake by the side of the road. There had been an early frost the night before and the snake had been caught out in it. The snake was stiff with the cold. The boy stopped to look at it, feeling sorry for the snake. Then a wonderful thing happened. The snake opened up its mouth and spoke to him.

"Help me," the rattlesnake said in a pitiful voice. "Pick me up, warm me or I will die."

"But if I pick you up, you will bite me," the boy said.

"No," said the snake, "I will not bite you. Pick me up, hold me close to you and warm me or I will die."

So the boy took pity on the snake. He picked it up. He held it close to him so that it would be warmed by his body. The snake grew warmer and less stiff and then, suddenly, it twisted in the boy's hands and—WHAH! It bit the boy on his arm. The boy dropped the snake and grasped his arm.

"Why did you bite me?" the boy said. "You said you would not bite me if I picked you up."

"That is so," said the snake, "but when you picked me up, you knew I was a rattlesnake."

DISCUSSION

Human beings have created images and beliefs about animals based on whether or not any particular animal is beautiful, cute or even homely in an endearing way. We also tend to put great stock in an animal's interactions with humans—warming to those we perceive as being friendly, nonthreatening or even helpful, and cowering from animals that can be dangerous if we do not respect their territory or means of existence. Our stories and myths develop these impressions even further, extending our acceptance or fear of animals, well-founded or otherwise, into the realm of fantasy. But animals are not made to appeal to human beings, their appearance is the result of a body and behavior that help to ensure survival. When it comes to our *aesthetic* appreciation of animals, beauty is in the eye of the beholder and truth is only revealed when we look beneath the surface.

Acting on our beliefs about animals without looking at them rationally often leads us to making *stereotypical* assumptions that are not necessarily accurate, and to taking actions that are often unwise. It is important to know what things in this world may, by their very nature, do harm to us if we get too close to them. Not only is this Apache story "The Boy and the Rattlesnake" told to Native

North American children to remind them to admire and respect such beautiful but potentially harmful fellow beings as the rattlesnake from a distance, it is a reminder that life always holds some dangers. By choosing wisely what to pick up, we may make our lives a little less dangerous. This story is also being widely used in drug and alcohol counseling with Native North American children. Just like the snake, alcohol and drugs may look good and we may tell ourselves that they will not hurt us, but they are capable of hurting us if treated unwisely.

The Choctaw story "How Poison Came Into the World" is also a good one for introducing this chapter on reptiles. Few animals are more frequently persecuted simply because people do not understand them, and even when they do, are not certain of how to act wisely when around them. As the story tells us, the leaders of the "small people" of the swamps, the bee, wasp, cottonmouth (water moccasin) and rattlesnake, were all given poison as a means of protecting themselves. And each of them issues a warning before using that poison. It is those who do not heed their warning or who do not understand the language of the animals who get hurt. When this happens, the animal is blamed. And that animal is often a reptile.

"Help me," the rattlesnake said in a pitiful voice. "Pick me up, warm me or I will die."

Reptiles

From turtles to crocodiles and from lizards to snakes, reptiles have captured the human imagination. Yet these amazing animals have been around far longer than humankind. About 250 million years ago, during the Paleozoic Era, reptiles became the first vertebrate animals to live a wholly terrestrial existence. Reptiles were the first animals to evolve the use of shelled eggs that provide the embryo with a tiny aquatic environment in which to develop away from the protection of the water. These early reptilian ancestors are thought to have come up on land in pursuit of insects to eat.

Turtles and crocodiles survived right through the great extinction of the dinosaurs at the end of the Cretaceous period around 63 million years ago. These two groups, oldest among the reptiles, have remained relatively unchanged for over 150 million years. Dinosaurs would likely be considered the most terrifying animals in the world were they alive today, yet they are one of the most popular groups of reptiles. They have even turned up as adorable creatures in recent cartoons and as cute, cuddly dolls on toy store shelves. One current thought is that dinosaurs became extinct when a gargantuan meteorite struck Earth. The impact caused such cataclysmic eruptions and sent so much dirt, dust, ash and other debris into the air that sunlight was blocked out for several years. Without the sun, many green plants died off and along with them, the great beasts that ate them, as well as their predators.

The long-term survival of other reptiles bears witness to their highly successful adaptations. Feathers and eggs, two adaptations that we tend to associate with birds, really originated among the early reptiles from which birds evolved. Feathers developed from reptilian (dinosaur) scales and have become diverse in color, shape and function among the birds. As many people now know, birds are thought to have evolved either from prehistoric, feathered dinosaurs or similar early reptiles that first developed the power of flight among vertebrate animals.

There are now over six thousand species of reptiles living around the world in nearly every kind of environment except extremely cold places. Virtually no reptiles live at high altitudes, while only three species can be found surviving the frigid chill of the Arctic. Some reptiles, such as the crocodilians (crocodiles, alligators and caimans), sea turtles and snakes of both fresh water and the sea, have returned to a life in an aquatic environment.

The study of reptiles is one branch of *herpetology*, along with the study of amphibians. *Reptiles* are cold-blooded vertebrate animals that are distinguished from other vertebrates by having:

- *skin covered with tough scales;*
- *claws* on their toes;
- *eggs with a flexible, leathery shell; and*
- *at least one lung* because they must breathe oxygen from the air.

FOOD AND FEEDING. Turtles, snakes, lizards and crocodiles are the major groups among reptiles. Reptiles eat a variety of food, ranging from plants to large animals. Turtles are omnivorous, eating plants and animals, both living and dead. These can range from tadpoles, fish, leeches and frogs to aquatic plants, berries and leaves. The major limiting factor among snakes is the size of the prey relative to the snake. Snakes will eat any living prey that is small enough to catch and swallow, including other snakes. Garter snakes (Figure 11-1) prefer to dine on earthworms, insects, frogs, toads and nestling birds. Fish and tadpoles often fall prey to water snakes. Some snakes are fond of eating eggs as well. Insects are the main source of food for most lizards along with earthworms, other small invertebrates, frogs and young mice. Horned lizards, however, subsist mostly on ants. The 2-foot- (61.0-centimeter-) long gila monster of the southwestern deserts eats bird eggs, mice, ground squirrels and other rodents, hares, rabbits and even Gambel's quail. Few predators are as feared as American crocodiles and American alligators of the southeastern United States. With one gulp they will eat small animals whole. If a bird or mammal is larger it will often be held underwater first. Crocodiles are known to guard a large prey for up to several days after it has been killed. Their food ranges from fish to other reptiles, mammals, birds, amphibians and even snails.

REPRODUCTION. Although all reptiles mate so that the embryo is fertilized internally, their reproductive strategies vary widely from that point on. Some simply lay eggs, bury them and abandon them. Others bear live young once the eggs have hatched inside, while some species produce live young without the aid of a shelled egg. Some female turtles can lay fertile eggs up to four years after their last mating.

Among reptiles, only female crocodilians and a few lizards and snakes are known to care for the eggs and young. The female American alligator, for instance, buries the egg in a nest of sand or plant material and stays nearby to guard them against predators such as raccoons and black bears. When the young begin to make sounds

Figure 11-1. Garter snakes, such as this eastern garter snake, feed on frogs, toads, earthworms, insects and, sometimes, small nestling birds. The snake in this photograph is seen with just the tip of its forked tongue protruding. A snake uses its tongue as a highly sensitive device for smelling and tasting. The tongue is flicked in and out of a small opening in the front of the mouth in order to pick up molecules of taste and scent in the air. When drawn back into the mouth, the tips of the tongue are inserted into a pair of cavities called the Jacobson's organ *on the roof of the mouth. Size: 18–26 inches (45.7–66.0 centimeters). Photo by Alan C. Graham.*

as they hatch, their mother uses her feet to scrape off the soil to expose the eggs so the young do not have to dig themselves out. Incredibly, she then lifts the newborn and hatching young out of the nest with her mouth and carries them gently down to the water where she releases them. Sometimes she even washes the pieces of egg from the babies or those nearly out of the shell by holding them gently between her jaws and swishing water around in her mouth for a bath!

ADAPTATIONS TO THE SEASONS. Being cold-blooded, reptiles must adjust their behavioral rhythms to maintain body temperatures in the midst of the vagaries of weather and season, as the child in the story "The Boy and the Rattlesnake" discovered. *Basking* helps them to maintain their body temperature by absorbing heat from the sun. Each reptile maintains an optimal body temperature that aids in digestion, as well as keeping it alert, active and mobile, as when it needs to escape from a predator. The increased heat of basking helps to keep the reptiles' skin or shell free of diseases, parasites and, among

aquatic turtles, decreases the growth of algae on the shell. It has been discovered that turtles are able to use the sunlight to make vitamin D.

Even among sun-loving reptiles it is possible to have too much of a good thing. Some desert reptiles, like the western diamondback rattlesnake and the desert tortoise, live in a burrow to avoid the hot, drying desert sun. The horned lizard can be seen resting buried in the sand with only its head exposed.

In temperate climates farther north reptiles respond to seasonal extremes in ways that reveal one advantage of cold-bloodedness: a slow metabolism that reduces dietary needs. Reptiles can become dormant for short periods of a few days to a few weeks or months, or they can overwinter for an entire season.[1] Most reptiles become dormant during the winter but there are exceptions and extremes. In the East, the spotted turtle may often become dormant to avoid July's heat, and will sometimes even remain dormant through the rest of the summer and

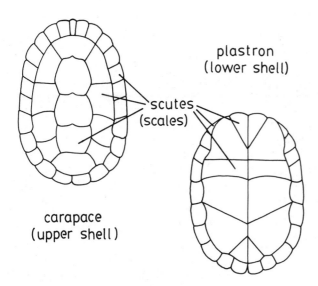

Figure 11-2. A turtle's shell and its parts.

into the winter, only to emerge the following spring. A directly opposite reaction to the cold is found among the widespread painted turtle, which often remains active year-round and can occasionally be seen swimming around beneath the clear ice of a pond! Garter snakes will hibernate alone or, where burrows are scarce, in groups of up to several thousand. Some have even been found hibernating underwater at the edge of ponds.

A closer look at some of the remarkable adaptations of each reptilian group reveals the great variety that exists both within and between them.

TURTLES. *Turtles*, as a group, are more ancient than any other vertebrate animals alive today. As individuals they are the oldest living animals on Earth. Some sea turtles and land tortoises can live over one hundred years. Of the 250 species found around the world, approximately 48 live in the United States. The three main North American groups include the snapping turtles, mud and musk turtles, and the twenty-six species of pond and marsh turtles, such as the painted turtle, box turtle and slider. The more specific term of *tortoise* usually refers to turtles that live on land with large limbs that lack webbing between the toes. The small turtles that are hunted for food are often called *terrapins*.

A turtle's *shell* consists of a solidly fused set of bones made up of the front and back rib cages, covered by *scutes* or *plates* that are composed of a fingernail-like material (Figure 11-2). These scutes are shed and replaced as the shell grows. The upper shell is called the *carapace* and the lower is called the *plastron*. Turtles have a sharp beak and scales covering their exposed skin. The soft-shelled turtles have a flexible, leathery shell covered entirely by skin.

While turtles do not possess any striking sensory adaptations as a group, there are some amazing survival strategies found among them. They hear well and are able to sense vibrations in the water through their skin and shell. Turtles can see colors and have a keen sense of smell. Snappers hunt mostly by sight and smell. No turtles possess vocal chords and sounds are limited to some whistling, grunts and the hissing of air when the body is pulled quickly into the shell. The alligator snapper, North America's largest freshwater turtle, uses a worm-like lure on its tongue, which turns pinkish and wiggles when active, to lure fish into its gaping mouth. Some turtles can live up to two years between meals.

Sea turtles are fully aquatic reptiles that come ashore solely to dig a nest and lay their eggs. They include the four shelled sea turtles, the green turtle, hawksbill, loggerhead and ridley turtle. The leatherback is another sea turtle that can weigh up to 1,500 pounds (680.4 kilograms). Green turtles are herbivorous and travel up to 1,200 miles (1,931.2 kilometers) between their nesting beaches and feeding grounds where they graze on beds of turtle grass. During these migrations they can maintain a steady course over long stretches of open ocean, reaching their home beaches precisely after a thousand-mile journey. While it is known that smell does play some role in their incredible ability to orient, the sun and stars *may* also help them to navigate. Whereas sea turtles once invaded their nest beaches by the tens of thousands, they are now among the most endangered animals in the world.[2]

SNAKES. Nowhere does fact and fiction about an animal become so confused in peoples' minds as with snakes. People once believed that a snake held its tail in its mouth, formed a loop and rolled downhill. Some *still* believe the myth that milk snakes sneak into barns at night to suck milk from a cow. Milk snakes do frequent barns, but the result is fewer rats and mice (their favored food), *not* milked cows!

In fact, when snakes see a human being they *generally* slither away and hide. The hog-nosed snake even plays opossum—it goes belly-up, opens its mouth wide and even convulses to feign death! Of course, if cornered or stepped on a snake may strike in self-defense, so it is best to keep your distance and watch them from afar. Handling them can injure them internally and even damage developing embryos.

There are about 2,400 species of snakes in the world, ranging from some species that are full-grown at 5 inches (12.7 centimeters) to 30-foot (9.1-meter) pythons. In some regions there are no snakes at all, including Antarctica,

Figure 11–3. The head of a pit viper. Notice the "pit" between the eye and nostril. This sense organ detects minute temperature differences in the snake's environment, enabling the snake to locate the body heat of its prey and strike with a great deal of precision. even in the dark.

New Zealand, Ireland, Iceland and in extreme arctic environments.

Snakes have a head, body, tail and short neck that allows the head to turn somewhat. *Scales,* which are either smooth or bear a ridge or *keel* to lend a rough appearance, cover them entirely. The skin is shed from head to tail as the snake grows, often in one piece and turns inside out in the process. Snakes come in all colors and patterns. There is an opening or *cloaca* used for excretion, mating and laying eggs. Most snake's eyes have round pupils. Many venomous snakes have vertical pupils, but these can appear roundish in low light. Snakes do not have eyelids. The eyes are covered with a clear membrane called a *spectacle.* Snakes never blink. Lizards, however, *do* have eyelids, they also have legs and external ear openings—both of which snakes lack.

All snakes are carnivorous. They have specialized lower jaws that unhinge at the back and stretch at the chin, where the front of the two jawbones is connected by an elastic muscle. Muscles control each side of the jaw separately so an animal can be "walked in" by pulling it alternately with one side, then the other. Snakes are famous for eating prey even larger in diameter than their body! The prey is held by sharp teeth that curve backward and are found on both the upper and lower jaws. Pit vipers, such as the rattlesnake, also have two hollow fangs attached to the upper jaw through which venom is injected. Pit vipers poison or paralyze their prey, while other snakes either catch the victim and swallow it whole (and often still alive) or constrict the animal until it suffocates before it is eaten. Constrictors do not crush their victims.

Snakes find their prey with a keen sense of smell. Their forked tongues are "flicked" outward where minute particles adhere to them. The tongue is then drawn in and inserted into the *Jacobson's organ* in the roof of the mouth—a highly sensitive odor- and taste-detecting device. Pit vipers have a "pit" or depression between each eye and nostril that can detect extremely small temperature differences from one to several feet away (Figure 11-3). This *pit organ* allows vipers to pinpoint their prey with a high degree of precision even in total darkness.

Some snakes, such as the garter, water snake, copperhead and timber rattler, bear live young. Others, such as the milk snake and hog-nosed snake, lay eggs.

Many people are puzzled by the speed and agility with which a legless snake moves. Snakes travel forward by either pushing off from several contact points along the waves of its body, or by bending its belly scales forward and pulling its skin and body to follow. The sidewinder lifts and throws loops of its body forward and sideways in successive loops.

LIZARDS. Lizards number over three thousand species worldwide, living in habitats ranging from oceans to desert to rain forest. There are only around 115 species in North America, which are concentrated in the south and west. These range from the 2-foot (61-centimeter) gila monster to iguanids, skinks, anoles and horned lizards. The venomous gila monster is one of only two poisonous lizards on Earth.

Unlike salamanders, *lizards* have dry, scaly skin, claws on their feet and external ear openings. As they grow their old skin is sloughed off in patches. Lizards' eyes are keen at

Figure 11–4. The broad, rounded snout of the American alligator is a familiar site in the freshwater wetlands of the southeastern United States. Unlike its close relative, the endangered American crocodile which largely inhabits saltwater environments, the alligator has frequent encounters with human beings. As the alligator in this photograph demonstrated when it walked right by the photographer's tripod, these animals are not always shy! The photographer was unharmed. Size: 6–16-1/2 feet (1.8–5.0 meters). Photo by Cecil B. Hoisington.

detecting even the slightest movement. They hear well and are sensitive to vibrations in the ground. They make no sounds of their own, however, except for a few species. Lizards detect odors much like snakes do. Some lizards, like the famous chameleon, can change color to blend in with their environment and be well *camouflaged*.

Tails are the lizard's primary claim to fame—tails that some species easily part with. The long, brightly colored tail of a skink, for instance, helps it to keep its balance on tree branches and serves as a means of display. If caught by the tail, however, the tail snaps off and is left wiggling while the skink scampers off. These amazing tails, which also serve to store fat during lean times, can grow back!

CROCODILIANS. Alligators and crocodiles have won a place of mythic proportion in the imaginations of North Americans. The *American alligator* can grow to be 10 feet (3 meters) long, while the rare *American crocodile* has been known to reach nearly 20 feet (6.1 meters) in length. Alligators are capable of producing a loud hissing when they are threatened, and a loud roar during the mating season. The predaceous crocodilians, of which there are about twenty-two species worldwide, have a dinosaur-like appearance with several rows of large, hard plates running down their back and tail, and are famous for being able to float with only their eyes and nostrils exposed above water. The skin on their bellies is soft. Unlike the three-chambered heart of other reptiles, crocodilians have a four-chambered heart. Four webbed toes on each rear foot are used to keep them from sinking into the soft muds. Their immense tail propels them along while swimming. American alligators, which have a wide, blunt snout, inhabit mostly freshwater wetlands (Figure 11-4). The American crocodile sports a long, narrow snout and is most common in saltwater environments.

Although the American alligator and American crocodile were once widespread throughout the southeastern United States, they are rarely found now outside of parks and preserves. The American crocodile only occurs in extreme southern Florida and is quite rare. These fascinating, yet, at times, dangerous animals were hunted to near extinction to be sold for leather to make shoes and purses, among other commercial ventures. Even so, they have often been killed simply out of fear and ignorance.

Conservation of Reptiles

It seems that reptiles face a difficult fight to survive whether they are disdained or well loved. Beyond their natural predators, such as foxes and raccoons which love to dine on reptilian eggs, people have had a significant impact in driving many species to scarcity and some to the verge of extinction. While snakes and alligators are frequently killed out of fear, the turtles, lizards and other reptiles of which people are fond run the danger of being collected and spending their lives as a pet in the few square feet of someone's cage. Over 2 million reptiles are known to have been collected for pets in one particular year. Box turtles and sliders are especially favored. Snapping turtles and sea turtles have been hunted for food for many years. Other forces that are decimating reptile populations include:

- *habitat destruction*, especially wetlands in the southeast and deserts in the southwest
- *road kills*, as a result of reptile crossings because many roads are built through prime reptile habitat, and because reptiles have an affinity for the warm, dark pavement
- *egg collecting* as a source of income
- *ingestion of ocean trash*
- *capture of sea turtles in nets used by shrimp boats*

Obviously, it is going to take conscious, concerted efforts to ensure that these intriguing animals will survive into the future. Our love-hate relationship with reptiles needs to be healed—it has been to their detriment. Despite the numerous prejudices and stereotypes that people have ascribed to reptiles over the years, human beings can choose to respond in a positive way to alleviate the current plight of these remarkable animals.

QUESTIONS

1. The boy in "The Boy and the Rattlesnake" is trying to help the rattlesnake when he picks it up, but he makes a mistake in doing so. Why is it a mistake? Name times that we should stay clear of animals, and animals we should avoid getting too close to.

2. Why does the rattlesnake bite the boy even though the boy had just helped him?

3. In the story "How Poison Came Into the World," the wasp, bee, water moccasin and rattlesnake are all given poison by the vine. How do they intend to use this poison? What does each of them do to warn people of the poison? What happens to a bee (honeybee) when it stings someone?

4. Which animals do you like? Why? Which ones do you not like? Why? Which ones are you afraid of? Why?

5. Why do animals have painful bites, stings and other defenses? What are some other animals that have these kinds of defenses? What would happen to them if they didn't have these defenses?

6. What are some popular stories and fairy tales that portray animals in a positive or negative way? Are the things these stories say about animals true?

7. What is a reptile? What makes a reptile different from other animals? How does a reptile's skin feel? Name some animals that are reptiles.

8. Were dinosaurs reptiles? What happened to the dinosaurs?

9. How are baby reptiles born? Do all reptiles lay eggs?

10. What do reptiles eat? How do they catch and eat their food?

11. Are reptiles warm-blooded or cold-blooded? How does a reptile stay warm? How do they survive the cold winter weather? What do they do when it becomes too hot and dry during the summer, or in the desert?

12. What does a turtle use its shell for? Can a turtle crawl out of its shell? How old can turtles live to be?

13. Why do snakes flick their tongues out? How can they eat prey that are bigger around than their own bodies? How does a snake move without feet?

14. Are there any lizards that live near you? How is a lizard different from a snake? How is a lizard different from a salamander? What is special about a lizard's tail?

15. Are there any crocodiles or alligators living near you? What do they eat?

16. What are some natural predators upon reptiles? Do any animals eat reptile eggs?

17. What are people doing to reptiles? How are we causing their numbers to decline lower and lower? Which reptiles are endangered? Which ones are already extinct?

18. Which reptiles especially need our help right now? What can we do to help save the reptiles?

ACTIVITIES
Reptilian Riddles

ACTIVITY: Listen to riddles. Guess what a reptile is and the identities of specific kinds of reptiles.
GOALS: Realize what distinguishes reptiles from other kinds of animals. Understand the characteristics of the different reptile groups. Identify some common reptiles.
AGE: Younger children and older cihldren
MATERIALS: Copy of the "Reptilian Riddles" from this activity, photographs and/or illustrations of some examples of animals from each reptile group.
PROCEDURE: Tell the children you are going to explore

a certain kind of animal, and that they are to guess which kind. Explain to them that you are going to read a riddle. Have them listen to the whole riddle and raise their hands *after* you have read it through completely if they think they know the answer. Read the following riddle:

What kind of animal
- has eggs with a soft, leathery shell?
- has claws on its toes?
- has no feathers?
- has skin covered with scales?
- has no fur?
- is cold-blooded?

If no one guesses "reptile" right away give more hints until someone guesses correctly. Then review the various characteristics of a reptile, identified in the riddle, in greater detail.

Now follow the same procedure with the following four riddles. Tell the children that the riddles identify reptiles from each of the four major groups of reptiles. The answer is given in parentheses after each riddle. Hold up some photographs and/or illustrations of reptiles from each group right after the children guess the answer to that particular riddle. Allow them to ask questions about each group of reptiles before moving on to the next riddle.

- I have a hard beak for catching food.
- My four legs are short but very strong.
- I live a very long time.
- When danger is near I can pull my head and legs into my house for safety.
- I have a short, pointed tail.
- I have a built-on house that I carry wherever I go.
- I walk along very slo-o-o-owly with my belly close to the ground.
  I am a (turtle).

- I flick my tongue to smell your scent.
- I am not commonly seen by many people.
- I have four legs.
- My body is long and thin.
- My kind usually eat a lot of insects.
- My scaly skin is shed in patches.
- If you try to grab me by the back end I will crawl away and leave you holding only my tail, which will break off in your hands and wiggle around.
  I am a (lizard).

- People are often afraid of me, but I usually crawl away when a person comes near.
- I do not have eyelids.
- Whenever I eat, it is always meat.
- I have the biggest mouth around for my size.
- I always gulp my food.
- I have a fork in my mouth and I stick it out to smell and taste.
- I have no legs but I move my long, thin body very fast.
- My skin of scales is shed in one piece.
  I am a (snake).

- I like to laze around in the swamp.
- I eat small and sometimes large animals, swallowing the smaller ones whole.
- When full grown I can be up to 10 feet (3.0 meters) long.
- My long tail, sharp teeth and bony plates cause some people to say I look like a dinosaur.
- My long, powerful tail is used for swimming.
- I can float with only my eyes and nostrils sticking out above the water.
  I am an (alligator).

Defenders of Defenses

ACTIVITY: (A) Find and observe reptiles and their many defenses and warnings that alert other animals of danger. (B) Create your own reptile with powerful defenses to ward off dangerous animals, and warnings that will signal other animals to keep away.
GOALS: Realize the number and kinds of defenses and warnings used by reptiles. Understand how these help to ensure their survival.
AGE: Younger children and older children
MATERIALS: (A) Index cards, pencils, crayons, colored pencils. (B) Construction paper, tape, glue, pipe cleaners, felt-tipped markers, crayons, balloons, egg cartons, toothpicks, scissors, other materials as needed.
PROCEDURE A: *Discovering Defenses.* Visit reptiles in the wild, at a pet store, at a zoo or in several of these locations. Observe them from a distance and search for the defenses they use to ward off danger, and the warnings (if any) that signal the defenses. These defenses range from passive forms like a turtle's shell or a lizard's snap-off tail to the active defenses of a snake's venom or a snapping

turtle's bite. Warnings can range from bright coloration to a rattlesnake's rattle.

Have the children make up index cards, each with an illustration of a reptile along with its defense(s) and warning(s) on one side, and a description of how these are designed and how they function on the other side. You could also take instant photographs of the animals and write the information on the back. Once these cards are completed—at least a dozen or more—have the children share their discoveries with the rest of the group. Allow time for a question-and-answer period.

Lead a discussion of the wisdom of watching dangerous animals from afar. Point out the beautiful colors, shapes and markings on many of these animals, and how it is best in nature to not interfere with a dangerous animal, but to leave it alone and enjoy it from a distance.
PROCEDURE B: *Designing Defenders.* Now have the children work in small groups of two or three to design the "ultimate defender." Place materials in several piles and have the children use their wildest imaginations to turn one of their group members into a fictitious animal with the best defenses they can design. Whatever they decide to do is fine. There are no limitations. Each animal must also be equipped with at least one warning to ward off other animals from the danger presented by the defense(s).

Once the children have finished have them share and demonstrate how their "ultimate defender" can protect itself, as well as how it will warn other animals of its dangerous defenses.

In the Eyes of a Rattlesnake

ACTIVITY: Go on a fantasy journey as a rattlesnake who encounters a human being. Discuss the ways that people might be viewed by rattlesnakes.
GOALS: Empathize with an animal by seeing the world from its point of view. Understand that human stereotypes of animals are often based on fear and other negative feelings. Realize that seeing beauty in an animal can be learned despite the fact that the animal may be dangerous, or simply not attractive or cute by human standards.
AGE: Younger children and older children
MATERIALS: Copy of "In the Eyes of a Rattlesnake," rattle, drum or other surface and striker to create the "thump, thump, thump" sound of the giant's footsteps.
PROCEDURE: Ask the children how they would feel and

react if they were walking in the desert and came across a rattlesnake that coiled up and began shaking its rattle. How would the rattlesnake feel? How do they feel about snakes in general? Do they think they are pretty? Ugly?

Have them lie on their backs, relax and close their eyes. They are about to imagine being a rattlesnake that has an encounter with a person. As you read this story, use a rattle to make the rattlesnake's warning and strike a drum or other surface to imitate the "thump, thump, thump" of the person's ("giant's") footsteps:

IN THE EYES OF A RATTLESNAKE

You are a sidewinder rattlesnake basking in the hot, dry desert air in front of a large rock. It is a very bright day. There are not many plants growing in the dusty, gravelly soil around you—a few juicy cacti with thorns and pretty flowers and some scraggly bushes with a few small leaves on them are all you see.

Your skin is bumpy with sandy-colored scales. You have no arms and legs. A slim tail tapers to a point at the far end of your long, thin body. Your head is flat and triangular from front to back and your eyes are on the top and sides of your head. You can see all around you by moving your head just a little bit. Almost all of your teeth are small, sharp and curved back. You have two upper fangs that are long, thin and hollow to inject poison when you bite. There is a small hole between each eye and nostril that you use for sensing the body heat of other animals while you are hunting.

Long scales run across your belly from side-to-side, while smaller scales overlap to cover your head, back, sides and tail. The end of your tail has eight hard pieces of old skin that join together to form a kind of rattle.

You continue to bask in the sun. Its heat feels good and warms you all over. There are no thoughts going through your mind. You are content there, basking.

Thump, thump, thump! The ground begins to vibrate with approaching footsteps in the distance. They become heavier and louder—thump, THUMP, THUMP! Suddenly, from around a huge boulder, an enormous animal appears. It is one hundred times taller than you are and has strange, loose-looking skin of all different shades. It has a squared-off head with a narrow rim encircling it and strange feet, each with one large toe.

It doesn't notice you. Those giant feet are coming right at you! You look behind to slither away, but the large rock blocks your path. You must defend yourself or risk dying under the giant's feet.

Quickly and smoothly you roll your body into a coil. You raise your head and pull it back, ready to strike. Intesha, intesha, intesha, the rattle on your tail begins to

vibrate a warning to the stranger. Every muscle in your body becomes tense and alert. You are full of fear.

As soon as your tail begins to rattle, the gargantuan stranger stops moving, looks down at you and becomes perfectly still. Ever so slowly it backs away—first one large foot, then the other—until it is a good distance from you. You can hear the grains of sand gritting beneath each slow, heavy footstep. Then, in an instant the giant turns and runs away—THUMP, THUMP, Thump, thump, thump—until it is gone.

Now your tense body begins to relax. You lower your head and tail, then uncoil a little. Once again you feel the nice warm sun on your body and a sense of peace comes over you. Still, you keep an eye on the spot where the stranger disappeared.

Ask the children to open their eyes when ready. Now have them answer some questions:

- How did it feel to be a rattlesnake?
- Did you enjoy sunning yourself on the sand?
- What did you feel when the person (giant) appeared?
- What did you want to do?
- If rattlesnakes could think and talk like people, what do you think they would say about us?
- How would people be portrayed in rattlesnake stories?
- What kinds of myths and legends would rattlesnakes have about human beings?
- In what ways would rattlesnakes find each other to be beautiful?
- Do you think there is anything beautiful about a rattlesnake?

Now share with the children the illustrations of a pit viper's pits (Figure 11-3) and of a rattlesnake in a defensive position, ready to strike (Figure 11-5).

Figure 11–5. This rattlesnake is in a defensive position, ready to strike.

Beauty in the Beast

ACTIVITY: Read some traditional Western animal stories and examine how and why animals are portrayed the way they are. Rewrite one of your favorite animal stories to depict the animal(s) in a more realistic way.

GOAL: Understand that human stereotypes of animals are often founded on feelings that have little to do with the true nature of animals in the wild.

AGE: Older children

MATERIALS: Books containing some of the traditional Western stories listed in this activity, or other animal stories of your choice, chalkboard and chalk or newsprint and felt-tipped markers, pencils, index cards, paper, books describing the natural history of the animal(s) being studied, crayons, markers, construction paper.

PROCEDURE: Many traditional fairy tales and many recent stories portray animals in certain stereotypical ways and roles. Such animals as the wolf, fox, spider, lion, rabbit, crocodile, bear, whale and snake are often depicted as being unrealistically aggressive or threatening or overly cute and friendly.

Choose one or more animals about which to examine our stereotypes and read several stories about that or these animals. Here is a list of some stories to choose from to share with the children:

- *Beauty and the Beast*
- *Who's Afraid of the Big Bad Wolf?*
- *Little Red Riding Hood*
- *Three Little Pigs*
- *The Wolf and the Three Kids*
- *Peter and the Wolf*
- *Peter Rabbit*
- *Peter Pan*
- *Bambi*
- *The Wizard of Oz*
- *Little Miss Muffet*
- *Charlotte's Web*
- *The Gingerbread Man*
- *The Fox and the Crow* (Aesop's Fable)
- *The Fox and the Grapes* (Aesop's Fable)
- *Reynard the Fox*
- *Goldilocks and the Three Bears*
- *Jonah and the Whale* (Old Testament in the *Bible*)
- *The Serpent in the Garden of Eden* (Old Testament in the *Bible*)

After you have shared the story, brainstorm with the children a list of character traits that the animal has in that story, for instance, hungry, mean, vicious, cute, beautiful, cuddly, scary, helpful or deceitful. Focus on how the animal is portrayed in both text and in the illustrations. Which animals are "good" and which are "bad" in the stories?

Now have the children read about and observe, if possible, the real natural history of that animal. Tell them to focus on compiling a set of cards describing the actual nature of that animal. Use all of these findings to write a report about the animal, including its habits for feeding, seeking shelter, getting water, catching prey, interacting with animals of its own kind as well as other kinds of animals and interaction with human beings. Share the findings of the report with the group. Ask them what about the *real* nature of that animal could have resulted in the stereotypes found in the stories. Ask them whether an animal is really beautiful or ugly, cute or vicious because people think so. Are there other eyes with which to see the animals, such as those of another of its kind?

It is time for the children to try using realistic eyes with which to view this animal. Have them rewrite and reillustrate the story or stories, so that the animal reacts and interacts as the children would imagine it's true nature would have it behave. Encourage them to illustrate their stories.

When the stories are finished ask each child to share her/his story and illustrations. Allow time for comments and reactions after each story is read.[3]

By the Skin of Their Scales: Conserving Reptiles

ACTIVITY: Learn about and practice a variety of conservation measures to help protect reptiles.

GOALS: Realize that the way we live our lives and the things we do that hurt reptiles as well as the things we fail to do to help reptiles have an impact on their numbers and survival worldwide. Learn and practice activities and ways of life that help to conserve reptiles.

AGE: Younger children and older children

MATERIALS: As needed for the specific project(s) chosen to conserve reptiles.

PROCEDURE: There are many ways that we can all help to assure the survival of turtles, lizards, snakes and crocodilians. Some of these actions may be local, regional or national, while others may involve reptiles, such as sea turtles, that are an international concern. Here are a few suggestions: (1) *Boycotts* are an effective way to put pressure on those people or companies who are engaged in activities that are harming reptiles. For instance, do not buy purses, shoes and other garments or objects made of reptile leather (skin). Alligators were once hunted nearly to extinction to satisfy the demand for alligator shoes and purses. Although the American alligator is once again fairly abundant in some areas due to rigorous conservation efforts, the American crocodile is still endangered. It is hard to discern whether a particular object was obtained from an animal hunted legally or from one killed by a poacher in North America or even overseas. Also be careful of the indirect ways that we can affect reptiles. As of this writing, endangered sea turtles, such as the Kemp's ridley turtle, are being inadvertently caught in the nets used by shrimp catchers. A battle rages over using turtle-excluding devices in shrimp nets, which some shrimpers say cuts down on their catch. Eating shrimp at this time can contribute to the endangerment and possible extinction of certain sea turtles. Keep reading newspapers and magazines to be aware of how this and other issues develop that affect reptile populations. (2) *Buy pets that are raised domestically*, if you must buy a pet, and not ones that are caught in the wild. *Never buy a pet that you know is a threatened or endangered species.* We encourage children to observe animals in the wild. If they *must* have a pet, have them collect an abundant, local animal, keep it for a week or two and care for it well (see Chapter 2, pages 21 to 24), and then release it in season back where it was found. (3) *Protect reptile habitat* by getting involved in habitat protection at the local, regional, national or international levels. Contact your local or national conservation groups, such as the Audubon Society, Nature Conservancy, National Wildlife Federation, Canadian Wildlife Federation or State or Provincial Department of Fisheries and Wildlife and request information to identify vital reptile habitats in need of preservation.[4] Pass the word using this information to help make other people aware. This can be done with posters, press releases, letters to the editor and presentations to local scout groups, fishing and hunting clubs, conservation groups, etc. Write letters to state, provincial and federal government representatives to encourage and/or support legislation and funding allocations to purchase land for conservation. Use your imagination to think of other ways to get involved. (4) *Protect reptiles at road crossings* by informing your parents and other drivers of places where roads cut through wetlands and other important reptile habitats. Encourage people to drive slowly through these areas. Try to get local authorities to erect "Drive Carefully, Animal Crossing" signs in these locations to alert traffic. Work on getting tunnels installed under the road in places where reptiles cross it in large numbers.

EXTENDING THE EXPERIENCE

• Write and perform a play or puppet show in which a turtle and a crocodile survive from over 150 million years ago, right through the origin and extinction of the dinosaurs and to the present day.

• Read any of the vast number of books on dinosaurs. Play some of the dinosaur games that are available. Create your own dinosaur stories and toys. Go dinosaur crazy!

• Draw a blank outline of a colored snake. Give each child a copy and have her or him color these in to create a real or imaginary snake.

• Visit a natural history museum to look at exhibits on dinosaurs and other reptiles.

• Go for a walk to a local pond and look for turtles.

• Visit a local dump and look for snakes under rocks, shingles, boards, etc.

• Adapt the activity from this chapter called "Defenders of Defenses" to use with other animal groups.

• Adapt the activity in Chapter 10 called "Amphibian Alert" on the conservation of amphibians to use for conserving reptiles.

• Use "Whither the Winter of Turtle and Beaver" in Chapter 6 as a supplemental activity to study dormancy and hibernation in reptiles.

• Follow up the activities and stories in this chapter with a Reptile Festival or Reptile Party. Make reptile models, reptile costumes, reptile cupcakes or cakes, write reptile songs and more. Celebrate reptiles!

NOTES

1. See Chapter 6 for more information and activities about reptiles and dormancy.

2. See the "Discussion" section in Chapter 17 for more detailed information about endangered sea turtles.

3. This activity is adapted from Mary Lynne Bowman, *Values Activities in Environmental Education* (Columbus, Ohio: The Ohio State University, Clearinghouse for Science, Mathematics and Environmental Education [ERIC], 1979), 45–48.

4. See the list of addresses at the end of Chapter 10.

CHAPTER 12

✤ The First Flute ✤

(Lakota {Sioux}—Plains)

Long ago, it is said, a young man saw a young woman in his village and longed to find some way to talk to her. But he was too shy to approach her directly. She was the daughter of a chief and it was well known that she was very proud. Many men tried to court her, but she sent them all away.

One day, this young man went on a hunting trip. He found the tracks of an elk and began to follow it. Although he caught sight of it now and then, it stayed far ahead of him, leading him away from the village until he was deep in the hills. Finally night came and he made a camp. He was far from home and the sounds in the night made him feel very lonely. He listened to the owls and rustling of the leaves, the creaking of the tree branches and the whistling of the wind. Then he heard a sound he had never heard before. It was a strange sound, like the call of a bird and yet different from any bird. It sounded as if it came from the land of the spirits. Strange as it was, that call was also beautiful. It was like a song and he listened closely to it. Soon he fell asleep and dreamed.

In his dream, a red-headed woodpecker came and sang that strange and beautiful song. Then the woodpecker spoke. "Follow me," it said. "Follow me and I will give you something. Follow me, follow me."

When the young man woke, the sun was two hands high. There in the branches of the tree above him was the red-headed woodpecker. It began to fly from tree to tree, stopping and looking back. The young man followed. Finally the woodpecker landed on the straight dead branch of a cedar tree. It began drumming with its beak on that hollow limb, which was full of holes made by the woodpecker. Just then a wind came up and blew through the hollow branch. It made the song that the hunter had heard!

Now the hunter saw what he should do. He climbed the tree and carefully broke off that branch. He thanked the red-headed woodpecker for giving him this gift and he took it home to his lodge. But he could not make it sing, no matter what he did. Finally he went to a hilltop and fasted for four days. On the fourth day a vision came to him. It was the woodpecker and it spoke again, telling him what to do. He must carve the likeness of the woodpecker and fasten it in a certain way near one end of the branch. He must shape the other end of the flute so it looked like the head and open mouth of a bird. Then when he blew into that end of the flute and covered the holes with his fingers, he would be able to play that song.

The man did as his vision told him. He carved the flute so that it looked like the head and open mouth of a bird. He tied on the bird reed near the other end and when he blew into the flute it made music. Then he began to practice long and hard, listening to the sounds of the wind and the trees, the rippling of the waters and the calls of the birds, making them all part

She went straight to where he was playing. She walked up to him and stood close to him and he lifted his blanket and wrapped it around them both.

of his playing. Soon he was able to play a beautiful song. Now when he hunted and camped far from the village he had his flute with him and could play it to keep himself company.

Finally, he knew that he was ready to visit that young woman he had liked so long from afar. He went and stood behind her lodge and played his best song on the flute. She heard that song and came out into the moonlight. She went straight to where he was playing. She walked up to him and stood close to him and he lifted his blanket and wrapped it around them both.

So it was that the young hunter became the husband of the chief's daughter. He became a great man among his people. Ever since then, young men who wish to go courting have learned to make the cedar flute and play those magical songs. And many of those flutes, to give honor to the red-headed woodpecker that gave such a special gift, have been shaped like the head and open mouth of a bird.

Manabozho and the Woodpecker

(Anishinabe {Ojibway or Chippewa}—Eastern Woodland)

Manabozho lived with his grandmother, Nokomis, in their lodge near the big water. As Manabozho grew older, his grandmother taught him many things. One day she told him about Megissogwon, the Spirit of Fever.

"Megissogwon is very strong," she told him. "He is the one who killed your grandfather."

When Manabozho learned about Megissogwon he decided that he should destroy him. "Things will be hard for the people to come," Manabozho said. "I will go and kill this monster."

Nokomis warned her grandson that it would not be easy to do. The way to Megissogwon's island was a dangerous one. It was guarded by two great serpents that waited on either side and breathed fire on anyone who tried to pass through. If one got past them, the waters of the lake turned into black mud and pitch that would stop the passage of any canoe. However, Manabozho was determined.

"Grandmother," he said, "I must go and fight Megissogwon."

Then Manabozho fasted and prayed for four days. He loaded his birchbark canoe with many arrows. He took with him a bag made from the bladder of the sturgeon which was filled with fish oil. He spoke a single word to his canoe and it shot forward across the water. It went so swiftly that he was soon to the place where the lake narrowed and the two great snakes waited on either side.

"Manabozho," the great snakes said, "if you pass between us we shall destroy you with our fire."

"That is true," Manabozho said. "I can see that your power is stronger than mine. But what about that other one there behind you?"

The two great serpents turned their heads to look behind them. As soon as they did so Manabozho spoke another word to his canoe and it shot between the two great serpents. He lifted his bow and fired his flint-tipped arrows, killing both of the serpents. Then he went on his way.

"Shoot at the top of his head," Woodpecker called, "his power is there, wrapped up in the knot of his hair."

Now he came to the place where the waters turned into black mud and pitch. He took out the fish bladder and poured the slippery fish oil all over the sides of his canoe. Then he spoke another word and his canoe shot forward, sliding through the mud and pitch.

At last Manabozho came to the island of Megissogwon. Only a single tree still stood on the island, for Megissogwon hated the birds and had destroyed all the other trees to keep them away. On that tree there was a single branch and on it sat Woodpecker.

"My friend," Manabozho said to Woodpecker, "I am glad to see you. I have come to destroy that one who hates us."

Then Manabozho called out in a loud voice as if speaking to many men. "My warriors," he said, "surround this island. I shall fight the monster first, but be ready to attack when I call for help."

Megissogwon heard Manabozho's voice and came running to attack him. He was taller than any man and his face and his hands were painted black. His hair was bound up tightly in a knot on top of his head. His body was covered with wampum painted in bright stripes. He roared as he came and his voice was so loud that it shook the ground.

"You are the one who killed my grandfather," Manabozho shouted. "My men and I will destroy you."

Then they began to fight. Manabozho shot his arrows at Megissogwon. The monster had no weapons, but his breath was colder than winter ice and he tried to grasp Manabozho with his black hands. Each time he came close, though, Manabozho would shout out as if to other warriors. "Now, attack him from behind."

Whenever Manabozho shouted, Megissogwon would turn to look. Thus Manabozho would escape his grasp and shoot another arrow at the monster. But Megissogwon's armor of wampum was so strong that the arrows just bounced off.

So they fought all through the day. Now the sun was about to set and Manabozho had only three arrows left.

Then Woodpecker called down to Manabozho from the place where he sat on that one last tree.

"Shoot at the top of his head," Woodpecker called, "his power is there, wrapped up in the knot of his hair."

Megissogwon was reaching for Manabozho with his huge black hands. His breath was cold on Manabozho's face. Manabozho took careful aim and shot. His arrow grazed the giant's hair and Megissogwon staggered.

"Shoot again, shoot again!" Woodpecker called.

Manabozho shot his second arrow. It struck Megissogwon's topknot and the giant fell to his knees.

"Shoot again, shoot again!" Woodpecker cried.

Manabozho aimed at the center of the giant's knot of hair. His arrow flew straight to its mark and Megissogwon fell dead.

Manabozho called Woodpecker to him.

"My friend," he said, "this victory is also yours."

Then he took some of the giant's blood and placed it on Woodpecker's crest, making its head red. To this day, Woodpecker has a red head, reminding everyone of how it helped Manabozho defeat the Spirit of Fever, reminding the people to always respect the birds.

DISCUSSION

There are many gifts that have been given to human beings by the birds. It is said that the flight of the birds reminds us that our spirits, too, have wings and we can fly above our everyday troubles. In the Lakota story of "The First Flute," a red-headed woodpecker shows the young man how to make a flute on which to play his love song. The practice of making flutes and shaping them to resemble birds occurred throughout North America. In northeast North America, the Abenaki people made flutes that looked like the loon and Abenaki men would keep themselves company when far from home by playing "lonesome songs" on their flutes. The practice of using the flute for courting was especially common among the people of the Great Plains. It gave a young man and a young woman a way to find some privacy together even in the midst of a crowded village. A young man would play his flute and, it seemed, only the young woman he was playing it for could hear him (even though a mother might smile and a father rather pointedly look the other way when their daughter suddenly realized in the middle of the night that she had to go down to the spring for water). The young woman would walk out to where the young man stood with his blanket around his shoulders and then, standing close to him, he would lift the blanket so that it covered both of their heads. The two would then be "invisible" to everyone else in the village and could talk together in privacy.

Flute music is still important to Native North American people and there is a whole new generation of flute players from a number of different Native North American nations. Some of the best who have cassette tapes of their flute playing available include Stan Snake, Tom Mauchahty Ware, Kevin Locke and R. Carlos Nakai.

Stan Snake, who is of the Ponca nation, says about flute playing in the liner notes to his tape *Dawn of Love:* "Flute music is considered to be holy and has a power of its own when played by a man with his heart and mind in the right place. Much prayer accompanies the making and playing of a flute. It has been said that a bad person with a troubled soul cannot play his instrument. I have found this to be true."

Kevin Locke, whose Lakota ancestors passed down the traditional tale that opens this chapter, says this about the flute in the notes to his cassette album *Lakota Wiikijo Olowan:* "To the Lakota/Dakota the flute is the essence of the wind. The flute gives voice to the beauty of the land and is the sound of the wind as it rustles the grasses and leaves, scales the buttes and mountains, or skims the surface of lakes and streams."

It is also true that many of the old courting songs for the flute were composed by men who belonged to the society called by the Lakota, The Society of Elk Dreamers. In their visions, and in their lives, those men embodied the qualities which were associated with the bull elk—nobility, grace and gallantry. Thus, it is appropriate that the man who made the first flute was following the tracks of an elk when he encountered a red-headed woodpecker.

At the edge of the cornfield a bird will sing with them in the oneness of their happiness. So they will sing together in tune with the universal power, in harmony with the one Creator of all things. And the bird song and the people's song, and the song of life will become one.[1]

Song of the Long Hair Kachinas
—Hopi

In the Anishinabe (Chippewa or Ojibway) story of "Manabozho and the Woodpecker," Manabozho awards a red crest to the woodpecker for helping him defeat the giant Megissogwon, the Spirit of Fever. Manabozho places blood from the giant on the woodpecker's crest, which reminds us to show respect for the feathered ones.

As watchers of birds we are compelled to ask which woodpecker this really is. Many species of North American woodpeckers have at least some red on their heads, but only two have a prominent patch of red and are found in the territory traditionally inhabited by the Anishinabe—the red-headed woodpecker and the striking crow-sized pileated woodpecker. But only the pileated has a crest, while the red-headed's head is rounded. In this story, then, the pileated receives its bright red crest.

Birds

Birds glide easily between the realms of story and science. Who has never daydreamed of soaring high above

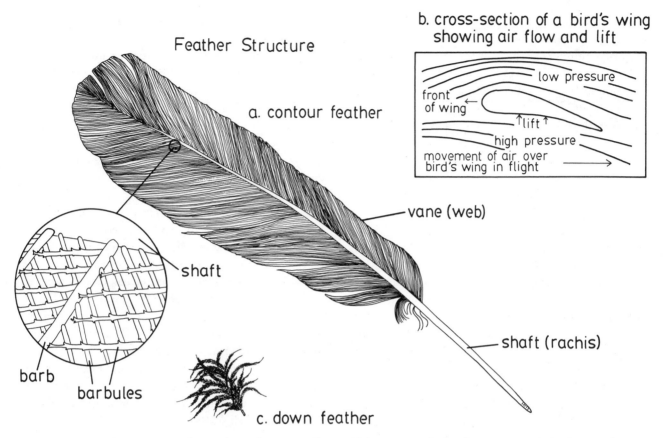

Feather Structure

a. contour feather

b. cross-section of a bird's wing showing air flow and lift

low pressure

front of wing

lift

high pressure

movement of air over bird's wing in flight

vane (web)

shaft

barb

barbules

shaft (rachis)

c. down feather

Figure 12–1. Feather structure and wing shape, showing air flow and lift: a. contour feather; b. cross-section of a bird's wing showing air flow and lift; c. down feather.

the ground like a hawk or eagle, surveying the land below with keen eyes, only to return to the hard reality of this existence with feet planted firmly upon Earth?[2]

These masters of flight have been around far longer than humans have been here to dream about them. *Birds* are vertebrate animals that evolved from small reptiles of the dinosaur age 160 million years ago. Feathers are an adaptation of reptilian scales and wings are a specialized version of a bird's front limbs. Birds still have scales on their feet and legs. Eggs are another adaptation to life on land that birds inherited and adapted from reptiles. The structure of a bird's skull and ear bones is still similar to that of a reptile, except that birds, of course, have beaks in place of teeth. Birds have developed strong, hollow bones with cross-bracing inside which lighten their bodies for flight, and many of their bones are fused to make the skeleton stronger. The breastbone is an avian adaptation that anchors their flight muscles or *pectorals*. Birds are also thought to have developed into warm-blooded animals to maintain a consistently high level of energy and metabolism for flight. Many scientists today, however,

think that dinosaurs may well have been at least partly warm-blooded after all.

The approximately 9,021 species of birds in the world today comprise the class of *Aves* in the animal world. Over eight hundred of these species are known to breed in, visit or occasion the North American continent. They live in nearly every kind of environment except for the greater depths of the sea. Birds have developed a seemingly infinite variety of adaptations in form and habit to survive in their particular habitats. The power of flight allows them to use distant environments to live, sometimes migrating thousands of miles between their summer nesting sites and winter feeding grounds. The mourning dove is able to nest in the deserts of the southwestern United States because it flies many miles to obtain water and only needs to drink every day or two.

ADAPTATIONS FOR FLIGHT. In addition to wings and feathers, flight requires acute eyesight, a delicate sense of balance and awareness of air flow over the body and superb muscle coordination. The large volume of oxygen that is needed for the metabolism and energy of flight is provided by two lungs attached to a number of *air sacs*. These balloon-like structures connect to numerous places throughout the body and even into the larger hollow bones. The air sacs help to store air and push it through the lungs in order to bring oxygen to the bird's cells via their highly efficient respiratory system.

Even though other animals, such as bats and many insects, can fly, *feathers* are a unique adaptation of birds. The strong, flexible *contour feathers* (Figure 12-1a) have a strong hollow tube called the *shaft* or *rachis* which is made of *keratin*, the stuff of scales and fingernails. The *vane* or *web* provides the surface area of a feather used for flight, protection and coloration. Contour feathers give a bird's body its streamlined shape, create *lift* along the wing surface to make flight possible (Figure 12-1b) and offer a water-repellant coat to protect from wind and water. Soft, *down* feathers (Figure 12-1c) grow beneath the contours to help insulate the bird from heat and cold. Like hair each feather grows from a follicle. Once a feather is fully formed it dies, yet remains attached and functional until it falls off during the next molt.

When a bird molts, the feather will drop off, then a new feather grows in from the same follicle. Depending on the species of bird, *molting* occurs from once to several times each year and is triggered by changes in day length. Feathers are usually shed right after breeding and before the migration season begins. All feathers are lost during a full molt, though this usually happens gradually so the bird can continue flying. Some birds—certain species of waterfowl for instance—temporarily lose their full powers of flight when molting. Many birds change from a winter plumage to breeding plumage during a partial molt just before the breeding season begins.

Feathers are delicate structures that require regular maintenance. *Bathing* in water cleans the plumage and cools the bird down. Birds can often be seen taking a dust bath, which is thought to help rid the bird of mites, lice and other parasites, as well as increase the feathers' insulating ability. It seems that birds at rest are constantly *preening* by rubbing and working their feathers with the beak. Preening also helps to clean the bird, remove parasites and lock the *barbs* of the feather vanes together to keep them tight and well formed. While preening, birds also spread oil over the feathers from a gland located just above the base of the tail. This oil makes the feathers water-repellant and reacts with sunlight to create vitamin D, which the birds ingest. Birds can sometimes be seen rubbing ants, other insects or objects such as berries, nuts or fruit through their feathers, or even letting ants crawl over their plumage. This behavior, called *anting*, may repel parasites.

Since feathers provide such efficient insulation, birds must have a way to cool off. Birds lack sweat glands on their skin so they pant and cool down as water evaporates from the lungs, mouth and throat. The air sacs also aid in cooling. Bathing, resting in the shade and the circulation of air through air sacs also help to keep birds cool.

While not all birds can fly, they all have *wings*. Wings designed for flying are *streamlined* and are curved outward on top and are flat or curved inward on the bottom to provide the *lift* that makes flight possible. Air moving over the top of the wing has to travel farther, and so becomes less dense as it is dispersed. The denser air below pushes up on the wing to support it. A bird in flight uses its *flight feathers* or *primaries* on the end of each wing to help push it forward and steer it up, down or into a turn. Even birds that do not fly, such as the penguin and the ostrich, use their wings for flippers when swimming and for balance while running, respectively.

AVIAN SENSES. A bird's keen eyesight helps it make intricate and amazingly accurate maneuvers, whether on the wing or coming in for a pinpoint landing on a branch. Expressions such as "eyes like a hawk" attest to the legendary vision of hawks, owls and vultures. Although birds of prey can see two-and-one-half times better than human beings, other birds do not see as well as these lords of the sky. The intense awareness and quickness with which birds can scan and notice things makes them appear to see better than they really do. There are probably more myths about avian vision than about any of their other senses. Birds can see color very well and the eyes of certain birds are more sensitive to particular colors. An owl's eyes do gather light better than a person's, causing an object to appear two-and-one-half times brighter in their vision. In practice on a dimly lit night, however, owls do not see appreciably better than we do because there is so little light available. Owls cannot turn their heads all the way around, but they can turn them three-quarters of the way around in each direction from a forward-facing position. So if an owl were spotted with its head turned full left, it could conceivably be seen spinning its head around a dizzying one-and-one-half full turns to where it was turned all the way to the right! Like all birds, an owl's eyes are very large relative to their skull size so they have a limited ability to move in their sockets—birds must often turn their heads to look around. Some owls have eyes that are so large they nearly touch in the middle of the skull!

Most songbirds, waterfowl and others have eyes set on the sides of their heads, so there is little overlap between the fields of view of both eyes. A pigeon can see 340 degrees around it with a small blind spot to the rear, yet has only a 24-degree overlap between the field of vision of both eyes. On the average, people have a 180-degree field of vision with an overlap of about 100 degrees —a significant area that both eyes view simultaneously. Three-dimensional or *stereoscopic (binocular) vision* requires not only that the eyes must see a certain spot at the same time (from their slightly different angles), but also that the optic nerve fibers from each eye travel to both sides of the brain, as in human beings. Among birds, only owls are known to see three-dimensional images, other birds have optic nerve fibers that run from one eye to only one side of the brain.[3] An owl's eyes, which face forward, have a 60- to 70-degree overlap in their field of vision which is roughly similar to that of a human being.

Birds can hear about as well as people and their ears function similarly. An exception is the oilbird of northern South America, which uses echo-location to navigate through the dark caves in which it nests. Avian ears are located on each side of the head just below and behind each eye. The funnel-shaped *facial disks* on owls and some hawks serve to funnel sound toward the ears. Owls can hear well enough to hunt by sound at night.

Even though taste is thought to be partly dependent upon smell among humans, most birds do not smell well even though they have taste buds to sense flavors such as bitter, sweet, acid and salty. So if a chick falls out of its nest, try to put it back because the parents *will not* abandon it if it bears a human scent. Some birds—petrels, fulmars, albatrosses, vultures, shearwaters and kiwis, for example—have a keen sense of smell.

A bird's skin has a well-developed sense of touch. The movement of feathers transmits through the skin to give the bird a sense of wind direction and of the strength of air flow over the body surface. The fine muscle coordination among birds allows them to position feathers for optimal flight performance. That birds are sensitive to temperature can be seen when they perch and fluff up their feathers to increase their insulation on a cold day.

WOODPECKERS. Each bird uses its senses and its own specialized adaptations to survive in a particular environment. The red-headed woodpeckers in the stories opening this chapter, and their close relatives, are familiar to anyone who lives in or near a wooded area or who has visited there. The bird that is called the red-headed woodpecker can be seen feeding on fruits and nuts or

Figure 12–2. The sturdy, conical beak of the American tree sparrow is ideal for cracking open seeds to get at the food inside. This common sparrow has a red-brown cap and a single dark spot on its light breast. It frequents thickets, brushy hedgerows, marshes and other weedy places where seeds abound. It is a common visitor to the winter bird feeder. Size: 6–6 1/2 inches (15.2–16.5 centimeters). Photo by Don Blades.

darting out to catch flying insects. Downy woodpeckers use their relatively small beaks to feed among the treetops on bark beetles and other prey, while the red-crested pileated woodpecker chisels small chunks of wood several inches across from even healthy, living wood! Woodpeckers peck wood to search for their food of grubs, ants and other insects, and to build nests. A pileated's nest can be up to 8 inches (20.3 centimeters) wide and 2 feet (61.0 centimeters) deep!

The twenty-two species of Native North American woodpeckers eat a variety of foods from insects to nuts and berries. Their long tongues have a sharp tip and sometimes a sticky end to catch insects deep in a hole in the tree trunk. When they land and perch vertically on the trunk the claws on their strong, opposing toes hold them there while stiff tail feathers prop them up. A sturdy, sharp bill is set in a strong skull which enables these birds to more than live up to their name of "woodpecker."

The northern flicker and the smaller hairy and downy woodpeckers are widespread in North America, along with the four species of sapsuckers and both the three-toed and black-backed woodpecker to the north and in higher elevations. Yellow-bellied sapsuckers peck neat, horizontal rows of small holes into the bark of fruit trees, basswoods, maples and others while feeding on the inner bark, then they return later to these tree wounds to lick up the sap and dine on moths and other insects that have

Figure 12–3. The large treetop stick nests of the graceful great blue heron can be found from northern North America to the northern coast of South America. These gregarious birds nest in large colonies called "rookeries." They are commonly seen in shallow wetlands where they patiently stalk their prey of fish, amphibians, crayfish and other invertebrates. Size: 42–52 inches (106.7–132.1 centimeters). Illustration by D. D. Tyler.

arrived for a slightly sweet, wet meal. The stunning, crow-sized pileated woodpecker can be so unwary while feeding that it is sometimes seen on trees growing along the streets and in the parks of towns and small cities. When it is aware of an observer, however, the "pileated" is shy and elusive.

BEAKS AND FEET. There is a seemingly endless number of variations on beak shapes and sizes used to gather the foods of different birds. Finches, grosbeaks and sparrows have stout, conical beaks for cracking seeds (Figure 12-2). Birds of prey and vultures have beaks with sharp, curved tips for tearing flesh. The woodcock has a beak with a *prehensile* tip that can probe for and grab worms when it is pushed into the soil. Generalized beak shapes, such as that of the robin, work well for a varied diet of earthworms, insects, seeds, nuts and berries. Bird tongues are also used for drinking, holding, piercing and tearing.

In order to drink most birds must take water into their beaks, then lift their heads up and tilt them back so the water runs down into the throat. Pigeons and doves, however, can actually suck water up and swallow it without lifting their heads. Beaks are also used for defense, feeding the young, gathering nest material, preening, scratching, courting and attacking.

Most birds have four toes on each foot and all of these are equipped with a claw on the end. What is usually called a bird's foot is really made up of toes, with the ankle being further up the leg and appearing like a knee. Most birds have three toes facing forward and one back, but some, like woodpeckers, hold two forward and two back.

SURVIVAL ADAPTATIONS AND FEEDING. Beaks and feet also help a bird to defend itself or attack an enemy. In addition, birds have an array of survival adaptations and strategies. *Camouflage* provides some with colors and patterns on their plumage that blend in with the background environment. When danger is near many birds hide by *freezing*, becoming still and silent. Some *flock* together to make it harder for a predator to home in on a single bird, while others will *mob* a larger, fiercer predator to harass it and drive it away en masse, attacking or sometimes even killing it. Blue jays, crows and others use a variety of *alarms* that tell specifically whether a predator is appearing from above, below or is using some other approach. *Bluffing* may involve clapping bills as in barred owls, opening bills wide, hissing or extending the feathers and/or wings to look big and threatening. Killdeers will even feign a broken wing to draw a potential threat away from the nest or fledglings.

When a bird is able to catch or collect its food, excess can be stored in a sac called a *crop* located at the end of the esophagus. This food can be digested later or regurgitated to feed young birds. And since beaks have no teeth, birds are able to augment the primary (acid) digestion of the stomach by grinding their food, such as seeds, in a muscular stomach pouch called a *gizzard*. Birds can often be seen picking at and swallowing sand and small pebbles which help to grind food up in the gizzard. Since owls and hawks often swallow their prey whole, or gulp it down in large chunks, the bones, fur, teeth and other indigestibles are stored in the gizzard and later regurgitated as a *pellet*.

BIRD SONGS AND COMMUNICATION. Many people love birds for their beauty and their songs. It is usually the male who has the most colorful plumage to attract the female during courtship. As a result (in part), the female is less conspicuous and so spends more time on the nest incubating the eggs later on. Most birds are lighter below and darker above to better blend in when seen from the ground silhouetted on a light sky, or from the air against earth and plants, respectively.

Many birds have their own, unique mating song sung by the males when spring returns. *Songs* are patterns of notes that are often repeated with minor variations. Songs are used to attract a mate and mark out a nesting territory. Birds also have short *calls* to communicate when danger is near or when migrating or feeding. In addition, communication takes many forms. Woodpeckers tap rhythmically on a tree trunk. Grouse "drum" by beating their wings to send out drum-like waves of compressed air. Prairie chickens and wild turkeys display with colorful feathers and brilliant patches of skin. Many birds, such as the endangered whooping crane, have elaborate courtship dances that are performed in tandem.

Later in the breeding cycle, one or both of the parents-to-be constructs a *nest*. There are the familiar cup nests of mud and straw that robins create. Others make nests of sticks, reeds, moss or simply scrape out a hollow in the soil, sand, gravel or leaves. Nests are found seemingly everywhere—in trees, on narrow rock ledges, in caves, on the ground and even in the gravel on city rooftops (Figure 12-3). Cowbirds find a nest of eggs and lay their own among them in the early morning when the true parents are away and preoccupied with other nesting chores. Many owls and hawks use an old, abandoned crow or heron nest for a nursery. Nests range from the tiny jewel of hummingbirds to the mammoth construction of the bald eagle, which is often strong enough to hold the weight of an adult person.

Although a few birds lay their eggs near hot springs or bury them in dark sand or fermenting vegetation to keep them warm, most birds sit on the eggs to keep them warm and incubate them. Frequently, both parents take turns *incubating* the *clutch* of eggs, with the less conspicuous female doing most of the sitting. In anywhere from eleven to ninety days the young hatch by pecking their way out of the shell using a special egg tooth, which falls off soon after hatching. *Altricial* young are featherless and sightless at birth, such as those of many songbirds. They must be fed for about two weeks in the nest and two to three more once they have fledged. Geese, ducks, swans, loons and many ground-nesting birds have *precocial*, down-covered chicks that can run around and feed themselves soon after hatching. Chicks of other birds may fall somewhere between these two categories when they hatch.

Unlike the soft, leathery shell of reptilian eggs, bird eggs have a hard *shell* composed mostly of calcium carbonate. This shell protects the developing embryo and helps to prevent it from drying out. Inside, the embryo is supplied with liquid and nutrition (*yolk* and *albumen* or "egg white"). Oxygen enters via microscopic pores in the eggshell, while carbon dioxide passes to the outside. The egg is created layer by layer in the female bird's *oviduct*, with the shell and finally pigmentation applied last before laying.

ADAPTATIONS TO THE SEASONS. Increasing day length stimulates the mating urges in birds each spring, although the exact timing is also affected by the weather. As spring progresses, migrants arrive and join the year-round avian residents to establish nesting territories and attract a mate. Breeding behaviors, such as molting into spring breeding plumage and migrating north, are controlled by the increasing day length. As unbelievable as it sounds, day length is not sensed through the eyes but by the amount of light penetrating the skull directly into the brain.[4] Later in the season, the cessation of breeding activity, shortening days of summer and dropping temperatures of fall will trigger a full molt, then the accumulation of body fat for the long *migration* south to weather the winter.

Some of the most energy-demanding parts of a bird's yearly cycle—those of nesting and molting—correspond with the times of year when food is most abundant. Breeding, molting and migration consume a lot of energy. In temperate regions like most of North America this means summer. In tropical or desert environments it occurs during the wet season. Birds compete passively for the available food in an area by being active at different times. Owls, poorwills, whippoorwills and woodcocks are *nocturnal* and feed at night, while *diurnal* birds are most active during the day. Cold or dry seasons are weathered locally or the bird migrates to a more favorable climate. The poorwill, however, which lives in southwestern North America and Central America, actually hibernates. Hummingbirds become partially dormant on a daily basis during the heat of the day when stress is high. This is called *diurnation*.

MIGRATION. Most songbirds migrate under the protective cover of night. Many hawks and eagles take advantage of the rising, warm *thermals* that begin around midmorning each day, along with the updrafts formed when wind rushes up the face of a cliff or a mountain slope. These masters of flight can be seen soaring in circles as they work their way north or south. Geese and cormorants also migrate during the day in a V-shaped flight pattern with a lead bird flying at the point.

One of our most common birds, the American robin, breeds each summer throughout nearly all of North America and overwinters mainly south of Canada. The arctic tern, meanwhile, on its epic journey, each year flies over 20,000 miles (32,187 kilometers) round-trip from its breeding grounds in the Arctic to its wintering grounds in the Antarctic Ocean, and back again.

How do birds navigate on these long flights? Birds use one or more of these cues to find their bearings: the sun, the stars, the moon, landmarks (mountain ranges, coastlines, rivers, lakes) and Earth's magnetic force. There are many hazards en route: storms bringing rain, ice, snow and lightning; predators such as human hunters and hawks; tall buildings and other structures; windows; power lines and towers; aircraft; and pollution such as oil spills.

Conservation of Birds

The natural threats faced by birds are dwarfed by those posed by people and our activities. Some birds have not been able to adapt to people, while others have fared well. The ivory-billed woodpecker—once the largest woodpecker in North America (up to 20 inches [50.8 centimeters] long)—is now found only in the montane pine-oak forest of Cuba. In the United States it requires large tracts of mature river-forest, where it finds the dead and dying trees in which it nests and feeds on the larvae of wood-boring beetles. This forest has largely disappeared due to logging and clearing for farmland and other forms of development. Only a few thousand of the smaller, red-cockaded woodpeckers survive, despite the fact that its remaining habitat is carefully managed. This endangered species, also of the southeastern United States, uses diseased pine trees to nest in. These trees are selectively cut by loggers to manage the forest, inadvertently removing the woodpecker's breeding habitat. Other endangered birds include the California condor, whooping crane, bald eagle and peregrine falcon. The list of extinct species is sadly a long one; the Carolina parakeet, Labrador duck, dusky seaside sparrow, great auk, dodo and passenger pigeon are just a few.

Birds face numerous threats to their survival, including:

• *habitat destruction*, such as of wetlands and the cutting of tropical rain forests where many North American migrants overwinter;
• *hunting*, which kills birds directly and through *poisoning* when waterfowl, loons and others ingest lead shot;
• *egg collecting*;
• *the selling of bird parts*, such as beaks, skin and feathers;
• *pet trading*, which depletes rare birds in their native tropical forests and often results in their release in Florida and other warm areas where they compete with native birds;
• *harassment and killing of birds by domestic pets*, especially cats;
• *competition for food and habitat by introduced species*, such as the aggressive starlings and house sparrows;
• *pesticides and other forms of pollution*, such as DDT which wiped out the bald eagle, peregrine falcon and brown pelican over most of their former range; and
• *disease*, such as the avian malaria that has caused a large-scale extinction of native birds on the Hawaiian Islands.

Many people enjoy bird-watching because it is so much fun, and records of sightings can help conservationists to keep track of bird movements and populations. The conservation of birds depends on us to learn about them, provide them with the necessary habitat protection they need, build nesting boxes and grow appropriate plants for food and cover. Birds are close to the heart of many people. Their status is a good measure of how well we are taking care of some of our most highly valued animal friends.

QUESTIONS

1. Do you like birds? What do you like about them? What kind of gifts do we receive from them? What is your favorite bird?
2. Why do birds call and sing? Have you ever tried imitating a bird's call?
3. Why do the people in each of these two stories both go someplace to fast for four days? What is fasting and why do people fast?
4. Where did birds come from?
5. What makes a bird different from all other animals?
6. How does a bird fly? What does it use to fly?
7. What are feathers used for besides flight?
8. Can an owl really see in total darkness? Can an owl see better than we can at night?
9. Why do most birds have eyes on the sides of their heads? Which birds have eyes in the front of their heads?
10. Where are a bird's ears?
11. Can birds smell?
12. What does a robin eat? What does a woodpecker eat? A crow? A hawk? A goose?
13. Why do birds have so many different kinds of beaks?
14. What does a bird do when danger is near?
15. How does a chick break out of its egg? What tool does it use?
16. Why do birds migrate? How do they find their way? How do the birds that do not migrate survive the winter?
17. What are some of the dangers people create for birds today? What can we do to help birds survive into the future?

ACTIVITIES

Bird Song Bingo

ACTIVITY: Discuss the meaning and use of bird calls and songs. Play a game of bingo which helps you to learn and practice some common bird songs.
GOALS: Understand why birds use calls and songs. Recognize the songs of some familiar birds.
AGE: Younger children and older children
MATERIALS: One copy of Figure 12-4a for each child; one extra copy of Figure 12-4b; crayons or colored pencils; scissors; paper; paste; small bag of bird food (sunflower seeds); paper bag; books, posters, magazines or other sources of bird pictures to use as models for coloring; recordings of bird songs to play to the group (optional).
PROCEDURE: Beforehand, make one copy of Figure 12-4a for each child. Copy Figure 12-4b and cut evenly across the page to create separate strips, each with the name and matching song of one bird on it. Put these strips into a paper bag.

Use the "Discussion" section to review with the children the kinds of bird vocalizations, how they are used and why bird songs and calls are an important form of communication. Ask them to identify other ways that birds communicate, such as courtship displays and dances, defensive bluffing, feather coloration like the woodpecker's red crest and hammering such as a woodpecker does on a tree trunk.

BIRD	SONG		BIRD	SONG
• black-capped chickadee	"chick-a-dee-dee-dee"		• American crow	"CAW, CAW, CAW"
• Canada goose	"honk, honk, honk"		• American robin	"cheerily, cheer-UP-CHEERIo"
• mallard duck	"quack, quack, quack"		• red-eyed vireo	"going UP, COMING down"
• bald eagle	"kak, kak, kak"			
• mourning dove	"whooooooo-who-who-who"		• common yellowthroat	"wichity, wichity, wichity, wich"
• barred owl	"who cooks for You- who cooks for YOU alll"		• yellow warbler	"sweet sweet SWEET I'm so SWEET"
• pileated woodpecker	"CUCK, CUCK, CUCK-CUCK!"		• red-winged blackbird	"conk-la-REE!"
• eastern phoebe	"FEE-bee"			
• blue jay	"JAY, JAY, JAY"		• American goldfinch	"per-chickory, per-chickory"

Figure 12–4. a. Bingo card bird illustrations for "Bird Song Bingo." b. Bird names and matching songs for "Bird Song Bingo."

Pass out the copies of Figure 12-4a (one to each child) and have them color in each bird as true-to-life as possible while looking at pictures or illustrations of the birds. Now have them cut along the lines to separate the bird pictures. Then have them jumble the pictures up and paste them onto a different sheet of paper in a new order using the same square arrangement of four across and four up and down. This will be their "Bird Song Bingo" card. Pass out sunflower seeds for markers.

Have the children take turns coming up to the front of the group. Each child will reach into the paper bag, pull out a slip of paper, read the bird's name and present (read or imitate) its song to the group. Children in the group will find that bird name and drawing on their bingo cards and mark it off with a sunflower seed. With younger children who cannot yet read you may have the child choose the slip of paper and then read the bird's name and present its call yourself while holding up the picture of that bird.

Each child becomes a "winner" every time she or he fills a row across, up and down or diagonally on her or his card. These children are given an extra handful of seeds to feed the birds later in the activity. All of the children eventually get to "win" an equal number of times during the game, and altogether again at the end because their cards fill up at the same time.

When the game is over, have the children take all of their sunflower seeds outdoors to a place where birds are likely to feed, such as a hedgerow, forest, park or bird feeder. Have them all thank the birds for their beautiful songs and place the seeds out for the birds to eat.

Note: You can augment this activity by having the children *play* the bird's songs since there are numerous audio field guides with the calls of individual birds recorded on separate cards.

Pin the Beak on the Bird

ACTIVITY: Match up the birds with their correct beak by pinning the beak on the bird.
GOAL: Realize that each bird has a beak that is well adapted to its food and feeding habits.
AGE: Younger children and older children
MATERIALS: Field guides to North American birds, pencils, crayons, tempera paints, colored pencils, scissors, tacks, tape.
PROCEDURE: Have the children use field guides for

examples to model as they draw and color large pictures of birds, paying careful attention to the detail of each bird's beak. Hold up an illustration of a bird that fills a standard-sized sheet of paper and instruct them to draw each bird in a similar size. (Otherwise, the size discrepancies between their drawings will provide clues to matching up the birds with their corresponding beaks later in the activity.) Have the children draw pictures of the following birds:

- duck
- hawk
- heron
- pelican
- cardinal
- robin
- hummingbird
- kingfisher
- woodpecker
- sandpiper
- crossbill

Now have them carefully cut the beak off of each bird along the line where it joins the face. Tape or pin all of the birds' bodies on a wall and carefully mix the beaks up in a paper bag.

You are now ready to have the children take turns picking a beak out of the bag and pinning or taping it onto the correct bird on the wall. Give them some hints, such as the kind of food it eats, if they are having difficulty locating the correct bird. Once each child has the beak attached to the correct bird, have her or him describe the structure of that particular beak, how that bird uses it to eat and what kind of food it eats. Help the child to give the correct information with leading questions aimed at having him or her think of the answers.

Repeat the game one or two more times so that everyone has had a chance. This also serves as a helpful review of the different kinds of bird beaks and their functions.

Avian Adaptations Match-Up

ACTIVITY: Play a matching game to identify some survival adaptations of birds.
GOAL: Understand that every bird has specific adaptations to help it survive.

Avian Adaptations Match-Up

Connect the adaptation with the
bird silhouette that it describes.

• Long, pointed wings help this bird to be a fast flyer.

• Here is a bird diving fast toward the water to catch a fish.

• Flying around trees and bushes is easier with this bird's short, broad wings.

• This bird has long, broad wings for soaring.

• Stiff tail feathers help this bird to stay upright on tree trunks.

• The wings on this bird move so fast that they're just a blur.

• It is easy for this bird to swim because its body is shaped like the hull of a boat.

• A strutting posture and fanned tail tell you that this bird is trying to attract a mate.

• As this bird runs along it uses its wings for balance.

• This bird can't fly, but it can use its wings as flippers to swim underwater.

• The "ears" on this bird's head are really made out of feathers.

Figure 12–5. Avian Adaptations Match-Up.

AGE: Younger children and older children
MATERIALS: One copy of Figure 12-5 for each child, pencils.
PROCEDURE: Hand out a copy of Figure 12-5 to each child. Tell them to match each silhouette of a bird on the right with its survival adaptation on the left by drawing a line to connect the two. Once they have completed the match-up, lead a question-and-answer discussion about each bird and its adaptation(s).

Bird-Watchers

ACTIVITY: Go bird-watching to discover and learn about some of the common birds living nearby. Monitor local bird populations.
GOALS: Experience the fun of identifying and learning about which birds are living in your neighborhood. Understand that each bird in the field looks and lives like it does because of its adaptations for survival. Learn the basics of bird-watching and why it is important to monitor bird populations.
AGE: Older children
MATERIALS: Binoculars, field guides to birds, cassette of the calls of common songbirds, tape recorder/player, pencils, paper, cardboard backing to write on.
PROCEDURE: Beforehand, take a pair of binoculars and a field guide to birds in your area and walk around the learning center identifying some common birds. Make a list of these birds and take notes describing the calls you hear and the bird making each call. Note several adaptations that help each bird to survive in its habitat, including beak and foot shape, color, food habits, behavior, etc. Create some field sheets with a list of these birds and things each child should be aware of to find them.

Gather the group together and tell them you are all going out "bird-watching" or "birding." Tell them that this will require them to be quiet patient listeners and to be very observant. Bird-watching is fun, trains the eyes, ears and mind and is a good way to help keep track of local bird populations, which are good indicators of environmental health. If you plan to have the children use binoculars, give them an orientation as to their use.

Introduce the children to the kinds of things they should look and listen for in the field when identifying birds, including the bird's

- shape (beak or bill, feet, wings, tail, overall silhouette)
- size ("as big as a robin" or "as big as a sparrow")
- color
- field markings and distinctive patterns, such as eye rings, stripes, wing bars, tail patterns and rump patches
- behavior, such as wagging its tail, swimming, wading, climbing up or down tree bark
- flight pattern
- habitat (trees, shrubs, field, freshwater, seacoast . . .)
- calls and songs

Use a field guide to show the children pictures and/or illustrations of the common birds they can expect to find as "bird-watchers." Have the children research basic behavior, habitat, food preferences and other important facts about their birds. Use the tape player to play the calls of some of their birds and describe how the field guides represent bird calls for identification purposes.

When you first go outside have the children stand quietly in a circle, close their eyes, listen to and take note of the number of different bird songs they hear. Have them try to imitate or describe these calls and songs. Lead a short excursion as you point out a few birds, including their vocalizations and identifying traits. Pass out the field sheets you prepared, binoculars (optional), field guides to birds and pencils. Ask the children to identify as many birds as they can while bird-watching and to use the notes you put on the field sheets to guide their observations of each bird's activities. Demonstrate the bird call you will use to gather the group together after their excursion.

Now send the children off to bird-watch in pairs. Roam around from group to group with a field guide to help them and to answer any questions. After about twenty minutes, call the group in and allow them to share their sightings and observations. Encourage them to continue "birding" on their own and to report their findings to the local Audubon society or other conservation group. Many such groups lead bird walks and ask volunteers to participate in periodic bird counts.

The Woodpecker's Multi-Decker

ACTIVITY: Create a papier-mâché woodpecker and dead tree containing a cavity for a woodpecker's nest, insects and other plants and animals that would live on or in a dead tree.

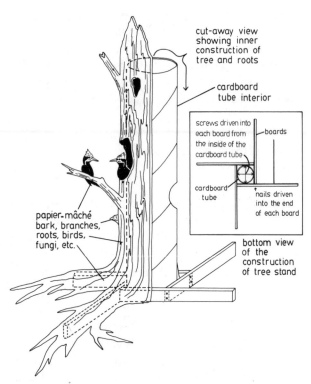

Figure 12–6. Creating "The Woodpecker's Multi-Decker."

GOALS: Understand the importance of forests and dead trees to cavity-nesting birds. Realize the diversity of plants and animals that make their home on or in a dead tree.

AGE: Younger children

MATERIALS: Sturdy, wide-diameter cardboard tube like those used for forms when pouring concrete columns; carving knife; four wooden studs measuring 2 inches (5.1 centimeters) by 4 inches (10.2 centimeters) by 4 feet (1.2 meters) to make the feet; nails; screws; hammer; screwdriver; saw; narrow-blade pruning saw to cut holes in cardboard tube; sandpaper; tape measure or yard (meter) stick; lots of newspaper strips; wheat paste; water; bucket; large spoon; enough crumpled newspaper to fill the tube; clay; stiff wire (such as a coat hanger) for bird feet; cutting pliers; pliers; tape; water-based paint; paintbrushes; pictures or illustrations of dead trees, birds, ants, etc., for the children to use as models while creating; paper; pencils; Figure 12-6.

PROCEDURE: Work with the children to make a nearly life-sized small tree, pair of nesting woodpeckers, nest with eggs and other inhabitants of the tree (Figure 12-6).

Take a sturdy wide-diameter cardboard tube, such as those used for the forms when pouring round cement columns, and cut several holes in it for the woodpecker's nest entrance, the nest holes of other birds or animals,

carpenter ant tunnels, etc. Make the nest holes large enough to reach in to build the nests.

Now fill the hollow tree with crumpled newspaper and pack it down. Use four 2-inch (5.1-centimeter) by 4-inch (10.2-centimeter) by 4-foot (1.2-meter) pieces of lumber to fashion a tree stand as shown in Figure 12-6. Nail or screw the cardboard tube onto the wood from the inside.

Use strips of newspaper and wheat paste to make the tube and feet into papier-mâché roots which support a tree that is broken off at the top, as if hit by lightning. Be sure to include the bark. Use the other materials to create fungi, ants and other insects that would be found living on or in a tree. Create nest cavities by reaching into the holes and pulling out some of the crumpled newspaper filling just inside each hole in the trunk. Line each nest cavity with a few layers of papier-mâché and build nests in these spaces.

Over the course of the next few days, while the tree is drying thoroughly, make clay and papier-mâché models of the pileated and/or red-headed woodpecker couples as well as other tree cavity nesters such as the black-capped chickadee and the beautiful wood duck. As you create, be sure to position the birds' bodies and feet properly so they can be made to perch or hang on the tree, or even incubate the eggs on the nest. Use wire for the feet and leave a piece sticking out beyond the end of each foot to hold the bird onto the tree trunk.

Paint the tree and all things attached to it while the wheat paste dries on the birds. Then paint the birds, let them dry and use the wire on their feet to attach them to the tree.

Once the tree and its inhabitants are completed, have each child write a story about her or his life and adventures as one of the woodpeckers or other animals of the tree.

Avoiding the Pane

ACTIVITY: Create a dark silhouette of a bird predator and stick it on a window to prevent other birds from crashing into the glass.

GOALS: Understand why birds sometimes fly into glass windows. Help to prevent them from doing so.

AGE: Younger children and older children

MATERIALS: Figure 12-7, scissors, black adhesive plastic shelf paper, tape, permanent felt-tipped marker.

PROCEDURE: Birds sometimes fly into window panes

Figure 12–7. Silhouette pattern for "Avoiding the Pane."

because the transparent glass tricks them into thinking that a window is just an opening in the wall. The glass also acts like a mirror that reflects trees and sky. This could cause the birds to think they're flying into an open space outdoors.

Children can do something that may help to prevent these close encounters between birds and windows. A dark silhouette shaped like a predaceous bird (such as a peregrine falcon) and attached to the outside of the window may help to keep birds away. The shape breaks up the reflection of the glass and may even cause the birds

to avoid the "predator" and stay clear of the glass.

Enlarge the shape shown in Figure 12-7 so that the wings are 12 inches (30.5 centimeters) from tip to tip. Have the children use a felt-tipped marker to trace the shape onto the plastic and then cut it out to form the silhouette. Help them to peel the protective backing off the adhesive and stick the shape onto the center of the window on the *outside* if possible, or on the inside if not. Tape the edge securely to help keep water from weakening the adhesive bond.

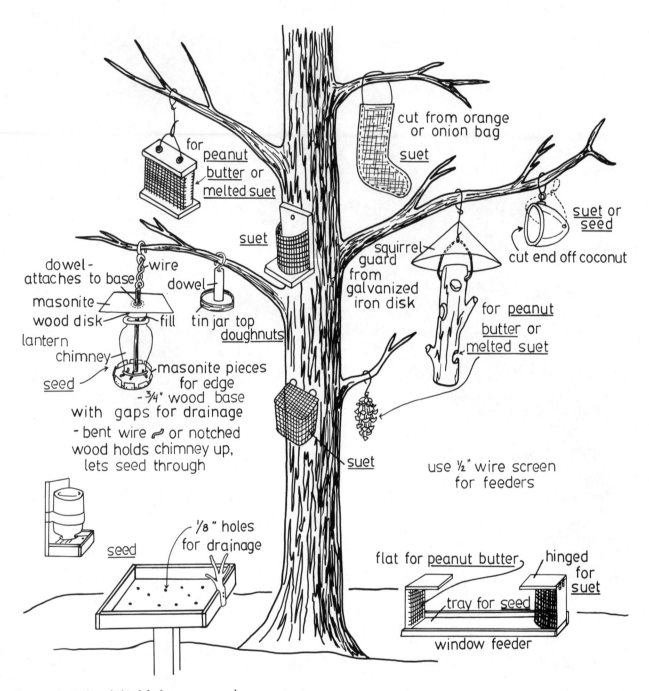

Figure 12–8. Simple bird feeders you can make.

EXTENDING THE EXPERIENCE

• *Home Tweet Home.* Make a mural of a forest, stream, field, lake and other habitats. Research the birds that nest in these places, including the kinds of eggs they lay and nests they build. Examples include tree cavities (chickadee, woodpecker, wood duck), shorelines (loon), floating nests (grebe), treetop nests (robin, vireo, oriole), seashore nests (plover, tern, gull) and bank nests (kingfisher, bank swallow).

• Use bird signals, such as coloration, songs, calls, tapping and displays, to create your own forms of nonverbal communication to convey messages. For instance, red could mean anger, blue cold, yellow happy, etc.

• Be careful when you find a young wild bird. If it is a

nestling that has fallen out, put it back in the nest. Parents *will not* abandon it if it has a human scent on its feathers. Leave fledglings on the ground when they have left the nest but are not yet ready to fly. The parents are nearby and will return to feed their offspring once you move away from it. Return a nest of young birds to the branch it fell from or as close by as possible if it has been blown or knocked down. Tie it up or even put it in a small box if you need to hold it up there. Parents will often return to carry on with raising the young. If you find a baby bird and cannot return it to the wild, contact a local Audubon society or other conservation group for details of where to bring it to be cared for or how to raise it properly yourself.

• Gather feathers from a zoo, park, farm or other location. Wash them thoroughly and dry them. Study them under a hand lens while looking at Figure 12-1.

• *Home Away From Home.* Even though it is best not to buy exotic birds as pets, some of you may already have one or more. Research where your pet bird comes from and what its natural habitat is. Redesign its cage to be as much like its natural habitat as possible. Create a better "Home Away From Home" for your pet bird.

• Get involved with projects to help conserve birds. Make a wood duck nesting box and (with permission) place it in a nearby marsh. Create a winter bird feeding station and keep it well stocked with feed (Figure 12-8). Plant native shrubs, trees, flowers and grasses in your yard or around the learning center to give native birds more food, cover and shelter. Provide them with water in a bird bath as well. Do not cut dead trees ("snags") in your forest. Save them for birds and other animals to use for finding food and shelter.

• See Chapter 5 for more information, activities and another story about birds, including the "Flight of Fantasy."

• See Chapter 6 for more information and activities about wintering and migration.

NOTES

1. Frank Waters, *Book of the Hopi* (New York: Ballantine Books, 1969), 211.
2. See "Flight of Fantasy" in Chapter 5.
3. Robert Burton, *Bird Behavior* (New York: Alfred A. Knopf, 1985), 43-44.
4. Ibid., 15.

He would sing a certain song. "Hiii aya, hiiiyahahey!" Then his eyes would fly right out of his head.

CHAPTER 13

❖ Why Coyote Has Yellow Eyes ❖

(Hopi—Southwest)

Coyote Woman lived near Skeleton Man. Skeleton Man lived near Coyote Woman. That is how it was. One day, as Coyote Woman was walking around, looking for food, she passed by Skeleton Man's place. Skeleton Man was sitting and doing something very strange. Coyote Woman stopped to watch him.

What Skeleton Man was doing was this. He would sing a certain song. "Hiii aya, hiiiyahahey!" Then his eyes would fly right out of his head. They would fly toward the south until they were out of sight. Then, as Coyote Woman watched, Skeleton Man's eyes came flying back and went right back into his head again!

"Ah," Skeleton Man said, "I have seen so many things."

Coyote Woman walked up to him. "I like that song you were singing," she said.

"Hep owiy!" Skeleton Man said. "Yes. It is a good song. When I sing it I see things I have not seen before. I saw a canyon and it was just filled with game animals. Deer and rabbits were there and all kinds of other animals."

Coyote Woman thought about all those game animals. "Will you teach me to sing that song also?" Coyote Woman said.

"It is easy," Skeleton Man said. "Just face to the south and sing like this." Then he sang again, "Hiii aya, hiiiyahahey." As he sang, his eyes flew out toward the south. He sat there and waited and before too long, his eyes came back again.

"That is easy," Coyote Woman said, "I can do that, too."

"Just be sure to face to the south and do not move," Skeleton Man said. Then he disappeared.

"I will see that canyon," Coyote Woman said. She sat down and faced south and she sang very hard. "Hiii aya hiiiyahahey." Her eyes came out of her head and flew toward the south. "Hep owiy!" Coyote Woman said, "I can see the game animals. This canyon is a good place." She got so excited that she began to move around. Soon she was facing toward the north.

"Now," Coyote Woman said, "it is time for my eyes to come back. Come back to me, eyes!" But her eyes did not come back. She called them again, but nothing happened. She called four times and now she could no longer see anything. "Is ohi!" she said. "What am I going to do? I can no longer see anything. Where are my eyes? I called them back to me."

Then Coyote Woman had an idea. She didn't realize that she was no longer facing south and that her eyes could not return to her because she was facing the wrong way. "I know what has happened," she said. "My eyes came back to me but they missed my head. They are on the ground here near me. I have to look for them."

Coyote Woman began to feel around for her lost eyes. She looked and looked and finally found something just the shape of one of her eyes on the end of a stalk. "Here is one of them," she said. Then she found another round thing which felt like an eye on the end of another stalk. "Here is the other one," she said. She lifted them up and popped them into her eye sockets. Now she could see, but everything looked yellow.

"Huih," she said, "my eyes are not working so well. They were outside of my head too long. I had better go find my children."

Then Coyote Woman trotted home. But as soon as her children saw her, they were afraid. Her eyes were big and yellow and frightened them. They ran in all directions to get away from her.

Coyote Woman chased her children. "Come back," she called. But they continued to run away. Coyote Woman had put two big gourds in her head for eyes and now her eyes were big and yellow and frightening. So it has been ever since then that all coyotes have yellow eyes and coyotes live scattered all over the place. And here is where this story has an end.

The Dogs Who Saved Their Master

(Seneca—Eastern Woodland)

There was a man who always treated his dogs well. He fed them good food and spoke kindly to them. He petted them and allowed them into his lodge. His four dogs were all great hunters, but the best of all was the smallest one. It had two black spots on its head, one over each eye. This dog he called Four Eyes.

One day, as the man was out hunting with his dogs in a place far to the north where he had never been before, he found a strange animal trail. Though his dogs whined and tried to draw him away, he began to follow that trail. Deeper into the thick forest he went. He saw how the branches on either side of the trail were broken as if some large animal had passed along this way.

At last he came to a clearing. There stood a giant dead tree broken off at its top. The dogs growled and the man looked up. There, crawling out of the hollow in the tree was a terrible animal. The man could not move at first, for it was looking right at him, but the four dogs pushed against the hunter. They turned him around and he was able to run. From behind him he heard the sound of a battle as his four dogs fought with the terrible animal. He turned back to help them, but the little white dog with the two black spots on its head blocked his way.

"My friend," the dog said, "you must run. My brothers and I will try to hold the monster."

The hunter was surprised. His dog had never spoken before. But he did as he was told. He ran as fast as he could, following the trail south. He ran until he could run no longer. Just as he stopped, the yelp of a dog came from the north followed by a terrible howl. He knew that one of his dogs had died. The hunter knelt, trying to regain his strength. His little white dog came out of the bushes.

"My friend," Four Eyes said, "the monster has killed my brother, Bear Killer. Now you must run. We will try to hold it here."

"My friend," the dog said, "you must run. My brothers and I will try to hold the monster."

The man rose to his feet and began to run again as Four Eyes bounded back up the trail. Again he heard the sound of fighting close behind him and he ran without stopping. He ran and ran until once more he heard the dying yelp of a dog followed by that terrible howl. The hunter fell to the ground, filled with despair. The little white dog came from the bushes and nudged him.

"My friend," Four Eyes said, "my brother Long Tooth is dead. The monster is closer now. You must run or our sacrifice will mean nothing."

The hunter forced himself to rise and the little white dog ran back up the trail. Stumbling as he ran, the man heard the sound of fighting close behind. He had only run for a short time when again he heard the yelp of a dog and the monster's howl. The hunter fell to his face. He had no strength to run further. He felt something licking his feet and turned his head to see his small white dog.

"My friend," Four Eyes said, "by licking your feet I have given you new strength to run. You have seen my brothers and me doing this in the past. It is part of our medicine. Now you must go. My brother, Holds Fast, is dead. I shall do my best to stop the monster. But before you go, if you escape, I must ask two favors of you."

The man looked at his little white dog. Its body was covered with wounds. Tears filled his eyes as he nodded his head.

"Ask anything," the hunter said, "and I shall try to do it."

"If you escape," Four Eyes said, "come back and gather our bones to give us proper burial. As a second favor, I ask that you take care of my wife. You may not know her, but the man who thinks of himself as her master does not feed her much and strikes her often. He is the heavy-footed one who does not know how to hunt. If you care for my wife, you may see my brothers and me again. Now, run fast. The monster is close."

The man leaped to his feet and ran. It was as if he had wings. Never had he run so swiftly before. He sped along the trail and as he ran he saw familiar landmarks. With his new speed he had traveled far. The sun now was near the western edge of the sky. His village was close. He had heard no sound of pursuit or battle behind him. He began to hope that he would escape.

Suddenly, from right behind him, came the terrible howl. His legs weakened. He felt the monster's hot breath on the back of his neck. But just as he began to fall, out from the bushes in front of him leaped his little white dog. It went straight for the monster's throat. The man rose and staggered on as the sound of the battle continued behind him. It was dark now, but he knew the path.

Ahead of him were lights, the fires of his village. Just as he reached its edge, a terrible cry split the air, louder than any of the howls before. Then all was silent.

The people of the village came out, frightened by that cry. The man fell down among them. When he woke the next morning, he led a party of men back along the trail. Not far from the village, they found the body of the little white dog. In Four Eyes' teeth was a great piece of skin torn from the monster. It was like no skin anyone had ever seen before. A great trail of blood led back toward the north. The hunter and the other men followed it. After a day's journey, they found the bones of Holds Fast. After another day's journey, they found the bones of Long Tooth and after another day those of Bear Killer. The blood trail continued on to the north, but they did not follow it.

The hunter brought the bones of his faithful dogs back home and buried them. He went to the lodge of Heavy Foot.

"I will trade you this old bear skin for your dog," the hunter said.

Heavy Foot thought at first to refuse. Then he saw the look in the hunter's eyes and he quickly agreed. His little white dog had never led him to any game anyway. She was no good as a hunter.

The hunter took the wife of Four Eyes home. He fed her well and cared for her. He saw that she was expecting and he began to understand the promise Four Eyes had made. When the four pups were born, one of them was a little white dog with two black spots over its eyes. When its eyes opened, they looked up at the hunter in a knowing way.

DISCUSSION

Native North Americans have always had a close relationship with their dogs, often treating them as if they were members of the family. Dogs helped with hunting, pulled peoples' belongings along while hitched to the front of a travois, provided companionship and playmates and were especially important when guarding boundaries of the village and of individual families. Many Native North Americans retain this close relationship with their dogs to this day.

In the story "The Dogs Who Saved Their Master," from the Seneca Nation of the Haudenosaunee (Iroquois) people, the hunter walks into danger because he does not listen to his dogs as they attempt to lure him from the trail. In the end he is saved by listening well to the little dog Four Eyes, which has two black spots over its eyes. Later, he keeps his promise to Four Eyes by burying the four dogs' bones and taking good care of Four Eyes' wife. The circle is further strengthened when she gives birth to a puppy with two familiar black spots over its eyes, just like its father. This story expresses some of the qualities that Native North Americans attribute to dogs, such as being faithful, trustworthy and self-sacrificing for the good of others. Dogs are also seen as being loyal, family-oriented animals.

In the Hopi story of "Why Coyote Has Yellow Eyes" we see a very different view of a wild dog, one which was called "God's Dog" by the neighboring Diné (Navajo) people. In Native North American stories Coyote appears in many forms, including that of a trickster, transformer and fool with its unique way of gaining wisdom through spectacular and superhuman experiences. Coyote can change form and is a smooth talker. In some stories Coyote, like Raven in Chapter 7, dies, only to return to life. Still, Coyote is regarded as having a certain malevolent benevolence and many good lessons are learned by those who listen well to Coyote's exploits and the outcomes.

Mammals

Coyote is a mammal—the class of animals that human beings are reliant upon for everything from food to companionship. Mammals also provide people with clothing, drink, transportation, power and shelter. Imagine a world without these mammals: dogs, cats, horses, cows and cattle, sheep, goats, oxen, pigs, deer and their relatives, dolphins, seals and whales.

There is a special bond between people and our closest relations among the animals. Human beings, science tells us, evolved, along with all other mammals, from common reptilian ancestors that dominated Earth 180 million years ago. The theory of *evolution* tells us that all living things are in one large family, and that the younger, more specialized forms of life descended from the older, simpler forms. Whenever an animal is born with an inheritable trait that increases its ability to survive in its environment, it is more likely to live to reproduce more of its kind in greater numbers than other individuals that lack this trait. In this way a particular trait, such as color or markings that provide better camouflage, is "selected" by nature and becomes more prevalent. This process of *natural selection* occurs over many generations and millions of years as species *evolve* that are well suited to life in their particular environment.

Modern mammals evolved from the first true, mouse-sized mammals of antiquity. About 65 million years ago mammals dominated Earth. Some of these lived in the treetops where the muscle coordination needed to survive required the development of complex brains among these early ancestors of monkeys, apes and people. The first true ancestors of the modern dog family appeared about 37 million years ago.

There are now roughly 4,300 species of mammals living in every habitat around the world, from desert to polar ice cap, from underground to the open sky, from mountain peaks to the depths of the sea, to forest and freshwater environments. Among vertebrates, only amphibians, with about 3,850 species worldwide, are less diverse than mammals. North America is home for about four hundred species of mammals.

Mammals are the only animals that produce milk to suckle their young, deriving their name from the Latin word *mamma*, meaning "breast" (Figure 13-1). Only mammals grow true *hair*, proteinaceous strands that emerge from *papillae* located in the outer layer of skin. Hair insulates mammals from the cold and protects against rain, snow and ice. Oil-producing glands in the skin help to keep the hair water-resistant. Many mammals have an *undercoat* made of thick, shorter hairs and an outer layer of longer *guard hairs*. Hair is shed seasonally or year-round and, in temperate areas, is thicker and often of a different color during the cold winter months. All mammals have hair at some stage of their development. Some adult whales lack hair and, possibly, only possess hair in an early embryonic stage. Whales have developed a layer of blubber up to 15 inches (38.1 centimeters) thick for insulation and protection from the elements.

While hair or *fur* helps to keep mammals warm, sweating from *sweat glands* and, in some cases, *panting*, helps to keep them cool. Since dogs have few sweat glands in their skin, they are cooled by the evaporation of water from the pads of their feet and from the pores on their tongue while panting. As a result of this efficient temperature regulation, mammals can tolerate and remain active in a wide range of temperature extremes.

Figure 13–1. The moose is the largest deer in the world and can run up to 35 miles per hour (56.3 kilometers per hour) on land. During the winter it feeds on the browse of woody plants, such as twigs, buds, bark and saplings. Much of its summer feeding time is spent in lakes where it eats water plants. A full-grown adult male may consume up to 60 pounds (27.2 kilograms) of food in one day. A cow moose, such as the one in this picture, usually gives birth in May to June to one calf, rarely two. The calf follows its mother after about three days. Size: height to 6-1/2 feet (2.0 meters); antler spread to over 6 feet (1.8 meters). Photo by Alan C. Graham.

Other characteristics of mammals include warm-bloodedness, a flexible backbone, a four-chambered heart and, of course, the need to breathe air. Internally, mammals have paired lungs and a *diaphragm* (a smooth muscle between the chest and abdominal cavities), specialized teeth for different functions, a lower jaw composed of two individual bones, with each comprising one half, and a smaller number of skull bones than other vertebrates.

A mammal's brain is more advanced than that of any other kind of vertebrate. The highly developed *cerebral cortex* is responsible for memory and enables mammals to perform intricate activities. This requires a constant body temperature. Everyone is familiar with the learning ability of dogs, who eventually seem to learn how to outwit even their owners. A visit to a marine aquarium performance is an occasion to witness the sophistication of the learning ability, motor skills and social awareness of whales, seals, sea lions and dolphins. The intricate social behavior, communication and learning skills of monkeys, baboons, chimpanzees and apes in the wild and at any zoo reveals a highly developed mind for reasoning. Among these primates and human beings the intellect and emotions are, supposedly, most highly developed.

From the aerial acrobatics of a bat to the majestic motion of a whale, mammals are diverse and fascinating to watch. There are three major groups of mammals that are distinguished by their anatomy and method of giving birth. The *monotremes* are the only mammals to lay eggs. This group is composed of the spiny anteater of Australia, Tasmania and New Guinea and the duckbill platypus of Australia and Tasmania. Monotremes use one opening for both reproduction and eliminating waste. Although the mother has milk-producing glands she lacks a true breast, so the young lap milk from pore-like openings on her abdomen. There are no representatives of this group living in North America.

Marsupials give birth to near-embryonic young that crawl up from the vaginal canal and attach to a teat for a number of weeks where they nurse and complete their development. At this stage of its life a baby opossum, for instance, weighs 7/100 of an ounce (2 grams). Many marsupials have a bag or pouch, called a *marsupium*, in which the young are sheltered as they nurse and grow. The female has two separate uteri and vaginal canals. A marsupial's brain is similar in form to that of a reptile. The only marsupials living in North America are the opossums. There are several marsupials living in Central and South America, including shrew-like animals and an aquatic opossum. In Australia, however, there seems to be a marsupial counterpart for most North American mammals, including marsupial cats, moles, squirrels (phalangers), rats, mice, marsupial groundhogs (wombats) and wolves (Tasmanian wolves). There is also a marsupial counterpart to the anteater. Kangaroos and the koala are perhaps the best-known marsupials.

In North America, when we refer to a native "mammal" we usually mean one of the *placentals*. These mammals have a *placenta* which connects the blood stream of both mother and embryo, allowing it to grow and develop inside her body and increasing the time the young has for its brain and body to develop. Most of the mammals living today are placentals.

Mammals of North America

In North America, mammals range from the 2-inch (5.1-centimeter) pygmy shrew which weighs 1/10 of an ounce (2.8 grams) to the blue whale at up to 100 feet (30.5 meters) and 150 tons (136.1 metric tons)! Mammals live in a wide range of North American environments, from treetops to the sky, and from the open sea to below the ground. In general, the smaller mammals are more abundant, in both species and total numbers, than larger ones. For example, rodents comprise roughly a third to half of all living species of terrestrial mammals on Earth. Bats are the second most abundant group with nine hundred species worldwide. There are sixteen orders of placental mammals around the world, including several that do not occur in North America such as the flying lemur (*Dermoptera*) of Southeast Asia, aardvarks (*Tubulidentata*) of Africa south of the Sahara and pangolins (*Pholidota*) of Southeast Asia and Africa. The armadillo of the southeastern and southcentral United States is the only North American representative of the *Edentata*, which also includes the sloths and the anteaters of Central and South America. Although some monkeys have been introduced around Silver Springs in Florida, there are no native *primates* in North America, such as monkeys, chimpanzees, gorillas, orangutans, gibbons, tarsiers or lemurs.

The twelve orders of mammals found in North America are:

- opossums (*Marsupialia*)
- shrews and moles (*Insectivora*)
- bats (*Chiroptera* or "hand wings")
- hares, rabbits and pikas (*Lagomorpha*)
- cats, dogs, wolves, foxes, bears, weasels, skunks, raccoons and coatis and ringtails (*Carnivora* or "flesh-eaters")
- squirrels, mice, rats, gophers, beaver, muskrat, lemmings,

moles, jumping mice, porcupine and nutria (*Rodentia* from the Latin *rodere* or "to gnaw")
• armadillo (*Edentata*)
• deer, pronghorn, bison, goats, sheep, muskox, swine, peccaries and most domestic animals such as cattle (*Artiodactyla*, the even-toed hoofed mammals, sometimes grouped with *Perissodactyla* as the *Ungulata*)
• horses (*Perissodactyla*, the odd-toed hoofed animals, sometimes grouped with the *Artiodactyla* as the *Ungulata*)
• manatee or "sea cow" (*Sirenia*)
• seals, sea lions and walrus (*Pinnipedia*)
• whales, dolphins and porpoises (*Cetacea*)

Each group of animals is known for its own particular habits and characteristics, although there is a lot of variation within each group. Cats tend to stalk and rush their prey, while the more social wolves and other dogs hunt in packs. Bears, while very quick when they need to hunt, also eat nuts, berries and other parts of plants as well as meat.

Most mammals move about on all four legs. Seals and their relatives, however, have developed flippers for propelling them along underwater, which causes them to be ungainly when walking on land. The flukes and streamlined bodies of whales, dolphins and porpoises make them the mammalian masters of the oceans, including the finback whale that is sometimes called the "greyhound of the sea." In contrast, the manatee, which is related to the dugong also of tropical estuaries and coastal waters, is a sluggish aquatic mammal that has paddle-shaped front limbs and no rear limbs at all. The related, 30-foot (9.1-meter) Steller's sea cow, a relative of the dugong and manatee, once of North Pacific waters, was hunted to extinction by whalers in the mid-eighteenth century who killed them mercilessly for food.

Bats, on the other hand, have developed the ability of true flight. "Flying" squirrels do not actually fly, but rather use flaps of skin stretched between their front and rear legs to glide from tree to tree.

Many of the smaller mammals, which can easily fall prey to a variety of predators, are *nocturnal*, being mostly active at night. These include bats, mice, shrews, moles and rats. We tend to see them at dusk and dawn, the times when *crepuscular* animals are also active. Tracks made by some of these animals are more commonly seen than the animals themselves. Other mammals are primarily nocturnal but can frequently be spotted during the day, such as foxes, coyotes, hares, rabbits and cats.

True *diurnal* or day-active mammals include the squirrels, chipmunks, prairie dogs, groundhogs and other

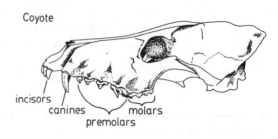

Figure 13–2. The four kinds of mammal teeth.

marmots. Many larger animals are also evident during the day, such as the deer, bison, caribou, elk, moose, pronghorn, muskox, sheep and goats, as well as the seals, whales, dolphins and sea lions.

FOOD AND FEEDING. The time when an animal is most active is largely determined by when it is best able to gather or catch its food, and when it can most readily avoid falling prey to another animal. Mammalian diets range from herbivorous to carnivorous to omnivorous. The food eaten at any particular time depends upon what is available in that season, the size and age of the animal, its state of health and how hungry it is.

Most mammals are plant eaters, subsisting on nuts and other seeds, fruit, leaves, nectar and even bark. Ruminants, such as cows and sheep, have a four-parted stomach to help them efficiently digest grass and other forage. Once the food is eaten and partially digested in the first two stomachs, it is brought back up to be rechewed as "cud." The largest order of mammals, the rodents, are also primarily herbivorous.

Carnivorous mammals eat insects and other invertebrates, fish, other mammals, reptiles, amphibians and even birds. Some meat eaters such as the bears, are omnivorous, also eating berries, nuts and other plant parts.

Bears store uneaten food in a *larder* for later consumption. Beavers, squirrels, chipmunks, deer mice and cats also gather more food than they need at a certain time and store it in a *cache*. Chipmunks and deer mice are able to store lots of seeds and berries in their cheek pouches, which they carry off to store for consumption later on.

There are four major kinds of mammal teeth, including *incisors* to the front of the mouth for gnawing, cutting and ripping; *canines* for seizing and tearing; *molars* and *premolars* for chewing and grinding (Figure 13-2). Some mammals have certain teeth that have evolved into prominence, such as a beaver's incisors, and not all mammals have all four kinds of teeth. Many rodents, for instance, lack canine teeth.

While most carnivorous mammals hunt alone, some have learned to cooperate to increase their chances at catching the prey. Gray (timber) wolves range single file in search of a moose or other large prey during the lean winter months. When an animal is spotted, the pack disperses downwind and act as pointers while standing still. A larger, lead animal rushes the prey while the others wait in the bush. When the prey flees, the pack pursues and bites at its legs and flanks. A large prey such as a moose, can often hold the pack off and survive if it stands its ground. Young wolves learn how to hunt by accompanying the pack, watching and gradually taking part. Cooperative hunting is also practiced by killer whales. Coyotes and badgers have even been seen hunting successfully together. In another cast that was not a form of cooperation, one coyote was seen stealing a woodchuck by driving away a northern harrier (marsh hawk) that had just swooped down upon its hapless prey.

When the prey is cornered it often uses a defensive strategy or adaptation. The opossum plays dead by lying motionless on its back with glassy eyes and mouth agape. Some animals *freeze* to avoid detection or to prevent attack, while the armadillo rolls up in a well-protected ball. Porcupines rely on their numerous, barbed quills to protect them while rabbits and hares can dole out a strong kick.

REPRODUCTION. Many small mammals, such as rodents, survive predation by producing large litters on a continual basis and having a short gestation period. Among other animals, such as deer, seals and weasels, the female enters *oestrus* or "heat" on a less frequent or even yearly basis. Among deer the breeding season or *rut* occurs in the fall in temperate climates. This way the young are born and the mother experiences the trying end of term, birth and nursing periods in spring when food is plentiful and weather is mild. The females of cats, squirrels, some bats and primates, including people, have oestrus periodically during the year.

During oestrus the *ovary* sheds the *egg* or eggs. The female also uses a scent and certain behaviors to attract and stimulate the male. The scent is produced by glands and is also spread in the urine. Both males and females use various devices to attract one another, such as coloration, size (males are usually larger), antlers, courtship dances and displays, vocalizations, caresses and kisses.

Mammalian babies are usually born head first, except for porpoises and whales which emerge tail first. Young of species that are often hunted, such as deer, can generally stand and get around soon after birth. The offspring of predaceous animals are often virtually helpless and must be cared for by the parents for a longer period of time.

ADAPTATIONS TO THE SEASONS. The reproductive cycle is timed to avoid raising young during the cold days of winter, when food is scarce. Each fall in the height of the rut, the white-tailed deer has already begun to prepare for winter. Their coat has changed to a dark brown and a thick coat of hollow, insulative guard hairs have replaced the reddish hairs of summer. This change and others are stimulated by the increasing lack of food, decreasing daylength and dropping temperatures. Mammals survive the winter by either staying active, becoming dormant or migrating to a more favorable climate.[1] Bears, skunks, opossums, chipmunks, raccoons and many squirrels enter a state of partial dormancy or *torpor*. During this winter sleep their body temperatures often drop less than that of the true hibernators. Groundhogs (woodchucks), jumping mice and some ground squirrels enter *deep hibernation*. The body temperature of some ground squirrels drops to a few degrees above freezing, their heartbeat rate decreases from two hundred to four hundred times per minute to five per minute, and their rate of respiration slows from two hundred breaths per minute to four or less. Bats gather in caves to hibernate en masse. They are also capable of *diurnation*, a brief period of daily dormancy, during hot summer days.

Beavers remain active all winter long even during the coldest parts of the winter. They keep warm in their lodges and eat the bark of green sticks that were stuck in the mud and stored underwater before ice encrusted the pond. Foxes continue to hunt as the snow grows deeper, while snowshoe hares feed on the green inner bark of winter twigs.

Some mammals migrate great distances to warmer winter environments where food abounds. Caribou travel from 400 to 500 miles (644 to 805 kilometers) on their dramatic migrations. Females of the Alaskan fur seals swim 6,000 miles (9,656 kilometers) round-trip from their breeding grounds in the Pribilof Islands to the coast of California and back again. Male fur seals overwinter in the Gulf of Alaska close to the breeding grounds. Blue whales are known to travel 300 miles (483 kilometers) in one month's time during their migration.

Dogs

Human beings figure prominently in the lives of these migrating mammals, as well as all species with whom we share Earth. We, too, are mammals, and it would be good to look at how we interact with the wild and domestic dogs that appear in the opening stories of this chapter.

We lavish much love and attention on our pet dogs, in turn for the affection and protection they return. We

Figure 13–3. The first domestic dogs in North America are thought to have been bred from wild stock of the gray (timber) wolf at least ten thousand years ago. Gray wolves are the largest wild dogs in North America. Their fur is commonly gray, but varies from almost completely white to nearly black. When light reflects off their eyes at night, it produces a greenish orange eyeshine. Size (including tail): 4.6–5.6 feet (1.4–1.7 meters); 26–28 inches (66.0–71.1 centimeters) high at the shoulders. Illustration by D. D. Tyler.

talk to them, pet them, learn from them and often share our living space with them. These remarkable dogs return our favors by sometimes making great sacrifices. Many people have been saved when their dog woke them up during a fire. Some dogs have been lost hundreds of miles or more away from home, only to appear mysteriously on their own doorstep weeks or months later.

Dogs were the first animals to be domesticated. The dogs that became an integral part of village life were most likely bred, at least 10,000 years ago, from wild stock of the gray wolf or one or more of the other species of wild dogs (Figure 13-3). Today there are thirty-seven different species worldwide in the dog family, *Canidae*, which live on every continent except Australia and Antarctica.

There are nine species of wild dogs in North America, including some from each of the three groups into which wild dogs are classified according to form and structure. The similarities of the dogs in each of these three groups correlate closely with their hunting strategies. The red

and gray fox are solitary hunters that eat small prey, such as cottontail rabbits and rodents, as well as both insects and plant matter. Coyotes will also hunt small game alone and, when in pairs or in a family unit, will pursue larger animals such as deer or elk. Gray wolves are capable of hunting alone for small game, or in small groups, but they can kill prey as large as a moose when hunting in a pack. Wild dogs are capable pursuers which run along on the four pads of their toes. The fifth toe is reduced to a dew claw on each front foot and is absent on the rear feet.

Dogs are master *communicators*. They will learn how to bark if raised alone but can only learn the subtleties of barking language from other dogs. We talk to our dogs and they do understand. In time, we learn to understand their whines, barks, cries and sounds of joy. We can learn to listen to and understand wild animals as well. The coyote is a good example of a wild dog that lives closely with human beings. **COYOTES.** Coyotes are adaptable hunters of both daytime and nighttime. They will hunt in packs or alone and

Figure 13–4. The coyote is a beautiful and graceful wild dog that ranges throughout most of North America. Its fur is gray to reddish gray with a whitish underside and rusty-colored ears, legs and feet. Coyotes are known for their haunting howls that penetrate the night air. Although coyotes can be seen during the day, they feed mostly at night on their chief food of small rabbits and rodents. True scavengers, coyotes will eat most kinds of plant and animal food. Size (including tail): 3.6–4.4 feet (1.1–1.3 meters). Photo by Peter Hope.

feed on live prey, carrion, wild fruit and nuts or city trash. Coyotes thrive in the wilderness and have been known to capture poodles in the streets of Los Angeles. They can den up in a drainage pipe, a cave, a hollow log or in a large fox burrow. Perhaps it is the coyote's remarkable adaptability that inspired its role as a trickster who takes many forms in Native North American stories.

There are up to nineteen subspecies of coyote in North America, which is the only continent to which they are native (Figure 13-4). Coyotes have the most extensive range of any carnivores of the Western Hemisphere, stretching from the Arctic Circle to northern South America and from the Atlantic to the Pacific Oceans.

Affectionate, sociable and cooperative, coyotes mate for life and remain together as a pair year-round. When the six to eight pups disperse in the fall or late summer, one young remains behind with the parents to help raise next year's litter in the spring, in case something should happen to one of the parents before the young are old enough to fend for themselves.

Although coyotes do kill sheep, it is an abnormal behavior carried out by renegade animals. Most coyotes living near farms actually help to drive away potential threats to livestock. Their normal food consists of woodchucks, rabbits, mice and voles, fruit, corn, dead animals and, occasionally, a stray pet.

Coyotes began to arrive from western North America into New York State, other northeastern states and the eastern provinces of Canada in the 1930s. Since that time they have saturated their habitat and are now spreading down river valleys to the mid-Atlantic states and further south. They did not fill the old niche of the wolf, which was systematically killed off in these regions, since the wolf required a different habitat of extensive forestland and prey of large game animals. Coyotes in the East are larger than those out West because food is so plentiful there and habitats more favorable. Some biologists also suspect that eastern coyotes may be larger because they have bred with gray wolves, which can weigh from 70 to 120 pounds (31.8 to 54.4 kilograms). New Mexican coyotes average 24.4 pounds (11.1 kilograms) while Vermont's average 39.1 pounds (17.7 kilograms).

Far from being vicious animals that attack people in packs, as is erroneously rumored, coyotes will often roll over belly-up when captured.

Perhaps only human beings are as capable of *change*, of adapting our behavior, food sources and rhythms for survival's sake, as our close neighbor the coyote. But we have responded to the coyote and to both the gray and red wolf, by declaring war on them—shooting, trapping, snaring, hunting, gassing and poisoning these wild dogs not to mention levelling, paving, flooding and developing their habitat. The gray wolf has been exterminated over much of its former range and the red wolf is now on the verge of extinction.

Many people have come to the coyote's defense. A battle still continues between those who want to kill off or drive out coyotes and animals that they perceive as competing with people, and those that struggle to help others to appreciate and enjoy coyotes, foxes, groundhogs, mice and other mammals who share our habitat.

QUESTIONS

1. Why are dogs important to Native North Americans? How do they treat their dogs?

2. What is sacrificed by the little dog Four Eyes and his companions Bear Killer, Long Tooth and Holds Fast to save the hunter in "The Dogs Who Saved Their Master"?

3. Why does the puppy with "four eyes," born at the end of the story, look up at the hunter in a "knowing way"?

4. How does the hunter return this gift from his dogs, particularly Four Eyes?

5. Do you like dogs? Why or why not? What are some of the qualities that dogs possess?

6. What does it mean when Coyote is called a trickster in Native North American stories?

7. What kind of animal is a dog? Can you think of other kinds of mammals besides wild and domestic dogs? Name them.

8. What makes a mammal different from other kinds of animals, such as birds, reptiles, amphibians and fish?

9. What kind of animal are people? How are we different from other mammals?

10. Name a mammal that lays eggs. Name some mammals that carry their young around in a pouch and some that give birth to young which have fully developed inside their mother's body.

11. What kinds of foods do different mammals eat? How do these mammals catch their food?

12. What do we call an animal that is active mostly at night? During the day? In the evening? Can you give some examples of each of these kinds of mammals?

13. What kinds of things does a mammal do to survive when it is being hunted?

14. How do mammals mate and reproduce? Where does the baby emerge out of its mother?

15. What are the different ways that mammals survive the winter?

16. How well do people treat their pet mammals, such as dogs and cats?

17. How well are people treating wild mammals, such as the wolf and coyote?

18. Do you have coyotes living near you? How do you feel about coyotes? What do you really know about them?

19. Why are coyotes able to live in so many different kinds of places, from deserts to cities to forests? What does it mean to be adaptable?

20. What can people do to take care of wild mammals?

ACTIVITIES

Mammal Masks

ACTIVITY: Take a walk to search for and observe mammals near the home or learning center. Work in pairs to create masks of common mammals in your area and guess which mammal each mask represents.

GOALS: Become familiar with local mammals and their differences in appearance and habits. Realize the importance of cooperating to complete a group task.

AGE: Younger children

MATERIALS: Strips of newspaper, slips of paper, pencil or pen, hat, pictures and/or illustrations of each of these mammals, wheat paste, newspaper to crumple, tempera paints, water, paintbrushes, scissors.

PROCEDURE: Beforehand, tear up a number of newspaper strips to be used for making papier-mâché masks.

Take a walk with the children around the home or learning center grounds to look for mammals and signs of mammals, such as squirrels, chipmunks, dogs, rabbits and cats. Take some time to watch the ones you see, paying close attention to what they are eating, where they are living and how they are communicating with each other and with your group.

Return to the home or learning center and brainstorm a list of local mammals which children have seen at one time, including those you have spotted on your walk. You will need a list of mammals equal to at least one-half the number of children in your group. Write the names of each mammal onto separate slips of paper and jumble them up in a hat. Now review the characteristics of these animals that distinguish them from other animals—what makes a mammal a mammal?

Divide the children into pairs and have someone from each pair come up and pull the name of a mammal out of the hat. Tell them to keep the identity of the animal *secret* from everyone else. Discuss the importance of cooperation and how many mammals, such as wolves when hunting, have learned to cooperate to get things done.

Using pictures and photographs of the various animals as models, have each pair work cooperatively to make a facial mask of papier-mâché of that particular animal. Stress the importance of cooperation when working together. Have each group mold a thin mask consisting of several layers of pasted strips of newspaper formed around a base of crumpled newspaper. Once the mask has dried thoroughly, usually in a couple of days, have the children gently pull the crumpled newspaper out of the inside and trim the edges neatly with scissors. Now have them paint their masks.

Have each pair come up to the front of the group with their mask. One child will hold the mask over her or his face, while the other will answer questions from the rest of the group as they try to guess which mammal the mask depicts. They can ask any questions they like, such as: "What does it eat?" "How does it move?" "Where does it live?" "How big is it?" As soon as someone thinks he or she has identified the animal, have him or her call out its name. The pair that has just correctly guessed the animal's identity will come up next with their mask. Keep this pattern flowing as long as possible, then call upon the pairs who have not presented to come up until all have had a turn to share their masks.

Unscrambling Mammals

ACTIVITY: Go on a "search and observe" walk near the home or learning center to find and learn about mammals living nearby. Play a cooperative puzzle game to unscramble and reassemble jumbled up mammals.

GOALS: Familiarize yourself with some mammals living nearby and understand how they survive in their habitat. Realize the importance of cooperation, listening and communication when completing a group task.

AGE: Older children

MATERIALS: Large sheets of poster board, pencils, crayons, colored pencils, scissors, chalkboard and chalk or newsprint and markers for listing ground rules for round two of the game.

PROCEDURE: Lead a guided walk to search for and observe local mammals, as described at the beginning of the previous activity "Mammal Masks."

Return to the learning center or home, and divide the children into an even number of small groups of three or four children. Assign each group a local mammal by whispering its name to them so that other groups cannot hear its identity. Have the groups make big illustrations of their animals on a large sheet of poster board, working out-of-sight and in secrecy from the other groups. Once the mammal illustrations are completed, have each group cut around their mammal, then have them cut it into about one dozen puzzle pieces. Before proceeding further, review the characteristics of an animal that cause it to be a mammal.

Discuss the importance of cooperation in animals and give several examples of how mammals cooperate, such as in raising the young, defending their territory or hunting together (e.g., wolves).

Each group will now exchange their puzzle with another group without revealing the identity of the mammal. Have each group place the puzzle pieces on the ground or floor and sit around them. They will work *in silence* as they cooperatively assemble their puzzle.[2]

When all groups are done with their puzzles, go around to each group and have them reveal the identity of their mammal. Hold a final discussion with everyone involved to explore what it was like to work on a puzzle in silence asking: "Did you really share the work?" "What did you do when someone was trying to do more than everyone else?" "How did you feel during this exercise?"

"How could your group have worked more efficiently in a cooperative manner?"

Now make up some ground rules and forms of nonverbal communication for this game and have each group work in silence on a different puzzle using those ground rules. For example, distribute the pieces of one puzzle evenly among the children in each group so that each child is in charge of some pieces and the assembling is truly a shared effort. Have each group assemble its puzzle in the middle of the circle, with each child working only on fitting in her or his own pieces, while allowing the others in that group to try to fit theirs into the puzzle as it takes shape. Children cannot take someone else's pieces, but can help if someone (in silence) offers her or his pieces as a way of asking for help. The only form of communication allowed is that of giving someone your puzzle pieces in silence: no talking, sign language, etc. Groups must stay together.

Reexamine how this exercise went the second time around.

Animal Talk

ACTIVITY: (A) Study the language of a pet or other domestic animal and create a dictionary translating the meaning of that animal's sounds and movements into your language. Create a second part to this dictionary including the things you say and do and what they mean to the animal. Practice using this dictionary to communicate with this animal. Create (write) an imaginary conversation between you and the animal by using the sounds and motions from both parts of the dictionary as the "speech." (B) Repeat the procedure for part "A" to create a dictionary that translates the meanings of the sounds and motions of a common wild animal near your home into your language. Write a story about a day in the life of that animal.

GOALS: Understand how domestic animals communicate with us and how we "speak" to them. Realize that wild animals use specific movements and sounds to communicate with people and with each other. Sharpen the skills of observation and listening.

AGE: (A) Younger children and older children, (B) older children

MATERIALS: (A) Pencils, index cards, tape recorder and tape (optional), camera and film (optional), crayons or colored pencils, sketch pad, writing paper. (B) Same materials as used in "A" plus books and other sources of information about the communications of wild animals.

PROCEDURE A: *Tongues of the Tamed.* Domestic animals, such as dogs, cats, horses, pigs, cows, goats, gerbils, mice, rats, are constantly "speaking" to us with body language and vocalizations. Dogs bark, beg, cower, confront, show affection and share many other messages with us. We in turn pet them, scold them, teach them and communicate in many different ways. These conversations occur between people and their domesticated animal friends every day.

Have the children spend time closely watching their chosen animal, such as a house cat. They are to record each action the animal takes when it is doing something to communicate, such as rubbing up against their legs to show and seek affection, turning its purring "motor" on to show how much it enjoys being petted, hissing or showing its teeth and/or claws when threatened, standing near the door and staring at it or circling around in front of it to show it wants to go outside or rubbing up against its dish when hungry. This record can be kept in the form of index cards containing a written description or illustration of what the animal is doing, with the meaning of that action or sound written next to it. Have them use one card for each communication. The communication can also be tape recorded, photographed and illustrated. As the completed cards and other records pile up over the course of observing the animal for a few days, the dictionary is being created.

At the same time another dictionary is to be made showing what the child says and/or does to communicate certain things to the animal, such as shaking a bowl of food to call it when its time to eat, rubbing its head and talking softly to show affection or talking loudly and sternly to tell the animal it has done something wrong.

Once the child feels both dictionaries are complete, have him or her ask someone else to help practice "tongues of the tamed." This helper will use the dictionaries to "speak" to the animal, as well as to listen to (interpret) the "language" that animal is "speaking."

Now have the child create a conversation, a kind of story, which occurs as she or he goes out and has an imaginary adventure with the animal. When this is done, have the child share it with others, and vice versa.

PROCEDURE B: *Wild Language.* Wild animals also communicate with each other and with people. Native North American creation stories often say that people could at first speak to the animals because we knew their language, but we have since forgotten. Such things as the number of times a crow is "cawing," or the number of

them in a flock and the direction they are flying, are given strong meaning by Native North Americans.

Repeat the same general procedure as described for "Tongues of the Tamed," with the following modifications.

Have the child create just one dictionary giving sounds and movements of some common wild animals of his or her choice and the possible meanings of these communications. There will be two possible meanings for each communication: the message intended for other animals, particularly its own kind, and the message intended for people. For example, this could include why a white-tailed deer snorts or lifts its tail to show the white underside when people come near, why a rabbit sometimes thumps its foot on the ground or why a squirrel cries out while sitting on a tree branch. Have the children read about their animals to enhance their learning and check their discoveries in the field.

Once they have completed a meaningful dictionary of the language of some common wild animals in your area, have them write and illustrate a story that includes as many of the sounds and motions of these animals as possible. Have them share the completed stories by reading them and showing the pictures to others.

Adapt and Survive

ACTIVITY: Play a game of choices to see if you are as adaptable as the coyote—to see if you can adapt to survive in a changing world.

GOALS: Understand that change—both natural and human-made—is a normal part of an animal's existence, and that adapting to change is necessary to survive.

AGE: Younger children and older children

MATERIALS: "Discussion" section from this chapter, copy or copies of "Coyote's Choice: Adapt and Survive," other materials as needed depending upon the format you use for this activity, such as a game for each child to play individually (one copy for each child) or a course that children will walk through while making the decisions (index cards, each with one of the numbered situations set up as separate stations and any props you may want to add to create a more life-like course for the children to experience), Figure 13-4.

PROCEDURE: Use information from the "Discussion" section to review with the children the adaptability of coyotes, the expansion of their range and the many changes that are constantly occurring around them to threaten their existence. These changes can be natural, such as floods, fire created by lightning, drought or a food shortage. Change can also be caused by people, for example, clear cutting a forest, damming a river or setting out traps or poisoned bait to kill animals. Coyotes are experts at adapting to change, moving to a new habitat when they need to or sensing danger when it is near and avoiding it, even if it means turning away from food that looks suspicious when they are hungry. They do not always make the right choice, however, and cannot always adapt successfully. Sometimes they survive, sometimes they do not. Share the photograph of a coyote in Figure 13-4 with the children.

Have each child read the following story, making choices along the way as they think a coyote might make. Even if a child makes the wrong survival choice at a certain point in the story, he or she is to continue on to the next station, and so on, until reaching the end of the story. When all of the children are through, have them share their choices, adaptations and experiences. How many of them *honestly* made *all* of the right choices and were able to make the necessary changes to survive each time? Which choices made it most difficult to make the right survival decisions? Which choices were the easiest?

Note: This activity can also be set up as a fun series of stations in which the initial situation is described and illustrated and children must choose one course or another by turning over a card or lifting up a flap to reveal the consequences of their decision. Then they can move on to the next station to test their wits there.

COYOTE'S CHOICE: ADAPT AND SURVIVE

1.   You are a tiny coyote pup and your mother has gone off to hunt for food. While you wait in the burrow a strange piece of thin wire on the end of a stick is pushed toward you from the door of your den. You see it coming and are afraid of it so you
     a.   cower back against the wall of the burrow to escape.
     b.   attack the wire by biting it.

If you chose (a) you survived. If you chose (b) you were snared and taken away by a hunter.

2.   You are now old enough to do some hunting on your own. There, up ahead, you see a dead animal that looks like it is more than big enough for a whole meal. When you get closer you see some strange tracks in the soil and smell an animal you have never smelled before. You are

very hungry, but afraid to go closer to the dead animal. After watching a while and looking for signs of danger you decide to
     a.   eat the meat of the animal.
     b.   turn away and search for another meal.

If you chose (a) the meat was a poisoned trap set by a farmer and you are a goner. If you chose (b) you survived.

3.   It has not rained for a long time, the plants are dying and animals are becoming scarce. You are very weak, yet you feel an urge to travel to look for food. You begin to walk away from your burrow but you find it hard to walk. You decide to
     a.   push ahead and look for water and food elsewhere even though it means risking using up your last energy.
     b.   return to the burrow and wait for the rain and food to return.

If you chose (a) you survived. If you chose (b) starvation set in and you became too weak to leave your burrow. You did not survive.

4.   You come to a place where people are living because you know there is usually some food nearby. There is a place up ahead where the smell of food is strong, yet danger is very near and threatening. As night slowly advances with the setting sun, you decide to
     a.   sneak in and eat as much of the food as you can under the cover of darkness.
     b.   turn around and seek food elsewhere.

If you chose (a) you were able to eat safely while protected by the darkness. You survived. If you chose (b) your last strength was used when searching for food in another spot. You did not survive.

5.   With your strength restored you travel a short distance seeking shelter—a place to sleep and digest your meal. There is a strange burrow above ground up ahead. It is large and the morning sun reflects off the strange smooth skin into your eyes. You climb up into it and try walking through the place that looks like the entrance, but you bump into something you cannot see. Finally you find an opening in the skin on the side and walk in, only to find many strange smells meet your nostrils. You sniff a few times and suddenly feel very tired. You decide to
     a.   lie down and sleep here.
     b.   move on to look for a safer place.

If you chose (a) you slept in an old abandoned car and made it your temporary shelter. You survived. If you chose (b) you found a large hollow tree to rest in and slept safely all day. You survived.

6. When you wake up the sun is setting and you are hungry again, but not starving like before. You leave your burrow and walk until you come to the edge of the woods. You see a field with some furry animals in it eating the plants, but you are not sure it is safe to enter the field or whether those animals are food or not. As you move closer you notice a freshly killed rabbit in front of you. There are those strange tracks around it, like the ones you saw near that dead animal with the strange smell some time ago. But this meat smells good as you approach it and your hunger deepens. Then, as you move even closer, you notice something sticking out of the ground near the rabbit. It looks like it has large teeth and is made of the strange skin of that burrow with the smooth shiny skin. You look all around one more time to make sure that none of the dangerous animals who walk on two feet are around, then you

    a.   pounce on the rabbit.
    b.   run off into the underbrush, sensing danger.

If you chose (a) you felt a sharp, cold pain climb up your leg from one of your feet. Your foot is in a steel trap and there is no way out. You did not survive. If you chose (b) you survived.

7. If you have successfully survived by making all of the right choices so far, you will now raise a new coyote family. On the way back to your burrow you meet a coyote and decide to take her or him as a mate. Soon the next generation of coyotes is born and you have pups of your own to feed.

EXTENDING THE EXPERIENCE

• Hold a festival of milk in celebration of one of mammal's unique creations. Eat *ice cream* with *whipped cream*, *cheese* and crackers, *yogurt*, *cottage cheese* and other milk products. Make butter by filling baby food jars with cream and shaking or "churning" them until the butter is formed.

• Create an illustration of what you imagine the monster to look like in the story of "The Dogs Who Saved Their Master."

• Keep a journal of all the wild mammals you see. Add to the notes about each of these mammals every time you learn something new by your own observation, by reading about it or from some other source.

• Visit places where coyotes live near you and listen for their calls at dusk.

• Work on learning how your pet or other domestic animal communicates and try duplicating these sounds and movements to speak its language.

NOTES

1. See Chapter 6 for more information and activities about overwintering strategies among mammals.
2. This procedure for assembling puzzles is adapted from William B. Stapp and Dorothy A. Cox, *Environmental Education Activities Manual* (Dexter, Mich.: Thomson-Shore, 1979), 130-32. To obtain a copy write to Environmental Education Activities Manual, 2050 Delaware, Ann Arbor, MI 48103.

CHAPTER 14

✤ Why Possum Has a Naked Tail ✤

(Cherokee—Southeast)

In the old days, Possum had the most beautiful tail of all the animals. It was covered with long silky hair and Possum liked nothing better than to wave it around when the Animal People met together in council. He would hold up his tail and show it to the Animal People.

"You see my tail," he would say. "Is it not the most beautiful tail you have ever seen? Surely it is finer than any other animal's!"

He was so proud of his tail that the other animals became tired of hearing him brag about it. Finally, Rabbit decided to do something about it. Rabbit was the messenger for the animals and he was the one who always told them when there was to be a council meeting. He went to Possum's house.

"My friend," Rabbit said, "there is going to be a great meeting. Our chief, Bear, wants you to sit next to him in council. He wants you to be the first one to speak because you have such a beautiful tail."

Possum was flattered. "It is true," he said, "one who has such a beautiful and perfect tail as I have should be the first one to speak in council." He held up his tail, combing it with his long fingers. "Is not my tail the most wonderful thing you have ever seen?"

Rabbit looked close at Possum's tail.

"My friend," Rabbit said, "it seems to me as if your tail is just a little dirty. I think that it would look even better if you would allow me to clean it. I have some special medicine that will make your tail look just the way it should look."

Possum looked close at his tail. It did seem as if it was a little bit dirty. "Yes," Possum said, "that is a good idea. I want all of the animals to admire my tail when I speak in council."

Then Rabbit mixed up his medicine. It was very strong, so strong that it loosened all of the hair on Possum's tail. But as he put the medicine on Possum's tail he wrapped the tail in the skin which had been shed by a snake.

"This snakeskin will make sure the medicine works well," Rabbit said. "Do not take it off until you speak in council tomorrow. Then the people will all see your tail just as it should be seen."

Possum did as Rabbit said. He kept the snakeskin wrapped tightly around his tail all through the night.

The next day, when the animals met for council, Possum sat next to Chief Bear. As soon as the meeting began, he stood up to speak. As he spoke, he walked back and forth, swinging his tail, which was wrapped in the snakeskin. He smiled as he thought of how good his tail would look because of the medicine Rabbit put on it. All of the animals were watching him very closely, looking at his tail. Possum grinned at the thought of how beautiful his tail would look. The time was right.

KAHIONHES

Possum pulled off the snakeskin wrapping and as he did so, all of the hair fell off his tail.

"My friends," Possum said, holding up his tail and beginning to unwrap the snakeskin, "I have been chosen to start this council because of my tail. It is the finest of all the tails. Look at my beautiful tail!"

Possum pulled off the snakeskin wrapping and as he did so, all of the hair fell off his tail. His tail was naked and ugly and when Possum saw it, the grin froze on his face. All of the animals were looking at him. Possum was so ashamed, that he fell down on the ground and pretended to be dead. He did not move until long after all the other animals had gone.

To this day, Possum still has that foolish grin on his face and whenever he feels threatened, he pretends that he is dead. And, because he was so vain, Possum has the ugliest tail of all the animals.

DISCUSSION
Animals of the City and Suburb

The possum, or opossum, which inspired this Cherokee story "Why Possum Has a Naked Tail," is one of the many animals that has adapted to life in close proximity to human beings. Throughout any suburb or city there is an amazing number of animals going about their business in seeming harmony with, or tolerance of, people's activities. When cities and suburbs were first built some animals perished or were forced to seek a home elsewhere as natural food supplies, watering holes, nest sites and escape cover diminished. Others adapted well to the restrictive, often small habitats of lawns, parks, cemeteries, roof tops and alleys that replaced their natural habitat. Natural predators were supplanted by traffic accidents and "road kills," cats and dogs, pollution and electric wires. Some of our urban animals in North America were introduced from Europe and other regions where they had already adapted to life amid buildings and roadways. These *exotic species*—alien invaders from other shores—such as the starling, house sparrow, Norway rat and house mouse, are now well established on their adopted continent. Zoos provide yet another environment for animals and are usually situated within the city limits.

Although some people view urban and suburban animals as pests and lower-class inferiors to their relatives in the wild, they can in fact be a continual source of enjoyment, beauty and fascination once we accept and appreciate them. City critters, too, are part of the great web of life—the part many people are most likely to see and experience. The following discussion looks more closely at some urban and suburban animals, zoos and the animal relationships these close contacts afford people whose surroundings consist of lawn, pavement and concrete rather than forest, field and wetland.

GRAY SQUIRREL. Few city animals are more common and enthusiastic in their interaction with people as the gray squirrel. This bushy-tailed nutkin of forest and park which sometimes appears as the "black squirrel" (a genetic strain of the gray squirrel), spends most of its time gathering food, especially nuts. The gray squirrel has adapted well to life in the city from its natural home in the hardwood forest. During the summer they live in ball-shaped, treetop nests made of twigs and leaves and lined with grasses. The entrance is on the side. As late summer fades into fall they can be seen scurrying around carefully burying nuts in the ground. They dig a hole, drop the nut in, tamp dirt over the nut using their front paws, then conceal this *cache* with grass or leaves. When winter arrives they take up residence in a hollow tree with the entrance up 40 to 60 feet (12.2 to 18.3 meters) from the ground. Or in park settings where hollow trees can be scarce, they may live in a larger winter nest with thicker walls than the summer versions. Gray squirrels do not hibernate, they remain active all winter long foraging for food and digging up the nuts they have stored in the ground. They seem to locate the nuts by smell.

For some reason gray squirrels often run away when confronted with the more aggressive, but much smaller red squirrels. The red squirrel frequents more secluded groves of evergreen trees and prefers the seeds of cones. Gray squirrels are denizens of hardwood groves where oak, maple, hickory, ash, butternut, black walnut and other nut-producing trees abound. The black strain of the gray squirrel is found in certain urban parks, such as the population living in the Bronx Zoo in New York City.

Some urban gray squirrels and their beautiful ruddy cousin, the larger fox squirrel, are almost completely dependent on humans for survival, especially during the winter. In many cases, attics have replaced hollow trees as

Figure 14–1. The raccoon's masked face is a familiar site in city and suburb. Size (including tail): 26–40 inches (66.0–101.6 centimeters). Photo by Peter Hope.

winter shelters from cold, wind and snow. On almost any winter day these squirrels can be seen eating from people's hands in local parks or availing themselves of bird seed at a backyard feeder. This habit, along with a tendency to occasionally raid bird nests, are the few traits that detract from the appeal of this well-loved animal.

CHIPMUNK. Chipmunks, like the red squirrel, can be found in somewhat more remote corners of the urban environment, such as the fringe of a large park or the wild borders of a cemetery. Their vociferous "chuck-chuck-chuck" rings out as they call back and forth to each other while perched up on a stone or cement wall or gravestone. Whenever people come too close they let out a shrill whistle to sound the alarm, then scamper down into their burrow or disappear into a wall. Their burrows have several chambers branching off the main tunnel that are used for nesting and for storing a sizeable underground cache of food. Burrows have several secret entrances for safety and there is no tell-tale mound of dirt outside since

the tailings are carried off somewhere else during excavation. Chipmunks seem to be forever filling their cheek pouches with food and scurrying off to add to their subterranean cache, which can be as large as a half bushel of seeds, nuts, raisins and other foodstuffs of both natural and human-derived origins. Once while on a camping trip, we returned from a hike to find that a chipmunk got into our supplies and made off with 12 ounces (340 grams) of raisins, leaving us the empty box. These food stores are used for sustenance during the winter when chipmunks awake periodically from their deep sleep with a ravenous appetite.

RACCOON. Raccoons have penetrated deeply into many urban areas (Figure 14-1). They often take up residence in attics and basements in place of the hollow trees and small caves they inhabit in the wild. Easily recognized by their black mask and ringed tail, raccoons are nocturnal and are usually spotted at the end of a flashlight beam when they're caught raiding a garden, garbage can or dumpster.

These black markings on face and tail help to camouflage them amid the shadows of branches in the treetops where they spend a lot of their time, being excellent climbers with sharp claws. Since raccoons like to be around wet areas such as rivers, marshes and swamps, they often leave their tiny, human-like paw prints in the sand or mud as they forage in parks for their natural food of insects, fish, crayfish, snakes, mollusks, frogs, berries and nuts. They are catholic eaters who also love corn and grains. They have been known to eat young squirrels, birds and eggs, and will even raid bumblebee and wasp nests! Raccoons are famous for washing their food before eating it when water is available. In the wild, raccoons become dormant during the winter months, but they are not a deep hibernator. They will emerge from their sleep to forage during warm spells.

WOODCHUCK. The woodchuck or groundhog and opossum are two more mammals that have adapted well to life among human beings. Woodchucks create their infamous burrows by digging with the strong muscles and sharp claws of their front feet and pushing the loose dirt out of the tunnel with their hind feet. This leaves the trademark mound of dirt at the mouth of the main tunnel. These substantial burrows are dug in woodlands, fields and hedgerows, under stone walls, ledges, old stumps or at the top of a small rise in the middle of a field. Tunnels vary from 10 to 25 feet (3.0 to 7.6 meters) long and run 2 to 3 feet (.6 to .9 meters) below the surface. Several grass- or leaf-lined galleries lie off the main tunnel and there are also several well-concealed escape tunnels. These holes are dug from the inside and the soil is pulled back inside the burrow to keep the entrance as inconspicuous as possible. Such escape routes are necessary because an immature or adult woodchuck makes a good meal for a fox, mink or weasel, and it is not uncommon for a skunk to wander in to set up house.

Not long after the adults emerge from their deep winter sleep, the young woodchucks are born, usually by the first of May. Since woodchucks often rest to escape the heat of the day, they can best be seen at dawn and at dusk eating the tender greens of grass, roots, leaves and bark. Many people enjoy the site of these furry mammals, but some consider them to be a garden pest which they wage war on—shooting, gassing, trapping or even burning them. Native North Americans often planted a substantial extra measure of the crops in their gardens to be shared with the other animals, a practice that works well. Still, if you must, woodchucks can be controlled by installing a fence around the garden and burying it at least 3 or 4 feet

(.9 or 1.2 meters) in the ground. As a last resort the intruder can be live-trapped and transplanted safely to a lush hedgerow or field away from other houses.

OPOSSUM. Sometimes the clattering of garbage cans heard soon after nightfall turns out to be a hungry opossum, which, like the raccoon, is mostly nocturnal. When confronted with a flashlight an opossum will often stare down its opponent with a strange grin as it stands its ground. Or it may bare its teeth and hiss, presenting a threatening, unattractive sight which drives most people back inside. People and dogs, however, are among the opossum's greatest predators and, if cornered, it will indeed "play possum" by rolling over onto its back, opening its mouth and even faking convulsions before "dying." Opossums prefer the open woods and swamps in the wild, but are now well adapted to living in and near waste lands, backyards and gardens, having extended their range far to the north from the southeast where the story of "Why Possum Has a Naked Tail" originated among the Cherokee. Upon spotting the opossum's long, rat-like tail with its rough skin and short, sparse, bristly hairs, it is clear why someone would wonder why an animal would have such an unprotected appendage. Opossums are adept at climbing trees and thus the rough tail skin is very useful for gripping since the tail is *prehensile* and can grab a branch to hold fast just like the tail of a monkey. Sometimes a mother opossum carries its young by holding her tail over her back as they grab onto it with their own. Opossums live in hollow trees, caves and buildings.[1]

MICE AND RATS. No discussion of urban and suburban animals would be complete without mentioning rats and mice. Some of our native species, such as the deer mouse, white-footed mouse and woodrats, have become well adapted to life alongside people.

Deer mice and white-footed mice are found throughout much of North America. In addition to their natural homes in logs and stumps, hollow trees and ground burrows, they have taken well to living in buildings. A reproductive rate of two to four litters of two to six young per year ensures an abundance of these mice scurrying around eating seeds, nuts and insects and storing great quantities of food in their caches.

The house mouse, which was introduced to North America from Europe, is now found all over the globe. Although house mice do eat our food, create messes and chew up the furniture at times, they also devour a lot of nuisance insects.

Our two alien introduced rats are the black rat, which is originally from the Orient, and the Norway (brown) rat from Eurasia. The sight of any rat distresses many people,

Figure 14–2. The pigeon or rock dove is equally at home on the ledge of a city building as it is beneath a highway overpass, in a barn or on a cliff in the wild. Its soft, cooing notes are a welcome sound amid the noises of the city. Size: 13 inches (33.0 centimeters). Photo by Alan C. Graham.

and rats do often carry contagious diseases. Norway rats are especially harmful because they devour great quantities of food while it is in storage.

HOUSE SPARROW. Like the house mouse and Norway rat, the house sparrow and starling crossed the Atlantic with European immigrants. House sparrows were introduced into New York City by Eugene Schieffelin, who also introduced song thrushes, nightingales, skylarks, chaffinches, bullfinches and the now ubiquitous starling. Only the house sparrow and starling were adaptable enough to become permanent inhabitants of North America.

House sparrows were first introduced into New York City in 1851 as a reminder of the European homeland, and possibly as a form of insect control. When listening to their songs in the morning and at dusk it is understandable that early immigrants missed them. These common birds feed on seeds, insects and food scraps such as bread crumbs. Their domed nests are built in the crevices of buildings, in climbing plants along walls and occasionally in trees. Because they remain in their habitat all winter, house sparrows quite naturally take possession of nesting spots before migrating birds like wrens, swallows and purple martins return in the spring. Not only do they out-compete other species of birds for nesting sites, but they will attack robins, chickadees, song sparrows and others as they feed and nest. Given this aggressiveness and

their high reproductive rates (two to five broods per season with four eggs per brood), it is no surprise that there seems to be a house sparrow perched on every brick and branch in some communities. These sedentary, territorial birds mate for life.

STARLING. Few people realize that the now common starlings are descended from the flocks that were brought to New York City's Central Park in 1890 and 1891 in an attempt to bring Shakespeare's birds to North America. These starlings spread quickly and they now number in the millions and range from coast to coast and from southern Canada to northern Mexico. Like house sparrows, starlings may, in part, have been introduced to North America to control insects. In fact a family of starlings can devour several thousand insects in one week. Also like the house sparrow, these birds are hardy, prolific breeders and adaptable to many different environments. Although in the wild they subsist on insects, fruits and berries, their city foods include just about anything they can get their beaks on. Unfortunately, their strong competitiveness for food and especially for nesting sites in hollow trees, has caused them to displace many of our native bluebirds and flickers. The holes under the eaves of buildings also do nicely for entryways to starling nest sites.

Starlings are master mimics and can imitate a variety of bird songs and other calls ranging from bobwhites to blue jays, robins, crows, goldfinches, northern orioles, bluebirds and even dogs and cats.

PIGEON. Pigeons, believed to be the first birds ever domesticated, had roots in city life long before they were brought to North America from the east (Figure 14-2). As early as the fifth century, people of Palestine and Syria constructed dovecots (chambers resembling rocky caves) for pigeons to nest in; the birds were used for food and as message carriers. Some of their natural nesting sites were found in England on the cliffs of Dover. It is possible that the eaves of buildings and constant din of traffic are reminiscent of the Dover cliffs and the incessant breaking of waves below. Rhythmic, rowing wing beats carry these birds as gracefully from rooftop to highway underpass as they do between their cliff-side roosts.

Have you ever stopped and noticed a colony of pigeons? Old, decrepit bricks and ledges, as well as steel girders under bridges make excellent nesting, breeding and roosting sites. Food, in the form of organic scraps found in litter and garbage, is plentiful in the city.

If you watch a colony of pigeons closely, you can get a feeling for the workings of their complex society. Pigeons have a *pecking order* that determines each individual bird's level of social dominance. Pecking is not usually an aggressive act but merely a symbolic statement saying, "This is just to remind you that I'm boss here so out of my way!" Social bigwigs get their choice of the best roosts, those sheltered from the wind and rain. Dominant pigeons are not necessarily the strongest, but those who are older (street pigeons can live to be thirty years old), more established and willing to assert their influence. With time, newcomers begin to contest for the better sites, thus the pecking order is always changing.

CHIMNEY SWIFT. Chimney swifts are native seasonal residents that have also adapted to city life. They build nests on the vertical walls inside of abandoned chimneys, and in buildings such as barns, by using saliva to cement twigs together. These speedy, darting birds, sometimes likened to "flying cigars," rest by clinging to the vertical walls of buildings that are usually abandoned. Swifts feed exclusively on insects caught on the wing.

NIGHTHAWK. Several species of native birds are less-known seasonal residents of cities and towns. Night-hawks, family relatives to the whippoorwill, arrive around the middle of May from their wintering grounds in South America. The flat, gravelly roofs of buildings and parking structures are often chosen as nesting sites. Night-hawks build no nest, they simply lay their eggs on a flat surface, such as a stump or even on the ground in the wild. Their sporadic flight high over the city is conspicuous as are their two distinct sounds, sometimes audible on a quiet street. During the breeding season, from mid-May until early June, the male nighthawk performs a mating display. He rises to a considerable height and then plunges downward. As he suddenly checks this rapid fall, the air rushing past his wings produces a peculiar roaring sound. In the spring we are more likely to hear the nasal "peent" that the nighthawk frequently makes while hunting. Mostly active at dusk, dawn and at night, these unusual birds eat insects on the wing. Moths, flies and other insects that collect around city lights provide an abundant food supply. They have long, pointed wings with a white band running across each wing.

WAXWINGS AND OTHER BIRDS. Flocks of cedar waxwings grace the branches of city trees in much of North America. These are among our most beautiful birds and are worth looking out for. They nest in open habitats with fruiting shrubs. In late fall and winter cedar waxwings are nomadic; some migrate to the West Indies and Costa Rica, while many overwinter in wandering flocks over much of this continent. A little smaller than a starling, they have a regal coat of fine, buff-brown feathers, a yellow-banded tail and a crested, black-masked head that makes them appear as a small cardinal with a pointed beak. Cedar waxwings are named for one of their favorite winter foods, the berries of the red cedar. A close relative, the bohemian waxwing, is an abundant winter visitor to Canadian cities, especially Calgary, Edmonton and Winnipeg.

Many other birds have adapted to living in urban and suburban areas, including the American robin, crow, mourning dove, purple martin, herring gull, grackle, mockingbird and hummingbird. It is hard to imagine life in the city without the colors, songs and characters of these adaptable birds.

CARP. Still another resident of many cities has it roots in the old world. Carp, first successfully introduced to America in 1877, eventually found their way into many waterways. Although these fish were, and still are, widely eaten in Europe, they never acquired widespread appeal in the United States. Their habit of churning up the river bottom and roiling the waters makes the river less hospitable for some native species of fish, especially trout. Presently, much controversy exists over whether or not to periodically poison certain rivers and kill the carp, which also results in the death of most other fish present, to allow the restocking of trout, walleye and other native species. In many cities and their environs, however, carp have become well established as a source of food for local people who enjoy fishing.

SUNFISH. The scrappy little native sunfish is a beautiful resident of urban lakes, ponds and rivers. A coat of scales with iridescent blue and green, orange speckles and olive bars makes them an attractive sight as they dart among the sunlit shallows along the shore. Their second name of "pumpkinseed" comes from the scarlet, seed-shaped spot on their gill covers. Each spring the male hollows out a nest in the shallows which is about 1 foot (30.5 centimeters) across and a few inches deep. It makes this nest by fanning the sand off to the side with its tail and picking up larger grains and small pebbles in its mouth to move them elsewhere. Courtship begins as the male spreads its gill covers to show the scarlet spots and fans the fins on its belly in display. Both male and female swim in a circle around the nest as the female lays the eggs and the male fertilizes them. After the female swims off the male remains to care for the eggs by driving away intruders and fanning the eggs with its fins to keep them well aerated and free of silt.

TOADS. While some urban animals are well regarded and others have earned a bad reputation, few are so undeservedly loathed as the toad. Even though 88 percent of its diet consists of flies, beetles, grasshoppers, grubs, ants, crickets, slugs and other invertebrates that many gardeners consider pests, the toad is unappreciated and even disdained. It lives quietly in moist, shady places and hunts at dusk, dawn and at night when the air is cooler and more damp. The low regard that most people have for the toad comes from the misbelief that the bumps on its skin, which is dry to the touch and not slimy at all, can cause warts. While these bumps, especially the large *paratoid gland* behind each eye, do emit an irritant that tastes bad and will inflame mucous membranes such as those around the eyes and mouth, people *do not* get warts from toads. A toad *will* usually release its bladder when picked up in order to startle a would-be predator.

INSECTS AND OTHER ARTHROPODS. Some of the least respected, much maligned and most numerous forms of urban wildlife are the insects and other arthropods. Cicadas and katydids, spiders, house flies, bees and butterflies are all part of our wildlife community. The spider in the corner of your bedroom ceiling may not be attractive, but its web will capture other insects, including mosquitoes, black flies and roaches. Bees—seen perhaps as no more than a potential sting—help form seeds for next year's plants by pollinating many kinds of flowers. And who can deny the appeal of a monarch butterfly, the flash of a firefly or the notes of cicadas and katydids on a warm summer evening?

Many people encounter a praying mantis while working in the yard or garden. These intriguing insects hold their front legs in a position that looks like they are praying. These legs are, however, quick to "prey" upon any likely insect meal that happens to wander into the mantis's ambush. Mantises eat a lot of harmful garden pests. The female will sometimes even devour its mate after mating if it is not quick enough to escape. A mantis egg mass appears like a mass of dried foam stuck to a twig or stem.

Dragonflies or "darning needles" sometimes happen by. The aquatic nymphs mature in a pond, lake or stream, but the adults are extremely accomplished flyers that can sometimes range a good distance from water and can use their two pairs of wings to reach speeds of up to 35 miles (56.3 kilometers) per hour! They can fly forward, backward, sideways, up or down and can even hover. These "mosquito hawks" eat many mosquitos and other biting insects and are completely harmless to human beings. They spend most of their time patrolling a territory over the surface of the water, where they catch food in a "basket" formed by the six legs beneath their bodies. Sometimes the food is eaten in mid-flight, at other times the dragonfly lands and then devours its hapless victim. Females can often be seen laying eggs by flying over the water and dipping the tips of their abdomens in here and there, or landing on a plant near the surface and sticking the abdomen beneath the surface to deposit the eggs.

Admittedly, there are some forms of urban and suburban wildlife that are hard for almost any person to tolerate, such as cockroaches and the many kinds of true flies. There are the biting flies like mosquitos, deer flies, black flies or buffalo gnats and "no-see-ums" or punkies, of which only the females bite. House flies do not bite, but they breed in garbage, excrement and carrion and can spread a number of diseases such as dysentery, cholera, typhoid and tuberculosis. Bluebottle and greenbottle flies are some of nature's recyclers, laying their eggs primarily in decaying plant and animal material. Tiny fruit flies proliferate in and around any overripe fruit that is left exposed. There are also the beautifully colored flower flies that feed on nectar, as well as the nectar-feeding crane fly that looks like an inch-long (2.5-centimeter) mosquito, but does not bite people at all. About fifteen thousand species of true flies inhabit North America.

True flies, a species which excludes dragonflies and many others with "fly" in their names, have one pair of wings and a pair of *halteres*, which are knobbed structures that provide equilibrium. Many flies, when seen through a hand lens, are covered by thick hair. Their *compound* eyes have several thousand hexagonal facets through which they view the world. Some flies, such as houseflies, have a sticky fluid exuded through hollow hairs located between the claws on their feet that enables them to walk up smooth, vertical walls or cling to ceilings.

OTHER URBAN WILDLIFE. There are many more kinds of animals that live in cities and their surroundings. The list is seemingly endless including earthworms, spiders and harvestmen (daddy longlegs), skunks, snails, garter snakes, slugs, garden snails, field crickets, honeybees, paper and mud wasps, yellowjackets, bumblebees, carpenter ants and their insect predators the ant lion, ladybird beetles ("ladybugs"), bullfrogs, green frogs, rats and mice, water striders, horned pout or catfish, bats, chickadees and cardinals. Even the peregrine falcon, which is now recovering from near extinction over its range in the eastern United States and southeastern Canada, has taken to nesting on the ledges of skyscrapers in several cities where there is an abundant supply of birds to prey upon.[2]

Figure 14–3. This female red wolf, an endangered species, is photographed here in its zoo habitat. The color of individuals can range from reddish-gray to nearly black. Originally ranging over southcentral North America, the red wolf's natural habitat is along river bottoms and in brushy and forested areas. The few remaining red wolves are being bred in captivity, and attempts are being made to reestablish populations in the wild. Size (including tail): 3.8–4.8 feet (1.2–1.5 meters). Photo by Adrienne Miller, courtesy Roger Williams Park Zoo, Providence, Rhode Island.

Conservation of Urban Wildlife

Granted we have mixed feelings about city wildlife. Watching a squirrel may be heart-warming, but few people will tolerate that same squirrel if it moves into their attic for the winter. Bats, on the other hand, are regarded by many as one of the least desirable animals, yet mosquitoes are among the hundreds of insects they eat each night. Have you ever had your garbage scattered by a raccoon or an uncontrolled dog? Do rabbit raids on your flower beds detract from the enjoyment you get from having them around? Did you ever think that the pigeon who is eating garbage on the street is also helping to keep the city clean, leaving less food for mice and rats?

One solution to conflicts between people and wildlife is to use good sanitary practices so as not to attract pests with human refuse. You can also encourage animals where they are wanted and discourage them elsewhere, but this should be done humanely. If you find a squirrel or raccoon living in your attic, wait until it has gone outside, then block the entry hole securely. Mice, squirrels, raccoons and other animals can be trapped with a humane live trap, then transported and released in a suitable wild habitat. These traps should be lined with nest material and checked twice daily. Since wild animals may carry rabies and/or other diseases, you should *never* handle them directly. Set the cage up on a board and lift the board to move the cage safely. Wear gloves when transporting any cage and use caution to avoid being bitten. Keep the cage covered with a heavy cloth to calm the animal while it is being moved.

Plantings that provide food and cover are usually the best way to attract desirable birds and other animals. Evergreens and dense shrubs afford protective cover and shelter from the elements. Shrubs such as highbush cranberry and other viburnums, dogwoods and winter-berry produce berries for winter bird food. Many trees can provide for the needs of animals, birds and insects—oak, hickory, hawthorn, beech, holly, mountain ash, black cherry, crabapple, maple, white pine and spruce are among the best known. Daisies, sunflowers, asters, black-eyed susans, petunias, columbine and other flowers add to the value of planted habitat. In a book called *Gardening With Wildlife*, the National Wildlife Federation describes how to attract wildlife with planting schemes that provide the correct balance of food, shelter and open space.[3]

An easy project is to place nest boxes and shelters in trees and on telephone poles to encourage wildlife. Bat boxes offer a form of shelter that is an alternative to an attic. Bird feeders are another enjoyable way to bring birds and small mammals close to home. There are few simple pleasures as rewarding and entertaining as watching the behavior of the many birds and small mammals that show up at the feeder.

FEEDER

Each time I fill
the bird feeder I made
from old cellar wood
nailed to the cut-off
stub of an ancient
lilac tree

I feel the claws
of the chickadees
on my finger, their beaks
prodding the crevices
of my hands which hold
seeds of the sun.

They are perfectly solemn
full of purpose and joy,
and I watch them
from my human distance
which does not always
come between us.[4]

—Joseph Bruchac
Near the Mountains

Zoos and Endangered Species

Strangely enough, cities are the only place that many people can go to see certain forms of exotic and rare wildlife. In one of the great ironies of our time and as one example of how people can sometimes turn nature on its head, the zoos found in metropolitan areas are now one of the last havens for endangered animals that are rare or even extinct in the wild (Figure 14-3). Zoos are, however, changing from the wildlife prisons of concrete and steel bars that they used to be into places where many animals are kept in elaborate and expensive simulations of their native habitats. Moats, steep-walled trenches and, in some cases, mere open space are now serving to confine people and keep them separate from the relatively free-roaming animals.

Zoos are no longer the form of dreary "entertainment" they once were. Many zoos now bring people and animals together in a way that educates and helps a bond of understanding and empathy to form. Children of all ages come to see both abundant and endangered species in habitats sporting waterfalls, lush vegetation of the tropical rain forest, air-conditioned rocky coasts of the arctic and hot, dry desert environments.

Yet what kind of experience does a zoo provide? What does it teach a child to see a rare animal seemingly content to live in a confined artificial environment? Do they value an endangered species more deeply when they understand that they could be looking at one of the last of its kind, or do they feel its value is less because they can simply walk or ride to a nearby zoo to see that animal?

In today's zoos in the United States, 90 percent of the mammals and 75 percent of the birds were bred in captivity versus being captured in the wild. Some zoos are now being used to breed endangered species for reintroduction into the wild in order to strengthen wild populations. In some cases, such as the California condor, an animal now exists *only* in captivity in zoos. Biologists hope to raise enough individuals in captivity to reestablish a wild population at a later time. Some conservation groups, such as the Nature Conservancy and Wildlife Conservation International, are saving entire ecosystems to conserve biodiversity and provide safe habitat for endangered species.

Modern zoos are providing an essential function by educating people about wildlife and by acting as a survival safety net by preserving some endangered species in captivity. And even though zoos provide another wildlife experience for urban children, zoos are not the true homes for those animals. Zoos are at once a source of hope for endangered

City Animal Search

Directions: Place a mark next to each of the animals and items found. Take time to observe each discovery and have fun. Do not worry about trying to see everything. Draw pictures of the animals and their homes on the index cards.

Find an animal that:

__has six legs

__has two legs

__has no legs

__has eight legs

__has more than eight legs

__has two wings

__has four wings (two pairs of wings)

__has two eyes

__has more than two eyes (write the number of eyes here ___)

__has antennae

__can walk

__has ears

__can fly

__has a tongue

__has a nose

__has lips

__can crawl

__lives on a wall

__lives in a crack of the sidewalk

__lives in the grass

__lives on the tree's bark

__lives up high in a tree

__lives in a house

__lives under the eaves of a roof

__lives in a chimney

__lives on a flower

__is native to this land

__came originally from another country and was introduced here

__eats leaves

__eats grass

__eats insects

__eats other animals

__eats seeds

__is eaten by other animals

__eats nuts

__bites people

__has a bushy tail

__is cute

__is not so cute

__you like (write down why you like it here and what the animal is): _____

_____

_____

_____

__you do not like (describe why not here and what it is): _____

_____

_____

__you neither like nor dislike (tell what it is here):_____

__has paws

__has claws

__has fur

__has feathers

__has naked skin

__has a hard shell

__is tiny

__is large

__is medium-sized

—is someone's pet

Find some threats to animals that make their lives dangerous:

__a car, bus or other form of moving vehicle

__litter

__water pollution

__dirty air

__dogs

__cats

__poison

__traps

Find a source of water for animals:

_____

Figure 14–4. City Animal Search.

animals and a sad testament to what human beings have done to push those animals to the brink. It is only when an animal is experienced free and wild in its native home that it is seen whole as the animal that it truly is.

The song of the bird in the open tree is the one that brings true music to the ear, while that of the one in the cage is but a sad imitation. The one brings to its song something of the wide expanse of the sky, the voice of the wind, the sound of water; the other's song can be only the song of captivity, of the bars that limit freedom, and the pain that is in the heart.[5]

—Old Keyam
Voices of the Plains Cree

QUESTIONS

1. What does an animal need to live close to people in a city, town or suburb?

2. How does a specific animal, such as an American robin, meet its specific needs for food, water and shelter in the city?

3. What are some animals that you can think of who live in cities and towns? Where did those animals come from?

4. What does it mean to say that an animal, such as a pigeon, is an "alien" from another country? Can you name some city animals that came from other lands? How did they get here to North America?

5. Are city animals as important to the web of life on Earth as animals that live in the wild? Why or why not?

6. Which are your favorite city animals? Which are your least favorite? (See the "Discussion" for examples.) Why do you like or dislike each of these animals?

7. How and why does a wild animal like the gray squirrel end up living in a city?

8. Why do you think that opossum has a naked tail? Why does it pretend it is dead or "play possum" sometimes? How does it do this?

9. What are some of the threats and dangers that animals face in the city?

10. How could you help to take care of animals of the city and suburb?

11. Have you ever been to a zoo? What animals do you remember seeing there?

12. Did you or do you like zoos? Why? Why not? How do you feel seeing animals in a zoo?

13. Where did the animals living in zoos come from?

14. Zoos are helping endangered species today. Can you think of how they are doing so? Is it good for animals to live in zoos?

15. If an animal can live in a zoo, does that mean it does not need or want to live in the wild?

ACTIVITIES
City Animal Search

ACTIVITY: Go on a walk to search for and observe some animals and the conditions they live under in your neighborhood.

GOALS: Understand which animals live nearby in the city, where they live and how they survive in that environment.

AGE: Younger children and older children

MATERIALS: Copies of "City Animal Search" (Figure 14-4), pencils, cardboard backings or clipboards to write on, hand lenses, index cards.

PROCEDURE: Beforehand, scout out the area(s) where you will lead this activity and look for some specific animals or animal signs that children may be expected to find. Add these to the "City Animal Search."

Note: This activity is to be conducted under the close supervision of adults, during daylight hours, and in areas known to be relatively "safe," such as a public park, residential street, school yard or large vacant lot. The children are to stay close to an adult at all times. A ratio of one adult per two or three children is recommended.

Once you have gathered the children together, ask them some questions about the wildlife they may expect to find: What kinds of animals live in our neighborhood? Can you name some you would expect to find? What kinds of food do they eat? Where do they live—in what sort of shelter? What kinds of threats do they face, such as predators, disease, food shortages, etc.?

See the "Discussion" section in this chapter for descriptions of many urban and suburban animals. Here is a partial list of some of the common, well-known ones:

- gray squirrel
- fox squirrel
- red squirrel
- chipmunk
- raccoon
- house sparrow
- pigeon
- starling
- American robin
- mockingbird
- gull
- nighthawk
- toad
- fly

- mice (white-footed, deer and house mice)
- rats (Norway rat, black rat and woodrat)
- bullfrog
- green frog
- bumblebee
- honeybee
- yellow jacket
- wasp
- carpenter and other ants
- cricket
- earthworm
- sunfish

and have them take turns sharing their findings with the entire group. Have the small groups lead everyone over to see any particularly exciting findings, such as a spider in its web, a praying mantis, a toad or a colony of ants.

City Animal Survey

ACTIVITY: Conduct a simple survey in your neighborhood of people's attitudes toward animals.
GOALS: Discover which animals are more or less well liked than others, why this is so and how and where people interact with animals.
AGE: Older children
MATERIALS: Copies of "City Animal Survey," pencils, cardboard backings or clipboards to write upon, chalkboard and chalk or newsprint and felt-tipped markers.
PROCEDURE: *Note:* This activity is to be conducted under the close supervision of adults. Children and adults will work in groups as in "City Animal Search," with one adult accompanying each group of two or three children at all times. The object is to complete the "City Animal Survey" during daylight hours along the streets in a safe part of your neighborhood or in a convenient place, such as a shopping mall. Malls are good locations because many of the people there are just passing time and may be willing to answer a few questions to help out. Places like supermarkets, where people are usually in a hurry to finish their shopping, are not good locations for this survey. *Get permission beforehand* if you plan to visit a mall or other shopping area.

Before you conduct the survey, have the children predict what people's answers will be to each question. Record these predictions and set them aside for use later.

Once you arrive at the site, have children work in their small groups as they mill around, introduce themselves to people walking by and describe briefly the nature of their project and why they are conducting the survey. Then have the children ask people who are willing to participate to answer the following questions, keeping in mind that *animals* refers to everything from insects to birds to toads to squirrels. Have them record all of the answers.

CITY ANIMAL SURVEY

1. Name some of your favorite animals that live in the city.
2. Why do you like having these animals around?
3. Name some of your least favorite city animals.

Seeking Shelter

Rural Animal Shelter	Urban Animal Shelter
dense shrub	gravel rooftop
hollow tree	chimney
	attic
underground	mattress
cave	a flower in someone's
	flower bed
under a rock	ivy growing up a wall
hollow log	space under a porch
crack in tree bark	duck pond in a park
	basement
tree branches	insulation in attic or walls
	in a wall of a house
among tree roots	stone wall
gravelly riverbed	under the eaves of a roof
crotch of tree branches	bushes in someone's yard
	garbage dump
bed of pine needles	crack in a cement wall
	soil in a vacant lot
on top of the ground	in a drain pipe
underside of leaves	under a loose piece of side-
	walk or a loose brick
field grasses	trees in a vacant lot
stone wall	a television antenna
	on the crosspole on top
pond or marsh	of a telephone pole
	weeds in a vacant lot
on a flower	crack in a sidewalk

Figure 14–5. Seeking Shelter.

- praying mantis
- butterfly
- bat
- woodpecker
- mallard duck
- horned pout (catfish)
- carp
- spider
- garter snake
- mosquitoe

Now divide the group up and assign two or three children to each adult leader. Pass out one copy of the "City Animal Search" sheets (Figure 14-4) to each group along with pencils, hand lenses and index cards. Once you have oriented them to the activity, emphasizing that the goal is to observe and leave the animals in their own homes, send the groups off on their excursions.

Gather the small groups together in about 20 minutes

4. What do you not like about these animals?

5. Do you ever spend time watching city animals? Which ones?

6. Do you ever feed the animals? Which ones?

7. Where do you go to watch and feed animals?

8. What would the city be like without any animals living here? Why do you feel this way?

Thank you for helping us by answering these questions!

Once you are back home or in the learning center, have the children in each group take turns sharing the responses they received to each question. Start with the answers to the first question and have all groups share responses, then move on to question two, and so on. Meanwhile, record the responses up front to put together a profile of how a particular group of people view and relate to city animals.

Now compare the real answers with what the children predicted people would say. How did they do on their predictions? Are there any surprises among real answers?

Seeking Shelter

ACTIVITY: Match up some forms of shelter for animals in the city to their counterpart shelters in the wild.

GOAL: Understand how animals have adapted to urban environments by finding shelters that meet their needs in the city.

AGE: Younger children and older children

MATERIALS: Copies of Figure 14-5 "Seeking Shelter," pencils.

PROCEDURE: Discuss the many ways that animals must meet their basic needs for food, shelter and water in the city. Ask the children to give some examples of specific city animals and how they meet their needs. Ask them to describe how populations of that animal which live in rural areas meet their needs.

Pass out copies of "Seeking Shelter" (Figure 14-5) and have the children draw lines to connect the rural forms of animal shelter on the left with their counterparts in the city. Each form of shelter on the left may correlate with more than one on the right, and vice versa.

Take a field trip to look at urban wildlife in some of these habitats as a follow-up to the matching experience.

Zoos and Endangered Species

ACTIVITY: Research some endangered or exotic species that are housed at a nearby zoo and discuss the issues surrounding the keeping of animals in zoos. Visit these animals in their zoo habitat to observe and interact with them. Write a story, draw a picture or create a poem describing your thoughts and feelings about seeing animals in a zoo, and what/how you imagine the animal might feel being there.

GOALS: Understand the issues involved in keeping animals, especially endangered species, in zoos. Realize, through "direct" experience, the nature of conditions in zoo habitats for these animals. Empathize with the plight of these animals.

AGE: Younger children and older children

MATERIALS: "Discussion" section from this chapter; list of endangered (or threatened) and/or exotic species housed at a nearby zoo; books, articles, filmstrips, videos and other sources of information about each species; pencils; paper; clipboards and cardboard backing; sketch pads; crayons; colored pencils; clay; tape recorders and cassettes; video camera and tape; camera and film; other equipment as needed to supply the children's needs for the zoo visit part of their projects and for presenting their reports.

PROCEDURE: Acquire a list of the exotic and endangered (or threatened) species found in a nearby zoo. If the zoo does not house endangered species, simply focus on the exotics. Have each child pick one animal from the list, being sure some of the endangered species are chosen. Help them to research and learn about their chosen species. Discuss the issues surrounding endangered species in zoos as described in the "Discussion" section of this chapter.

Visit the zoo and station the child or children who have chosen a certain species, along with an accompanying adult, in front of each animal's zoo habitat. Have them record with notes, tape recording, illustrations, photographs or videotape the movement, habits and vocalizations of the animal. Encourage them to consider all that they have learned about the animal as they watch it and to try to put themselves in the animal's place. Have them attempt to interact with the animal by making eye contact, attempting to respond by imitating the animal's sounds and by talking *softly* to the animal. Instruct them *not* to feed or touch the animal; these animals are on special diets. Also warn them that the animals may bite if approached too closely. Allow from 20 minutes to 1 hour or more for this observation and interaction, depending upon the age and attention span of the children. Spend the day at the zoo, have fun and encourage the children to return periodically during the visit to further the contact with their chosen animal.

While the children are either still at the zoo or back home or in the learning center, have each child respond creatively to the experience with her or his exotic and/or endangered animal. This may take the form of a poem, illustration, story, sculpture, slide show, video narrative or other creative and informative expression. It could be a report, or an artistic work or story. The object is for each child to express her or his feelings and thoughts about the plight and experience of that animal, with a particular focus on whether or not he or she believes that zoos are a logical or appropriate home for endangered and exotic species.

This empathy and understanding for their animal can be furthered by a follow-up involving taking action to help protect that species, to let the zoo officials know of the children's opinions and feelings resulting from the activity, or an educational project to inform them about the animal or any other idea you or the children may have.[6]

Urbanimal

ACTIVITY: Create a fantastic urban animal that is *incredibly* well adapted to surviving the challenging environmental conditions of life in an urban environment.
GOALS: Understand the environmental conditions to which an urban animal must adapt if it is to survive. Understand the survival adaptations that enable urban animals to survive.
AGE: Younger children and older children
MATERIALS: Balloons, clay, egg cartons, straws, yarn, pipe cleaners, tape, glue, paste, construction paper, cardboard, scissors, tubes from empty rolls of toilet paper or gift wrapping, crayons, any other materials you or the children think of or need for their urbanimals.
PROCEDURE: Brainstorm with the children a list of environmental conditions in the city. Ask them to describe the qualities of the air, water, food and shelter, as well as the threats to safety, noise level and other harsh conditions faced by an animal living in a city.

Have them work in small groups to create an urban animal that is *incredibly* well adapted to living under the city conditions they thought of, such as:

- polluted air;
- polluted water;
- food found in dumpsters and other unpleasant places;
- shelter in dark dirty places;
- loud noise much of the time; and
- numerous threats to survival such as cars, buses, trains, trucks, dogs, cats, electric wires, mouse traps, poison and other devices set out by people to kill animals.

The children can either create their own animal from scratch, using a balloon, clay, egg carton or other object as the body, or they can turn one of the group members into an "urbanimal." Have them attach as many devices or (adaptations) to the animal as they desire to help the animal survive in the city. They may think of, for instance, a mouth with a water filter, ears with plugs or tiny openings, no ears at all, insulated fur to protect the animal from being electrocuted or feet that cannot walk on pavement to avoid being hit by a car.

Once their urbanimals are done, have each group explain its many adaptations and how they help that urbanimal to survive.

Adopt an Urban Animal

ACTIVITY: Get involved in hands-on projects to provide good habitat (food, water and shelter) for urban animals.
GOALS: Understand that urban animals have basic needs. Realize how people can take action to help them meet those needs.
AGE: Younger children and older children
MATERIALS: Appropriate supplies for the particular animals and projects chosen.
PROCEDURE: Have each child choose a certain animal to adopt that frequents her or his backyard and the space around it. This could include a bluejay, pigeon, toad, bat, cricket, squirrel, English house sparrow, garter snake or any other animal the child chooses from the list in "City Animal Search" or from animals mentioned in the "Discussion" section. Help each child to learn about what that animal eats, where it lives, how it acquires water to drink and what it does to survive the winter.

Now have the children choose a project that will help their adopted animal, such as:

- wildlife plantings;
- a nest box;

- a watering hole or bird bath;
- a winter shelter;
- a winter feeding station; or
- a summer shelter.

Emphasize that the idea is to help a wild animal to meet its needs while it lives free and independent in its home outdoors. Tell the children they are not to try to touch or catch the animal, especially since some animals carry and spread diseases and parasites.

EXTENDING THE EXPERIENCE
• *Twenty Questions:* Choose a city animal that you like. Stand in front of the rest of the group while everyone else asks you questions about your animal that can be answered with "yes" or "no" only. The group has twenty questions to try to guess which city animal you are.
• *Urban Ant Trails:* Ants mark scent trails to lead other ants in their colony to food. Set out a treat of food for someone and use a ball of string to mark an imaginary "scent" trail to the food. Make the trail long, winding and tricky, from room to room, outdoors—all over! Have someone follow the trail to find his or her reward!
• Play possum: Just for the fun of it, practice "playing possum" by rolling over onto your back, opening your mouth and going into convulsions. Be dramatic! See who is the most convincing!
• Write your own "why" stories to explain things about different animals, like Possum's tail in "Why Possum Has a Naked Tail."
• Calculate the temperature of any urban or suburban environment by using the "Cricket Thermometer" in Chapter 8. This activity can be conducted wherever snowy tree crickets are calling, including vacant lots, parks and ballfields.
• See Chapter 3 for stories, information and activities about spiders and harvestmen (daddy longlegs), common residents of city and suburb.

NOTES
1. See the "Discussion" section in Chapter 13 for more information about the opossum and other marsupials.
2. See Chapter 17 for the story of the peregrine falcon.
3. National Wildlife Federation, *Gardening With Wildlife* (Washington, D.C.: National Wildlife Federation, 1974).
4. Joseph Bruchac, *Near the Mountains* (Fredonia, N.Y.: White Pine Press, 1987), 22.
5. Edward Ahenakew, *Voices of the Plains Cree*, edited by Ruth M. Buck (Toronto: McClelland & Stewart Limited, 1973), 80. Quoted in Frances G. Lombardi and Gerald Scott Lombardi, *Circle Without End* (Happy Camp, Calif.: Naturegraph Publishers, 1982), 21.
6. See Chapter 17 for more information and activities involving threatened and endangered species.

✛ SURVIVAL ✛

He painted spots upon the fawn's body so that, when she lay still, her color blended in with the earth and she could not be seen. Then Wakan Tanka breathed upon her, taking away her scent.

Chapter 15

❖ How the Fawn Got Its Spots ❖

(Dakota {Sioux}—Plains)

Long ago, when the world was new, Wakan Tanka, The Great Mystery, was walking around. As he walked, he spoke to himself of the many things he had done to help the four-legged ones and the birds survive.

"It is good," Wakan Tanka said. "I have given Mountain Lion sharp claws and Grizzly Bear great strength. It is much easier now for them to survive. I have given Wolf sharp teeth and I have given his little brother, Coyote, quick wits. It is much easier now for them to survive. I have given Beaver a flat tail and webbed feet to swim beneath the water and teeth which can cut down the trees and I have given slow-moving Porcupine quills to protect itself. Now it is easier for them to survive. I have given the birds their feathers and the ability to fly so that they may escape their enemies. I have given speed to the deer and the rabbit so that it will be hard for their enemies to catch them. Truly it is now much easier for them to survive."

However, as Wakan Tanka spoke, a mother deer came up to him. Behind her was her small fawn, wobbling on weak new legs.

"Great One," she said. "It is true that you have given many gifts to the four-leggeds and the winged ones to help them survive. It is true that you gave me great speed and now my enemies find it hard to catch me. My speed is a great protection, indeed. But what of my little one here? She does not yet have speed. It is easy for our enemies, with their sharp teeth and their claws, to catch her. If my children do not survive, how can my people live?"

"Wica yaka pelo!" said Wakan Tanka. "You have spoken truly; you are right. Have your little one come here and I will help her."

Then Wakan Tanka made paint from the earth and the plants. He painted spots upon the fawn's body so that, when she lay still, her color blended in with the earth and she could not be seen. Then Wakan Tanka breathed upon her, taking away her scent.

"Now," Wakan Tanka said, "your little ones will always be safe if they only remain still when they are away from your side. None of your enemies will see your little ones or be able to catch their scent."

So it has been from that day on. When a young deer is too small and weak to run swiftly, it is covered with spots that blend in with the earth. It has no scent and it remains very still and close to the earth when its mother is not by its side. And when it has grown enough to have the speed Wakan Tanka gave its people, then it loses those spots it once needed to survive.

"Come close so I can talk to you," said the alligator. "I will not harm you. Help me and I will also help you."

The Alligator and the Hunter

(Choctaw—Southeast)

There once was a man who had very bad luck when he hunted. Although the other hunters in his village were always able to bring home deer, this man never succeeded. He was the strongest of the men in the village and he knew the forest well, but his luck was never good. Each time he came close to the deer, something bad would happen. A jay would call from the trees and the deer would take flight. He would step on dry leaves and the deer would run before he could shoot. His arrow would glance off a twig and miss the deer. It seemed there was no end to his troubles. Finally the man decided he would go deep into the swamps where there were many deer. He would continue hunting until he either succeeded or lost his own life.

The man hunted for three days without success. At noon on the fourth day, he came to a place in the swamp where there had once been a deep pool. The late summer had been a very dry one, however, and now there was only hot sand where once there had been water. There, resting on the sand, was a huge alligator. It had been without water for many days. It was so dry and weak that it was almost dead. Although the hunter's own luck had been bad, he saw that this alligator's luck was even worse.

"My brother," said the man, "I pity you."

Then the alligator spoke. Its voice was so weak that the man could barely hear it. "Is there water nearby?" said the alligator.

"Yes," said the man. "There is a deep pool of clear cool water not far from here. It is just beyond that small stand of trees to the west. There the springs never dry up and the water always runs. If you go to that place, you will survive."

"I cannot travel there by myself," said the alligator. "I am too weak. Come close so I can talk to you. I will not harm you. Help me and I will also help you."

The hunter was afraid of the great alligator, but he came a bit closer. As soon as he was close, the alligator spoke again.

"I know that you are a hunter but the deer always escape from you. If you help me, I will make you a great hunter. I will give you the power to kill many deer."

This sounded good to the hunter, but he still feared the alligator's great jaws. "My brother," the man said, "I believe that you will help me, but you are still an alligator. I will carry you to that place, but you must allow me to bind your legs and bind your jaws so that you can do me no harm."

Immediately the alligator rolled over to its back and held up its legs. "Do as you wish," the alligator said.

The man bound the alligator's jaws firmly with his sash. He made a bark strap and bound the alligator's legs together. Then, with his great strength, he lifted the big alligator to his shoulders and carried it to the deep cool water where the springs never dried. He placed the alligator on its back close to the water and he untied its feet. He untied the alligator's jaws, but still held those jaws together with one hand. Then he jumped back quickly. The alligator rolled into the pool and dove underwater. It stayed under a long time and then came up. Three more times the alligator dove, staying down longer each time. At last it came to the surface and floated there, looking up at the hunter who was seated high on the bank.

"You have done as you said you would," said the alligator. "You have saved me. Now I shall help you, also. Listen closely to me now and you will become a great hunter. Go now into the woods with your bow and arrows. Soon you will meet a small doe. That doe has not yet grown large enough to have young ones. Do not kill that deer. Only greet it and then continue on and your power as a hunter will increase. Soon after that you will meet a large doe. That doe has fawns and will continue to have young ones each year. Do not kill that deer. Greet it and continue on and you will be an even greater hunter. Next you will meet a small buck. That buck will father many young ones. Do not kill it. Greet it and continue on and your power as a hunter will become greater still. At last you will meet an old buck, larger than any of the others. Its time on Earth has been useful. Now it is ready to give itself to you. Go close to that deer and shoot it. Then greet it and thank it for giving itself to you. Do this and you will be the greatest of hunters."

The hunter did as the alligator said. He went into the forest and met the deer, killing only the old buck. He became the greatest of the hunters in his village. He told this story to his people. Many of them understood the alligator's wisdom and hunted in that way. That is why the Choctaws became great hunters of the deer. As long as they remembered to follow the alligator's teachings, they were never hungry.

DISCUSSION

Predator and Prey: Survival Adaptations

Many Native North American stories deal with survival and the interactions and adaptations that have developed between animals that relate as predator and prey. *Adaptations* are physical and behavioral traits that help animals to survive. The Dakota story "How the Fawn Got Its Spots" is rich in the knowledge of the survival adaptations of several animals. This brief story mentions a number of important adaptations, including those that show how animals have adapted to living with each other and in their particular environments:

- sharp claws of the mountain lion
- strength of the grizzly bear
- sharp teeth of the wolf
- quick wits of the coyote
- flat tail and webbed feet of the beaver
- quills of the porcupine
- feathers and ability to fly of the birds
- speed of the deer and rabbit

When the mother deer points out to Wakan Tanka that her little fawn has no way to protect itself from predators, the fawn is endowed with its *camouflage* of white spots, an adaptation that helps it to blend in with its surroundings to avoid detection. These spots and the fawn's lack of a scent help it to hide effectively from its enemies. In maturity, the fawn gains its speed to flee from danger. A white-tailed deer, for instance, can run at speeds of up to 50 miles (80.5 kilometers) per hour.

It is no wonder then that the hunter in the second story, the Choctaw tale "The Alligator and the Hunter," has trouble catching a deer! On the *fourth* day of the life-or-death journey in which he is committed to hunting a deer, he meets an alligator who is dying of thirst. The alligator offers to help the hunter succeed in exchange for being carried to a water hole to save its life. Yet, as the Apache story "The Boy and the Rattlesnake" shows in Chapter 11, animals are almost always true to their nature, so the man ties up the alligator's feet and jaws to be safe.

Upon reaching the pool of cool, clear water the alligator dives and surfaces *four times* before remaining afloat to teach the hunter the secrets of catching a deer. The alligator tells the hunter to greet, but not kill young does, older pregnant does, older does capable of bearing fawns and younger bucks who will father many fawns. Only an older buck that has lived out its life, who is "ready to give itself" to the hunter, can be killed. It must then be greeted and thanked. Only those Choctaws who remember to follow the teachings of the alligator become great hunters.

INTERRELATIONSHIPS. Both the alligator and the hunter demonstrate some important realities of survival. First, we are all *interdependent* upon our own kind as well as on the plants and other animals around us. Some of these *interrelationships* may seem hard and cruel because one animal benefits at the expense of another. *Predators* catch and devour their *prey*, while parasites, such as the lamprey or a tick, slowly feed on a host while it is still alive. Sometimes the host lives, sometimes it becomes so weak that it eventually perishes and the parasite moves on to find another. *Competition* results when two animals vie for the same resource, such as food or space, in any habitat. Eventually, one competitor wins out over the other, or one either adapts to using an alternative resource or dies. No two animals can occupy the same exact niche or use identical resources in any environment. *Amensalism* occurs when an inhibitor's actions affect another animal negatively without bringing any benefit to the first animal. For instance, a groundhog may dig up an ant nest while excavating a new burrow.

Some interactions between animals benefit at least one of them while bringing no harm to either. Certain animals, such as the coyote and badger, will hunt together cooperatively, but these partners in *protocooperation* can easily survive without each other's help. *Commensalism* describes how one animal benefits from another as a necessity while the host is seemingly unaffected. The small fish called the remora attaches to a shark's underside with a suction disk on top of its head and feeds on the scraps of the sharks meals, but the shark seems to take little notice. In some cases two partners depend upon each other for survival. This is called *mutualism*. Termites, for example, have single-celled protozoans living in their guts that enable them to digest lignin and cellulose, two components of wood. These protozoans need the unique conditions in termite guts to survive and are supplied with food while the termite feeds.

It is said that there is a third category of interaction between animals called *neutralism*. These independents supposedly do not affect each other in any way. To our minds, while it *may* be possible for two animals to be so ecologically separate that they have no discernible direct effect upon each other, *every* interaction between two species of animals has some effect, either positive or negative, no matter how minor it may be. All living things on Earth are interconnected no matter how remote they may live from one another and how seemingly small the effect each has on the other's life.

Offense—Defense

Both predator and prey must, at certain times and in different situations, use the tactics of offense and defense to survive—to kill and avoid being killed. Many adaptations, can serve either purpose. A weasel's sharp teeth, for instance, may be used to kill a deer mouse or to defend itself against a great horned owl that tries to turn the smaller, but extremely aggressive weasel into a meal of its own.

OFFENSIVE ADAPTATIONS. *Offensive adaptations* are some of nature's most impressive. An owl's or hawk's sharp talons are made for attacking its prey, and its bill for tearing off pieces of flesh small enough to be gulped down. The undigested bits of the prey's teeth, bone, fur or feathers are regurgitated later in the form of a neat, oblong *pellet*. Pellets sometimes contain the entire skeletal remains of one or more small animals such as a mouse, vole or shrew.

Teeth made for attacking range from the hollow fangs of a poisonous pit viper to the tusks of a walrus, and from the canine teeth of a wolf or bear to the rows of razor sharp teeth on a shark's jaw that are periodically shed and replaced throughout the shark's life.

The arsenal of offensive adaptations includes a heron's bill and a cat's claws, a snake's or gila monster's poison or a spider's paralyzing venom.

Horns and antlers are weapons that come in many sizes and shapes. Horns are found on sheep, bison or buffalo, musk ox and antelopes. In most cases both male and female possess horns that are never shed and continue growing throughout the animal's life. Bone forms the core of a horn, which is covered with a material called *keratin*. This material is also the stuff of claws, fingernails and hair. Deer, moose, caribou and elk are among the animals that grow a new set of antlers each year prior to the mating season, only to shed these imposing weapons during the winter after the fall *rut* is over. In most cases, except for caribou and reindeer, only the male grows antlers. The male uses them to fight other males over the selection of a certain mate, as well as to display and attract the female. *Antlers* are made purely of bone. They are covered with soft, blood-rich "velvet" that nourishes the antlers as they grow. The velvet is usually rubbed off against a tree once the antlers are mature. This scraping, plus the sharpening of antlers against trees, leaves a characteristic naked patch on trees called a "rub." Antlers grow large and more impressive with the age of the animal until it has reached its peak. Nutrition also affects antler size—a well-fed deer grows a larger *rack* of antlers than another of similar age that is undernourished. As the vigor of older animals begins to fade, the size of their rack declines.

Hunting techniques are another form of offensive adaptation. Cats and other predators stalk their prey, often *freezing* in patient stillness or creeping slowly up on its victim, only to rush and pursue it at the right moment of opportunity. Wolves, conversely, hunt in packs that rely on exhausting the prey, then moving in for the kill. Insects use different strategies as well. Damselflies wait quietly until they see an opportunity to *ambush* their prey, then they return to a perch to consume it, while dragonflies catch, and sometimes even devour their prey on the wing.

DEFENSIVE ADAPTATIONS. Freezing to avoid being detected not only serves predators well, it is also widely used by rabbits, deer and other prey as a *defensive adaptation.* When a rabbit takes *flight* but finds itself in immediate danger of being caught, it will turn quickly on its pursuer and throw it a few swift kicks. This often confuses the predator and gives the rabbit another chance to reach safety. Musk ox are famous for their habit of forming a circle, with the adults facing out and the young in the middle, when threatened by predators such as wolves. Many animals avoid predators before they are even in sight because of the warning calls of others, such as a blue jay's or crow's call or the slap of a beaver's tail.

Some relatively slow-moving animals use *armor,* an effective means of protection from predators. Turtles can pull themselves into their shells while armadillos roll up into a well-protected ball.

Porcupines, skunks, toads and others survive by making each predator's encounter with them a most unpleasant one. A toad's bumps are really glands that emit a foul-tasting substance that irritates mucous membranes, such as those in the mouth and around the eyes. (These bumps *do not* cause warts, however.) Skunks are capable of spraying their overpowering musky scent up to 10 to 12 feet (3.0 to 3.7 meters) with pinpoint accuracy. Porcupines have up to thirty thousand barbed *quills,* a specialized form of hair, that will pull off, stick into an attacker's skin and work their way deep into an animal's soft tissues. Lost quills can grow back again.

Many of the animals possessing the most unpleasant, and even deadly, defenses provide a warning to keep away. The striped skunk will stomp its feet and display the white of its tail clearly before spraying. A rattlesnake's warning signal—the vibrating "rattle" on the end of its tail—tells others to beware. Some animals have a poor flavor when eaten combined with bright warning colors to advertise this fact to avoid becoming a meal. Most of these animals are also poisonous when eaten. These include the brightly colored red eft (the terrestrial stage of

the red-spotted newt) and the monarch butterfly caterpillar. Monarch caterpillars feed exclusively on the milkweed plant with its milky, bitter-tasting, poisonous sap. The animals that eat monarch butterflies experience a severe fit of vomiting.

An opposite strategy is the fine art of concealment, which is practiced by both predator and prey alike. *Camouflage* derives from the French verb *camoufler,* "to disguise." The fawn's spots in the opening story of this chapter are a form of camouflage (Figure 15-1), as is the snowshoe or varying hare's white winter coat and the adult deer's dull, gray winter fur. The arctic fox, ptarmigan and short-tailed weasel (ermine) also change color seasonally to a white coat that blends in with the snow. Some animals, such as the polar bear and the northern races of the arctic wolf and arctic hare, have white coats year-round. The desert relatives of many animals that also live in the forest tend to be relatively light in color. Some animals, like the "walking stick" insect, are shaped and colored like a twig, leaf or other part of the environment.

If a predator does spot its prey it is better to *bluff* and look like an imposing enemy than a tasty meal. The green caterpillar of the spicebush swallowtail butterfly has two pairs of large orange "eyespots" to scare away potential

Figure 15-1. The spotted patterning of these two fawns is a highly effective form of camouflage amid the dappling of sunlight and shade in the underbrush. Fawns remain inactive during the first three or four days of life, except when they are nursing. They instinctively "freeze" or become motionless when sensing danger. An additional survival adaptation that protects fawns from being detected by predators is the fact that they are odorless during their first three or four days of life. Photo courtesy Vermont Institute of Natural Science.

predators. The front spots even have a pair of menacing pupils. Many species of moths have eyespots in the color patterns on their wings. This may startle an attacking bird just long enough for a moth to drop off of a tree and out of sight in the confusion. Most insects attempt to escape predators by simply dropping like a stone off a leaf or twig when the perch is disturbed.

Some animals employ a form of *mimicry* for protection from predators. The adult viceroy butterfly mimics the orange and black colors of the monarch butterfly. Monarchs are both noxious and poisonous when eaten by predators, and so are avoided by them. As a result, the viceroy mimics, which *are* edible, seldom fall prey to birds.

Certain animals can even escape once they are caught. Skinks, a kind of lizard, have colorful tails that attract a predator's attention to that less vulnerable end. The tail snaps off and wiggles, allowing the skink to scuttle off largely intact, only to grow its tail back again. Field mice can slip out of and shed the thin skin of their tails when caught by a predator. The tail remains, though it dries up and falls off afterward.

Tracking and Nature Observation

All of these remarkable adaptations arise from the relationships of predator and prey. The elements of the hunt involve a heightened sensory awareness for the act of stalking or of escaping the stalker. There are many instinctive and learned behaviors used by animals to survive. Many of these skills of the four-leggeds have been mastered by those who stalk about up on two feet. The skills of the human hunters of the traditional peoples of North America can be used by those who want to observe, experience and learn more about wildlife in the outdoors. They are some of the basic components of *tracking* and *nature observation*. Some Native North Americans played a deer stalking game to heighten the senses and sharpen skills and reflexes. The stalker would sneak up so close to a deer that, with one quick motion, a tuft of hair would be pulled from the deer before it could sense the intruder and flee. Each tuft was tied tightly into a small bundle and strung onto a necklace. The more tufts of deer hair on the necklace, the greater the honor and recognition that person had as a skilled tracker and stalker.

At first, to an unskilled tracker, this game might seem highly implausible, even fictitious. This is simply because most of us are out of touch with the essential skills of tracking and their effectiveness when mastered and used in a good, balanced way.

Days or even weeks of preparation would precede the moment of success in the deer stalking game. The stalker would refrain from bathing and would obtain some scent of the deer to be rubbed onto the skin to mask the human scent. Clothes would be kept outdoors, again to rid them of human scent.

The habits and habitat of the deer in that region would be studied carefully. Where were they at different times of day? Where did they feed? When? Where did they bed down and leave scrapes? Where did they go to seek water? What were the prevailing wind conditions in the deer's habitat at different times of day and in different locations.

A period of four days of fasting and praying would often precede the game, during which the stalker would only drink fluids. The stalker would watch, learn and master the movements of the deer. Finally, when all was ready, in the dim light of dusk or dawn, the stalker proceeded from the downwind side, along the edge of a grazing herd while covered with a deer skin. The stalker frequently wore antlers and used white paint on the chest to resemble the deer's white belly fur. In this way, the stalker walked deer-like into the herd and finally got close enough to suddenly reach out and pull a tuft of hair from a deer's back.

TRACKING AND STALKING. The essential elements of tracking and stalking include:

- *learning* and *remembering* the ways and movements of the animals and the signs of the trail;
- close *observation*;
- unbroken and intense *concentration*; and
- using instinct to tell you when to *stalk actively* by moving ahead and exactly when to make your final move to get as close as you can, or when to *wait, passively and patiently,* for the animal to come to you.

It is important to remember that certain animal's senses are far more acute than those of human beings. There is, for instance, a world of scents to which we are mostly oblivious. Most people have seen domestic dogs marking a territory by urinating on a bush, hydrant or car tire. Mammals communicate and mark the boundaries of their territories in urine, scat (droppings) and from glands located on the tail, anal region, head, feet and sides of the body. Scents serve to mark a home range and food supply and to express the condition of the animal sexually and emotionally.

We can slightly improve on our inferior sense of smell by wetting our nose with a finger. We can also avoid being detected by staying downwind of the animals we are trying to observe. Check the wind direction before going out, but keep in mind that, during the morning, warm air near the surface is rising up from the valley.

Work from up above. In the evening, cold air is sinking, so work from downslope.

Some people use fire or a light to attract animals at night for observation, hiding out of sight behind a *blind*. A moose call can be made from a megaphone and squirrels are attracted to the rubbing together of two smooth stones, which sounds like a squirrel chewing through the husk of a hard-shelled nut. There are turkey calls and owl calls and many others that can be used to draw an animal in for a closer look. However, attracting an animal with artificial calls is an intrusion upon the animal's natural behavior. This practice causes animals to expend a good deal of energy investigating or even defending against a phantom "animal" that is not really present.

Nothing can replace simple watchfulness and patience for observing animals in their undisturbed behavior. Tracking is more than an art; it is a way of being that involves body, mind and spirit. It is a special way of joining with our relations in the wild. There will be many times when the tracker senses the common bonds that run deep between the stalker and the stalked. It is only when a tracker has taken the reality of an animal and its environment into himself or herself, and becomes one with them both, that the animal can truly be seen.

TRACKING

Walking
with eyes closed,
the way of touch
is truer than sight.

Barefooted, that slow stalk
extends the center of your breath
into the earth, each blade of grass.
Bend through the tangle
of small spruce and
blend into an older motion
beyond those forms defined
by circles of fire.

With no moon, no stars,
no human light
there are no shadows.
The only shapes are those
beyond your eyes.[1]

—Joseph Bruchac
Tracking

OBSERVING ANIMAL TRACKS AND SIGNS. Lacking these tracking skills and seeing animals primarily during the day, most people see animals such as domestic dogs and cats, chipmunks, squirrels, birds, insects and turtles. Many animals are rarely seen because they are nocturnal and/or crepuscular, spend the day in caves, hollow trees, burrows, attics and other places out of sight, are animals of the wilderness or are simply too small and inconspicuous to human eyes. The closest that many people come to these animals is an encounter with some of their *tracks* and other *signs*.

Everyone knows animal signs. Many of them are common and easy to find with practice and patience. First look around and ask yourself what animals live in the habitat you are visiting. Then have fun searching for some of these common animal signs:

- *tracks* or *prints* in the sand, mud, snow (wet, shallow snow is best) or even dust;
- *scat* or *droppings* of all kinds, including the familiar round pellets of rabbits and the "castings" of earthworms outside their burrow entrances;
- *homes* such as beaver dams, squirrel nests, chipmunk holes and woodchuck burrows;
- *nests* of birds, mice and others;
- *digging* and *tunneling signs* such as molehills and tunnels and skunk holes in the lawn or vole tunnels through tall grass;
- *food* and *feeding signs* including mouse caches of seeds, popcorn, raisins or nuts; red squirrel middens of pine cones and seeds; beaver-chewed tree stumps or branches (Figure 15-2); horizontal rows of sapsucker holes drilled into the sides of a tree trunk; browsed branches where deer (that make a rough, torn-off chew) or rabbits (that leave a clean, angular cut) have been feeding;
- *claw marks on tree trunk* made by a porcupine, bear or other tree climber;
- old or still-occupied *spider webs*;
- *remains of animals* such as feathers, bones, fur caught on a thorn or barbed wire and quills; and
- *vocalizations* of unseen birds, mammals, insects and others.

Some signs can only be learned from first-hand experience. One afternoon we were down by a pond eating lunch while sitting in the grass. A paper wasp landed on the backrest of a bench in front of us that was made of butternut. We watched in amazement as the wasp used its mouthparts to methodically scrape a line of wood fibers off the backrest to use for constructing the wasp nest. After a while, it flew off with its material, then returned—time and again. A closer look at the wood revealed distinct lines where the wood fibers

Figure 15-2. A patient and attentive eye will discover many signs of animal activity, such as this beaver-chewed stump. Photo by Alan C. Graham.

were chewed up. We still notice lines on old fence posts, shingles and other pieces of weathered wood where wasps have been collecting.

Many people are familiar with a few simple animal tracks. There is, however, some basic terminology that is important to know for serious tracking. A *track* or *print* refers to the imprint left by one foot falling on the substrate. A series of tracks makes up the distinct *pattern* of that animal's movement. An animal that walked by left a *trail* of tracks. Animals walk with a certain distance or *straddle* between tracks from side-to-side. The *stride* is the distance from track to track along the length of a trail (Figure 15-3).

Tracks can also be told apart by the shape, number of toes and the presence or absence of toenails in the print. Cats and dogs both have four toes per track. Cats walk with their claws retracted, leaving no claw marks. Dog tracks have a claw

mark before each toe print, as do a number of other kinds of animals. Weasel, raccoon, bear, beaver and otter tracks all have five toes. Deer, moose, elk, goats, sheep and most hoofed farm animals have two-toed tracks. Although in deep snow and other soft substrates, such as mud, the "dew claws" on deer hooves appear in the tracks, creating a four-toed imprint. Some animals, such as squirrels, chipmunks, mice and groundhogs, have four-toed tracks in front and five-toed tracks in the rear. A horse, of course, walks up on one toenail.

Track patterns can be deceiving. When certain animals, such as rabbits, hares and squirrels, move quickly their hind feet land in front of their front feet. The track pattern appears to indicate the animal was going in reverse. Squirrel tracks look similar to rabbit tracks. If the track begins or ends at a tree, however, you can be sure it was not an arboreal hare!

Keep your eyes open for other signs. Look for a fresh deer *rub* on young trees in the fall when the bucks are scraping off the velvet and sharpening their antlers against the bark. Burrows are all around. Groundhogs leave a pile of earth outside their main entrance but dig their escape routes from below so that no telltale sign is seen from above. How big is the burrow? What size animal may have made it? Check to see if it is still active by looking for spider webs across the doorway? Is the original owner still using a woodchuck burrow or has a skunk or fox moved in? If you are looking at a single 5- or 6-inch (12.7- or 15.2- centimeter) hole high up a riverbank it could be a kingfisher's nest. A colony of smaller holes in the same environment could be the nests of bank swallows. Is there a pile of grass in the meadow where a mouse or vole has nested? Do you notice any seeds, nuts or old animal bones in a nearby rock crevice or cave or in a hollow log or tree? Identifying this kind of bird's nest in your neighborhood trees is a sport unto itself.

Many people enjoy trying to identify animal *scat* or *droppings*. Rabbits and hares leave round pellets, deer often leave oval-shaped ones or small clumps if they've been feeding on berries or fruit. Domestic dogs leave flat-ended scats but fox and coyotes produce scat that are pointed on the ends. Fish scales in a scat along river or lake side could well mean an otter lives nearby. Bear scat is large and tube-shaped with lots of seeds, plant fibers and other bits of plants intermingled.

Tracking Stewardship

While tracking is fun and challenging, it is always good to remind ourselves that we are visiting the homes of the animals around us. The adaptations of the squirrel

Raccoon

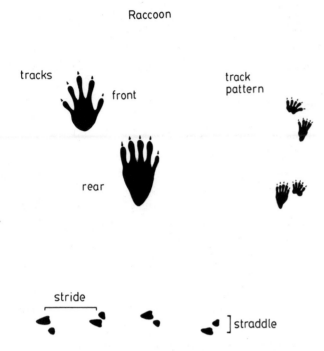

Figure 15-3. Some details and terms to focus on when tracking animals (a raccoon in this case): tracks, track pattern, stride and straddle. Sizes of raccoon tracks: front tracks are 2–3 inches (5.1–7.6 centimeters) long; rear tracks are 3–4 inches (7.6–10.2 centimeters) long; stride ranges from 6–20 inches (15.2–50.8 centimeters) or more.

next door or the fox at the end of a field remind us that all wild animals are adapted to survive in the interdependent wild communities of which they are a part.

What is a measure of how well human beings are adapting to our stewardship role for the wildlife around us? In Native North American tradition the care and conduct of the tracker and hunter was one such measure. Imagine how hard it would be to be the hunter in the story "The Alligator and the Hunter," and pass by three deer after waiting all of your life to kill one. Having faith that a deer at the right stage of life would appear would take an enormous amount of belief, patience and trust.

As human beings, tracking is a journey inward to ones' own center as well as outward to connect with the life around us. Some animals are able to adapt well to the changes people are bringing to Earth, others cannot. Tracking entails much more than observation and enjoyment, it includes elements of empathy, concern and care-taking.

The native vision, the gift of seeing truly, with wonder and delight into the natural world, is informed by a certain attitude of reverence and respect. It is a matter of extra-sensory as well as sensory perception. In addition to the

eye, it involves the intelligence, the instinct, and the imagination. It is the perception not only of objects and forms but also essences and ideals.[2]

—N. Scott Momaday
Kiowa

QUESTIONS

1. What does it mean to say an animal is well adapted for surviving? What is an adaptation?

2. What are some adaptations of a squirrel? An owl? A butterfly? A snake? The fawn in "How the Fawn Got Its Spots"? What are the fawn's spots made from in the story?

3. What are the two things that happen in fours in "The Alligator and the Hunter"? Why is four an important number in many Native North American traditions? Can you think of things that come in or happen in fours? What are some other stories in this book that focus on an important number?

4. Why does the alligator trust the hunter to tie him up in "The Alligator and the Hunter"?

5. What is the gift that the hunter receives in return for saving the alligator? What does the alligator teach the hunter?

6. Name some ways that certain animals have a positive or helpful effect on other animals. Name some ways that certain animals harm other animals. What does it mean to say animals are all interrelated?

7. What are some ways that predators attack and kill their prey? How do the prey defend themselves?

8. What is camouflage? How else do animals hide themselves?

9. How can you stalk an animal to sneak up for a closer look at it? What are some techniques used by Native North Americans to get close to animals?

10. What kinds of animal tracks have you seen before? What did they look like? What are some other signs of animals that tell you they have been around?

11. What does it mean to say someone is a tracker?

12. How should a good tracker treat the animals?

ACTIVITIES

Prey, Tell Me

ACTIVITY: Solve some riddles that describe the survival adaptations of some prey animals by guessing each animal's identity.

GOALS: Understand what a survival adaptation is and

learn some defenses of certain prey animals.

AGE: Younger children and older children

MATERIALS: Riddles and kids.

PROCEDURE: Discuss the meaning of interrelationships and give examples (from the "Discussion" section) of different kinds of animal relationships. Be sure to include examples of animals that have both positive and negative effects on each other. Ask the children to think of their own examples.

Define and discuss the concept of survival adaptation with the children. Have them call out some examples of offensive adaptations of predators and defensive adaptations of prey animals.

Now tell them they are going to hear some riddles which describe some adaptations of animals that are often hunted as prey. With older children, have them come up and take turns reading the riddles. You will need to do the reading for young children. The riddles vary from easy to challenging.

PREY, TELL ME (RIDDLES)

• My home is a burrow in the ground. I only come out at night when it is cool and damp and when I am not likely to be seen. *Lots* of animals, especially early birds, love to eat me, but I can scoot down my burrow quickly if someone tries to grab me, and I am very sensitive to vibrations in the ground. Don't fish around too long for the answer.

I am a *(worm)*.

• I am a great swimmer from the minute I am born, I float almost as well as a cork. If something comes after me I use my webbed feet and tiny wings to skate quickly away over the water. The predators who spot me and try to attack from below see *down* when they look up. You may see me eating plants or fish.

I am a *(duckling)*.

• My long ears, keen hearing and sensitive nose help me to detect danger from far off. I can make a fast getaway if spotted. Still, I come out from sunset to sunrise with darkness as my cover. I have a habit of twitching my nose. My tail is short and my feet are lucky.

I am a *(rabbit)*.

• I sing my song when summertime is aging and fall is on the way. I don't sing with my voice though. Some people know I *wing* it. My long antennae help me to sense when danger is around. Still, my kind often become lunch for birds, shrews and even tiny snakes. I might live under a rock or spend my time in a clump of grass.

I am a *(cricket)*.

• You know me well around your garden. My skin is bumpy and bad to taste. I eat ants and flies with a long, sticky tongue. When you pick me up I release the contents of my bladder to startle you into putting me down.

I am a *(toad)*.

• My skin of scales is a good hint. I am small and quick with a colorful tail. When a predator comes and grabs at the tip, I snap it off like the flick of a whip.

I am a *(skink)*.

The Alligator and the Duckling

ACTIVITY: Listen to a story in which you are an alligator hunting a duckling, then a duckling being hunted by an alligator. Choose how you want the story to end, write it down and discuss what you have written.

GOALS: Understand the plight of both the predator and the prey. Learn some adaptations of both predator and prey. Examine how you feel in a story when you are in the role of first the hunter and then the hunted.

AGE: Younger children and older children

MATERIALS: Copy of "The Alligator and the Duckling," paper, pencils, chalk and chalkboard or newsprint and felt-tipped marker.

PROCEDURE: Prepare the children for this guided fantasy by having them lie on their backs, close their eyes and relax in a comfortable position. Ask them to clear their minds and prepare to enter the worlds of the hunter and the hunted. Now read them the following story:

THE ALLIGATOR AND THE DUCKLING

You are a huge old alligator with bumpy scales and two ridges of plates running down the tough skin on your back. As you sit on the bank of a marsh sunning yourself, the sounds of splashing drift across the water. On the opposite shore you see a duck and her ducklings playing and flitting across the water that sprays up off their little downy wings and webbed feet.

You have not eaten for many days because food is scarce and your reflexes are not as good as when you were younger, smaller and quicker to strike. Hunger is gnawing at your belly.

Slowly, smoothly, you ease your long body beneath the water. You can feel it cool against your soft white belly as you slip along underwater, propelled by stroke after stroke of your powerful tail. About halfway across the marsh you stick only your eyes and nostrils out above the surface to breathe and locate the ducklings again. Now they are farther out into the marsh; an easy target.

Underwater once again, you swim toward the sounds of the ducklings playing and splashing. Finally, very close now, you surface one last time and prepare to attack. All of your energy is focused on the one duckling closest to you. Steady now, closer, almost ready to strike, you begin to open your mouth and push ahead as fast as you can!

But wait! Suddenly you are changing. You are now very small. Your body is covered with soft, downy feathers. Your rear feet are webbed and your front limbs form little wings. You now have a tiny duck's bill on a small head with little eyes. Your tail is just a little, stubby, feathered duckling tail on a round, down-covered body.

Now you are a duckling looking out across the marsh. An enormous alligator is coming right toward you with its mouth beginning to open. Just as it lunges you turn and skirt across the water, moving your wings and feet as fast as you can. Your brothers and sisters flee in all directions. Water is spraying up everywhere and ducklings are peeping for their mother. Your little heart is racing and thumping in your chest. The shore is getting closer, very close, but the alligator is just behind you and gaining. Right as you leap for shore the alligator lurches with its mouth wide open, its rows of teeth and pink skin a breath away. You scream out one loud PEEP!! to your mother and then . . .

Stop the story and have the children keep their eyes closed for a few more minutes while they imagine how the story ends. Have them write their endings down and share them with the rest of the class. Then have each one write the entire story from either the alligator's or duckling's point of view, whichever they choose.

As they share their stories ask them to explain why they chose to be that character. Record a list of answers to these questions too: How did it feel to be the alligator/duckling? How did it feel to eat the duckling/be eaten by the alligator? How did it feel to miss your prey and go hungry/escape the alligator and live? Would you rather be a predator or prey? Why? Are people predators? Do people eat animals? What kind of animals do people eat? Where do these animals come from? How is this the same as a wild animal catching and eating its prey? How is it different?

Tracking

ACTIVITY: (A) Learn about the essentials of tracking and explore a natural area for animal tracks and other signs of animals. Record and map your findings on a large piece of paper. (B) Write a story about or draw a picture of these animals, showing some of the events that happened in their habitat as revealed by the animal tracks and signs you discovered.

GOALS: Experience firsthand the excitement of discovering animal tracks and other signs of animals. Understand how these signs can be interpreted to recreate the events that happened in that habitat before you arrived.

AGE: Younger children and older children

MATERIALS: Index cards, pencils, one copy of Figure 15-3 for each group, tracking field guides, chalkboard and chalk or newsprint and felt-tipped markers, large roll of paper for the habitat map such as postal wrapping paper, large piece of cardboard to tape paper onto, masking tape, crayons, felt-tipped markers, hand lenses, rulers for measuring sticks, paper, pencils and cardboard backing or clipboards to write on.

PROCEDURE A: *Track Trails.* Beforehand: Scout out a natural area that is rich in animal tracks and signs. This could be the mud along the edge of a marsh, the sand of a dry riverbed, a snowy border between forest and field, etc. Use the list of animal signs in the "Discussion" section to prepare checklists on index cards for children to carry into the field. Create a simple track story on a chalkboard or large sheet of paper, using drawings of several different kinds of animal tracks and as many other "signs" as possible.

Lead a question-and-answer session to discuss the different kinds of tracks and other animal signs that the children may find on their visit. Use the checklists of animal signs you have prepared to review each kind of animal sign and answer any questions the children may have. Share and discuss Figure 15-3 with the children. Use some tracing guides or charts to point out the particular tracks that they may expect to see outdoors in your area. Some excellent guides for tracking include *Tom Brown's Field Guide to Nature Observation and Tracking,*[3] *A Guide to Animal Tracking and Behavior*[4] and *A Field Guide to Animal Tracks.*[5] Have the children familiarize themselves with these tracks. Now present your track story to the children and ask them to interpret it by using the signs to piece together the events and the sequence in which they occurred.

Travel to the habitat you will be studying. Take a brief walk around and point out some of the animal signs in the area. Ask the children to be careful not to step on any animal tracks or other signs they may find. Pick up at least two different sets of tracks and follow them as a group, having the children try to answer such questions as: Where was the animal coming from and going to? Which set(s) of tracks were made first? What kind of animal made the tracks? What was the animal doing? Was it moving fast or slow? What happened to it along the way?

Roll out the large sheet of paper in a flat area and tape the corners down onto the cardboard. Put out crayons or felt-tipped markers. Create a rough sketch of the habitat and explain it to the children. They are to return to draw in any tracks, trails and other animal signs onto this simple map of the habitat.

Divide the children into pairs and pass out the checklists to help the children recall the signs for which they will be searching. Give each pair a hand lens, a copy of Figure 15-3, paper, a pencil and backing on which to write. Assign each pair a certain part of the habitat to observe, making sure the area is well covered. Remind them not to step on any animal tracks and signs they find. You may need to lead younger children over to their particular areas of observation since it is hard for them to discern position from a map. Adults need to be careful to stay close by to younger children.

Send them out into the field for a half hour or so, or until the habitat map begins to be well marked with tracks and signs. Ask them to pay close attention to time. Which tracks were made when? They should also ask themselves: Which animal was it? What was it doing? Where did it go? How was it moving? Did it meet any other animals along the way? Why was this animal there? What was it looking for? Are there any signs that it was feeding, or of what it had been eating?

When the map has taken shape, gather everyone together to discuss the animal tracks, trails and signs they found and have each pair explain what they found and what they think it is. Make sure everything is recorded on the map. Visit the sites of any particularly notable findings. Make sure the children have left each animal's home and the entire area as they found it.

PROCEDURE B: *Tracking Tales.* Return home or to the learning center and hang the map up for all to see. Have the children take turns telling "Track Tales," as they interpret the story of the events revealed by the tracks and other signs. Notice how many different ways the signs can be interpreted.

Stalking

ACTIVITY: (A) Stalk by sitting still for so long the animals come close by. (B) Stalk an animal to observe it by approaching it slowly, from a direction and in a way that is to your advantage.
GOALS: Learn and practice some of the skills needed for stalking and observing wild animals.
AGE: Older children
MATERIALS: (A) A clock with a large face and sweep seconds hand; dry mats to sit upon outdoors such as small carpet squares; long pants, long-sleeved shirts and hats to protect against biting insects; gift of sunflower seeds or other

natural object. (B) Clothing of muted camouflage colors that have been airing outdoors in a dry place for a few days, insect repellant clothing as in "A"; gift for the animals.
PROCEDURE A: *Still Stalkers.* Lead a discussion about stalking. Share the story of the deer stalker from the "Discussion" section and review the skills needed for successful stalking, also in the "Discussion" section, including:

• *learning* and *remembering* the ways, movements, and signs of the animals;
• *observing* closely;
• *concentrating* well; and
• *using your instincts* to tell you what to do and when to do it.

Practice the skills of concentration and sitting still. Have the children assume a comfortable sitting position. They are not to move at all except for turning their heads around slowly to observe. Begin by having the children watch the second hand of a clock as it moves around the clock face. That speed is the *maximum* rate at which they are to move when turning their heads. The idea is to avoid any quick motion that would scare an animal away. Now have the children look straight ahead, then gradually and smoothly turn to look to the right. Then have them look off to the left. The slower the motion, the better. It is possible to move so slowly that even an animal looking right at you cannot detect the motion. Have the children sit absolutely still for about 5 minutes while they practice their slow head movements.

Discuss *peripheral vision*. Have the children look straight ahead again. Begin from in front of them and walk around, behind and back to the front of the group from the other side. How much of the time could they see you? Peripheral vision is especially important when tracking because we see better in dim light with our peripheral vision than when we are looking at objects directly.

You could also test to see how strong their sixth sense is. Stand behind the group, out of sight, and raise your hand every so often. Without turning to look at you and with their eyes closed, have them raise their hands when they think yours is up and put theirs down when yours is down. Are any of them in synchrony with your movements?

Before going outside, make sure the children are wearing insect repellant clothing as described in "Materials." Now go down to the shore of an active beaver pond, farm pond or other place where there is a lot of animal activity. Give each child a dry mat to sit on. Acquaint them with the sound you will use to call them in.

Station each child along the shore and have her or him sit down and face out over the water. They are to practice their *still stalking* until you give a signal to call them in. There can be no talking or noise of any kind! Allow at least 10 minutes the first time, but not much more. Then call them in and allow them to share their experiences. Encourage the children to leave a small gift of thanks, such as some sunflower seeds, acorns or other natural objects.

Extend the length of this *still stalking* on subsequent visits. Longer sits mean more exciting close encounters with the animals that live there.

PROCEDURE B: *Stalk Walkers.* Beforehand, scout out a habitat animals frequent at dusk. A field where deer feed or a meadow where rabbits congregate both work well. Have the children store a pair of medium gray or dark brown clothes in a dry place in the outside air for a few days before you plan to take your field trip.

Once the children have mastered the patience of *still stalking* they are ready for a more challenging activity. Have them practice walking and crawling with that same slow motion. It will help if they imagine a very slow animal stalking its prey, such as a heron in a marsh. They should concentrate their focus straight ahead and imagine their energy coming from the center of the body just below the diaphragm, while still being keenly aware of whatever enters their peripheral vision as well.

There is also a simple but useful technique for enhancing the ability to hear more acutely. Have the children cup their hands and then hold them, palms forward, behind the flaps of their ears as extensions. By looking straight at the source of sound while wearing these "deer ears," every noise sounds louder, while some very soft sounds can be heard that would not otherwise have been detected.

Study the natural history of the animals you will be stalking. Visit the area by day and plan an approach. Look for good cover such as shrubs and tall grass, especially clumps that extend into the field. Note the compass directions. Plan to come up from below toward the animals (if dusk), or down from above (if early dawn). Also prepare to move in from downwind of the prevailing breeze at the time you arrive. Finally, locate or mark a trail to the habitat.

Have the children wear their camouflage clothes on the evening of the excursion. Park your vehicles well away from the habitat, and slowly and quietly follow the trail in. Approach the edge of the field, meadow or other habitat you may have chosen from downwind. Watch and wait.

Once you have watched the animals for a time and your eyes have adjusted to the low light, begin to inch gradually closer to the animals. Listen to them, watch them, smell them if you can (being downwind). Move in a bit more, staying concealed, until you are quite close but still unnoticed. This takes practice and will undoubtedly require several visits to do successfully.

There is a certain thrill just to be close to wild animals; it is a rare chance to watch their natural behavior when they are unaware of your presence. The stillness of the night air, the calls of the insects and other wildlife, the wonderful smells that carry strongly on the humid evening air—all of these sensory experiences add to the magic of sharing the night with animals that are simply going about their way. There is much to be grateful for and we always encourage the children to leave a gift and a few words of thanks to the animals before departing.

EXTENDING THE EXPERIENCE

• Create your own story of animal tracks on a large sheet of paper. Can anyone decipher the story correctly?
• After reading "How the Fawn Got Its Spots," ask the children to identify the gifts given to the "four-leggeds" and "winged ones" by Wakan Tanka. Discuss these gifts and define them as *adaptations for survival*. Hand out photographs, illustrations or even puppets of certain animals to small groups of children. Have each group identify and explain the adaptation of their animal to the rest of the group.
• Go on a "deer walk" as described on page 19.
• Play the camouflage game described on page 20.
• Play the "Predator and Prey" and "Hiders and Seekers" camouflage games on pages 170-71 in *Keepers of the Earth.*

NOTES

1. Joseph Bruchac, *Tracking* (Memphis, Tenn.: Ion Books, Inc./Raccoon, 1986), 21.
2. Marion E. Gridley, *Contemporary American Indian Leaders* (New York: Dodd Mead & Co., 1972), 138. Quoted in Frances G. Lombardi and Gerald Scott Lombardi, *Circle Without End* (Happy Camp, Calif.: Naturegraph Publishers, 1982), 12.
3. Tom Brown, *Tom Brown's Field Guide to Nature Observation and Tracking* (New York: Berkley Publishing Group, 1983).
4. Donald Stokes and Lillian Stokes, *A Guide to Animal Tracking and Behavior* (Stokes Nature Guides) (Boston: Little, Brown & Co., 1986).
5. Murie J. Olaus, *A Field Guide to Animal Tracks* (Peterson Field Guide Series) (Boston: Houghton Mifflin, 1975).

CHAPTER 16

✛ The Gift of the Whale ✛

(Inuit-Inupiaq—Arctic)

When the Great Spirit created this land, he made many beautiful and good things. He made the sun and moon and stars. He made the wide land, white with snow, and the mountains and the ocean. He made fish of all kinds and the many birds. He made the seals and the walrus and the great bears. Then the Great Spirit made the Inupiaq. He had a special love for the people and showed them how to live, using everything around them.

Then, after making all this, the Great Spirit decided to make one thing more. This would be the best creation of all. The Great Spirit made this being with great care. It was the Bowhead Whale. It was, indeed, the most beautiful and the finest of the things made by the Great Spirit. As it swam, it flowed through the ocean. It sang as it went, and it was in perfect balance with everything around it.

But the Great Spirit saw something else. He saw that the Inupiaq people needed the Bowhead Whale. Without the whale, it would be hard for them to survive. They needed to eat muktuk, the flesh of the whale, to keep warm and healthy during the long, cold nights. They needed its bones to help build their homes. They needed every part of the great whale.

So the Great Spirit gave the Bowhead to the Inupiaq. He gave them a way to hunt it from their boats covered with walrus hide. He made a special time each spring, when the ice of the ocean would break apart to form a road where the whales would swim. In that whale road, the Open Lead, the whales would come to the surface and wait there to be struck by the harpoons of the Inupiaq. They would continue to do so every year as long as the Inupiaq showed respect to the Bowhead, as long as the Inupiaq only took the few whales that they needed in order to survive.

But the Great Spirit decided this also. At that time each year when the Open Lead formed, when the whales came to the surface to be hunted, the Great Spirit made it so that a heavy cloud of thick mist would hang just above the ice, just above the heads of the whales and the Inupiaq. That thick mist would hang there between the sea and the sky. "Though I give you permission to kill my most perfect creation," the Great Spirit said, "I do not wish to watch it."

DISCUSSION

The Inuit-Inupiaq are the peoples of northern Alaska. Although many know them as Eskimos, they call themselves *Inuit*, meaning "the people." *Eskimo* comes from a Cree word meaning "fish eaters." The Inuit do not regard themselves as American Indian but of another race entirely. Their language and their culture are distinct from those of other Native North American peoples, and they are circumpolar.

The relationship between the Inupiaq and the bowhead whales goes back further than anyone can remember.

These people of the Arctic lands are careful observers of nature. In what has been described as the most unforgiving environment in North America, the regions of the Polar ice cap, they developed a way of life that offered them material comfort and the leisure to develop a strong storytelling tradition. Their ability to observe nature enabled them to survive in a land covered with snow and ice for most of the year. Often, their survival depended upon copying the animals that were their instructors in survival. They did so in their games as well as their methods of hunting and fishing. Each year an "Eskimo

So the Great Spirit gave the Bowhead to the Inupiaq. He gave them a way to hunt it from their boats covered with walrus hide.

Olympics" is held in Alaska with highly trained Inupiaq athletes competing against each other in events that draw from the old ways of hunting and survival, events that stress agility, the ability to stand pain and great strength. Events such as the three-man carry, the seal race (in which men extend their bodies like seals and run on their knuckles) or another challenge during which men leap from a standing position to kick a ball hung 10 feet (3.0 meters) overhead all draw on time-honored skills the early hunters needed to survive.

Traditional Whale Hunting

Respect for the natural world and the animals was an important part of that old way of life, and no animal was given more respect than the great bowhead whale. Its thick fat or muktuk could feed a community and provide necessary vitamins in a land where no green plants grew. It was not easy to kill a whale; it required great courage and strength to spear the whale from a small boat. One young Inuit man told us how he killed his first whale while out with his uncle. They were next to the whale and had struck it several times. It did not dive but continued swimming. It was wounded but not dying. Things were not going well. The whale was suffering. Our friend, Tommy, asked that his uncle give him the harpoon. Taking it, he jumped from the boat onto the whale's back and walked along it—the icy water washing up to his thighs—until he came to the place where a small indentation marked the junction of the whale's neck and head. He spoke then to the whale, asking it to forgive them for causing it pain and asking it to understand that they needed to kill it to live themselves. Then he drove the harpoon down into that spot, and the whale quivered and died.

He told us that when he was a very small child, his grandfather had taken him out to a bowhead that had been killed and drawn up onto the ice. "I want you," his grandfather said, "to touch every part of this whale. I don't care how long it takes." And so he did it, even though it took him many hours. And that night he dreamed he was a bowhead, swimming beneath the ice, ready to sacrifice himself to the Inupiaq.

On St. Lawrence Island, one of the islands between Alaska and Siberia, when a whale is killed, even after that whale is dragged up on the ice, it must be given proper respect. Grace Slwooko, a Yupik storyteller from St. Lawrence Island, explained to us that when the whale is cut up, each part must be placed on the ice with care and the parts not separated from each other until everything has been completed. That way when the Whale People

look up from below the ice, they would see that it was not such a bad thing to sacrifice themselves and that the Inupiaq people were trustworthy.

In a world where most people no longer kill the meat they consume, it may be hard for some to understand the strong, even loving, feeling that the Inupiaq people have for the whales. They know them so well that some years ago when the International Whaling Congress released statistics about the numbers of bowhead whales in the Arctic near Alaska, the Inupiaq disagreed.

"No," the Inupiaq people said, "there are twenty times as many whales as you say there are."

"How do you know?" asked the International Whaling Congress people.

"We know because we count them each year. If there were as few as you say there were, then we would no longer hunt for them."

It turned out, in fact, that the Inupiaq were right about the numbers of bowhead whales. After considering the special relationship the Inupiaq have with the whales, it was agreed that they—and no one else—would be allowed to hunt the bowhead. The Inupiaq themselves agreed to very strict controls on the numbers of whales that they would strike in any given year. Some Inupiaq villages along the northwest coast of Alaska and the adjoining islands are allowed to kill only two or three whales each per year. Further, if they strike a whale and it escapes, that whale is part of their count. The whales are not sold, but divided up among the hunters and the people of each village.

During the winter of 1988–89, the plight of three gray whales (which the Inupiaq do not hunt) caught the eye of the world press. The whales were caught by early freezing ice and could not swim far enough under the ice to reach the open sea and safety. The Inupiaq people came close to the place where those whales were trapped and spoke to them, encouraging them to survive. The picture of an Inupiaq woman gently touching the front of a whale was broadcast all over the world. The eventual rescue of two of the three whales was due in part to the Inupiaq hunters, who suggested ways of breaking a path through the ice for the whales to follow until they reached the channel being cut for them by a Russian icebreaker. For a time, the hearts of Americans and Russians and Inupiaq people all joined together to save those whales. Some thought it stranger that Inuit whale hunters would save whales than that Russians and Americans would work together. But those who truly knew the Inupiaq people did not think that. They knew that the Inuit people had love and respect for the great whales—the most perfect creations of the Great Spirit.

Whales are fascinating creatures that figure prominently in the myth, music and art of many cultures. We recently saw a pair of Atlantic right whales—a mother and calf—swimming gracefully, side-by-side, in the coastal waters off Massachusetts. First the mother would surface and exhale her V-shaped blow, then the calf would follow and blow a little V. Time and again they dove and surfaced in tandem near our boat. It brought tears to our eyes to see these breathtaking animals and know that they were 2 of only about 350 left of the entire race of Atlantic right whales, which once numbered many thousands. All told, there are now only about three thousand right whales left. They are the most endangered whale on Earth.

These beautiful mammals of the sea were given the name "right" whale because they were docile, easy to harpoon and floated once they were killed, making it easy to retrieve them. Bowhead whales also float when they are killed. For thousands of years the Inuit hunters killed whales as a necessity for survival. Blubber and flesh were used as food, with oil serving as a kind of "butter." The sinews became bowstrings, cords and ropes, while stomach and intestines were dried, inflated and fashioned into vessels for storing oil.

The hunting, however, was done in a respectful, reverential manner, as is the way with the traditional hunting practices of Native North American peoples. Ivory harpoons were thrown from skin boats. Sealskin buoys were tied to the whale to float it. At this level, Native North Americans fulfilled an ecological niche much like that of other predatory animals that hunt out of need, not want. Animals were not regarded as *objects* or resources to be consumed but as *subjects* and part of the circle of life of which we are all a part.

Modern Whaling

Whales and whale hunting or *whaling* have since become symbols of what can happen when people hunt out of greed and for economic gain rather than as a matter of survival. In many countries where whaling was a traditional subsistence activity, it was transformed into a means of trade and commercial gain. Since then, during the seventeenth, eighteenth and nineteenth centuries and up until recent times, whaling boats from around the world have hunted these majestic animals with abandon. Blubber was rendered and the oil used for heat, lamps, soaps and lubricants. *Spermaceti* oil, from sperm whales, was highly prized and valued for use in candle-making, as a lamp oil and as a base for perfumes. Whale bones were used for tools, the meat for food and the intestines to make twine. Baleen was made into a number of consumer products, including corset stays. Whale products once supplied the economy with many items that are now produced from petroleum and plastics.

The right whale was hunted until it became scarce. Then, humpback whales, which could be reached more easily from shore than other species, were hunted heavily. When humpbacks were depleted, whalers turned seaward for sperm and bowhead whales. No limits were set on the numbers or species of whale taken until many were near extinction. As a result, many North American whales are now endangered, including the blue, bowhead, beluga, finback, gray, humpback, right, Sei and sperm whales (Figure 16-1). Sowerby's beaked whale is now classified as rare or vulnerable in Canada. Most countries now honor the International Whaling Commission's worldwide ban on all commercial whaling, but some countries continue to protest the ban and defy it by hunting a large number of endangered whales, ostensibly for "research."

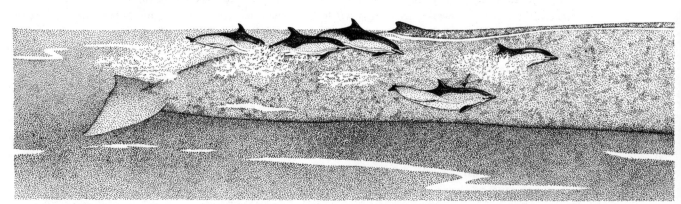

Figure 16-1. The blue whale is the largest mammal that has ever lived. It is also an endangered species. Common dolphins are shown swimming alongside with sooty shearwaters overhead. Size: to 100 feet (30.5 meters); weight to 150 tons (136.1 metric tons).

Hunting Issues

The Inupiaq and some other peoples continue to hunt as a means of *survival*. For many others, however, hunting is not done out of need, rather, it has become a matter of *choice, sport* and, oftentimes, *commerce*. Sixteen million people, 7 percent of the population of the United States, bought hunting licenses in 1989. Many of these licenses went to the people who hunt for recreation, sport, trophy and trade purposes. Native North American traditions say that it is right to kill only out of a need for survival, not for sport or other reasons that do not relate to subsistence.

Earlier in this century many people supported hunting. The Federal Wildlife Refuge System was started in 1903 by President Theodore Roosevelt, himself an avid hunter, to preserve habitat and increase populations of wild game animals. Many of these species had been in decline due to uncontrolled overhunting, rampant development of their habitat and pollution. Hunters have since invested billions of dollars for research, habitat protection and management of nonendangered game animals. These programs have also benefited many nongame animals and those who enjoy them.

However, people are increasingly questioning the wisdom and ethics of "blood sports," including many environmental groups. One survey found that, while 80 percent of U.S. citizens approve of hunting out of necessity for food, 80 percent say trophy hunting is wrong and 60 percent disapprove of hunting for sport and recreation. One out of every three people in the United States would like to see hunting banned altogether.[1] Many people would like to see animals granted the right to exist.

The populations of some animals, which are in trouble in certain regions, would be helped by a ban on hunting, for example, bighorn sheep, mountain lion, antelope, black bear and many species of waterfowl. Due to hunting

pressures and a heavy loss of vital wetland habitat, the breeding populations of nine out of the ten species of the major migratory ducks decreased in 1989, as part of an overall downward trend in the numbers of waterfowl in recent years.[2] This makes the numbers of these species especially sensitive to hunting pressures.

One program that demonstrates a particularly heinous disregard for animal life is the U.S. Department of Agriculture's (USDA's) Animal Damage Control (ADC) program. With a combined federal and state budget of well over 30 million dollars in 1990, this program aims to kill "pests" and "predators" that consume crops, feedlot grains and young livestock, as well as fouling their roosts in parks and on buildings. To this end, certain animals are systematically hunted, gassed, burned, poisoned, trapped, snared and chased with everything from dogs to helicopters. Although the program does control predators on some endangered species and keep airways relatively free of dangerous pest birds, it also kills many species that need to be protected in certain areas. In 1988 the government contracted professional ADC hunters who killed two hundred mountain lions; three hundred black bears; thirty thousand beavers, skunks and raccoons; seventy-six thousand coyotes; 4.6 million birds, especially starlings and blackbirds; and (accidentally) around four hundred pet dogs and one hundred pet cats.[3] The ADC program, and its predecessor under the U.S. Fish and Wildlife Service, has contributed to the extirpation of the mountain lion east of the Rocky Mountains (except for a few local occurrences), killed many western eagles and has all but wiped out the gray wolf and grizzly bear in the lower forty-eight states.

A MATTER OF SURVIVAL. Many of our currently threatened, endangered and even extinct animals were once in a similar state as some of the game, commercial and "pest" species of today. Whether it is an organized

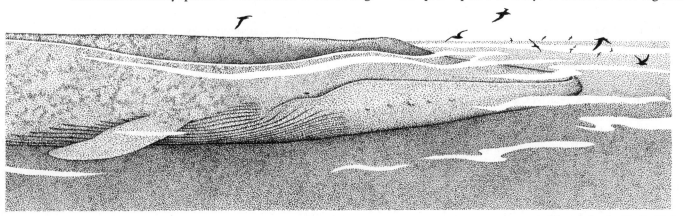

Illustration by D. D. Tyler.

sport hunting or fishing expedition, or a commercial hunt to provide a set of alligator shoes or a fur coat, today's economy places a certain demand upon wildlife populations to supply the markets with material wildlife "products." But materialism has often elevated human *want* to the same level of importance as *need* and, sometimes, even puts desire above necessity. These priorities have created a greater demand for wildlife than the existing supply can sustain. Using hunting technologies that are so efficient that a species can be wiped out entirely, hunting and fishing industries are frequently dipping into the pool that populations need to reproduce and maintain their numbers for the sake of survival. Once the harvest of an animal has exceeded its *carrying capacity*—the population level at which the animal can reproduce and sustain its numbers—that species begins to decline precipitously. It is no longer a *renewable* but a *nonrenewable* species or resource—it is not capable of replenishing itself fast enough to keep up with the rate at which it is being depleted. Perhaps the 200 million birds and animals being killed each year are more than nature can provide, especially given the additional pressures of habitat destruction and ecological pollution. When international economies and trade, such as the world-wide demand for ivory from the African elephant and for rhinoceros horn (which is thought to have medicinal and even aphrodisiacal properties) are figured in, these animals come under harvesting pressure that far exceeds their ability to sustain numbers.

Whales and Other Marine Mammals

The whales that are now endangered due to the actions of humankind have been around for eons. Whales evolved from ancestors that are common to all mammals—amphibians that came up out of the sea onto land about 350 million years ago during the Carboniferous Period. Some mammals, including whales, dolphins, porpoises, seals and manatees, later returned to life in the sea. Toothed whales date back to 54 million years ago, while the baleen whales, such as the right and bowhead whales (25 million years ago) and the humpback (10 millions years ago), are relatively recent.

Whales and their relatives, *porpoises* and *dolphins*, comprise an order of marine mammals called the *Cetaceans*. There are two major groups of Cetaceans: the suborder *Odontoceti* or *toothed whales*, and the *baleen whales* of the suborder *Mysticeti*. Cetaceans are streamlined like fish, but they have horizontal tails, or *flukes,* and must surface to breathe air (Figure 16-2). Being mammals, Cetaceans are warm-blooded, have hair and bear live young, which they suckle. Normally, one calf is born to a mature female every other year. Calves nurse from the mother's mammaries, which literally inject milk of a "cottage cheese" consistency into the calf's mouth.

When whales surface and exhale through a *blowhole* on top of the head, the *blow* can be seen as a cloud of moisture condensing in the air. After taking a breath, the nostrils are closed and the animal dives. Toothed whales have a single external blowhole, while baleen whales have two external blowhole openings. *Flippers* are used for locomotion and steering. Cetaceans are well insulated from the cold oceanic waters by a thick layer of fat called *blubber*, lying just under the skin. Blubber also stores a tremendous amount of energy. Once submerged, they conserve oxygen by decreasing blood flow to those areas where it is not essential and by slowing down other bodily functions. Oxygen is stored in the myoglobin in the muscles and released slowly as needed.

Toothed whales navigate using a form of sonar called *echo-location*. Sounds, made by air forced through closed nasal passages, reflect off objects to reveal the location of the objects.

Whales are highly intelligent animals capable of learning intricate tasks. They also possess a well-developed sense of reasoning and a certain degree of creative thinking. For example, one form of hunting used by humpback whales consists of blowing large bubbles in a circle while submerged to form a kind of *bubble net* that herds together fish, krill (tiny, shrimp-like crustaceans) and other prey. The whales then swim up the center of the bubble net with mouths agape to devour their meals. Although it is now widespread, bubble netting is thought to be a relatively recent phenomenon. It is a skill that was first observed in 1978 and has been "learned" by hundreds of whales since that time. Humpbacks also use a *cloud net* consisting of individual 5-foot (1.5-meter) bubbles of air, which are followed to the surface. When whales swim, the action of their flukes at the water's surface leaves a flat spot of upwelling water called a *footprint*, which is especially pronounced in the spot from which the whale dove. Dives can last from 2 to 30 minutes. The average length of a humpback's dive is from 5 to 7 minutes. Upon surfacing, whales sometimes *breach*—come partly or completely out of the water. Breaching could be a response to excitement, an aggressive display, a way of shocking fish beneath to make them easier to catch or a form of auditory communication as the sound travels great distances underwater. Toothed whales are frequently seen in herds or *pods*, and the killer whale or orca actually practices a form of cooperative hunting. Baleen whales are found in groups of two or more individuals.

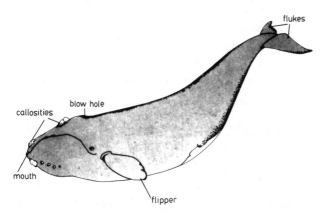

Figure 16-2. The parts of a whale. A right whale is shown here. Size: to 70 feet (21.3 meters).

TOOTHED WHALES. Altogether there are sixty-five species of toothed whale, including dolphins and porpoises, beaked whales, sperm whales, narwhals and killer whales. All these toothed whales have regular, peg-like teeth. Another characteristic is the deposit of waxy tissue that forms the bulk of the head above the upper jaw. This tissue, which is sometimes called a *melon* when it is prominent, senses vibrations in the water as part of the animal's echo-location apparatus. Toothed whales eat relatively large prey, such as squid and fish, which are caught individually. It is thought that the difficulty in catching a large volume of food in this manner may explain why, as a group (with the exception of the 60-foot [18.3-meter] sperm whale), the toothed whales have never attained the size of the baleen whales.

There are several species of sperm whale, including the sperm whale and pygmy sperm whale. Sperm whales are named for the spermaceti oil found in the whale's head that hunters used for candle wax and lamp oil. Sperm whales can dive down to 2,000 feet (610 meters) and can remain down for 60 to 90 minutes. As the whales dive the spermaceti oil thickens in the cold waters and decreases the whales' buoyancy. Fish, octopus and giant squid are their primary foods. Sperm whales are found worldwide, and they now number about 600,000.

Porpoises and dolphins will often approach divers and swimmers closely and, when in large groups, will swim alongside boats. They can ply the water at up to 20 miles per hour (32.2 kilometers per hour). Dolphins have conical teeth and a long beak, while porpoises have relatively rounded teeth and no beak. Bottlenose dolphins are the best known of the lot and are often featured in aquarium performances. They can leap vertically out of the water up to 16 feet (4.9 meters) high! These highly intelligent animals love to swim and play around boats; they have an excellent facility for memorizing, solving problems and mimicking. Their echo-location is so efficient that they can navigate a maze blindfolded.

Dolphins are often found swimming with schools of yellow-finned tuna. In one of the tragedies of modern-day fishing, a great number of dolphins are inadvertently caught and drowned each year when these tuna are captured using drift-gill nets or purse-seine nets. This happens in around 10 percent of U.S. tuna catches and 70 percent of foreign tuna catches.

The *orca* or killer whale is a large dolphin found worldwide. Orcas can swim up to 23 miles per hour (37 kilometers per hour) in search of their food of fish, squid, sea lions, seals, porpoises and even seabirds, which they swallow whole. Male orcas grow up to 30 feet (9.1 meters) long, while females are smaller at about 20 feet (6.1 meters). Orcas are beautifully marked with large zones of black-and-white coloring, although both all-white and all-black individuals are sometimes spotted. They have one prominent fin, which measures up to 6 feet (1.8 meters) long in males, on their backs. Gregarious in nature, they travel in packs of five to fifty and practice a form of cooperative hunting—attacking even the great whales. Killer whales will sometimes "spyhop" to look around by standing vertically with head and much of their body out of the water, held aloft by thrusts of their powerful tails. Humpbacks, one of the baleen whales, also exhibit this behavior.

BALEEN WHALES. In place of teeth the baleen whales have strips of *baleen* hanging from the roof of their mouths. There are two hundred to three hundred plates of baleen on each side of the upper jaw only. Composed of fingernail-like *keratin*, the frayed edges of baleen are used to capture small animals. When the whale opens its mouth, plankton and food such as krill pour in along with an enormous volume of water. The prey are trapped when the whale partly closes its mouth, then forces the water out through the plates of baleen. The tongue is then used to wipe the prey off the inside of the baleen. Prey are then gulped down whole. The *rorquals* or finback whales, including the blue, humpback, Sei, finback and minke whales, have expandable grooves called *ventral pleats* on the throat, which allow a tremendous volume of water to be taken in with each gulp.

Baleen whales are the largest animals in the world. They are comprised of the rorquals and the right whales—the right and bowhead whales. At a length that sometimes reaches 100 feet (30.5 meters) and a weight of up to 150 tons (136.1 metric tons), the blue whale is the largest animal that has ever existed on Earth. Baleen whales, such as the humpback, create beautiful and intricate sounds. They are calls, some short and some long, which are learned by all males each season and are repeated as "songs." With each new season the song changes. In addition, baleen whales will often "sound" just before surfacing.

The humpback whale is a global species that is perhaps the most commonly seen of the large whales. It grows up to be nearly 50 feet (15.2 meters) long, with an average weight of 29 tons (26.3 metric tons). The flukes of the humpbacks have markings that are so distinctive and unique that individuals can be identified by them. Humpbacks have knobs on their heads, each of which bears one gray hair that is 3/4 to 1-1/2 inches (1.9 to 3.8 centimeters) long. Some knobs lack hair but do contain a hair sac. Humpback whales breed and calve in tropical seas during the winter, but they do not eat in tropical waters. They migrate north to temperate seas to feed come summertime. Females calve every other year, and a pregnancy lasts about twelve months. Humpbacks tend to be active at the surface and they are commonly seen breaching (Figure 16-3).

TRUE SEALS, SEA LIONS AND THE WALRUS. Other marine mammals include the true seals, sea lions and walrus. Their front and hind legs form excellent flippers for swimming, and the flippers enable these animals to walk clumsily on land. These marine mammals are members of the order *Pinnipedia* ("wing-footed"). Some, such as the walrus, sea lions and certain seals, gather in great "rookeries" to breed and raise their young. Mothers nurse their single pups on high-fat milk. Certain species spend a good deal of time on land, while others are out to sea for eight months of the year. In the sea they are amazingly quick and agile as they hunt for squid, fish and a number of invertebrate animals, remaining underwater for up to 15 minutes at a time.

MANATEE. A discussion of North American marine mammals would be incomplete without mentioning the manatee or "sea cow" which, in the United States, is now confined strictly to the waters of southern Florida. Slow-moving and herbivorous, the manatee lives in shallow, warm coastal waters where it may eat up to 100 pounds (45.4 kilograms) of seaweed, grass and weeds each day. They have a single, spatulate fluke in the rear and two wide flippers in the front. Although they once were found as far north as North Carolina, manatees were overhunted and are now an endangered species found only in southern Florida. While they do have their natural predators, including sharks and crocodiles, their biggest threats today are habitat destruction, siltation of their feeding grounds and boat propellers. Since manatees tend to lie just under the surface, coming up for a breath every 15 minutes or so, there are frequent collisions with boats that can leave the manatees with serious deep wounds. This has happened so often that researchers now identify individual manatees by the patterns of the scars on their backs.

Conservation of Marine Mammals

As with any animals, the survival of marine mammals depends upon their abilities to adapt to changes occurring in their environments. Some are better equipped to adapt than others. Blue whales, for example, have a specialized form of fine baleen to strain krill from the water in great volumes. But krill are now being harvested by South Korea, the Soviet Union and Japan. Once the krill are gone, or severely depleted, the blue whale will see a similar fate. Humpback whales, however, with their coarser baleen, are capable of catching krill, as well as larval mollusks and fish, such as their favorite fish food, the sand lance. Their dietary variety gives them an adaptive advantage.

Figure 16-3. This humpback whale calf is breaching—a term that describes a whale coming entirely or almost entirely out of the water. Young whales often breach more than their parents. Notice the white flippers and white undermarkings on the "chin" and "chest" areas. The lines toward the front of the underside are the ventral pleats, which expand when the whale feeds. The long flippers of the humpback have inspired its nickname of "wings of the sea." Whales do not land on their ventral (belly) surfaces when they breach—they nearly always land on their sides. This prevents monumental "belly flops." Breaching could be either a response to excitement, a demonstration of playfulness, an aggressive display meant to threaten or scare off an enemy, a way of stunning fish beneath to make them easier to catch or a form of auditory communication as the sound travels great distances underwater. Size: adult to 50 feet (15.2 meters). Photo by John Korejwa.

Further threats to marine mammals include pollution and harassment by people. Long-lived pesticides such as DDT and PCBs are being found in high concentration in whale tissues and in mother's milk. What effect these poisons may have on the health, longevity and reproductive success of whales is presently unknown. No one is certain what long-term ills may befall marine mammals as a result of the toxics entering the food chain during oil spills. Even when well-meaning curiosity seekers and people who care deeply about whales try to catch a glimpse of them on a "whale watch," the whales are intruded upon. The effects on feeding and child-rearing of the ever-increasing volume of whale watch boats that track whales each day in their feeding grounds are unclear.

Biologists and conservationists are beginning to call for the creation of marine sanctuaries, curtailment of whale watch boats, protection of marine mammal food stocks and a permanent ban on all whale hunting, among other measures, in order to assure the future of these magnificent mammals of the sea. After surviving the long evolutionary journey from sea to land and back again, the fate of these awesome giants and their relatives now rests in the hands of humankind.

THE RIGHT WHALE

There,
    off the bow,
    the haze of mid-June
    split by the tell-tale "V"
    of a Right Whale's blow.

Then suddenly,
    a rare sight in the sea
    a Right Whale calf blows a smaller "v."

Slow and steady
    they break the swells
    as tears well up
    and mix with saltspray
    drying on sun-baked cheeks.

Knowing that human hands
    have taken their bounty,
    their beauty and wisdom,
    and traded them in an economy
    that lacks eyes for
    awe and mystery.

Still,
    with trust unflagging,
    this mother and child

mark time
between two whaleboats
whose forebears hunted
more than a "sighting"
and wrote off
their once-abundance
to history.

Will we now look on
    as they swim
    gracefully along
    until we have silenced
    their last song?

A powerful presence
    swimming in tandem;
    spouting "V's" for victory
    in hope that the heavy heart we feel today
    will empower us to save
    those we may have lost to the fight
    had we forgotten how deeply
    we have wronged
    the Right.

—Michael J. Caduto

QUESTIONS

1. In the story "The Gift of the Whale" the Great Spirit creates a thick cloud of mist that hangs over the sea during the whale hunting season. Why does he create this mist?

2. Where do the Inupiaq live? What is the name that the Eskimos call themselves? What does that name mean?

3. What is the climate like where the Inupiaq live? How do they survive in such a harsh environment?

4. Why do the Inupiaq hunt the bowhead whale? What do they do to show respect for the whale?

5. How did the "right whale" get its name?

6. Why did whale hunters of the past three hundred years hunt whales until they were nearly extinct? What did they get from the whales? Was this hunting done out of need?

7. What other whales can you name that are now endangered species?

8. In the Native American tradition, is it right for people to hunt because they need to hunt to survive? Why?

9. In the Native American tradition, is it right for people to hunt for recreation or sport? Why? Is it right, in the Native American tradition, for people to hunt because they want a trophy for their wall?

10. What does the *carrying capacity* of a population of animals mean?

11. What is a renewable resource? A nonrenewable resource?

12. Where did whales originally come from? How long have they been on Earth?

13. What kind of animal is a whale? Can you think of any other marine (ocean) mammals?

14. How does a whale breathe? How does it keep warm? How does it find its way around in dark or murky waters?

15. What are the two main groups of whales? Can you name a few of each? To which group do dolphins and porpoises belong?

16. What is baleen? How is it used by whales?

17. What are manatees? Where are they found? How well are they doing today?

18. What are some threats to the future of whales?

19. What can people do to help protect and conserve whales for the future?

ACTIVITIES
An Ocean of Mammals

ACTIVITY: Create models of marine mammals, other ocean animals (including food of the marine mammals) and props that simulate their under-the-sea environment. Use these models to turn a space into a room-sized diorama of the sea and its creatures.

GOALS: Understand the external anatomy of the various kinds of marine mammals. Realize what these mammals eat. Visualize the habitat of marine mammals. Visualize the relative size of marine mammals and other ocean animals. Have an ocean of fun!

AGE: Younger children and older children

MATERIALS: Tape measure; yardstick; ruler; calculator; strong monofilament fishing line; ropes hung from side-to-side across the ceiling, screwhooks twisted in or other means of hanging creatures up; wallpaper or a roll of parcel post paper; scissors; cardboard; umbrella; balloons; newspaper strips, wheat paste and water for papier-mâché; construction paper of all colors; clay; pipe cleaners; lots of old sheets; fabric shears; needle and thread and/or sewing machine; crumpled newspapers; pencils; chalk for tracing onto sheets; crayons; tempera paint, water, containers and paintbrushes; fabric paint; field guides and other books providing the correct sizes of marine fish and mammals as well as information about their natural history; other materials as needed for original ideas; creativity and energy. Figure 9-6; Figures 16-1, 16-2 and 16-4.

PROCEDURE: Beforehand, choose a scale to work in so that everything can be made in accurate sizes relative to each other. We suggest a scale of one to four. To create the scene and the animals at this scale, simply divide the normal size of everything by four. The entire scene will be one-fourth life-size. Begin by turning a large room into a giant ocean scene. Use a combination of the techniques of fastening props to the walls, hanging them from the ceiling on strong fishing line and resting them on the floor. Be sure to include a seashore with rocks and seaweed, beds of giant kelp and the open ocean. Look at the diagram in Figure 9-6 for ideas on how this is done on a smaller scale, which can be adapted for this activity.

Use your imaginations to create this scene. Have the children cut up strips of green wallpaper or green-painted parcel post paper to hang from the ceiling as giant kelp. Make a giant Portuguese Man-of-War jellyfish from the hanging "bell" of a small, opened umbrella by creating long tentacles to hang from beneath the bell. Create fish and other creatures out of balloons, cardboard, papier-mâché or by sewing two pieces of an old sheet together in the shape of each creature and filling with newspaper to form stuffed animals. Be sure to include numerous kinds of fish, giant squid, octopus, seabirds, krill, capelin and other marine mammal food (see "Discussion" section and Figures 16-1, 16-2 and 16-4 for some ideas). Paste the silhouette of the bottom of a boat on the ceiling!

Now trace two outlines of each marine mammal onto an old sheet. Cut these out and sew the edges together but leave one end open. Now turn this inside out. Color the features onto the animal and attach flippers, flukes, etc., then stuff it with crumpled newspaper. A larger animal, such as a whale, will need an old broomstick or longer board stuck through the middle inside to give it enough rigidity to hold its shape. Hang these on strong fishline from the ceiling. Be sure to include at least one marine mammal from each of these groups:

• toothed whales (sperm whales, killer whales, beaked whales, dolphins, porpoises and narwhals)
• baleen whales (blue, humpback, finback, minke, Sei, right and bowhead whales)
• seals, sea lions, walruses
• manatee or "sea cow"

Once the entire scene is complete, have the children lead others on an under-the-sea nature walk describing all they know about each marine mammal and its way of surviving.

Sonar Swim

ACTIVITY: Play a simulation echo-location game to find your way through an obstacle course while blindfolded.

GOALS: Understand how echo-location works and get a sense of how to use it.

AGE: Younger children and older children

MATERIALS: Medium-sized room, chairs, blindfold, clickers or other materials for creating the sonar sound chosen.

PROCEDURE: Beforehand, set up an obstacle course in the open space of a medium-sized room. With younger children, place only four to five obstacles (objects) well apart from each other and randomly scattered throughout the space. Chairs work well. With older children, place a larger number of chairs closer together to make the course more challenging. Rearrange the chairs between each round so that the children cannot memorize a safe route through them.

Discuss echo-location and sonar with the children (see the "Discussion" section) and how marine mammals (and bats) use this device for detecting objects around them. Ask the children how useful this would be if they lived underwater, and why it would be important and even necessary.

Now ask for the first volunteer to be a marine mammal navigating by sonar. Have her or him choose which mammal (toothed whale, porpoise or dolphin) he or she wants to be. (We will imagine a whale was chosen here.) Have that child go to one corner of the room and blindfold her or him. The child is to keep eyes closed at all times. No peeking!

At this point emphasize to all children present that *only* the "marine mammal" and the "echoing" obstacles can make *any* noise during the game or it will not work. All the other children are to be *absolutely quiet* until it is their turn to play.

Arrange the chairs and have one child go and sit in each chair, facing the blindfolded "whale." The whale will begin walking across the space, making periodic "beeps," while holding her or his hand out in front to feel around. Whenever the whale beeps while facing in the direction of one of the seated children, she or he will immediately respond with a beep to simulate the reflecting of sound back to the whale. Children in the chairs will respond *only* when a beep is made while the moving whale is directly facing them. The object is for the whale to traverse the room without even touching one of the

obstacles. When children do bump into an obstacle, give them a chance or two to try the game over, or let them simply continue on to reach the other side. Continue through successive rounds of the game until everyone has had a chance to be both a mammal and an obstacle.

Note: In place of "beeps" children could navigate using metal clickers, finger-snapping or other sounds, as long as everyone involved is making the same sound.

Color the Sea With Mammals

ACTIVITY: Make a coloring book with all kinds of marine mammals and color in it. Research and report on the natural history of these marine mammals. Create booklets out of these illustrations and reports.

GOALS: Recognize the appearances of the different kinds of marine mammals. Understand some basic natural history of these marine mammals.

AGE: Younger children

MATERIALS: Tracing paper or thin typing paper for tracing, pencils, paper and photocopies of masters (optional), staples (optional), crayons, copies of Figure 16-4, children's and adult books and other resources that teach the basic natural history of marine mammals.

PROCEDURE: Gather pictures or illustrations of marine mammals from each of the groups listed under "An Ocean of Mammals." Have the children use thin typing paper to trace or even enlarge at least one mammal from each group; one per sheet of paper. If the children are very young, you may want to create some masters and staple some coloring books together out of photocopies of the masters. Figure 16-4 provides some marine mammals for tracing and for using as masters.

Have the children color in their mammals. When the coloring books are completed, allow time for the children to research and share what they have learned about their mammals. Compile these illustrations and reports into booklets and publish copies for the children.

A Hunt to Drive You Crackers

ACTIVITY: Working in small groups, play a game that simulates the results of different levels of hunting pressure on

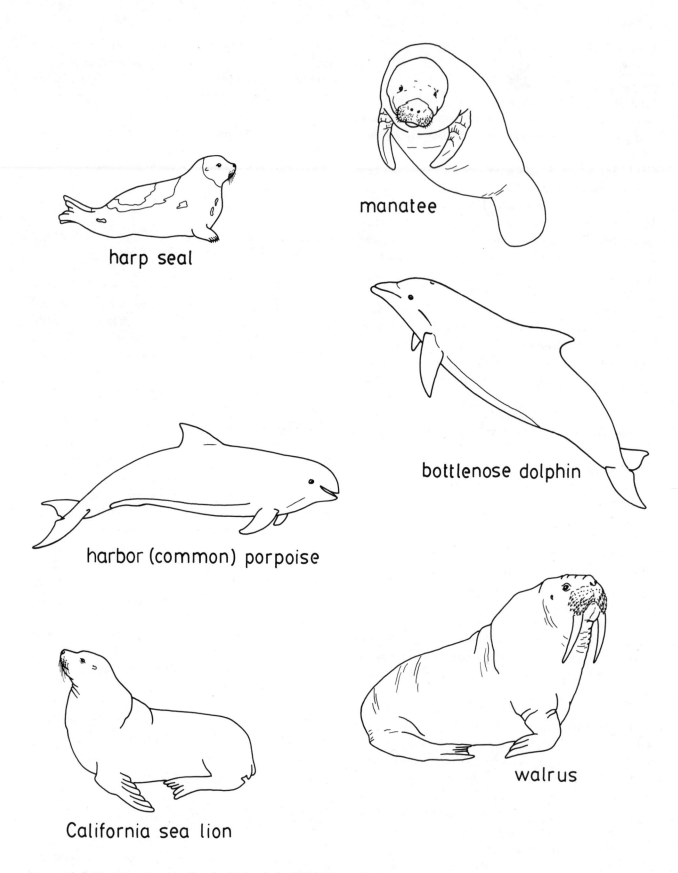

harp seal

manatee

bottlenose dolphin

harbor (common) porpoise

California sea lion

walrus

Figure 16-4. Marine mammal outlines for "Color the Sea With Mammals."

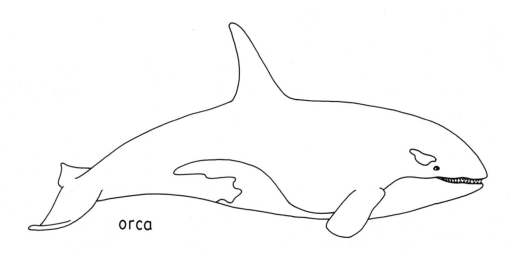

orca

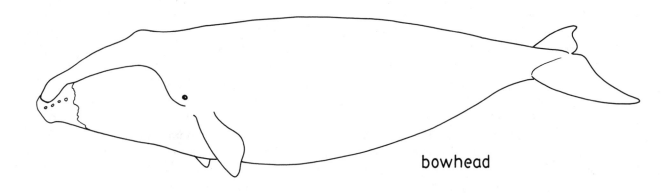

bowhead

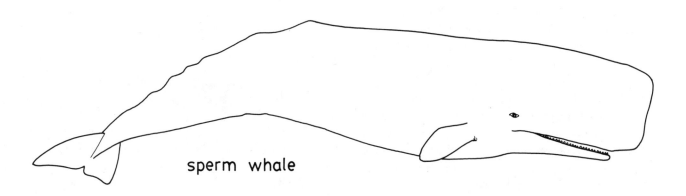

sperm whale

marine mammal populations. Discuss these findings and decide which groups are better wildlife stewards.

GOALS: Explore the ways that the demands of hunting can directly affect the food supply of the hunters and the survival of the prey. Understand the importance of the sustainability of a population and what is meant by carrying capacity and both renewable and nonrenewable resources. Understand the concepts of wildlife management and game versus nongame animals.

AGE: Older children

MATERIALS: At least eighty-seven *whole* crackers of the fish-shaped variety for each set of nine children (three groups of three children each) (extra fish crackers are recommended!), chalkboard and chalk, paper and pencils, Figure 16-5.

PROCEDURE: Explain that, with the marine mammals in this activity, the population present at any given time will have an equal number of both males and females. There will, however, be one extra animal at times when there is an odd number present. There will, for the purposes of this activity, be an equal number of males and females born every year. In other words the *sex ratio*—the relative number of both sexes present in the population—will always be equal if the number of animals is even. This is not realistic in the wild, but it simplifies the calculations needed for the activity and still teaches the basic concept.

The following process may seem complex but it is not. The children in each group will simply add one young mammal per pair in the herd each spring and will hunt (subtract) their assigned number of mammals from the herd each year.

Divide the children into sets of nine. There will be three small groups per set, and each of these small groups will consist of three children. Designate the groups in each set as Group 1, Group 2 and Group 3. The directions that follow describe what will happen in *each set* of nine children.

Write down the present year where all can see it. Each small group of three will start the year with a "herd" of ten marine mammals (fish crackers). Start by putting ten fish crackers in front of each small group and then ask them how many young those animals will produce that spring (five in all cases—one for each pair of "adults" in the herd of ten). Add five animals to each group's herd.

Now have each group "hunt" (subtract) their assigned number of animals for that year. Group 1 will hunt four per year, Group 2 five per year and Group 3 will hunt six per year. Then have them count how many animals are left. (Point out that there would normally be additional deaths due to accidents and injury, disease, natural predation and other

factors.) Each cycle of "birth" and "hunt" marks one round of the game or year in the life of the herds.

Add another year to the date and have the children in each group of three figure out how many young their herd can now produce. Add this number of animals to each group's herd. While it is not always true in the wild, in this activity each pair of animals will produce one young so any odd number of adults leaves one unproductive animal. Now have each group hunt its assigned number of animals again. Repeat this whole cycle until the group that hunts six animals per year (Group 3) has no herd left to hunt (four years). The numbers over this four-year period are calculated in Figure 16-5.

Now discuss what happened and explain that Group 3 has exterminated its mammals in that hunting range. If Group 3 represents a group of people hunting the whole population of that animal, then the animal would now be extinct. Ask the children which group(s) they think is(are) doing a good job of making sure that the animals will survive into the future. These are the *wildlife managers* who are keeping a balance between the demands of their hunting practices and the birth, growth and survival of new animals in the population. Discuss the concepts of carrying capacity, sustainability and both renewable and nonrenewable resources (see the "Discussion" section). What is the carrying capacity of these herds of marine mammals? What is a game animal? What is a nongame animal?

It is important to discuss that hunting alone does not usually drive a species of animal to extinction if suitable habitat is available, stable and of high quality. Animals become more susceptible to extinction by hunting when habitat is reduced in quality and quantity. Whales, however, are an exception where overhunting has driven some species to the brink of extinction. This is also true with some sea birds that are vulnerable to overhunting when they congregate in great numbers to nest each year. These nesting grounds can contain hundreds of thousands of birds that, in some cases, comprise almost the total population of that species.

Hunting for a Resolution

ACTIVITY: Conduct a role-playing exercise during which the players air their views, take and defend a particular stand regarding hunting and the issues surrounding hunting, and engage in a simulation of a cross-cultural dialogue.

GOALS: Understand the various stands that people take for and against hunting. Explore the issues and controversies surrounding hunting, such as hunting out of need versus want, traditional Native North American versus high-tech hunting techniques, materialism and economics and their affects on the demand for animals and animal products. Practice sharing your ideas and opinions and listening to the ideas and opinions of those with whom you do not agree as you search for a common solution to a difficult problem. Consider the needs, wants and beliefs of a traditional Native North American culture during a decision making process affecting one of their important sources of food, cultural context and meaning.

AGE: Older children

MATERIALS: Pencils, large index cards, cardboard and felt-tipped marking pens to create name plates for government officials, props and clothing for children to use to dress up in the roles they are playing, large table or desk for Department of Environmental Management (DEM) representatives of the federal government to sit at as they preside over the meeting. Copies of the "History of the Gray Seal," the "Gray Seal Management Plan" and the "Descriptions of the Interest Groups" from this activity.

PROCEDURE: *Note:* Begin this activity at least one week before you want the children to conduct the actual role-playing exercise. This will give them time for research, interviews and other background preparation. We find that when the children are heavily invested in their roles, they take the entire exercise more seriously and really "get into" their role-playing identities.

Beforehand, prepare the cards describing each interest group's identity and position regarding the Gray Seal Management Plan.

Share the Inuit-Inupiaq story "The Gift of the Whale" with the children. Have each of them take turns reading as you review the parts of the "Discussion" section that deal with hunting and related issues.

Now tell the children that they are each going to prepare for a role-playing activity during which they will take on the identity of a person with a particular stand about hunting. Emphasize that they are going to take the roles *seriously* and defend their positions as if they *really are* those persons. Read the following fictitious scenario.

HISTORY OF THE GRAY SEAL

For thousands of years the Inuit of Seal Harbor have hunted the gray seal as an essential source of food, clothing and shelter. The meat and fat were eaten, the oil was used for lamps and the skin for clothing and shelter. The Inuit never took more seals than they needed. They always hunted in the traditional way: asking permission of the Creator and the seals, taking only the weaker individuals and leaving stronger ones to reproduce, wasting nothing and giving thanks for the gift of life from the seals.

Gradually, over the last one hundred years, the gray seal has come under increasing pressure exerted by hunters from outside the region. In particular, the gray seal pups are killed in great numbers each spring to supply the European fur-trade market. Now, the Inuit are finding it difficult to hunt

---

Calculations for "A Hunt to Drive You Crackers"

The numbers look like this over four years:

	Year 1	Year 2	Year 3	Year 4
group 1 (hunts 4/year)	$10+5=15(-4)=$	$11+5=16(-4)=$	$12+6=18(-4)=$	$14+7=21(-4)=17$
group 2 (hunts 5/year)	$10+5=15(-5)=$	$10+5=15(-5)=$	$10+5=15(-5)=$	$10+5=15(-5)=10$
group 3 (hunts 6/year)	$10+5=15(-6)=$	$9+4=13(-6)=$	$7+3=10(-6)=$	$4+2=6(-6)=0$

Figure 16-5. Calculations for "A Hunt to Drive You Crackers."

their food because there are so few left. If these trends continue, the gray seal may soon become an endangered species.

GRAY SEAL MANAGEMENT PLAN

Due to pressure from the Inuit, several conservation groups, provincial authorities and the general public, the federal government has proposed a complete ban on all hunting of the gray seal, except for a certain quota to be taken by the Inuit for their survival needs. This will assure that the population of gray seals will remain healthy while providing for the survival needs of the Inuit peoples, traditional hunters of this gray seal. A public hearing has been scheduled to consider the issues surrounding this proposal, known as the Gray Seal Management Plan.

Have the children choose their roles and pass out the cards that identify the interest groups and their positions to players so that all sides are represented. Now allow the children a week or longer to prepare for their roles through research and (if possible) interviews with people involved with similar issues in real-life situations. It is important to set aside specific time for this background preparation and to offer as much support and guidance as possible. During this period of preparation, the children need to decide who will be the spokesperson for their group and what comments of support the other members of the group will make at the hearing. Help the children representing the provincial authorities to decide which of the four positions they want to advocate at the hearing.

When the time for the role-playing finally arrives, the children will play their roles as people present at the public hearing, which will be presided over by the three representatives from the federal government's Department of Environmental Management (DEM). During the hearing, each side will be given a maximum of ten minutes to present its views, until all sides have been heard.

The three children who receive the DEM cards will (1) conduct the hearing; (2) retire for a few minutes to consider the testimony; (3) take a vote on the resolution and decide either to support or reject the Gray Seal Management Plan, or to offer an alternative course of action; and (4) report their decision to the group as a whole.

After the decision is rendered, ask the various members of each group to share how they felt about the process and what their thoughts and feelings are about the decision.

Finally, facilitate a discussion that includes the concepts of need versus want, traditional hunting techniques versus high-tech hunting methods, materialism and economic demand upon animal populations and products and game versus nongame animals.

DESCRIPTIONS OF THE INTEREST GROUPS

These descriptions of the interest groups and their stands on the issues are to be written on index cards and passed out to the children. Make up as many cards as indicated so that each player has his or her own card.

• *Department of Environmental Management Officials* (3)

You are a representative of the federal government's Department of Environmental Management (DEM). You are to work with the other two DEM representatives. First, read the Gray Seal Management Plan to the entire group that has assembled. Then, tell the assembly that each interest group will be allowed *five minutes only* to submit testimony during the hearing, until all who want to have shared. Appoint an official timekeeper from among yourselves to stop testimony after five minutes for each group. Once all testimony has been received, retire to consider all viewpoints and take a vote among the three of you to either approve or disapprove the Gray Seal Management Plan.

• *Inuit* (one spokesperson plus any number of representatives)

We have hunted the gray seal for thousands of years, as far back as the memory of our people goes. The seal is part of us, and we are part of the seal. We have always treated the seal with great respect, have never taken more than we needed or wasted any part of the seal. We continue to hunt with a modern form of our traditional hunting techniques. There was never any problem with the numbers of seals until the fur hunters came and killed the young in great numbers using modern methods that kill many animals and cause them much pain. How can the seal survive if its young are slaughtered? We support this ban and will follow the management quotas as written to keep the gray seal strong. (Other Inuit people add their own comments.)

• *Seal fur hunters* (one spokesperson plus any number of representatives)

Why should a ban on gray seal hunting exclude only those that hunt for fur? Most of us are willing to accept limits on the hunt and use humane hunting techniques. We are entitled to make a living too. It is only a few selfish and insensitive fur sealers who have hunted without regard for the seals' well-being and who have given us all a bad name. We strongly urge the federal government to allow a limited, regulated hunt by fur sealers as an amendment to the Gray Seal Management Plan. (Other fur seal hunters add their comments.)

• *Conservationists for the Protection of Gray Seals* (a spokesperson plus any number of representatives)

For many years we have watched in dismay as the number of gray seals has declined year-by-year. Each springtime the wanton slaughter of these magnificent pups continues. If the fur seal hunters have not been able to control themselves, then how can we trust them to honor any regulations that would be set forth in a management plan? Our calculations tell us that the gray seal will be driven to the verge of extinction within ten to fifteen years if the Gray Seal Management Plan is not approved and enforced. We strongly recommend approval of this plan as it is now written. (Other conservationists add their comments.)

• *Members of the general public* (nonnative local hunters and trappers, animal rights activists and others)

Some of you will be for, and some against, the Gray Seal Management Plan. Decide who will take which stand and take your five minutes to say how you feel about the issues and why. Be sure there are some representatives present from each side of the issue.

• *Provincial authorities* (one spokesperson, two present)

Four possible courses of action by the provincial authorities are offered here: (1) a decision in support of the Gray Seal Management Plan (GSMP); (2) a decision to reject support of the proposed GSMP, but to propose instead to monitor the existing situation more closely; (3) a decision during which the provincial authorities offer their support for an amended version (of their own design) of the GSMP; and (4) an open option in which the provincial authorities design a completely original response to the GSMP and the situation at hand.

1. Position in support of the proposed GSMP:

We have debated long and hard at the provincial level about the issues surrounding the harvest of fur seals. There are many conflicting interests and no one plan can satisfy everyone's needs and desires. We have decided that the most crucial factor is the preservation of the gray seal, which is an important animal to all who live within its range and beyond. Secondly, we find that the livelihood of the Inuit, long-time hunters of the gray seal, is closely tied to their continued hunting of this animal in a wise and prudent manner that will assure its survival. Seal fur hunters do have a vested interest in the gray seal but it is not as crucial as these two concerns that I previously mentioned. The provincial government, therefore, has decided to support the Gray Seal Management Plan in its original language.

2. Position rejecting support of the GSMP:

We have debated long and hard at the provincial level about the issues surrounding the harvest of fur seals. There are many conflicting interests and no one plan can satisfy everyone's needs and desires. We have decided that the most crucial factor is the health of the economy of Seal Harbor. While the well-being of the seal population is an important consideration, we do not feel that the evidence warrants the support of a plan as restrictive as the Gray Seal Management Plan. We will, however, do everything in our power to monitor the population of the gray seal and to make sure that the fur sealers carry out the gray seal hunt in a humane fashion. We do not support the Gray Seal Management Plan as it is written.

3. Position offering an amended version of the GSMP:

We have debated long and hard at the provincial level about the issues surrounding the harvest of fur seals. There are many conflicting interests and no one plan can satisfy everyone's needs and desires. We have decided that these are our major concerns and priorities:

•

•

•

•

Therefore we have decided to support an amended version of the Gray Seal Management Plan with the following changes:

•

•

•

•

4. This position will be completely original. It will be designed and agreed upon by the children representing the provincial authorities.

A Whale of a Gift

ACTIVITY: Create something simple, original and from the heart to show appreciation for the gifts of the whales and to help preserve them for the future.

GOALS: Complete the circle of giving and receiving between whales and yourself. Realize that we can all help to assure that whales survive.

AGE: Younger children and older children

MATERIALS: As needed for the specific project chosen.

PROCEDURE: Have the children choose one or more

projects to express their thanks and appreciation to whales and to help protect them for future generations. Here are some examples:

• Create a small whale sculpture out of clay and other natural materials such as milkweed pods, pecans, acorns or other nuts, locust seed pods, feathers, etc. It could also be carved out of wood. Take the gift to the sea (if you live nearby) or a special place outdoors, say thank you to the whales for their many gifts and offer the gift to them by throwing it into the sea or burying it in the ground.

• Write to the federal government office in charge of endangered species (see page 243 in Chapter 17 for addresses) and other government representatives to express your support for legal protection of whales and other endangered species and their habitats.

• Write a story, puppet show, play or poem (in the shape of a whale) that expresses the many gifts we receive from whales.

• Create your own fantasy journey of a visit with the whales beneath the waves.

• Create a whale journal with a section on each kind of whale, a picture or illustration of each species and notes recording everything you have learned about each whale and what you have done to help save it.

• Study traditional whaling cultures, such as the Inuit, and their practices for thanking the whales. Make up your own ways to thank the whales with these practices in mind.

EXTENDING THE EXPERIENCE

• Cut pieces of string to the actual, life-sized length of the animals modeled in "An Ocean of Mammals." For example, a blue whale grows up to 100 feet (30.5 meters) long. Stretch the strings out next to each other in a large open area to compare the relative sizes of these marine mammals. Have a child stand at each end of each string to graphically mark its length for the rest of the group.

• Compare the size of the blue whale, the largest animal that ever lived, to the size of other forms of ocean life by conducting the activity called "Ocean Life, The Large and the Small of It" on page 99 in *Keepers of the Earth*.

• Visit a marine aquarium and have fun while you learn all you can about marine mammals.

• Play whale charades. Hang up pictures of several different whales, dolphins, porpoises, seals, sea lions, walruses and manatees and have small groups imitate these marine mammals while others try to guess which ones they are imitating.

• Write a paper on the *rights* of whales and other animal species. Review the constitutional rights guaranteed citizens by the federal government first, then make up your own bill of rights for animals.

• Have fun playing and learning about whale songs that have been recorded.

• Write for more information and activities about marine animals to:

Center for Marine Conservation
P.O. Box 96003
Washington, D.C. 20077-7172

Canadian Museum of Nature
P.O. Box 3443
Station D
Ottawa, Ontario K1P 6P4

• Continue the experience with the ocean stories and activities in Chapter 11, pp. 93–101 in *Keepers of the Earth*.

• Go on a traditional hunt in "A Journey With the Abenakis" on page 169 in *Keepers of the Earth*.

NOTES

1. Michael Satchell, "The American Hunter Under Fire," *U.S. News and World Report* 108, no. 5 (February 5, 1990): 30–36.
2. Ibid.
3. Michael Satchell and Joannie M. Schrof, "Uncle Sam's War on Wildlife," *U.S. News and World Report* 108, no. 5 (February 5, 1990): 36–37.

CHAPTER 17

❖ The Passing of the Buffalo ❖

(Kiowa—Plains)

Once, not long ago, the buffalo were everywhere. Wherever the people were, there were the buffalo. They loved the people and the people loved the buffalo. When the people killed a buffalo, they did it with reverence. They gave thanks to the buffalo's spirit. They used every part of the buffalo they killed. The meat was their food. The skins were used for clothing and to cover their tipis. The hair stuffed their pillows and saddlebags. The sinews became their bowstrings. From the hooves they made glue. They carried water in the bladders and stomachs. To give the buffalo honor, they painted the skull and placed it facing the rising sun.

Then the whites came. They were new people, as beautiful and as deadly as the black spider. The whites took the lands of the people. They built the railroad to cut the lands of the people in half. It made life hard for the people and so the buffalo fought the railroad. The buffalo tore up the railroad tracks. They chased away the cattle of the whites. The buffalo loved the people and tried to protect their way of life. So the army was sent to kill the buffalo. But even the soldiers could not hold the buffalo back. Then the army hired hunters. The hunters came and killed and killed. Soon the bones of the buffalo covered the land to the height of a tall man. The buffalo saw they could fight no longer.

One morning, a Kiowa woman whose family was running from the Army rose early from their camp deep in the hills. She went down to the spring near the mountainside to get water. She went quietly, alert for enemies. The morning mist was thick, but as she bent to fill her bucket she saw something. It was something moving in the mist. As she watched, the mist parted and out of it came an old buffalo cow. It was one of the old buffalo women who always led the herds. Behind her came the last few young buffalo warriors, their horns scarred from fighting, some of them wounded. Among them were a few calves and young cows.

Straight toward the side of the mountain, the old buffalo cow led that last herd. As the Kiowa woman watched, the mountain opened up in front of them and the buffalo walked into the mountain. Within the mountain the earth was green and new. The sun shone and the meadowlarks were singing. It was as it had been before the whites came. Then the mountain closed behind them. The buffalo were gone.

DISCUSSION
American Bison

The destruction of the herds of American bison (buffalo) was in part a deliberate action taken by the U.S. Army as a means of bringing the Indians under their control. Western movies to the contrary, fewer Native North Americans were actually defeated by the U.S.

Cavalry than is generally believed. The majority of casualties among the Native North Americans of the West came from European-introduced diseases and starvation. Because the life of the Plains people depended so heavily upon the bison, killing the bison was decided upon as a final solution.

The Indians of the Plains knew well just how important a resource the bison were and the love and respect for

Straight toward the side of the mountain, the old buffalo cow led that last herd.

the bison shown in their traditions was grounded in ecological common sense. The great Lakota (Sioux) Chief Red Cloud had been successful in turning back the U.S. Army who had helped build the "Thieves' Road" into the Black Hills, breaking a treaty made with the Lakota (Sioux) guaranteeing them that land. George Armstrong Custer had been instrumental in building that road (which led to rich gold deposits) and several forts had been built.

Fortunately for the Lakota, when they won their war against the Army the commissioner of Indian Affairs was Ely Parker, a Seneca Indian who had been a General in the Civil War. Parker had proposed a peace policy with the western Indians and President Grant followed his advice, producing one of the few times of peace between white and Indian during the nineteenth century. The forts in the Black Hills were abandoned and the Lakotas burned them.

Once again, the Lakota controlled a large area. It was then that something that has seldom been discussed began. Recognizing the danger faced by the remaining bison, the Lakotas began to herd them. They would keep their friends, the bison, in the north, preventing them from following the old migration paths south. Then they would not be killed by the bison hunters who were being kept out of the lands of the Lakota.

From the Killdeer Mountains to the Missouri River, the Lakota kept a herd line. Any animals that tried to head south were moved back. From 1864 until the Custer Battle in 1876, the Lakotas kept that herd line. South of the line, all of the bison were gone, but the northern herd was growing again in strength.

After the fight at Little Big Horn, half of the entire U. S. Army moved into the plains seeking to capture Sitting Bull and Crazy Horse. Many of the Lakota were forced to flee north and the herd lines were broken. Once more, the bison began to gather and follow their old trail to the south. Some of the Native North American people of the southern plains thought that the Great Spirit had opened the caves in Earth from which the bison originally came according to their old traditions. They thought the bison had been given back to them. Sadly, it was not so. It was only the great Lakota herd, drifting down from Montana and the Dakotas, coming back again into range of the high-caliber "sharps" rifles of the bison skinners.

In the southern plains, the Comanches and Kiowas had joined together to fight the bison hunters and the U.S. Army. They tried to save the bison and their fight was called the Buffalo War. But they were outnumbered. Between 1872 and 1874, 4 million bison were killed on the southern plains. Of that number, less than 5 percent were killed by Native North Americans. The white people of Texas saw what was happening and asked General Sheridan to end the slaughter of the bison. His reply was, "Let them kill, skin and sell until the buffalo is exterminated." It was the first deliberate act of ecocide in our history. By 1875 all the bison were gone from the southern plains.

Then, in 1876, the northern herd came south and it began again—for a short time. In 1881, fifty thousand bison hides were shipped east from the southern plains. In 1882, two hundred thousand hides were shipped. In 1883, fifty thousand were shipped, and in 1884, only three hundred. Thereafter, there were none.

The original population of from 50 to 60 million plains bison, which may have been the largest population of any great mammal since Earth first formed, was close to extinction by 1900 (Figure 17-1). Plains bison have been protected since 1893 and the herds have been managed since the 1920s. These magnificent animals, which once travelled several hundred miles across the prairie during their yearly migration, are now confined to captive herds in Canada and the United States, which total several thousand individuals. Historic skulls and bones of the bison are found on the western plains to this day.

Less known is the plight of the wood bison, a larger, darker, nonmigratory subspecies of bison that originally lived in northcentral Canada. The original population of a few hundred thousand individuals was decimated until there were about three hundred left by 1891. The creation of the Wood Buffalo National Park, which straddles the Alberta/Northwest Territories border, helped this population to increase to around fifteen hundred to two thousand animals by 1922. But this group interbred with a larger herd of 6,673 plains bison that were released in the park in the mid-twenties, and the wood bison had all but disappeared by the 1940s. There are now about three thousand wood bison on the Mackenzie Bison Sanctuary in the Northwest Territories, bred from eighteen of the small herd of about two hundred wood bison found isolated in the northern margin of the Wood Buffalo National Park in 1957. The wood bison is now listed as threatened in Canada and as endangered in the United States.[1]

* * * *

The following discussion delves into such topics as wildlife management, animal populations, endangered species and the causes of endangerment and extinction.

Figure 17-1. Due to overhunting and wanton slaughter during the 1800s, the plains bison, whose population once numbered 50 to 60 million, was on the verge of extinction by the year 1900. Size: height 5–6 feet (1.5–1.8 meters) and up to 2,000 pounds (907.2 kilograms). Illustration by D. D. Tyler.

Any discussion of endangered species and extinction evokes feelings of sadness and, at times, even despair. However, there is indeed *hope* for endangered species and for us, the human beings who hold their fate in our hands. This chapter ends with a discussion of some success stories describing species that have been saved from extinction—some of which are no longer in immediate danger. There is also a section describing the many ways that people can work to make Earth a safe habitat for the animals and specific actions that can help to save endangered species.

Wildlife Management

The face of North America and the fate of the animals that live here have changed dramatically since the time when Native North Americans were the sole inhabitants of this land. Prior to the arrival of Europeans to North America, and the effects that their cultures, economy and technology had upon the indigenous cultures and wildlife of this continent, the native people of the plains were the caretakers of the land inhabited by the great herds of bison and many other animals. They were concerned with the numbers of animals they hunted and the quality of habitat the animals had to live in. It is now known that in many areas, Native North Americans, by burning, maintained a diverse patchwork of open brushy clearings, forests and fields to provide good habitat, especially food and cover, for deer, bison and other animals.[2] Some of these practices created habitat that enhanced what modern wildlife managers call the *edge effect*, creating places where several different habitats meet to better provide for certain animals' basic needs for food, water and shelter.

Native North Americans, by virtue of their spiritual, physical and emotional connections to the animals and all of their surroundings, lived in a *sustainable* relationship with nature. The Native North American consciousness goes beyond that of *wildlife management*, which tends to treat animals as resources for meeting human needs and wants, to a deeper belief that people, animals and all of nature are one in the great circle of life with the Creator at its center, who is the source and inspiration to all those who live therein.

Conversely, European-based cultures and religions frequently view the natural world as a separate, subservient resource to serve human beings. This has historically led to a manipulative, controlling relationship spurred on by technological breakthroughs which enhanced a false sense of being more powerful than nature.

The Values of Species

Increasingly, however, as people realize how deeply we are interconnected with all life on Earth, the immeasurable richness and importance of the plant and animal life with which we share this common home are coming to light. There is no way to measure the full value of any species' continued existence. With each extinction Earth and all of its denizens are diminished. Still, the questions of value are often asked, "Why should we care so much about animals—endangered species in particular? Why are they so important?" Consider the many ways that any species is of irreplaceable value:

- *ecological*, as sources of genetic and biological diversity and stability and as warnings or signs of environmental health, as threads in the web of life;
- *utilitarian and economic (commercial)*, since animals are used for food, clothing, shelter and more;
- *educational and scientific*, as teachers to help us better understand our environment and ourselves;
- *historical*, connecting us with our own cultural past and that of Earth;
- *recreational*, for our enjoyment while engaged in outdoor activities;
- *aesthetic and symbolic*, as sources of beauty, inspiration and wildness;
- *spiritual*, as sources of our connection with all our relations on Earth, both human and wild;
- *inherent or intrinsic*, the value a species possesses simply by virtue of its existence and being, regardless of whatever values people do or do not attribute to it; and
- *ethical*, that species have the right to exist, and that human beings play a stewardship role to preserve, not destroy, other species.

Biological diversity or *biodiversity* is a value that people are particularly concerned about today who are mindful of the present rate of extinction and the ever-growing number of endangered species. Every species is unique and possesses the full range of values just described. Every time a species is lost, then so too are its particular values gone forever, thus decreasing the biological diversity of an ecosystem. Biodiversity is a measure of the adaptability of any ecosystem, even the global ecosphere, and is a major determinant of whether or not that ecosystem can survive. The greater the number of species, the greater chance an ecosystem has to adapt to and survive change. The increasing population of humanity and the stresses we place on the ecosphere are decreasing biodiversity to a level not seen since the dinosaurs disappeared 65 million years ago at the end of the Mesozoic Era.[3] It took 5 to 10 million years for Earth's diversity to recover after that great extinction occurred. Since tropical rain forests are home to over half of all species on Earth, and since these environments cover only 7 percent of the Earth's land surface, it is crucial to protect the species that live there and their precious habitat. An area of tropical forest the size of the state of West Virginia is being cleared each year. It is estimated that at least 2 million species live in the world's forests, and these are currently being wiped out at the rate of four to six thousand per year—ten thousand times faster than the natural rate of extinction.[4]

Obviously, human beings cannot afford to ignore the disappearance or endangerment of any one species or group of species. Their survival is of utmost concern to our own future and quality of life upon Earth. Each economic activity must be tailored to ecological stability and sustainability.

Animal Populations

Human beings, however, are not the only force affecting animal populations. Even when left to its own rhythms, a population of animals experiences ups and downs. The number of animals in any given *population*, a group of animals of a certain species living in a particular ecosystem, could fluctuate cyclically (may reach a peak every seven years with declines in between), explode to great numbers periodically with dramatic declines in between or maintain a fairly constant size through time. Natural populations increase due to births and immigration from neighboring groups. Decreases can be due to emigration or *dispersal* and death due to aging, disease, accidents, predators and starvation. The size of any population of animals depends upon these factors, plus the quantity and quality of food, water and shelter available and its distribution; weather and climate; and the behavior of those animals such as territoriality, stress tolerance, mating behavior, social interactions, food preferences and the animal's ability to adapt to new food sources. Often there is a certain *limiting factor*, such as a low tolerance for crowding among a species or a limited food supply, which keeps a population below the maximum level it could reach in an ecosystem, and often prevents overpopulation and habitat destruction from overuse.

THREATS TO SPECIES SURVIVAL. These natural checks and balances, however, have been upset by the enormous pressures placed upon animals by the presence and activity of human beings, whether intentional or not.

While some human influences have favored highly adaptable forms of wildlife, such as those that can survive in urban, suburban and other built environments, the overall effects of people on wild animal populations have been devastating. And, although human beings are a part of nature, the extent and intensity of the changes we bring to the natural world are so far-reaching as to exert a degree of influence far beyond that of any other living things.

Threats to the continued well-being, and even existence, of many species of animals are serious and widespread, including:

- *habitat destruction and decimation*, including urbanization, deforestation, desertification and the resulting erosion
- *overhunting and overfishing*
- *pesticides, herbicides and other toxic compounds* that poison the food chain
- *global warming* (the "greenhouse effect")
- *acid rain* and other forms of *air pollution*
- *toxic waste* buildup and environmental contamination
- *ozone depletion* and the resulting increase of exposure to harmful ultraviolet radiation from the sun
- *surface- and groundwater pollution*
- *the over-collecting of animals* for pets and other commercial wildlife "products"
- *poaching and other uncontrolled, illegal activities* that decimate wildlife populations
- *the introduction of exotic species* that compete with indigenous animals for food, water and cover
- *hazardous human refuse*, such as plastic waste, that entangle animals and cause internal injuries and death when ingested
- *burgeoning human populations* and competition with animals for available resources
- *disturbance and stress* caused by contact with humans while involved in hiking, photographing, bird-watching, boating and other nonconsumptive forms of contact with wildlife
- *the gradually deteriorating quality of the ecosphere* that all of these problems are working together to produce

Habitat destruction is causing unestimable damage to wildlife. Without a home to live in and an environment to meet the basic needs of an animal, there is little hope for its survival. Vast amounts of natural habitat are converted for use in logging, grazing, agriculture and urban development. Tropical rain forests, home for many of North America's migrating birds, are being destroyed at the rate of 23,000 square miles (59,570 square kilometers) per year, which is equal to the land area of West Virginia. Sixty thousand acres of ancient forest are being cut every year in the United States. Most of this wood is exported to Japan and its neighboring countries in the Pacific rim. As much as 50 percent of the prime forestland in Alaska's Tongass National Forest has been cut since 1950.

In 1987 alone 5.5 billion boardfeet of timber was cut in the Pacific northwestern United States. The old growth forests of western Oregon, western Washington and northern California are part of this timberland. This habitat is also home to the northern spotted owl, which is decreasing at the rate of up to 12 percent per year according to Cornell University scientists. This 2-foot (61-centimeter) tall bird now numbers only three to five thousand pairs and has been placed on the list of threatened species in the United States. It is also listed as an endangered species in Canada. The threatened species designation makes it illegal to harm the spotted owl or destroy any of its habitat. The federal government must be consulted before undertaking any action that would have an impact on the northern spotted owl or its environment.

The activities associated with energy production have altered, polluted and even destroyed significant amounts of wildlife habitat. Oil drilling disrupts the behavior patterns of local wildlife. Oil spills take a disastrous toll on marine wildlife and habitat, killing scores of animals outright and degrading the quality of the affected habitat for years to come.

The development of enormous hydroelectric dams and reservoirs in the James Bay region of Canada is having catastrophic impacts on the indigenous wildlife, as well as the native cultures of the Cree Indians and Inuit peoples of that region. Phase one of this project flooded 4,440 square miles (11,500 square kilometers) of fish spawning areas, caribou calving grounds and migratory bird habitat, as well as greatly diminishing the food supply of marine mammals. Other impacts of this project beyond habitat destruction include:[5]

• the leaching of naturally occurring mercury out of flooded soils, causing this heavy metal to enter the food chain, poisoning people, fish and other wildlife;
• the loss of vast areas of forestland, increasing the greenhouse effect as the carbon dioxide absorption capacity of those trees is lost and the decaying vegetation releases carbon dioxide, methane and other "greenhouse gases," further accelerating the greenhouse effect;
• the drowning in September 1984 of ten thousand

caribou of the George's River herd as they tried to cross the river along their ancient migration route, where it is suspected that the caribou were trapped when a massive amount of water was released from the Caniapiscau Reservoir upstream; and
• the disappearance of a rare species of mollusk that inhabited La Grande River, which was dammed in three places as part of phase one of the James Bay project.

The proposed James Bay II project would flood an additional 1,614 square miles (4,180 square kilometers) of land, in addition to creating a 774-square-mile (2,004-square-kilometer) storage reservoir by flooding Lake Bienville. If James Bay II is completed, the total area that is actually flooded (the *impacted* area will be far greater) by both James Bay projects will exceed the combined land area of the states of Connecticut and Rhode Island. The Great Whale Project of James Bay II threatens a unique population of freshwater seals that live in two lakes which could be destroyed when the Nastapoca River is diverted. It is suspected that these seals may be a separate subspecies of the harbor seal.

Habitat destruction on this scale affects not only wildlife, but the peoples who have led a subsistence existence in this region for thousands of years. The Cree Indians and Inuit peoples of northern Quebec have also suffered greatly, including:

• the flooding of villages, as well as hunting, trapping and fishing grounds;
• the depletion and destruction of native fisheries due to mercury poisoning and the destruction of spawning grounds; and
• mercury poisoning among people who have eaten tainted fish and wildlife, particularly children, who are the most susceptible and for whom, traditionally, the first solid food is mashed whitefish.

Changes of this kind are eroding the native cultural and spiritual context that is so tightly intertwined with the local environment and wildlife. These impacts have also contributed to a shift from the traditional subsistence way of life of many Cree and Inuit families and villages to a monetary economy. Tragically, a cash-based economy is not viable in the harsh Arctic environment. This is due to, among other factors, the extremely high cost of imports, the unavailability of many items previously derived from the land and the difficulties involved with shipping supplies during extended periods of extreme inclement weather.

Global warming—the greenhouse effect—is predicted to have a profound affect upon wildlife, especially those species living in the cold temperate and polar regions. Carbon dioxide (CO_2) is accumulating in the upper atmosphere due to the burning of coal, gasoline and other fossil fuels, as well as the emission of CO_2 from the large-scale burning of tropical forests. This layer of CO_2 is acting like the glass of a greenhouse. The sun's shortwave radiation passes through and heats up the Earth's surface. This heat, or longwave radiation, which is given off by Earth, is reflected back by the layer of CO_2 and is gradually warming the global temperature. If CO_2 continues to build up at present rates the average global temperature could rise by about 7°F (4°C) by the year 2050.[6] As the climate warms, those animals living in arctic and subarctic habitats, especially those that could not adapt or migrate fast enough to better climates, could perish. In addition, as the polar ice caps melt and sea levels rise several feet, coastal habitat would be flooded and weather patterns around the globe would be altered, resulting in widespread drought and floods.

Acid rain is a pervasive form of air pollution that is the leading edge of a general decline in the quality of the global environment. Nitric and sulfuric acid form overhead from the emissions released by the burning of fossil fuels, and these contaminate fog and rain to create acid-fallout. This acidity is killing life in hundreds of waterways worldwide, especially in industrialized nations. The decline of the endangered Aurora trout and Acadian whitefish in Canada, for instance, is a direct result of the acidification of our waterways. Acid rain is considered by many to be one of the leading causes of the overall degradation of the global environment, which is leading to, among other effects, a worldwide decline in populations of amphibians (frogs, toads and salamanders).

Another atmospheric pollution problem, *depletion of the ozone layer* in the upper atmosphere, will also affect animals. Certain chemicals called chlorofluorocarbons (CFCs), used in refrigerators and air-conditioning units, destroy Earth's protective ozone layer that shields us from the sun's harmful ultraviolet radiation. Immense holes in the ozone layer have now been found at both the north and south polar regions. Exposure to excessive levels of ultraviolet radiation increases the risk of skin cancer and lowers the resistance of plants and animals to diseases and the harmful effects of other forms of pollution.

The combined effects of several environmental hazards often produces a *synergistic* effect, in which the damage done is greater than the sum total of the harm expected to be caused by the two agents. A plant or animal whose resistance has been lowered is, for example, more susceptible to the ill-effects of environmental contamination in the form of pesticides, herbicides and PCBs.

DDT and other contaminants pose a serious threat to many species and have brought some perilously close to extinction. The coelacanth is a 5-foot- (1.5-meter-) long fish found in the waters of the Indian Ocean around the Comoro Islands off the southeast coast of Africa. It is an ancient fish that has remained nearly unchanged for 380 million years. Coelacanths are thought by some to represent an evolutionary link between fish and "tetrapods," air-breathing, four-legged terrestrial animals and people. Up until one was caught in a fishing net and identified in 1938, the coelacanth was thought to have been extinct for 70 million years. Scientists have now discovered that coelacanth tissues are highly contaminated with DDT and PCBs. Between the effects of these toxins, and the fact that up to one dozen or so coelacanths are caught and killed by local fishermen each year (it is believed that their spinal fluid can prolong a person's lifespan), it is now thought that these marvelous fish of antiquity will become extinct within thirty years.

In 1967 the once abundant bald eagle's population was so decimated that it was listed as an endangered species throughout much of the lower forty-eight United States and in parts of Canada. This inspiring bird's image appears as everything from the national symbol of the United States to the face of coins and the logo for many businesses and products. In the province of Ontario alone, at least forty places and nineteen lakes have "eagle" in their names. Still, the bald eagle was frequently shot for sport and profit. It has been accidentally killed by everything from getting tangled in fishing line (fish is an important part of the eagle's diet) and electrocuted on power lines, to being poisoned by contaminated bait meant for coyotes, wolves, foxes and bobcats and inadvertently caught in leg-hold traps set for other animals. The eagle's habitat has been severely reduced. Other contaminant-related impacts include lead poisoning from the ingestion of the spent pellets from shotgun shells and acid rain, which is decreasing fish populations.

Bald eagles have been contaminated by PCBs and other industrial compounds, but it was poisoning by the pesticide DDT that nearly led to their complete demise in the United States. DDT was used widely to kill insect pests on crops in the mid-twentieth century in the United States and Canada. Rains washed it off of fields and into waterways where it contaminated the food chain. Through

Figure 17-2. The sight of an immature peregrine falcon, such as the one in this photograph, was once a rare event. More and more peregrine nests failed due to the poisoning of the adults by DDT-tainted food. By 1960 in the United States all peregrine nesting sites east of the Mississippi River were vacant, as were 90 percent of those in the West. In Canada a 1975 survey showed that the peregrine was virtually extirpated in the East, and only a few western provinces showed evidence of an active breeding population. The peregrine was placed on the United States Endangered Species List in 1969 and , in the early 1970s, most uses of DDT were banned in Canada and the United States. Since the peregrine falcon's plight first came to light, biologists and conservationists, such as those at the United States Fish and Wildlife Service, federal and provincial authorities in Canada, the Peregrine Fund in Boise, Idaho. Cornell University Laboratory of Ornithology and numerous other professionals and concerned volunteers, have been working together to restore the peregrine to its native habitats. These swift and magnificent birds of prey are once again breeding in over twenty-three states and in a growing number of provinces. Size of body (adult): 15–20 inches (38.1–50.8 centimeters). Photo by David F. Boehlke.

a process called *biomagnification*, DDT became highly concentrated in the tissues of those animals near the top of the food chain. Each time a trout or bass, for instance, ate a minnow or other small fish, the predator acquired more and more DDT from its prey. Eagles and other predators at the top of the food chain ate trout, bass and other animals with concentrated levels of DDT in their tissues, and so accumulated still greater amounts in their own body tissues. DDT caused widespread nest failures due to females laying thin eggshells that cracked when incubated, poor embryonic development and abnormal behavior among adult nesting birds.

In certain areas, the bald eagle and other birds such as the peregrine falcon (Figure 17-2) and brown pelican that suffered similar fates had completely disappeared by the time DDT was largely banned throughout North America in the early 1970s. As levels of this pesticide have decreased in the food chain, and as the birds have been gradually reintroduced into some of their ancestral habitat, these species have begun a dramatic recovery from the brink. The decline of these species, as well as the songbirds and others affected by DDT, is an excellent example of how animals function as sensitive indicators of environmental health.

Unfortunately, the negative effects of human activity upon animals is not always inadvertent. Many threatened and endangered animals are collected for international *commercial trade*, including the lucrative *pet trade*. Certain animal parts or *wildlife products* are bought and sold illegally at great profit, such as bald eagle feathers, the gall bladders of bears, rhinoceros horns (believed to possess aphrodisiacal properties) and elephant tusks (ivory). As an example of how profit-seeking can lead people to practice ecocidal acts of frightening barbarity, witness the wholesale severing of shark fins to be served in shark's-fin soup in exclusive restaurants worldwide. The dorsal and pectoral fins and lower lobes are cut off of more than a dozen species of shark, including lemon sharks, makos, blues, tigers and duskies. Not only is this practice brutal (often the shark is caught and "finned" by cutting off the fin and tossing the mutilated shark overboard to die), but along with fishing for the burgeoning shark filet market, it is causing a rapid decline in the populations of the Atlantic's sharks. At the current rate many species of sharks will be facing extinction in twenty to thirty years. Ecologically, if a top oceanic predator like the shark were eliminated it could cause an explosion of other predators and prey species lower on the food chain, disastrously upsetting the balance of life in the sea.

Sharks, it seems, could one day go the way of the whales. Whaling is an archetypal example of how ignorance and wanton greed can result in overhunting that is so severe that species are nearly wiped out. Many species of whale found in North American waters are now listed as endangered as a result of centuries of relentless hunting. This includes the beluga, bowhead, finback, gray, humpback, right, Sei, sperm and blue whale, the largest animal on Earth. While the International Whaling Commission has instituted a worldwide ban on all commercial whaling, some countries continue to protest this ban and are engaged in hunting a significant number of endangered whales for "research" purposes.

Introducing *exotic species* to an area can contribute to major declines in native animal populations and significant ecological disturbances. Starlings, house sparrows and other aliens compete so aggressively and successfully with native bluebirds and other songbirds for food and nesting space, that the populations of some native species declined when these foreign birds were introduced and have never fully recovered. Florida's warm climate has become an adopted home to numerous animals that have been purposefully or accidentally released there and have managed to survive, reproduce and prosper. Some species of local wildlife have suffered as a result.

The *overpopulation* of human beings represents the single greatest threat to the continued existence of many species of wildlife due to the effects of our direct contact with animals, habitat destruction and the aforementioned consequences of our actions. People have been around for about 2 million years. By the year 1800 there were 1 billion people on Earth. This figure doubled to 2 billion by 1930 and again to 4 billion by 1975. There were over 5 billion people in 1989 and, at the present rate of growth, this number will double by the year 2029. We compete intensely with the animals for available food, water, habitat and other resources on Earth. We hunt and fish for them; we use them for food, clothing, shelter, adornment and ornamentation, and to fulfill other needs and wants. Wild animals are also our companions in times of leisure; we seek them while camping, hiking, boating and bird-watching among other *recreational activities*. Even this well-meaning contact, because of our sheer numbers, often disrupts their lives. Endangered species watching is a particularly popular sport nowadays. It helps people to be more aware of the plight of these animals, but how does it affect their chances for survival? Even some forms of nonconsumptive recreation, such as skiing, compete directly for the resources wildlife needs to live.

Endangerment and Extinction

Since the rest of this discussion and chapter deals with those animals that are losing the struggle to survive alongside humanity, there are some terms that need to be clearly defined. Rare or vulnerable species do not face an immediate threat but could be at risk because their numbers are declining and/or they occur in a restricted range. Some species may be listed as rare in one region while they may even be abundant somewhere else. If the surviving population of a species is so low that it could face extinction if it declined further, it is a *threatened species*. Members of an *endangered species* are so rare they are in immediate danger of becoming *extinct*, of being wiped out completely from the face of Earth. A species has been *extirpated* from part of its range when it no longer exists in an area it once inhabited.

Prior to the great decline of North·American wildlife over the past 150 years, there were

- 60 million bison
- 100,000 grizzly bears
- more than 150,000 bald eagles
- expansive herds of elk, antelope and bighorn sheep
- prairie dog towns 25 miles (40.2 kilometers) across
- flocks of passenger pigeons that blackened the skies like a cloud for two to three hours at a time as they migrated past
- populations of bobcat, mountain lion, black bear, wolf, beaver, mink, otter and many species of waterfowl that were far more abundant than they are today [7]

It is estimated that several species became extinct every *year* during the two thousand years leading up to the seventeenth century, when the numbers of extinct species started to increase dramatically. In the late twentieth century the rate of extinction may be exceeding one species per *hour*.[8] Of Earth's estimated 30 million species of plants, animals, microbes and fungi (only 1.4 million have been identified and named to date), one-quarter or more will become extinct by 2010 if we do not act to ensure their survival. Some of these will have yet to be discovered before they are gone forever.

The North American species that have already become extinct is growing larger by the hour:

- great auk (1844)
- Labrador duck (1874)
- sea mink (1894)
- Carolina parakeet (early 1900s)

- passenger pigeon (1914)
- blue walleye (1960s)
- dusky seaside sparrow (1987)

The ivory-billed woodpecker is widely believed to have been extirpated from its home in the bottomland swamps of southeastern North America and only a small population remains in Cuba. Gray whales of the North Atlantic have been extirpated leaving only their Pacific counterparts. The black-footed ferret has been extirpated from Canada and possibly from the United States. It may now be extinct in the wild, although there are some being bred in captivity. Fourteen species of birds have become extinct on the Hawaiian Islands in recent times, and virtually all other indigenous birds living in Hawaii are threatened or endangered.

Passenger pigeons are one of the most renowned species to have been driven to extinction. There were once so many of these beautiful birds that they blocked out the sunlight as they passed in great flocks during the spring and fall migrations. They were hunted relentlessly. One favorite technique was to attach torches to a long pole and raise them up into the treetops at night. The dazed birds were then knocked to the ground out of their perches. Overhunting and harassment in nesting colonies resulted in some years when there was almost complete nesting failure. Between the impacts of these actions and the cutting of their favored habitat of old growth forest of American beech, passenger pigeons had become rare by the 1890s. The last one died in the Cincinnati Zoo on September 1, 1914.

The dusky seaside sparrow is a recent endangered North American bird to become extinct, and the first one to do so since the United States Endangered Species List was created in 1966. In June 1987 the last full-blooded dusky died. The hybrids that it left, crosses between the dusky and Scott's seaside sparrows, perished in a thunderstorm when their cage was torn open on March 27, 1989.

THREATENED AND ENDANGERED NORTH AMERICAN ANIMALS. Many North Americans are familiar with the plight of some worldwide endangered species such as the giant panda of China, the Asian elephant and the great Indian rhinoceros, among others. But how many people are as informed about the state of North America's threatened and endangered wildlife?

In the United States, threatened and endangered species are protected by the Endangered Species Act of 1973 which is administered by the Endangered Species Program of the U. S. Department of the Interior, Fish and

Figure 17-3. The endangered cobblestone tiger beetle exists in small populations found in only a dozen or so locations throughout the world. It takes its name from the stony habitat where it lives along swift-flowing stretches of rivers and streams. The individual beetle in this picture is missing one of its six legs and exhibits a scar along the edge of its shell near where the right rear leg was apparently removed when injured in the wild sometime before this photograph was taken. Size: 1/2 inch (1.3 centimeters). Photo by Alan C. Graham.

Wildlife Service.[9] The Canadian government has organized a group charged with determining and monitoring the status of wildlife species, the Committee on the Status of Endangered Wildlife in Canada (COSEWIC).[10] This is a coalition of governmental conservation agencies and private environmental groups. Endangered species are further protected from international trade of endangered wildlife and wildlife products by the Convention on International Trade in Endangered Species of Wild Flora and Fauna (CITES).

Of the approximately eighteen hundred species of vertebrates in Canada, roughly one in forty is either threatened or endangered. In 1989 there were forty-four species of animals designated as threatened or endangered in Canada. These include the

- Attwater's greater prairie chicken
- woodland caribou
- beluga whale
- whooping crane
- wood bison
- burrowing owl
- spotted owl
- peregrine falcon
- Aurora trout
- Acadian whitefish
- eastern cougar
- Eskimo curlew
- piping plover
- swift fox

With the exception of the burrowing owl, beluga whale, Aurora trout and Acadian whitefish, of which the last three species do not occur in the United States, all of these species are also listed as endangered in the United States. The burrowing owl is found in Florida and in parts of the western United States. Although no one knows exactly how many species of animals are in danger of extinction in the United States, the number is undeniably far greater than the roughly 344 native animals that are officially listed as threatened or endangered by the federal government (Figure 17-3). Some additional species on this list include the Kemp's (Atlantic) ridley turtle, black-footed ferret, bald eagle, Florida manatee, gray (timber) wolf, red wolf, California condor and Everglade snail kite. The grizzly bear and desert tortoise are threatened species in the United States. Despite the fear with which grizzlies are regarded by many people, the number of people actually hurt each year by grizzlies is small, yet 84 percent of all grizzly deaths are caused by human beings.

Black-footed ferrets are one of the rarest mammals in North America. This beautiful, sleek member of the weasel family, with its black paws and facial marks and eyes that reflect an emerald hue at night, was once common through-out the prairies. It fell victim to habitat destruction, poisons set out to kill its main food of prairie dogs and a devastating sylvatic plague that decimated the prairie dog population in the mid-1980s. Prairie dogs have declined from an estimated population of 5 billion in the late 1800s to the point where the Utah prairie dog is now a threatened species in the United States. The Mexican prairie dog is endangered. Today, black-footed ferrets exist in captivity but researchers are having a difficult time locating any in the wild. In time, it is hoped that a wild population will be reestablished from captive bred animals.

The endangered California condor, the thunderbird of Native North American myths, now exists solely in captivity. This great bird, North America's largest with a wingspan of over 9 feet (2.7 meters) and a weight of up to 25 pounds (11.3 kilograms), is being captive bred in two zoos in the hopes of reintroducing it into its newly protected wild habitat.

The burrowing owl is an endangered species of the Canadian prairie region. This mostly ground-dwelling bird, which is about as large as a pigeon, lives in burrows dug by ground squirrels and badgers. There are now only 1,100 pairs left due to poisoning by pesticides used to control grasshoppers, road kills, shooting and habitat destruction.

Many people have a warm place in their hearts for turtles, some of which are among the most endangered species in North America. The desert tortoise population had declined sharply due to overgrazing by cattle and disruption of habitat by off-road vehicles. Then, in the summer of 1989, it was ravaged by a fatal disease, pushing it into the endangered status.

Sea turtles are in dire need of help. Every species is either endangered (E) or threatened (T), including the

- loggerhead sea (T)
- green sea (T)
- Kemp's (Atlantic) ridley sea (E)
- leatherback sea (E)
- hawksbill sea (E)
- olive ridley sea (T)

The fate of the Kemp's ridley turtle, the smallest and most endangered of the sea turtles (up to 3 feet [.9 meters] long and 100 pounds [45.4 kilograms]), typifies the fate of these gentle giants. Ninety-five percent of all ridleys migrate to a particular beach in eastern Mexico to lay their eggs in the sand along the shore. In 1948, forty thousand ridleys came ashore to nest in one day! While they were once hunted in great numbers, their primary nesting beach has been pro-tected by the Mexican government since 1966. Yet by 1989 only four to six hundred ridley females came ashore to nest. Despite the fact that researchers, since the late 1970s, have been collecting eggs, raising young and releasing them once they have passed the dangerous first year of life, the popula-tion is still declining by about 3 percent each year. It is estimated that there are now only about nine hundred adult female ridleys and an unknown number of males in existence.

The number of Kemp's ridley sea turtles continues to decline because commercial shrimp boats, working pri-marily in the Gulf of Mexico, inadvertently catch and drown over eleven thousand of the forty-eight thousand endangered sea turtles caught in the nets each year. Thirty dead ridleys washed up on Texas beaches during the height of shrimping season in 1989, and over twelve on Florida's beaches in 1988. Drowning in shrimp nets is the largest identifiable cause of sea turtle death.

The "turtle excluding devices," required on the nets by the United States Department of Commerce since May 1, 1989, have been vehemently fought in the courts by the shrimpers, who often defy the government by not using the devices. Shrimpers claim that using the devices reduces the size of their catch. Research has shown, however, that when these simple devices are used prop-erly, they allow the turtles to escape unharmed while having little or no effect on the shrimper's catch.

Back From the Brink: Species Recovery

Fortunately, in spite of the grim situation that many species are in, there have been many recent successes in helping endangered species to recover.

The magnificent whooping crane, a majestic and graceful bird that stands over 5 feet (1.5 meters) tall, was reduced to only twenty-three individuals by 1941. "Whoopers" nest in the Wood Buffalo National Park and winter in the Aransas National Wildlife Refuge on the Gulf Coast of Texas—a true symbol of a North American endangered species. Although these birds still face a long journey back from near elimination and many perils on the way, habitat protection and a captive breeding–reintroduction program have bolstered their numbers to over two hundred birds today.

All four of the endangered North American birds that were extirpated or nearly wiped out by DDT poisoning in many regions—the bald eagle, peregrine falcon, American white pelican and brown pelican—have made dramatic comebacks in recent years. Peregrines had been extirpated from their historical range in eastern North America by the early 1960s. These raptorial lords of the sky that can fly well over 200 miles per hour (322 kilometers per hour), have been reintroduced into parts of their eastern range and are now beginning to reestablish a small population of breeding individuals. Following a reintroduction program in thirteen states and the province of Ontario, the bald eagle, too, is coming back strong. It seems to be making a successful adjustment in many areas from a wilderness bird to the much-altered environment of today.

The American alligator of the southeastern United States is another story of a great comeback. It was once endangered due to overhunting and habitat destruction. Once it came under the protection of the Endangered Species Act it multiplied so successfully that, today, it is considered to have recovered in many parts of its range. The alligator is now so numerous in some parts of Florida that it is considered a pest. It is illegal to feed alligators because this causes them to relate food to people. A strictly controlled alligator hunting season is now allowed in some areas.

In Canada, the wood bison's status has improved (it has been "down-listed" from an endangered to a threatened species), and the swift fox has returned to the Canadian prairie after being extirpated for fifty years. A small number are now holding their own in the wild with the help of an intense monitoring and reintroduction program.

The Road to Recovery

The journey to recovery for an endangered species is a long, arduous, multifaceted process, often involving:

• legal protection and listing on the register of threatened and endangered species;

• the design and implementation of a recovery plan;
• habitat protection;
• habitat cleanup, such as the ban on DDT;
• habitat management to maintain and restore conditions required by that species;
• captive breeding;
• reintroduction into former habitat in the wild;
• a substantial investment of human energy and financial resources;
• coordinated efforts of both governmental and private conservation agencies and groups; and
• education for public awareness.

HOW TO HELP SAVE SPECIES. Our daily lives are a statement about how much we care about the survival of species and humankind. There are many actions we can take to be a positive force in helping to preserve animal species:

• *Use less electricity* to decrease the need for new power plants, which could mean one less hydroelectric dam destroying thousands of acres of habitat for wildlife and humans. It also means less of a need for nuclear power and the radioactive toxins it generates for future generations to care for. We are just now beginning to realize the unprecedented environmental contamination and number of environmental refugees created by the Chernobyl nuclear power plant disaster of 1986 in the Soviet Union.

• *Reduce* the demand for resources and *reuse* and *recycle* our waste products to place a smaller demand upon the environment, and help to prevent the pollution of groundwater, among other ecological effects.

• *Drive less, use more mass transit* and *buy fewer plastics and synthetic clothing* to decrease the need for oil and the resulting environmental and political disasters associated with extracting and transporting oil. Burning less gasoline, oil and other fossil fuels also decreases the contribution to acid rain and global warming.

• *Refuse to eat or use the products made from all animals that are threatened or endangered* to take pressure off their diminishing numbers.

• *Refrain from the use of goods produced from the habitats of endangered species and boycott foods that harm endangered species indirectly while the food is being captured, grown or processed.* Become informed and selective about the kind of wood used in the furniture you buy. Teak, mahogany, rosewood and other tropical species are harvested and manufactured into products often without regard for the impact the cutting of this timber has on the destruction of rapidly disappearing tropical rain forests. In some cases, certain products from tropical regions, such as nuts and other foodstuffs, can be obtained from producers, including many cooperatives, that use sustainable agricultural and forestry practices. Encourage these environmentally concerned producers by supporting their markets.

Habitat protection is extremely important. Threatened and endangered species, by virtue of their tenuous status, require a minimum of their *critical habitat*—the land, water and air space needed to fulfill their normal needs and assure their survival. There are now over four hundred wildlife refuges in the United States alone and critical habitat is being preserved in many areas where needed.

Saving the threatened and endangered species of the world is going to require

- *conservation*
- *habitat protection*, particularly critical habitat
- *sharing* of Earth's resources, not hoarding them to the exclusion of others
- *sacrifices* to help animals by getting back to our needs and doing without some of our *wants*
- a sustained *commitment*

Any less will jeopardize the future of Earth's biological survival.

QUESTIONS

1. How was the American bison (buffalo) important to Native North Americans?

2. What happened to the bison? Why did it happen? Who was responsible? How many are left today?

3. What are some ways that the numbers of any kind of animals increase? Decrease? How can the number stay the same over time?

4. What happens when there are too many of one kind of animal? What happens when the numbers become too small?

5. What happens to animals when people destroy their homes? Overhunt a species? Create acid rain and other kinds of pollution?

6. What is an endangered species? A threatened species? A rare or vulnerable species?

7. What happened to the bald eagle and peregrine falcon that caused them to disappear in many places? What have people done to remedy this situation and bring these birds back?

8. What is extinction? Name some animals you know

that have become extinct. Why did this happen? Will you ever see an extinct animal? Where?

9. How do you feel about extinction?

10. Name some North American animals that are threatened or endangered. Can you think of any that live near you? What do you know about these threatened and endangered species?

- whooping crane
- right whale
- spotted owl
- woodland caribou
- beluga whale
- brown pelican
- black-footed ferret
- gray (timber) wolf
- red wolf
- California condor
- piping plover
- grizzly bear
- shortnose sturgeon
- Kemp's (Atlantic) ridley turtle
- Plymouth red-bellied turtle

11. How do biologists save a species from extinction? What do they have to do?

12. Why are animals important to us? If there were no people at all living on Earth, why would the animals living here be important? Why are animals important to you?

13. What is biological diversity? Why is it important?

14. What can you do to save the animals? What will happen if people do not help the animals to survive?

ACTIVITIES
Plight of the Peregrine

ACTIVITY: (A) Journey through a brief fantasy in a few moments of the life of a peregrine falcon. Hear the story of the peregrine's journey to near extinction and back again. (B) Play a passing game to simulate the biological magnification that once wiped out the peregrine falcon over much of its former range.

GOALS: Experience the life of the peregrine falcon and understand how it has survived some serious threats to its existence. Understand how biological magnification works.

AGE: Younger children and older children

MATERIALS: (A) Copy of "Flight of the Peregrine," Figure 17-2. (B) Copy of "Plight of the Peregrine: Biomagnification," a number of whole dried peas depending upon the size of the group, one cup for each player. (Please do not use disposable cups!)

PROCEDURE A: *Flight of the Peregrine.* Have the children close their eyes and prepare them for a fantasy journey into a brief moment of the life of a peregrine falcon. Have them imagine that they are up on a tall mountain at sunrise looking through their binoculars, when suddenly they see something magnificent happening right before their eyes. Now read them this fictional, yet scientifically accurate story about a brief moment in the life of a peregrine falcon.

FLIGHT OF THE PEREGRINE

An orange halo glows above the eastern horizon, and in the cool, crisp spring morning air, before the thrushes have begun to sing their flute-like songs, a shrill cry goes out, then quickly fades into echos in the valley below.

A life has ended, a day begun. In the faint light of dawn, the colors of a falcon can be seen on a narrow ledge of the cliffs, his dark mustache bobbing up and down like a small chisel as he plucks the blue feathers from a jay he has just caught. Little puffs of steam drift downwind from the falcon's breath.

Always alert, the falcon looks to the sky and sees something moving quickly. He flies off of the cliff face and cries a loud "whichew," looking like a blue-gray streak across the blurred grays and greens of the forest and rock behind him.

The falcon flies back and forth in broad arcs in front of the cliff as a larger, darker falcon appears. Then he flaps in broad spirals and is carried upward on the rising warm air until he is high above the cliff. At the highest point of all, he folds his wings and shoots down before the cliff face, veers up, performs three loop-to-loops, flashes his cream-colored breast, and calls out a creaking, rusty-hinged note.

The larger, darker bird follows the male up higher and higher, then the two dive with the male in pursuit. They level off, dive again and level off again, low and in close to the cliff. Then, the female turns her breast up toward the male and they grapple with their talons while she is upside down in midair.

Finally, tired, they land in tall trees on the cliff face, panting, quietly watching each other's moves.

Courtship has begun. Soon the pair will mate.

Now have the children open their eyes. How did it feel to be "watching" the peregrine falcon? Could you picture what it looked like? Share the photograph of a peregrine falcon (Figure 17-2) with the children.

PROCEDURE B: *Plight of the Peregrine: Biomagnification.* Read the following true story to the children:

PLIGHT OF THE PEREGRINE: BIOMAGNIFICATION

Peregrine falcons once lived throughout much of North America, tracing their beautiful flight patterns through the skies. Then, in the late 1940s, peregrines began to disappear. By the early 1960s, less than twenty years later, peregrine falcons had died out completely from eastern North America and there were far fewer living elsewhere.

Peregrines, it turns out, had been poisoned by pesticides—chemicals that are sprayed on crops to kill insect pests. DDT, DDE, oxychlordane, dieldrin and PCBs are the names of some of these chemicals. These pesticides moved up the food chain and were eventually eaten in high concentrations when the peregrines devoured their contaminated prey. DDT caused the peregrines to lay eggs with shells so thin they cracked when the parents incubated them. The young birds in the eggs could not develop. Adults would abandon the nests and sometimes would not mate at all for the season.

Finally, in the early 1970s, DDT was banned in North America. From the mid-1970s and on into the early 1990s, biologists raised young peregrine chicks and released or "hacked" them on the old cliff sites where peregrines once nested. The biologists raised the young birds and fed them until they *fledged* or flew away at five to eight weeks old. These young peregrines grew and some nested and raised their own young on cliff sites in the East, and even on the ledges of skyscrapers in some cities. A new population of peregrines had begun.

Today, because of the ban on DDT and the work of dedicated biologists, peregrines are once more returning to nest on the cliffs of eastern North America. They are an endangered species rescued from the brink of extinction.

Now, discuss biomagnification, as described in the "Discussion" section, in preparation for a simple game simulating how biomagnification occurs.

Note: The rest of this activity can be done as written or as a tag/relay race during which the "earthworms" run up to pass their "Ps" to the "robins," who in turn run up to pass their "Ps" to the "peregrine."

Divide the group of seven or more children into three levels of a food chain. One child will be the peregrine falcon, several will be the robins and a still larger number will be earthworms. Use this setup time as an opportunity to introduce (or review) energy flow through a food chain and web. (See the information and activities in Chapter 6.) For example, a group of seven children would have one peregrine falcon, two robins and four earthworms. The exact

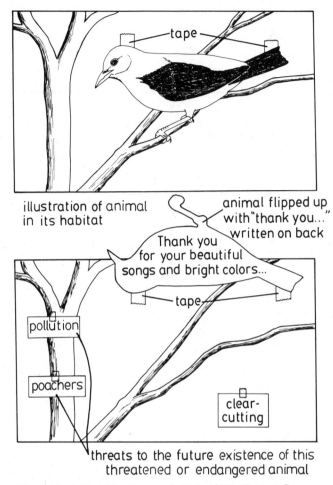

illustration of animal in its habitat

animal flipped up with "thank you..." written on back

Thank you for your beautiful songs and bright colors...

tape

pollution

poachers

clear-cutting

threats to the future existence of this threatened or endangered animal

Figure 17-4. Model for creating the "Thank You Species" flip-up.

Thank You Species

ACTIVITY: Create an illustration of a favorite endangered or threatened species and a large, separate drawing of its habitat. Tape the illustration of the animal onto its habitat to create a flip-up wallboard with a "thank you" for the many gifts of that animal written on the back of its illustration. Write out or illustrate the threats to that species' well-being and future survival, and tape these to its habitat.

GOALS: Realize the value and the many gifts of a favorite endangered species. Express gratitude for these gifts. Understand where that species lives and the kinds of threats it faces to its continued existence.

AGE: Younger children

MATERIALS: Pictures and illustrations of threatened and endangered species of North America clipped from natural history magazines and/or old wildlife calendars, white posterboard, posterboard of other colors to suit the various habitat backgrounds, scissors, crayons, pencils, paintbrushes, tempera paints, water, containers for paints and water, newspaper for a drop cloth, scissors, transparent tape, writing paper, list of threats to species from "The Population Shuffle" activity in this chapter, glue or paste, Figure 17-4.

PROCEDURE: Find as many pictures or illustrations as you can of the following threatened and endangered North American animals from the "Discussion" section or others you may know of:

- wood bison
- spotted owl
- burrowing owl
- bald eagle
- peregrine falcon
- ivory-billed woodpecker
- black-footed ferret
- woodland caribou
- Attwater's greater prairie chicken
- beluga whale
- humpback whale
- right whale
- bowhead whale
- whooping crane
- Aurora trout
- Acadian whitefish
- eastern cougar

- Eskimo curlew
- piping plover
- swift fox
- Kemp's (Atlantic) ridley turtle
- gray (timber) wolf
- red wolf
- California condor
- Everglade kite
- grizzly bear
- desert tortoise
- prairie dog
- leatherback sea turtle
- hawksbill sea turtle
- brown pelican
- American white pelican
- blue whale

numbers are not important, just the decreasing number of animals moving up the food chain from earthworm to peregrine. Arrange the children into the three groups.

Tell the children that a farmer has sprayed a pesticide (we'll call it "P") onto the field where these earthworms live. As they feed and pass the soil through their guts, the earthworms each absorb ten "Ps" into their bodies. Give each child a cup to hold the "Ps" in, then pass out ten "Ps" (ten whole dried peas) to each "earthworm" to represent the pesticide they have absorbed into their bodies. As the robins eat the worms, they pick up the total amount of pesticide absorbed by the worms. Have two earthworms give their "Ps" to each robin by pouring them into his or her cup. Each robin now has twenty "Ps." When the peregrine falcon catches and eats the robins, it ingests all of the "Ps" those robins have absorbed. Tell the two robins to give the peregrine all of their "Ps." The peregrine falcon ends up with forty "Ps" of pesticide in her or his cup. That is how biomagnification works.

Each child will pick one threatened or endangered animal that he or she would like to thank. Have him or her draw that animal on a piece of white poster board or cut out a picture of the animal and paste it on. Then, on a separate sheet of larger poster board, have each child illustrate the animal's habitat. Now have each child create a flip-up by taping the top edge of his or her animal to an appropriate place on its habitat (Figure 17-4).

Now review the list of some recognized values of animals from the "Discussion" section and add the children's own ideas about the values of animals. On the back of each illustration or picture of an animal, and along the bottom edge (so the words will read correctly when the animal is flipped up if a written "thank you" is used), have each child create a "thank you" for all of the gifts that animal gives to her or him and other people. This thank you could be a list, a poem, a story, an illustration—anything the child wants to use to express gratitude to the animal.

On small pieces of paper, have each child write down or illustrate all of the threats she or he can think of to the animals' future existence, one threat to each piece of paper. (See "The Population Shuffle" for a list of threats to consider.) Each threat should be glued or taped onto the habitat. When these steps are completed, have each child share her or his animal with the rest of the group, its habitat, the "thank you" presented to the animal and threats to the animal's survival.

The Population Shuffle

ACTIVITY: (A) Play a game with cards and beans to simulate the natural increases and decreases of a population whose numbers are in a stable balance. (B) Repeat the same game but add the kinds of human threats to animal species that decimate a population to simulate the endangerment and possible extinction of a species.
GOALS: Understand the factors that both add to and subtract from the total population numbers of wild animals. Realize how these factors can interplay in a system of checks and balances to create a stable population over time. Understand how human impacts can decimate a population, endanger a species and even drive it to extinction. Understand that endangered species have the same basic needs as other animals for food, water and shelter.

AGE: Older children
MATERIALS: Deck of playing cards, gummed peel-off labels that fit onto the face of the playing cards, pen, bag of at least 250 dried beans or peas, large pot, small dish.
PROCEDURE: *Note:* This game/simulation requires several hours of preparation time. The size of the group playing can range from two to eight players.

Beforehand, fill a small pot with 135 large dried beans and put aside in a dish a supply of another 100 of the same kind of bean to draw from during the game.

Obtain a standard deck of playing cards. To prepare for part "A," write or type each of the following sources of population increase and decrease onto separate gummed, peel-off labels that will fit neatly onto the face of each playing card or reduce the size of the list on a copier, put it onto a gummed sheet and trim to size. Put *one* factor of population increase or decrease onto *each* label and *each* card.

Factors that will directly or indirectly tend to increase a population include:

• some young animals arrive from a nearby group—*add 6*
• there are many births this year—*add 24*
• your habitat produces an abundant food supply this season—*add 12*
• a disease clears up that has been killing many animals—*add 7*
• very few animals have had accidents this year—*add 4*
• a disease kills many individuals among your worst species of predator—*add 18*
• rains keep your water supply clean and plentiful—*add 14*
• your habitat provides the best shelter in a long time for raising young—*add 10*

Factors that will directly or indirectly tend to decrease a population include:

• predators are more numerous lately—*subtract 18*
• many of the older animals die this year—*subtract 9*
• a disease sweeps through your population—*subtract 22*
• the habitat is being stressed by a large population—*subtract 10*
• some young animals leave for other places—*subtract 8*
• several animals have fatal accidents—*subtract 3*
• food is scarce: some animals die of starvation and sickness due to a weakened condition—*subtract 12*
• drought strikes—*subtract 6*
• a bad ice storm catches some animals off guard—*subtract 7*

Now to prepare for part "B," copy each of these human-caused threats onto separate gummed labels and stick each onto the face of one of the playing cards (keep these cards separate from the others):

• part of your forest habitat is destroyed by clear-cut logging—*subtract 23*

• pesticides are sprayed on the fields where your main insect food feeds—*subtract 9*

• toxic waste from a dump is leaching into one of your watering holes—*subtract 7*

• two animals are caught in traps—*subtract 7*

• a nearby marsh, an important source of food and water, is drained to use for farmland—*subtract 13*

• there have been more poachers over the past few years, killing more animals than usual—*subtract 15*

• a strange animal has been introduced into your habitat that is multiplying rapidly and using the best nesting places—*subtract 21*

• someone illegally collects some of your relatives to sell as pets—*subtract 8*

• acid rain is lowering the resistance of trees in your forest and insects are attacking the leaves, leaving less cover and fewer places to hide so more animals are caught by predators and human hunters—*subtract 12*

• a new shopping mall is built nearby, destroying habitat and stressing animals so fewer young are produced—*subtract 8*

• hikers put a trail through your habitat and add to the stress placed on the animals there—*subtract 2*

PROCEDURE A: *Beanpot Population Balance Game*. Use the information from the "Discussion" section to talk about animal populations. Discuss how wildlife populations cycle up and down over time because of some factors that cause changes in numbers. Ask the children to name some of these. Discuss how these factors work as a system of *checks and balances* to keep a population stable over time, and how many of these factors affect all animals' basic needs for food, water and shelter. Certain populations may have a natural limit on habitat space or food supply that naturally keeps the population levels where they are. This is the *limiting factor*. The checks on a populations' size prevent it from overpopulating an area. The factors that add to or help a population to grow keep it strong. Discuss the concept of *synergism* (see "Discussion" section, page 230).

Now place the animal "population" of 135 beans in the middle of the group. Tell the children the number of beans in the pot. Show them the dish of one hundred beans from which to draw to add to the population. Have the first dealer shuffle, then pass out all of the cards, one at a time, that contain the *natural* factors which cause, or tend to cause, populations to increase and decrease. The dealer will place the cards face down, making one pile in front of each player, until all of the cards are dealt. The children will take turns turning over a card, reading it and adding to or subtracting from the pot as the card indicates. When all cards have been read and acted upon, have the children count the number of beans in the dish. There will still be one hundred beans in the dish.

How many beans, then, are still in the pot, the population of "animals"? Count them. How could this be? What has happened? Has the population increased? Decreased? Stayed the same? Why?

PROCEDURE B: *"Dealing" a Blow to a Species*. Now have the next dealer add to the deck from part "A" by shuffling in the cards containing all of the *human-caused* threats to the animal population. All of the cards you created are now in the deck. Play the entire game over until all cards have been played once, as in part "A," or until the population of animals in the pot is driven to extinction.

The outcome of this part of the game will depend upon how the cards mix in the shuffle. If, by chance, a larger number of population decrease cards come up early on than the number of population increase cards, the animal could by wiped out at some point (the pot will be empty) and the game will end! If this happens the species has been driven to extinction. Discuss why this occurred in the second round of the game and not in the first round. What caused the extinction?

Another possible outcome is that the population will survive but be reduced to a much smaller size, with numbers occurring during the course of the game that could be even smaller than the final tally. How many "animals" are left in the population (pot) at the end of the game? (There should be ten.) Is that enough to reproduce and keep the population alive? What has happened along the way as a result of these human threats? What *could* happen to this small population of this now threatened or endangered species of animal? Have one of the children read off the list of threatened and endangered species from the activity called "Thank You Species." What is a threatened species? What is an endangered species? Play several rounds of "Dealing a Blow to a Species." What is extinction? Proceed to the activity called "Save a Species."

Biodiversity Breakdown

ACTIVITY: Construct ten or more small houses of cards to represent all of the species comprising the biodiversity of an ecosystem. Slowly remove cards from the bottoms of the houses to represent the loss of species from that ecosystem—decreasing biodiversity. Discuss the importance of each species to biodiversity, and the importance of biodiversity to the health of an ecosystem, to the ecosystem's ability to adapt to change and survive.

GOALS: Visualize the disappearance of species and the collapse of the biodiversity of an ecosystem. Understand why diversity is important to the adaptability and survival of an ecosystem.

AGE: Older children

MATERIALS: Deck of cards.

PROCEDURE: Define and discuss biodiversity using the information provided in the "Discussion" section under "The Values of Species" on page 227. Biodiversity is a measure of the number of different species and traits an ecosystem has to draw from to adapt and survive. For instance, there may be some animals in an ecosystem that are tolerant of human beings living nearby. They may survive if people expand into their home, but other species that may not be able to survive in the midst of a human presence will not survive, or if possible, will migrate to a new habitat. In an ecosystem, biodiversity of

Figure 17-5. All of the materials in this photograph can be recycled. Recycling reduces our need for raw materials as well as the volume of waste we throw away. Thus, recycling cuts down on pollution and decreases the destruction of vital animal habitats from which those raw materials must be mined, harvested, cut and otherwise extracted. Photo by Michael J. Caduto.

species represents how well that ecosystem can adapt to a changing environment. If there are only a few species present and each has specific and rigid needs, then any changes could cause the ecosystem to collapse.

Have the children build ten or more houses of cards. Each card represents a species and the collective houses represent the biodiversity and adaptability of an ecosystem.

Have the children come up and take turns removing a card from the bottom of one house. The loss of each card represents the loss of a species from that ecosystem due to, for instance, extinction or emigration out of the ecosystem, and thus a decrease in biodiversity. The collapse of each house marks a further decline in biodiversity and the ability of the ecosystem to adapt and survive.

Save a Species

ACTIVITY: Draw the physical outline of a threatened or endangered species you have chosen to save. List the values of this species inside the outline, along with a checklist of the steps you can take to save the species. Make a commitment to work to save the species and check off each step you have taken to do so as you complete it.

GOALS: Realize the value of an endangered or threatened species and understand what is needed to save it from extinction. Get involved in a vital conservation effort upon which the survival of a species depends.

AGE: Younger children and older children

MATERIALS: List of threatened and endangered species from the "Thank You Species" activity in this chapter, illustration or photograph of each species chosen by the children, large pieces of paper, crayons and other art supplies as needed, pencils, materials as needed for the projects the children become involved with, Figure 17-5.

PROCEDURE: *Note:* Since most very young children have not yet learned to write, they may draw in symbols to represent their ideas instead of writing, wherever possible. These children will need special attention during the writing components of this activity, such as writing their ideas down for them. The activity can also be simplified for younger children.

Have each child choose one animal from the list of threatened and endangered species found in the activity "Thank You Species." Or each child could choose another endangered or threatened species they are particularly excited about helping.

On a large piece of paper, have each child draw an outline of that animal. Review the values of a species (see "Discussion" section) with them and have (or help) each child write or draw inside their animal's outline starting at the top, a list of words or symbols representing all of the values (gifts) of that animal. Ask them to think of other values, share them with the group, and write or draw them in too.

Now ask what they think they could do to help save that species. Have them write down or draw these things, in the form of a list, inside the outline of their animals below the list of values (gifts). Now share the following list of other ways that people help to save endangered species and ask or help the children to write into their animal's outline any of these that they could become involved with:

• join a conservation group that helps save endangered animals;
• write to conservation groups that help save endangered animals and ask how you could help;
• use less electricity to reduce the need to build new power plants that use resources to generate electricity (turn off lights when not being used, keep the refrigerator door closed, turn the television off when not being watched, etc.);
• reduce our use of all resources by *using only what we need*: paper, glass, cans, bottles, wood, etc.;
• reuse and recycle those things which we can: paper, glass, cans, bottles, plastics, wood, etc. (Figure 17-5);
• do not litter since many forms of plastic trash can strangle animals or kill them if eaten, and other forms of trash, such as broken glass and jagged, rusty metal cans, can harm animals and people;
• pick up litter;
• promote legal protection to protect the animal, such as writing to a representative in Congress to tell them you care and want the animal to stay (or become) listed as endangered or threatened;
• use less gasoline, heating oil and other petroleum products; drive less frequently in cars; use buses, trains and other mass transit; ride a bicycle; use a skateboard, scooter or walk; keep our houses cooler in winter; use clothes of cotton and other natural fibers and less of synthetic fibers made from oil; use less plastic (made from oil) and reuse plastic articles over again (wash plastic bags, cups and bottles and reuse);
• refrain from buying products that, when produced, kill that animal or destroy its habitat;
• do not buy any pet that is threatened or endangered and report any pet store that is selling them to the federal government;

• share Earth's resources with the other animals that live here;
• help keep the animal's habitat clean and free of pollution by not using toxic chemicals such as pesticides, herbicides and other household toxic compounds;
• volunteer time and money to conservation groups that save endangered and threatened species; and
• make a commitment to keep doing everything you can to help the animal until it recovers and has a healthy population, or until it disappears and you have done all you can to save it.

Mention some other ways that biologists, governments and conservations groups and sometimes private citizens, get involved such as:

• protecting the animal's habitat;
• managing the animal's habitat to meet its needs better;
• passing laws to legally protect the animal and its habitat;
• designing a recovery plan to help the animal reproduce and grow in numbers;
• conducting a captive breeding program;
• reintroducing the animal into its former habitat; and
• cleaning up the habitat and banning the use of poisonous chemicals, such as DDT, that harm animals.

Have each child choose one or more projects to carry out to help save his or her chosen species. Now help the children to follow through on their commitments by providing the needed materials, support and expertise.

EXTENDING THE EXPERIENCE

• Conduct the activities in Chapter 14 on zoos and endangered species.
• Hold a celebration to honor those species that are threatened, endangered and extinct.
• Report any sightings of poaching in national parks to the toll-free hotline maintained by the National Parks and Conservation Association at 1-800-448-NPCA.
• For the most recent list of endangered and threatened wildlife and plants, and other pertinent information about threatened and endangered wildlife, contact the United States Department of the Interior, Fish and Wildlife Service, Endangered Species Program, Washington, D.C. 20240.
• For information on the current status of Canadian threatened and endangered species, contact Coordinator, Threatened Species, Environment Canada, Canadian Wildlife Service, Ottawa, Ontario K1A 0H3.

• For further information, contact Environment Canada, Government of Canada, Ottawa, Ontario K1A 0H3.

• For information about habitat protection in Canada, contact Wildlife Habitat Canada, 1704 Carling Avenue, Suite 301, Ottawa, Ontario K2A 1C7, (613) 722-2090.

• For a copy of the 1989-1990 supplement, Endangered Species, contact the Teachers Clearinghouse for Science and Society Education, Inc., 1 West 88th Street, New York, N.Y. 10024.

• For a copy of the comprehensive publication, "Endangered Means There Is Still Time," contact the U. S. Government Printing Office, Washington, D.C. 20402 (stock #024-010-005-26-2).

• For information about whales, seals and other marine species, contact the National Marine Fisheries Service, Department of Commerce, Washington, D.C. 20235.

• Contact the Department of Agriculture about importing or exporting pets and birds and federally regulated plant species.

• Check the reference books and directories at your local library.

NOTES

1. J. A. Burnett, C. T. Dauphiné, Jr., S. H. McCrindle, and T. Mosquin, *On the Brink: Endangered Species in Canada* (Saskatoon, Saskatchewan: Western Producer Prairie Books, 1989), 65-67.

2. Stephen J. Pyne, "Indian Fires," *Natural History* 92, no. 2 (February 1983): 6-11.

3. Edward O. Wilson, "Threats to Biodiversity," *Scientific American* 261, no. 3 (September 1989): 108-16.

4. Ibid.

5. According to figures from the Arctic to Amazonia Alliance, Strafford, Vermont.

6. Russell Wild (ed.), *The Earth Care Annual: 1991* (Emmaus, Penn.: Rodale Press, in conjunction with the National Wildlife Federation, Washington, D.C., 1991), 29.

7. Michael Satchell, "The American Hunter Under Fire," *U.S. News & World Report* 108, no. 5 (February 5, 1990): 30–36.

8. According to figures from the Nature Conservancy.

9. For more information about specific species and a list of endangered species, write to: U. S. Department of the Interior, Fish and Wildlife Service, Endangered Species Program, Washington, D.C. 20240.

10. For more information, write to: Coordinator, Threatened Species, Environment Canada, Canadian Wildlife Service, Ottawa, Ontario K1A 0H3.

✤ The Lake of the Wounded ✤

(Cherokee—Southeast)

Deep within the Smoky Mountains, the Aniyunwiya people say, west of the headwaters of the Ocanaluftee River, there is a lake called Ataga'hi. No hunter has ever seen this lake, for it is the place the animals go to heal themselves when they are wounded. Some men say they have been near that place. As they walked through the mists across what seemed to be a barren flat, they began to hear the wings of water birds and the sound of water falling. But they could not find Ataga'hi.

Some of those who have lived as friends of the animals have been granted a vision of the lake. After praying and fasting all through the night, they have seen the springs flowing down from the high cliffs of the mountains into the stream that feeds Ataga'hi. Then, just at dawn, they have caught a glimpse of wide purple waters and the birds and the animals bathing in those waters and growing well again. But as soon as they have seen it, that vision has faded away, for the animals keep the lake invisible to all hunters.

It is said that there are bear tracks everywhere around Ataga'hi, for the bear is a great healer. One of those who saw Ataga'hi in the old days said that she saw a wounded bear with a great spear wound in its side plunge into the purple water and come out whole and strong on the other shore.

It is hard today to see Ataga'hi, and some think that its sacred waters have dried. But it is still there, the Cherokee say, hidden deep in the mountains and guarded by the animals. If you treat all the animals with respect, live well and pray, it may be that some day you will see the purple waters of Ataga'hi, too.

Then, just at dawn, they have caught a glimpse of wide purple waters and the birds and the animals bathing in those waters and growing well again.

Glossary and Pronunciation Key
✦ to Native North American Words and Names ✦

The following rules are used for the phonetic description of how each word is pronounced:

1. A line appears over long vowels. Short vowels are unmarked. For instance, "date" would appear as dāt, while "bat" would appear as bat.
2. An accent mark (´) shows which syllable in each word or name is the one emphasized.
3. Syllables are broken with a hyphen (-).
4. Syllables are spelled out as they are pronounced. For instance, "Cherokee" appears as chair-oh-key.

Where appropriate, the culture from which each word or name comes is given in brackets [ ], followed by the meaning of that word or name or an explanation of its significance as it appears in the text.

Abenaki (Ab´-er-na-kee or Ab´-eh-na-kee). People living at the sunrise, "People of the Dawn." A northeastern Algonquian group.

Achumawi (Ah-shoo´-mah-wee). The Achumawi or Pit River Indian people's homeland is the area of northern California between Mount Shasta and Mount Lassen on one side and the Warner Range on the other. The name *Achumawi* means "River People."

adobe (ah-dō´-bey). [Spanish, from Arabic *atobe*] Sun-dried bricks.

Akwesasne (Ah-kwey-sahs´-nēē). Literally "where the partridge drums." The Mohawk name for their community along the St. Lawrence River in northern New York and southern Quebec and Ontario.

Aleut (Al´-ēē-ūt). *See* Aleutian Islands.

Aleutian Islands (Ah-lū´-shun). A string of islands stretching from the southwest tip of Alaska almost to the coast of Siberia. "Aleut" is the name the Russians gave to the people of these islands. They call themselves *Unangan*, literally "Those of the Seaside." They are related to the Inuit-Inupiaq people (Eskimo).

Algonquian (Al-gon´-kee-en). Large diverse grouping of Indian peoples related by a common linguistic root. Algonquian Indians live in the Atlantic coastal regions from what we now call the Maritime Provinces to the southeastern United States, west to the Prairie Provinces and down through the central states into Wyoming and Montana.

all my relations. Words spoken when entering or leaving a sweat lodge. A translation of the Lakota Sioux words *Mitakuye oyasin* (Mē-tah´-koo-yeh oh-yah´-seen).

American Indian. Term used to refer to the native aboriginal inhabitants of North America, Central and South America. Used interchangeably with the newer term "Native American" in the United States. In Canada, the terms "Native," "Indian," "Métis" or "Aboriginal" are commonly used rather than "Native American." In most cases in this book, we have used "Native North American" to refer to the native peoples of the United States and Canada. In all cases, it is best to refer first to the person with regard to the individual tribal nation—for example, "Lakota" or "Abenaki" or "Dine." *See also* Native American.

Anishinabe (Ah-nish-ih-nah´-bey) or Anishinabeg. The native people found in the central and northern Great Lakes areas of North America. They are the same people known as the Ojibway and the Chippewa, names applied to them in the last few centuries and used widely today by Anishinabe people themselves. *Ojibway* (O-jib´-i-weg) was a name given them by their neighbors and probably means "Those Who Make Pictographs." *Anishinabe* means "First Men" or "Original Men." *Chippewa* is a variant of Ojibway. (Ojibway is also translated as "puckered up" referring

to their moccasin style, puckered in front.) Currently the Anishinabe are one of the largest native groups, with a U.S. and Canadian population of over 160,000.

Apache (Ah-patch´ē). [Zuni Pueblo *Ahpachu*, meaning "The Enemy"] Word used commonly today to refer to the people who call themselves *Tineh* (Tih-ney)—"The People."

Ataga'hi (Ah-tah-gah´-hee). [Cherokee] "The Lake of the Wounded."

Azaban (Ahz-bahn´). Abenaki word for "raccoon," referring both to the animal itself and the trickster hero of Abenaki lesson stories.

Bear Clan. One of the three main clans of the Haudenosaunee (Iroquois) people—Turtle, Bear and Wolf—that are found among all five original Iroquois nations. Clan is inherited from the mother.

Black Elk (1863–1950). A Lakota (Sioux) visionary and medicine man of the late nineteenth and early twentieth century. The story of his life, as recorded by John Neihardt, *Black Elk Speaks: Being the Life Story of a Holy Man of the Oglala Sioux*, is regarded as a minor classic of American literature. The words of this *wichasha wakan* (holy man) are also recorded in *The Sacred Pipe* by Joseph Epes Brown and in *The Sixth Grandfather*, edited by Raymond J. DeMaille.

Cayuga (Kah´-yū-gah). [Iroquois] One of the six nations of the Iroquois confederacy, "People of the Swampy Land."

Cherokee (Chair-oh-kēy´). Corruption of a Lenni Lenape [Delaware] Indian name (*Talligewi* or *Tsa la gi*) for this very large southeastern tribe who called themselves *Ani Yunwiya* (Ah-nēē Yūhn-wi-yah)—"Real People." One of the so-called (by whites) "Five Civilized Tribes."

chief. This is one of the most widely used and misunderstood words applied to native people today. All too often, every Indian man is called "Chief" by non-Indians. In some cases, this can be seen as an insult, especially if that men is *not* a chief. Other native men, who, indeed, are "chiefs" do not mind having that word applied to them. Early Europeans thought a "chief" among the native people of the Americas was like a king, and they even called many traditional leaders "king" (e.g., King Philip, who was known as Metacomet by his own *Wampanoag* (Wom-pah-nō´-ag) people. In general, a chief was a person chosen by his people to lead them. He was not all-powerful and the roles of such "chiefs" varied widely from one part of North America to another. In many tribal nations, if a chief did not behave properly, he was taken out of office by the people. Sitting Bull once explained that a chief, by definition, has to be a poor man because he must share everything he has. "Chief," therefore, is not a term to be used lightly.

Chief Seattle (1786?–1866). Seattle, sometimes called Sealth, was a leader of the Duwamish League of Puget Sound and a strong American ally during the wars between the United States and a number of northwestern native nations between 1855 and 1860. The present-day city of Seattle, Washington, bears his name. He is best remembered for a speech ascribed to him which sets out eloquently the relation between human beings and the natural world.

Chippewa (Chip´-ah-wah). *See* Anishinabe.

Choctaw (Chock´-taw). A people of Mississippi and Alabama. One of the so-called "Five Civilized Tribes."

circle. The circle is seen as a special symbol for many native people. It is continuous and all-embracing. When people gather and form a circle, the circle can always be made larger to include more. Those who sit on the circle are all at the same height, and all are the same distance from the center—thus it promotes and stands for equality. The "Sacred Hoop" referred to by many of the native people of the Plains is another vision of the circle and stands for life itself, continuing, never-ending, as well as standing for "the nation."

clan. Among most native peoples the concept of "clan" exists. Loosely described as "clan," a term which also is applied to Scots and other European peoples, it refers to groups of people within a nation who are "born into" a particular group, though not necessarily related by blood. Among the Mohawk there are three clans— Turtle, Wolf and Bear. A person *always* belongs to the clan of his or her mother. If a person from another nation (including a white person) entered a tribal nation, that person had to be adopted by a clan mother and was then of her clan. Among many native nations, people were not supposed to marry someone of their own clan. Further, if a member of the Bear Clan among the Mohawk, for example, met a person of the Bear Clan from another native nation, she or he might regard that person as a sister or a brother. Clans, therefore, created links between people and nations, as well as a sense of belonging to a special group.

Clan Animal. In most cases, a clan is said to have "come from" a particular animal. That animal is regarded as having a special relation to the members of that clan, who may even exhibit some of that animal's characteristics such as being strong as the bear. These animals are regarded as ancestors and relatives, and many stories explain how a certain clan came to be when such an animal helped a human being long ago and then that person began that clan.

Clan Mother. Elder woman regarded as the head of a particular clan. Among matrilineal people such as the Haudenosaunee (Iroquois), a Clan Mother has great power and is a major political force. Among the Haudenosaunee, the women have a strong, central role. Each clan is headed by an elder woman, a Clan Mother, chosen by the others of her clan to lead. The Clan Mothers and the other women of the clan have many duties—such as choosing the men who will be "chiefs" among the Haudenosaunee. If a Haudenosaunee chief does not do his job well, the Clan Mother warns him three times and then, if he still fails to behave, she takes away his chieftaincy. The roles of Clan Mothers varied, and in some native nations of North America there were no Clan Mothers per se.

Comanche (Ko-man´-chē). Corruption of the Ute word *komon´teia*, "One Who Wants to Always Fight Me." A people of the southern Great Plains whose own name for themselves is *Nermurnuh* (New-mer´-noo) or "True Human Beings."

Coyote. Coyote is the trickster hero of many native stories throughout the west, southwest and northwest. Sometimes call "Old Man" he is regarded as both wise and foolish, dangerous and benevolent. Among some native people he is respected, while others regard him as untrustworthy. In this century, Coyote has become a sort of "Pan-Indian" symbol of native people themselves, and Coyote is the hero of many new contemporary tales that symbolize the struggle between native people and the government.

Crazy Horse (1842–1877). An Oglala Lakota (Sioux) noted for his reckless courage. Crazy Horse was one of the leaders of the native resistance against the U.S. encroachment on Lakota lands in the period following the American Civil War. As a war leader, he is credited with many victories, the most famous being the Battle of Little Big Horn in 1876. After surrendering to the army in 1877, he was bayoneted by a soldier while being taken forcibly into a prison cell and died shortly thereafter.

Cree (Krē). A primarily subarctic people whose various tribal nations stretch from Quebec in eastern Canada to Alberta in the west, a stretch of close to two thousand miles. In the area around Hudson Bay and James Bay, the traditional hunting and fishing subsistence lives of the Cree are threatened today by several James Bay power projects. The dams from these projects will block the major rivers of this region, creating a number of enormous lakes that will inundate much of that part of the North American continent, with disastrous ecological and cultural impacts.

Crow (Krō). Name usually applied to the native people of the northern Great Plains who call themselves *Absaroke* (Ahb-sah-rokuh), which means "Bird People," but could also mean "Crow."

da neho (dah ney-hō´) [Seneca] Literally "It is finished." A conventional way to end a story among the Iroquois.

Dakota (Dah-kō´-tah), "Sioux." One of the seven main "council fires" of the Sioux people. *Dakota* in the Santee Sioux dialect means "Allies" and refers to the Sioux of the eastern plains of Minnesota. Sioux called themselves *Ocheti Shakowin* (Oh-che-ti Shah-kō-win), "The Seven Council Fires."

Dine (Dih-nēy´), "Navajo." It means "The People."

Eskimo (Es´-kih-mo). Cree word meaning "Fish Eaters," applied to the people who call themselves *Inuit*—"The People."

John Fire/Lame Deer [Lakota]. A contemporary Lakota (Sioux) *wicaso wakan* (medicine man or holy man). With Richard Erdoes, he wrote *Lame Deer, Seeker of Visions* (New York: Simon and Schuster/ Touchstone Books, 1972), which was later published as *Lame Deer, Sioux Medicine Man*. This is a good book about the Lakota people and the ways of native spiritual practice.

Gitchee Manitou (Gih-chee´ Man´-ē-too). [Anishinabe] The Great Spirit.

Grandmother. The term "grandmother" is used among many native people to refer in a respectful way to a female elder, whether human or animal.

Grandmother Spider. Grandmother Spider is a central character in many of the stories of the Southwest. She is seen in some stories as the Creator of many things. She introduced weaving to the people, and the rays of the sun are sometimes seen as part of her great web. She is a benevolent force in the native world of such people as the Dine (Navajo) and Pueblo nations.

Great League, "Iroquois." The alliance of peace forged among the formerly warring five nations of the Iroquois about five hundred years or more ago by The Peacemaker and Hiawatha. The Great League is still active among Iroquois peoples.

Great Spirit. A translation of various native names for the Creator, for example, the Anishinabe term *Gitchee Manitou* or the Abenaki term *Ktsi Nwaskw* (T-see´ Nah-wahsk´).

hageota (hah-gey´-oh-tah). Iroquois word for a person, usually a man in middle age, who travels from lodge to lodge telling stories and being rewarded for his efforts by being given small gifts, food and a place to stay.

Haida (Hī´-dah). Pacific northwest Indian group of Queen Charlotte Islands, British Columbia, and the southern end of Prince of Wales Island, Alaska. Called *Kaigani* in Alaska, they are known for their beautiful carvings, paintings and totem poles.

Haudenosaunee (Ho-dē-nō-show´-nē). [Iroquois] Iroquois name for themselves, which means "People of the Longhouse."

Hep owiy (Hep oh-wi-ēē´). [Hopi] Literally means "yes" or "uh-hunh."

Hero Twins. Hopi, Navajo and Pueblo traditional stories have these two playful and powerful children as heroes who kill monsters.

Hiii aya hiiiyahahey (Hiii ah-yah´ hiii-yah´-ah-hey). [Hopi] Not translatable, a song made up of vocables like "tra-la-la" in English.

hogan (hō´-gun). [Navajo] Traditional dwelling made of logs and earth used by the Navajo.

Hopi (Hō´-pēē). Contraction of *Hopitu*, "The Peaceful Ones," the names used for themselves by a town-dwelling native people of northeastern Arizona.

huih (hoo-ee´). [Hopi] An exclamation like "ah-hah."

huli-i-i, hu-li-i-i, pa shish lakwa-a-a-a (hoo-lee-e´-e hoo-lee-e´-e pah-sheesh´ lah-kwah´-ah-ah-ah . . .). [Zuni] Farewell song sung by the eagle.

Huya Ania (Hoo-yah´ Ah-nee´-ah). [Yaqui] "The wilderness world."

Iitoi (Ē´ -e-tōy). [Papago] Elder Brother, Our Creator.

inallaaduwi (in-ahl´-lah-ah´-doo-ee) [Achumawi] "People Not Connected to Anything." An Achumawi word for white people.

Inuit (In´-you-it), "Eskimo." "The People," name used for themselves by the native peoples of the farthest Arctic regions, Iceland and Arctic Asia. Not regarded by themselves or Indians as American Indian.

Inupiaq (I-nōō´-pē-ak). One of the two major dialects of the Inuit (Eskimo) language spoken in Alaska. Inupiaq and Yupik are the two main Alaskan dialects of the Inuit language.

Iroquois (Ear´-oh-kwah). Corruption of an Algonquian word *ireohkwa*, meaning "real snakes." Applied commonly to the Six Nations, the "Haudenosaunee."

"is ohi" (ish o-hee´). [Hopi]. Literally "oh my" or "oh dear."

kachina (kah-chee´-nah) [Hopi] Sacred dancers or spirit people who bring rain, equated with ancestors and clouds.

Kahionhes (Gah-hē-yōn´-heys). [Mohawk (Iroquois)] Name meaning "Long River."

Kiowa (Kī´-yō-wah). Native people of southern Great Plains (southwest Oklahoma). Name means "Principal People."

kiva (kē´-vah). [Hopi] A chamber, usually underground, used for ceremonies.

Kwakiutl (Kwah-kē´-yūt-ul). A people of the Pacific northwest, British Columbia coast. Sometimes referred to as *Kwaguilth* or *Kwa-Gulth*.

Lakota (Lah-kō´-tah) (Sioux). *See Dakota.* "Sioux" native people of northern plains, Nebraska, Dakotas.

Lakota Wiikijo Olowan (Lah-kō´-tah Wē-ē´-key-jō Oh-lo-wahn´). Lakota flute music.

lap lap (lap-lap) [Nez Percé] Nez Percé word for butterfly.

Lapwai (Lap´-wī). [Nez Percé] "Valley of the Butterfly" in Nez Percé.

Little Loon or Mdawelasis (Meh-dah-wēē-lah-sis´). [Abenaki]. The Abenaki name of Maurice Dennis, an Abenaki elder from the Adirondack region.

Kevin Locke. [Lakota (Sioux)]. English name for *Tokaheya Inajin* (Ton-ka´hey-yah In-ah´-jeen) ("Stands First"), a Lakota storyteller, flute player and dancer.

longhouse. Large traditional dwelling of Iroquois people. Framework of saplings covered with elm bark with central fires and, to each side, compartments for families.

madagenilhas (mah-dah´-gen-ill-has´). [Abenaki] Word for bat, literally "fur-hide bird."

Manabozho (Man-ah-bō´-zo). [Algonquian] Algonquian trickster hero, "Old Man."

medicine lodge. Small lodge used for curing ceremonies among northeastern native peoples.

Medicine Man. General term used to refer to "Indian doctors" who effect cures with a blend of psychiatry and sound herbal remedies, as well as by use of spiritual means. Each Indian nation has its own word for this person.

Megissogwon (Meh-gis-sog-wahn´). [Anishinabe] Anishinabe Spirit of Fever.

Miwok (Mee´-wohk). Native people of the part of California surrounding the San Francisco Bay area and east of the bay.

Mōhawk (Mo´-hawk). Abenaki word *maquak*, used to refer to the Iroquois who lived in the area of Mohawk Valley in New York State and called themselves *Kanienkahageh* ("People of the Flint").

Name means "Cowards."

muktuk (muhk´-tuhk). The part of whale meat that includes the outer skin and the fat of the whale, also called "blubber."

Nanavits (Nah-navits´). [Paiute] "Moon of New Grass," month of April or May.

Native American. Native people of North, South and Central America who were aboriginal inhabitants prior to Columbus, and the descendants of these aboriginal inhabitants. Used interchangeably with the term "American Indian." In this book, we have used "Native North American" to refer to the native peoples of the United States and Canada.

Navajo (Nah´-vah-hō). *See Dine.*

Nez Percé (Nehz Purse). A native people of Idaho and western Washington. Name means "Pierced Nose" in French. The French confused the Nez Percé word for themselves, *Choo-pin-it-pa-loo* ("People of the Mountain"), with the Nez Percé word *chopunnish* (pierced noses).

Nokomis (Nok-koh´-miss). [Anishinabe] Anishinabe term for "Grandmother," grandmother of Manabozho in stories.

Nootka (Nōōt´-kah). Maritime people of the coast of what is now called British Columbia.

nyaweh gowah (nēēy-ah´-way gō´-uh). [Kanienkahageh (Mohawk)] "Great thanks."

Oglala Sioux (Ō-glo´-lah Sōō). One of the branches of the western Lakota people.

Ojibway (Oh-jib´-wah). *See Anishinabe.*

Oneida (Oh-ny´-dah). [Iroquois] One of the Six Nations. Their name for themselves was *Onayatakono*, "People of the Standing Stone."

Onondaga (On-un-dah´-gah). [Iroquois] The centralmost of the six nations, the "Fire-keepers." Name for themselves is *Onundagaono*, "People on the Hills."

Osage (Ō-sāj). The people who call themselves *Ni-U-kon´-Skah*, "The People of the Middle Waters." Their lands formerly included the area where Missouri, Kansas, Arkansas and Oklahoma meet, but today their communities are mostly in Osage County, Oklahoma.

Paiute (Pī´-yōōt). Native people of Nevada, Colorado, Arizona, California and Utah. The Northern Paiutes, sometimes referred to as the "Snakes," call themselves *Nu´ma* or *Ni´mi*, which means "People." The name *Paiute* is the modification of form borrowed into English and is probably misspelled.

Papago (Pah´-pah-gō). Southwest Indian group of southern Arizona. Nomadic horticulturalists and prolific basket weavers. Two-thirds of the roughly 13,500 Papagos today live on reservations located mostly in Pima County, Arizona, with some living in Sonora state, Mexico. Sometimes referred to as *Tohono O´odham*, "People of the Desert."

Parker, Ely (1828–1895). A grand Sachem of the Seneca Nation, Ely Parker's Seneca name was *Do-ne´-ho-ga-wa*, "Open Door." One of the best-educated men of his time, he was an engineer, fluent in Latin and Greek and a Brevet General in the Civil War, serving as General Grant's personal secretary.

Pawnee (Paw-nēē´). A people of the northern Great Plains, Nebraska. Name may mean "Horn" or "Hunters." They call themselves *Chahiksichohiks*—"Men of Men."

Pit River Indian people. *See Achumawi.*

Pueblo (Pweb´-lō). Spanish for town, refers to a number of "town-dwelling" native peoples along the Rio Grande in New Mexico who live in large adobe buildings like apartment complexes.

qaade-wade toolol aakaadzi (kwah-ah-deh-wah-deh tool-ohl ah-ank-ah-dah-zee) [Achumawi] "The Beings Which Are World-over, All-living."

Raven. Raven is the trickster hero of many of the tales of the people of the Northwest. His image is usually carved on the top of totem poles of the region.

Red Jacket. Name given by whites to *Sagoyewatha* (Sah-gó-ye-watha) "He Who Keeps Them Awake," one of the leaders of the Seneca nation in the late eighteenth and early nineteenth centuries. One of the greatest orators of his time, he is the author of a number of speeches that became famous in English translation.

Santee Sioux (San´-tee Soo). A division of the eastern Dakota (Sioux) peoples living in Minnesota.

Sealth. *See* Chief Seattle.

Seneca (Sen´-eh-ka). Corruption of Algonquian word *O-sin-in-ka*, meaning "People of the Stone." Refers to the westernmost of the Six Nations, "Keepers of the Western Door." The Iroquois who called themselves *Nundawaono*, "People of the Great Hill."

Seye Wailo (Seh´-yeh Wa-e´-loh). [Yaqui] Literally "The Flower World," the mystically beautiful natural world inhabited by the deer in Yaqui stories and songs.

shaman (shah´-mun). An Asian term referring to one who speaks with ancestral spirits in order to heal or gain power. Often applied by Europeans to Native North American medicine men.

Shoshone (Shō-shō´-nee). Native people living in Wyoming, Nevada, and parts of Utah. Also a term referring to the related nations of Shoshonean stock such as the Ute.

Sioux (Su). *See* Dakota. Corruption of an Anishinabe word meaning "Snakes," which refers to those who call themselves *Dakota* or *Lakota* or *Nakota* or *Ocheti Shakowin* (Oh-che-ti Shah-kō-win), "The Seven Council Fires."

Sitting Bull (1831–1890). Translation of the Hunkpapa Sioux name of *Tatanka Iyotake* (Tah-tan´-kah Ee-yō-tah´-kay), one of the great leaders of the Lakota people in the late 1800s.

Sonora. A state in northwest Mexico, also refers to the desert regions in southern Arizona.

Mount Tamalpais (Tam-ahl-pi´-us). California mountain, visible from the San Francisco area, which is a central feature in the Miwok creation story.

Tawa (Tah´-wah). [Hopi] The Sky God.

Tehanetorens (Dey´-ha-ne-dō-lens) [Mohawk (Iroquois)] Name of Ray Fadden, an Iroquois Mohawk teacher; it means "He Is Looking Through the Pine Trees."

Teton Sioux (Tē´-ton Soo). One of the western Lakota nations. Others included the Hunkpapa and the Oglala.

tipi (tee´pee). [Siouan] Plains Indian dwelling, a cone-shaped house of skins over a frame of poles; it means "dwelling."

Tirawa (Tee-rah´-wah). [Pawnee] The Creator.

Tlingit (Klin´-kit). A native people of the Pacific northwest.

totem (tō´-tum). [Anishinabe] Refers to the animal relatives regarded as ancestral to the lineage. Each person is born into a particular totem, inherited in many native cultures through the mother. Totem animals include Bear, Eagle, Deer, Turtle, Wolf, Snipe, Eel and many others. Common throughout North America.

tribe. From Latin *tribus*. A term used by both Indians and non-Indians to refer to groups of Native North Americans sharing a common linguistic and cultural heritage. Some Native North American people prefer to speak not of "tribe" but of *nation*.

Tsalagi. *See* Cherokee.

Tsimshian (Shim´-she-un). A native people of the Pacific northwest.

Turtle Clan. *See* Clan Animal, Bear Clan, clan.

Turtle Continent. North America, in many native stories, is placed on Great Turtle's back.

Tuscarora (Tus-ka-rō´-rah). The Sixth Nation of the Iroquois. The name means "Shirt-wearers." Driven by the Europeans from lands in North Carolina in the early eighteenth century, they resettled in western New York State.

Ute (Yoot). Native people for whom the state of Utah is named. Their homeland included Colorado, Utah and part of New Mexico. An important division of the Shoshonean nations, most live today in Colorado. They call themselves *Nu Ci* (New´ Chi), which means "Person." The word *Ute* is a corruption of the Spanish term *Yuta*, which is of unknown origin.

Wabanaki Confederacy (Wa´-bah-na-kee). A loose union of a number of Abenaki nations circa 1750–1850, possibly echoing an earlier confederacy and influenced by the Iroquois League. Allied Micmac, Maliseet, Passamaquoddy, Penobscot and Abenaki nations. Wampum belts were introduced and triannual meetings held at Caughnawaga, Quebec.

Wakan Tanka (Wah-kon´ Tōn´-kah). [Lakota (Siouan)] The Creator. "The Great Mystery."

Wampanoag (Wom-pah-nō´ag). Means "Dawn People," sometimes called *Pokanoket*. Algonquian linguistic group of eastern woodlands, which once occupied what are now Bristol County, Rhode Island, and Bristol County, Massachusetts. Many were killed, along with the Narragansetts, by the colonists in King Philip's War in 1675 (King Philip was the colonists' name for Chief Metacomet, son of Massasoit). At least five hundred Wampanoag live today on Martha's Vineyard, Nantucket and other places in the region.

wampum (wom´-pum). Purple-and-white beads made from shells, they are still used by the Haudenosaunee as devices to record agreements between nations and to symbolize aspects of Iroquois history and culture. Woven together in strings in pre-Columbian times and then, after the introduction of European machinery, made into beads and strung into belts. *Not* used as money by native people.

water drum. Type of drum used by some northeastern native people such as the Iroquois. A small, round wooden drum shaped like a small pot, which has water placed in it to moisten the drum head and change the tone of the drum.

wica yaka pelo! (wee-chah´ yah´-kah pā´-low). "You have spoken truly" or "you are right" in the Dakota language.

wigwam (wig´-wom). [Abenaki] Probably from *wetuom*, which means "dwelling." Dome-shaped house made from bent sticks covered with bark, common to northeastern Abenaki peoples.

Yaqui (Yah´-kee). Native people of Sonoran area of Mexico. Communities of Yaqui people also live in several regions of Arizona.

Yupik (Yoo´-pik). One of the Inuit (Eskimo) nations of the western coast of Alaska. Yupik and Inupiaq are the two main Alaskan dialects of the Inuit language. *Yupik* means "Authentic People." Yupik people are also found along the Siberian coast.

Zuni (Zoo´-ñee). [ñ = nasalized] A Pueblo people of New Mexico who call themselves *Ashiwi*, "The Flesh." Name comes from a Keresan Pueblo word whose meaning is unknown.

❖ Other Versions of Native North American Stories ❖

Joseph Bruchac

In choosing the stories to be included in this book and in its predecessor, I followed several rules. The first was to choose stories with levels of meaning relatively easy for a general audience to understand. (Each of these stories also may have additional levels of meaning that can only be perceived by those who are extremely close to the individual tribal nation each story comes from.) The second rule was to not tell "restricted" stories, stories only to be shared with those who are, in some way, "initiated." My third rule was to include only stories with earlier versions already in print or in public circulation through recordings or film. I do not wish to be the first to take a story out of the oral tradition. By this I do not mean to condemn those who first "document" such stories; I simply mean to make it clear that I do not see this as my role. Fourth, the versions included in this book (and in *Keepers of the Earth*) are my own retellings and may differ considerably from other versions already recorded. In general, this is because I have tried to make my versions closer to the oral traditions from which the stories come or to include important information left out in other recorded tellings.

The following list will lead the reader to some (but not all) other versions of many of the stories in *Keepers of the Animals.*

Silver Fox and Coyote Create Earth (Miwok). Those who have drawn on California Indian stories of Fox and Coyote include Mohawk poet Peter Blue Cloud. See Peter Blue Cloud, *Elderberry Flute Song* (Fredonia, N.Y.: White Pine Press, 1989). Other versions are Jane Louis Curry, *Back in the Beforetime* (New York: Macmillan, 1987); Jamie de Angulo, *Coyote Man and Old Docotor Loon* (San Francisco, Calif.: Turtle Island Foundation, 1973); and a compilation by Edward Gifford and Gwendoline Harris Block, *California Indian Nights* (Lincoln: University of Nebraska Press, 1990).

How the People Hunted the Moose (Cree). One of the best collectors of Cree traditions has been Howard Norman, whose books range from *The Wishing Bone Cycle* (New York: Stonehill Press, 1976) to a 1990 collection of traditional stories from the north. This particular story is found among the Abenaki and other Algonquin-speaking people. Versions include *Legends from the Forest,* told by Chief Thomas Fiddler (Moonbeam, Ontario: Penumbra Press, 1985).

How Grandmother Spider Named the Clans (Hopi). Other versions are found in G.W. Mullett, *Spider Woman Stories* (Tucson: University of Arizona, 1979); Edmund Nequatewa *Truth of a Hopi* (Northland Press, 1967); Frank Waters, *The Book of the Hopi* (New York: Viking Press, 1963); and *Meditations With the Hopi* (Santa Fe, N.M.: Bear & Company, 1986).

How the Spider Symbol Came to the People (Osage). Other versions are found in Robert Liebert, *Osage Life and Legends* (Happy Camp, Calif.: Naturegraph, 1987); and Francis LaFlesche, *The Osage Tribe* (Washington, D.C.: Bureau of American Ethnology Report 35, 1918).

The Rabbit Dance (Mohawk). Other versions are found in J.N.B. Hewitt, *Onondaga Mohawk and Seneca Myths* (Washington, D.C.: Bureau of American Ethnology Report 21, 1910–11); and Tehanetorens, *Tales of the Iroquois* (Mohawk Nation via Rooseveltown, N.Y.: Akwesasne Notes, 1976).

The Deer Dance (Yaqui). Other versions are found in Refugio Savala, *Autobiography of a Yaqui Poet* (Tucson: University of Arizona Press, 1980); and Larry Evers and Felipe S. Molina, *Yaqui Deer Songs/Maso Bwikam* (Tucson: University of Arizona Press, 1987).

Eagle Boy (Zuni). This story is found among more than one of the Pueblo nations. A Hopi version can be found in G.M. Mullett, *Spider Woman Stories.* Other Zuni versions are Frank Hamilton Cushing, *Zuni Folk Tales* (Tucson: University of Arizona Press, 1901); and the Zuni people, *The Zunis: Self-Portrayals* (Albuquerque: University of New Mexico, 1972).

Turtle Races with Beaver (Seneca). Versions of this tale are found among all of the Six Nations of the Iroquois and in various neighboring tribal nations such as the Lenape and the Abenaki. Two sources are Arthur C. Parker, *Skunny Wundy, Seneca Indian Tales* (Chicago: Albert Whitman and Co., 1970) and William M. Beauchamp, *Iroquois Folk Lore* (Port Washington, N.Y.: Kennikat Press, 1966).

Octopus and Raven (Nootka). Other versions are found in Franz Boaz, "The Nootka" (6th Report on the Indian Tribes of Canada, 1890); and David W. Ellis and Luke Swan, *Teachings of the Tides* (Nanaimo, B.C.: Theytus Books, 1981).

How the Butterflies Came to Be (Papago). Other versions are found in *American Indian Myths and Legends,* selected and edited by Richard Erdoes and Alfonso Ortiz (New York: Pantheon, 1984); and Mary I. Neff, "Pima and Papago Legends," *Journal of American Folklore* 25, 1912.

Salmon Boy (Haida). This story is widely told among the various tribal nations of the northwest coast including the Kwakiutl, the Tlingit and the Klallum. Versions include John Bierhorst, *The Mythology of North America* (New York: Quill, 1985); and John R. Swanton, *Contributions to the Ethnology of the Haida* (New York: American Museum of Natural History, 1905).

The Woman Who Married a Frog (Tlingit). Another version is by John R. Swanton, *Tlingit Mythos and Tales* (Washington, D.C.: Bureau of American Ethnology Report 39, 1909).

How Poison Came into the World (Choctaw). Other versions are found in *Native American Legends,* compiled and edited by George E. Lankford (Little Rock, Ark.: August House, 1987); and "Myths of the Louisiana Choctaw" by David I. Bushnell, *American Anthropologist,* No. 12, 1910.

The First Flute (Lakota). Versions in *American Indian Myths and Legends,* selected and edited by Richard Erdoes and Alfonso

Ortiz (New York: Pantheon, 1984); and Eugene Buechel, *Lakota Tales and Texts* (Pine Ridge, S.D.: Red Cloud Indian School, 1978).

Manabozho and the Woodpecker (Anishinabe). Other versions are found in Alden O. Deming, *Manabozho* (F.W. David Co., 1938); and Henry R. Schoolcraft, *Algic Researches* (New York: 1839).

Why Coyote Has Yellow Eyes (Hopi). Other versions are found in Hamilton A. Tyler, *Pueblo Animals and Myths* (Norman: University of Oklahoma Press, 1975); Ekkehart Malotki, *Gullible Coyote* (Tucson: University of Arizona Press, 1985); and Mark Bahti, *Pueblo Stories and Storytellers* (Tucson: Treasure Chest Publications, 1988).

The Dogs Who Saved Their Master (Seneca). Versions of *Seneca Myths and Legends* by Arthur C. Parker, (Buffalo Historical Society, 1923); and *Seneca Fiction Legends and Myths* by J.N.B. Hewitt (Washington, D.C.: Bureau of American Enthology Bulletin 32, 1911).

Why Possum Has a Naked Tail (Cherokee). Other versions are found in Traveller Bird, *The Path to Snowbird Mountain* (New York: Straus and Giroux, 1972); and James Mooney, *Myths of the Cherokee* (Washington, D.C.: Bureau of American Ethnology Report 21, 1900).

How the Fawn Got Its Spots (Dakota). Other versions are found in *Legends of the Mighty Sioux* by South Dakota Writers' Project, 1941; and Eugene Buechel, *Lakota Tales and Texts* (Pine Ridge, S.D.: Red Cloud Indian School, 1978).

The Alligator and the Hunter (Choctaw). Other versions are found in *The Choctaw of Bayou Lacomb* by David I. Bushnell (Washington, D.C.: Bureau of American Ethnology 48, 1909); *Native American Legends* compiled and edited by George E. Lankford (Little Rock, Ark.: August House, 1987); and John R. Swanton, *Myths and Tales of the Southeastern Indians* (Washington, D.C.: Bureau of American Ethnology Report 88, 1929).

The Passing of the Buffalo (Kiowa). Other versions are found in Alice Marriott and Carol K. Rachlin, *American Indian Mythology* (New York: Mentor Books, 1968); and Alice Marriott, *Saynday's People* (Lincoln: University of Nebraska Press, 1963).

The Lake of the Wounded (Cherokee). Other versions are found in James Mooney, *Myths of the Cherokee* (Washington, D.C.: Bureau of American Ethnology Report 19, 1902); and Douglas A. Rossman, *Where Legends Live* (Cherokee, N.C.: Cherokee Publications, 1988).

❖ Art and Photographic Credits ❖

All illustrations associated with the stories are by either John Kahionhes Fadden or David Kanietakeron Fadden and can be distinguished by each artist's signature.

Eight of the animal illustrations accompanying the "Discussion" sections throughout the book are by Diana Dee Tyler (D. D. Tyler) and can be distinguished by the credit line in the captions.

All illustrations that lack a credit line and are used in Chapters 1 and 2, and in the "Discussion," "Activities" and "Extending the Experience" sections are by Carol Wood.

The map *Native North America* © 1991 by Michael J. Caduto. Cartography by Stacy Miller of Upper Marlboro, Maryland.

Fig. 1-1. Alan C. Graham.

Fig. 2-2. Arthur Swoger, courtesy Audubon Society of Rhode Island.

Fig. 2-3. Courtesy Audubon Society of Rhode Island.

Fig. 2-4. Don Blades.

Fig. 2-5. Don Blades.

Fig. 2-7. Adapted with permission from Donald J. Borror and Richard E. White, *A Field Guide to the Insects.* Boston, Mass.: Houghton Mifflin Co., 1970, 25.

Fig. 3-1. Michael J. Caduto.

Fig. 4-1. Peter Hope.

Fig. 5-2. Cecil B. Hoisington.

Fig. 6-4. Don Blades.

Fig. 7-1. Adapted with permission from Deborah A. Coulombe, *The Seaside Naturalist.* Englewood Cliffs, N.J.: Prentice-Hall, 6.

Fig. 7-4. Adapted with permission from Deborah A. Coulombe, *The Seaside Naturalist.* Englewood Cliffs, N.J.: Prentice-Hall, 113.

Fig. 8-1. Courtesy Joseph Bruchac.

Fig. 8-3. Alan C. Graham.

Fig. 9-1. Adapted with permission from Deborah A. Coulombe, *The Seaside Naturalist.* Englewood Cliffs, N.J.: Prentice-Hall, 6.

Fig. 9-3. Robert S. Michelson.

Fig. 9-5. Michael J. Caduto.

Fig. 10-2. Alan C. Graham.

Fig. 10-3. Alan C. Graham.

Fig. 10-4. Peter Hope.

Fig. 11-1. Alan C. Graham.

Fig. 11-4. Cecil B. Hoisington.

Fig. 12-2. Don Blades.

Fig. 12-8. Adapted with permission from Massachusetts Audubon Society, *Curious Naturalist Supplement No. 2.* Lincoln, Mass.: Massachusetts Audubon Society.

Fig. 13-1. Alan C. Graham.

Fig. 13-4. Peter Hope.

Fig. 14-1. Peter Hope.

Fig. 14-2. Alan C. Graham.

Fig. 14-3. Adrienne Miller, courtesy Roger Williams Park Zoo, Providence, Rhode Island.

Fig. 15-1. Courtesy Vermont Institute of Natural Science.

Fig. 15-2. Alan C. Graham.

Fig. 16-3. John Korejwa.

Fig. 17-2. David F. Boehlke.

Fig. 17-3. Alan C. Graham.

Fig. 17-5. Michael J. Caduto.

✤ Index of Activities by Subject ✤

Mammals

Common mammals,
  differences in appearance and habits of in local environments, 44, 45
  familiarity with ones found in local environments, 44, 45
  survival adaptations of in local environments, 45
Communication between people and mammals,
  domestic mammals, 46
  wild mammals, 46
Coyote,
  adapting to a changing environment, 47
  adapting to human-caused changes to the environment, 47
  change as a part of its existence, 47
  change as essential for adapting and surviving, 47
  survival adaptations of, 47
Deer,
  communication with other deer, 1
  empathy for, 1
  sensory awareness of, 1
  stalking and being stalked, 1
Dogs, see also coyote
  communication between people and, 46
Marine mammals, see also whales
  as a natural resource— renewable versus non-renewable, 61, 62
  controversial issues surrounding hunting of, 62
  echo-location or "sonar" of—how and why it functions to aid in navigating around obstacles when sight is impaired, 59
  external anatomy of various species of, 58, 60
  external appearance of different species of, 60
  foods of, 58
  habitats of, 58
  hunting—effects of upon populations of, 61, 62
  importance of to Native American cultures, 62
  natural history of various species of, 60
  population dynamics of, 61, 62
  populations of—factors affecting the sustainability and carrying capacity of, 61, 62
  predator/prey relationships among, 61, 62
  relative size of compared to other ocean animals, 58
  wildlife management of, 61, 62
  wise stewardship practices toward, 61, 62
Stereotypes of mammals in children's literature, 36
Survival adaptations,
  of mammals living nearby, 45
Whales, see also marine mammals
  completing the circle of giving and receiving between people and whales, 63
  role of people in assuring survival of whales, 63
  showing appreciation for gifts of whales, 63

Natural Resources and Animals

Animals used as food,
  marine mammals, hunting of and sustainability of populations of, 61, 62
  traditional Native American hunting techniques for marine mammals versus modern, high-tech methods, 62
  salmon fishing, 27
Economics,
  issues, controversy and the effects of hunting out of need versus want, 62
Materialism, economics and the effects of these pressures on the demand for animals and animal products, 62

Natural Resources and Animals (continued)
Soil, 13
  importance of for plant and animal life, 13
  importance of nutrient cycle in, 13

Personal Relationship with Animals

Amphibians,
  keeping field records of, 32
  protection and conservation of, 32
Appreciation toward animals,
  for gifts from the sea, 28
  for gifts received from species that are endangered, 65
  for gifts of the whales, 63
  for gifts received from insects, 20
  for the values of endangered species, 65
Attitudes (likes and dislikes) toward,
  predators, 55
  prey animals, 55
  urban and suburban animals, 49
Beauty in animals, 36
  seeing in rattlesnake, 35
Celebration of animals,
  with the circle dance, 8
Circle of giving and receiving between people and animals,
  as practiced in a special place in nature, 10
  between traditional Native Americans and marine mammals hunted, 62
  celebrated with the circle dance, 8
  completion of with endangered species of animal, 65
  completion of with insects, 20
  completion of with the sea, 28
  completion of with whales, 63
  perverted by pesticide poisoning of animals, 64
Communication with animals,
  learning the "languages" of wild and domesticated animals, 46
  "speaking" to domesticated animals in their languages, 46
Community of people and all animals,
  celebrated with the circle dance, 8
Empathy for animals,
  endangered and threatened species, through first-hand experience and interaction with in zoos, 51
  found in western children's literature, 36
  predators, 55
  prey, 55
  rattlesnake, 35
Fear of animals,
  predator (alligator), 55
  rattlesnake, 35
Giving thanks to the animals, see appreciation of animals,
Gratitude toward animals,
  as demonstrated and experienced during the circle dance, 8
  for gifts from the sea, 28
  for gifts of species that are endangered, 65
  for gifts of the whales, 63
  for gifts received from insects, 20
Interconnectedness,
  between people and the sea, 2
  celebrated with the circle dance, 8
  pesticide poisoning of animals via biomagnification as evidence of interconnectedness, 64
  strengthened through solitude in nature, 10
Living in balance,

Personal Relationship with Animals (continued)
  by not wasting and using only what is needed, 20
  traditional relationship between Native Americans and marine mammals hunted, 62
Observation of animals,
  importance of to a personal relationship with animals, 10, 25, 57
Praise for animals,
  as part of the circle dance, 8
Reptiles,
  protection and conservation of, 37
Respect,
  for animals when stalking, 57
  for animals when tracking, 56
  for dangerous animals, 35, 55
  for gifts of the sea, 28
  for gifts of the whales, 63
  for predators, 55
  for prey, 55
  shown by traditional Native Americans for marine mammals that are hunted, 62
Seeking a helping animal, 3
  as guide, 3
  as source of strength, 3
  as source of wisdom, 3
  as teacher, 3
Self-knowledge,
  as found in solitude in a special place in nature, 10
Sense of place,
  developing a relationship with a special place in nature, 10
  developing in solitude with the sea, 28
  importance of solitude to developing a, 10, 28
Sensory awareness,
  importance of developing a sense of place, 10
  importance of when stalking animals to observe them, 57
  importance of when tracking animals, 56
Silence,
  as an important way of relating to animals, 10
  importance of to focusing and observing, 25
  importance of when stalking animals for observation, 57
  while observing the interactions of insects and plants, 25
Solitude,
  as a way of connecting with the sea, 28
  as an important way of relating to animals, 10
  while observing the interactions of insects and plants, 25
Spiders,
  acceptance of, 6
  learning patience from, 3, 6
  protection of, 6
Stereotypes of animals,
  based on distortions of animals' true natures, 36
  based on fear and other negative feelings toward rattlesnakes, 35
  found in western children's literature, 36
Symbols, using animals as symbols, 4
  of strength, 4
  of wisdom, 4
  of empowerment, 4
Urban and suburban animals,
  behavior toward, 49
  providing habitat (survival needs) for, 53

Plants and Animals
This part of the index lists those activities that

✦ General Index ✦

✤ Notes ✤